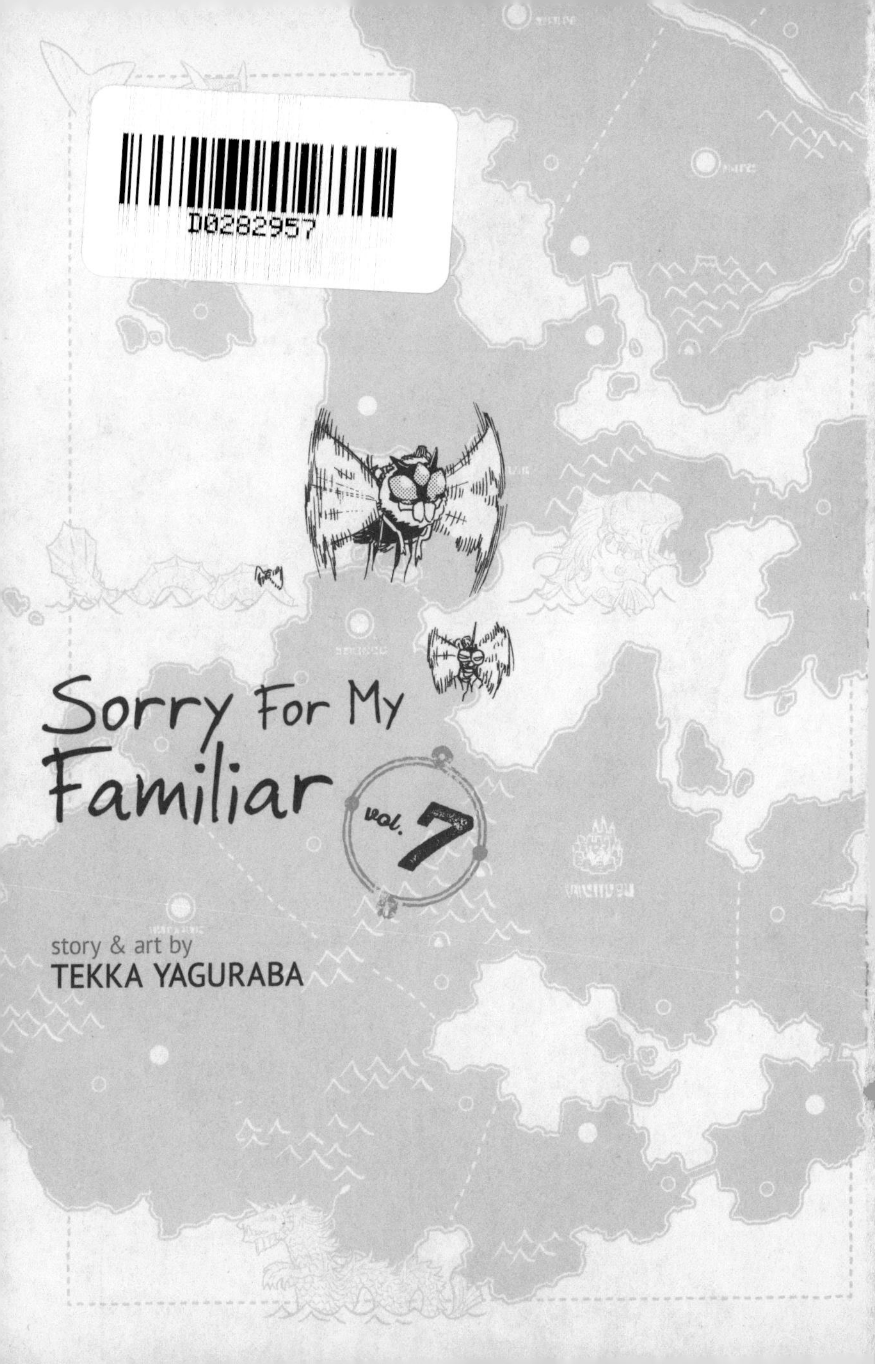

Sorry For My Familiar

vol. 7

story & art by
TEKKA YAGURABA

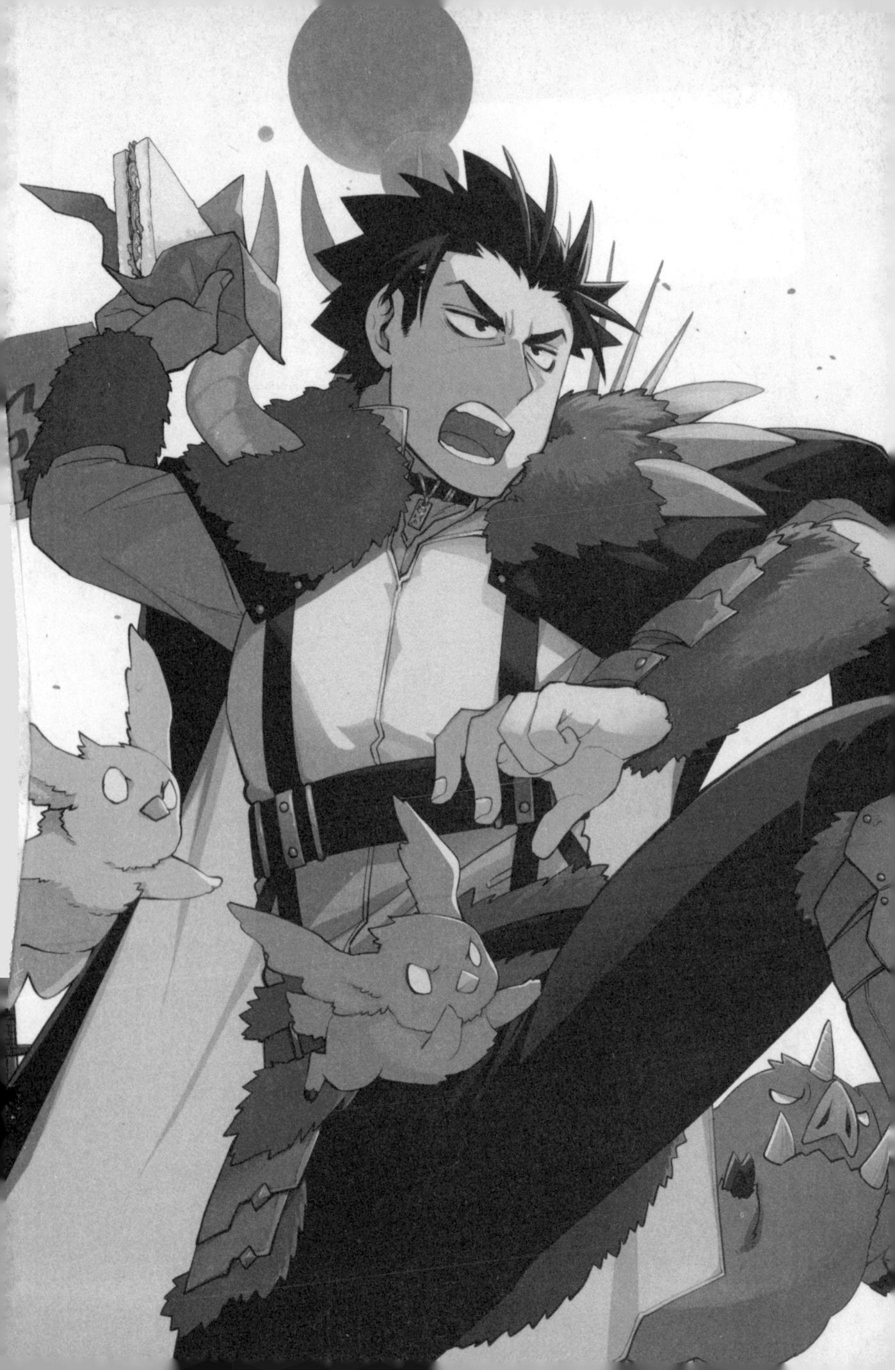

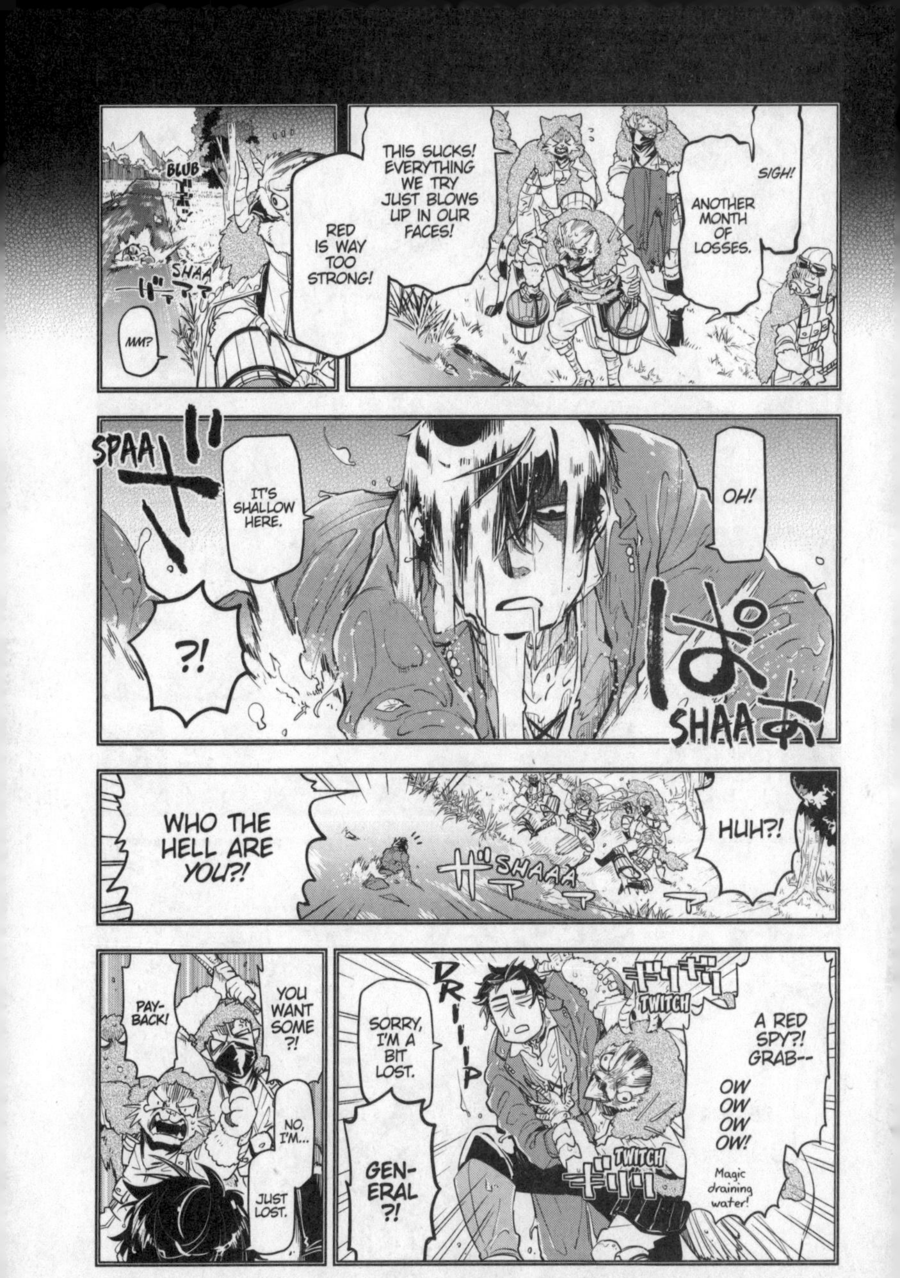
SIGH!
ANOTHER MONTH OF LOSSES.
THIS SUCKS! EVERYTHING WE TRY JUST BLOWS UP IN OUR FACES!
RED IS WAY TOO STRONG!
BLUB
SHAA
MM?
OH!
IT'S SHALLOW HERE.
SPAA
?!
SHAA
HUH?!
SHAAA
WHO THE HELL ARE YOU?!
A RED SPY?! GRAB--
OW OW OW OW!
Magic draining water!
TWITCH
SORRY, I'M A BIT LOST.
DRIIIP
GEN-ERAL ?!
TWITCH
YOU WANT SOME ?!
PAY-BACK!
NO, I'M...
JUST LOST.

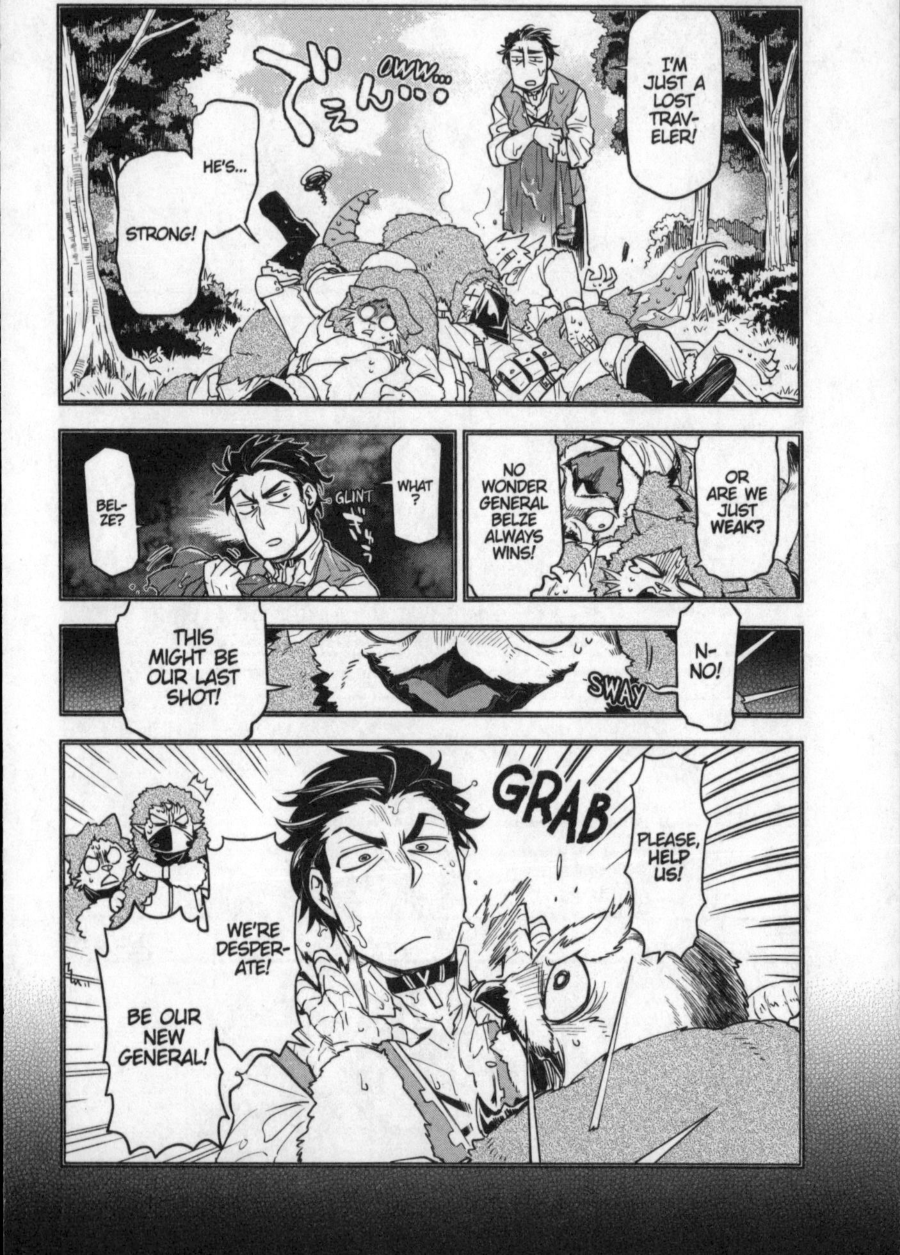
I'M JUST A LOST TRAVELER!
OWW...
HE'S...
STRONG!
OR ARE WE JUST WEAK?
NO WONDER GENERAL BELZE ALWAYS WINS!
WHAT?
GLINT
BELZE?
N-NO!
SWAY
THIS MIGHT BE OUR LAST SHOT!
GRAB
PLEASE, HELP US!
WE'RE DESPERATE!
BE OUR NEW GENERAL!

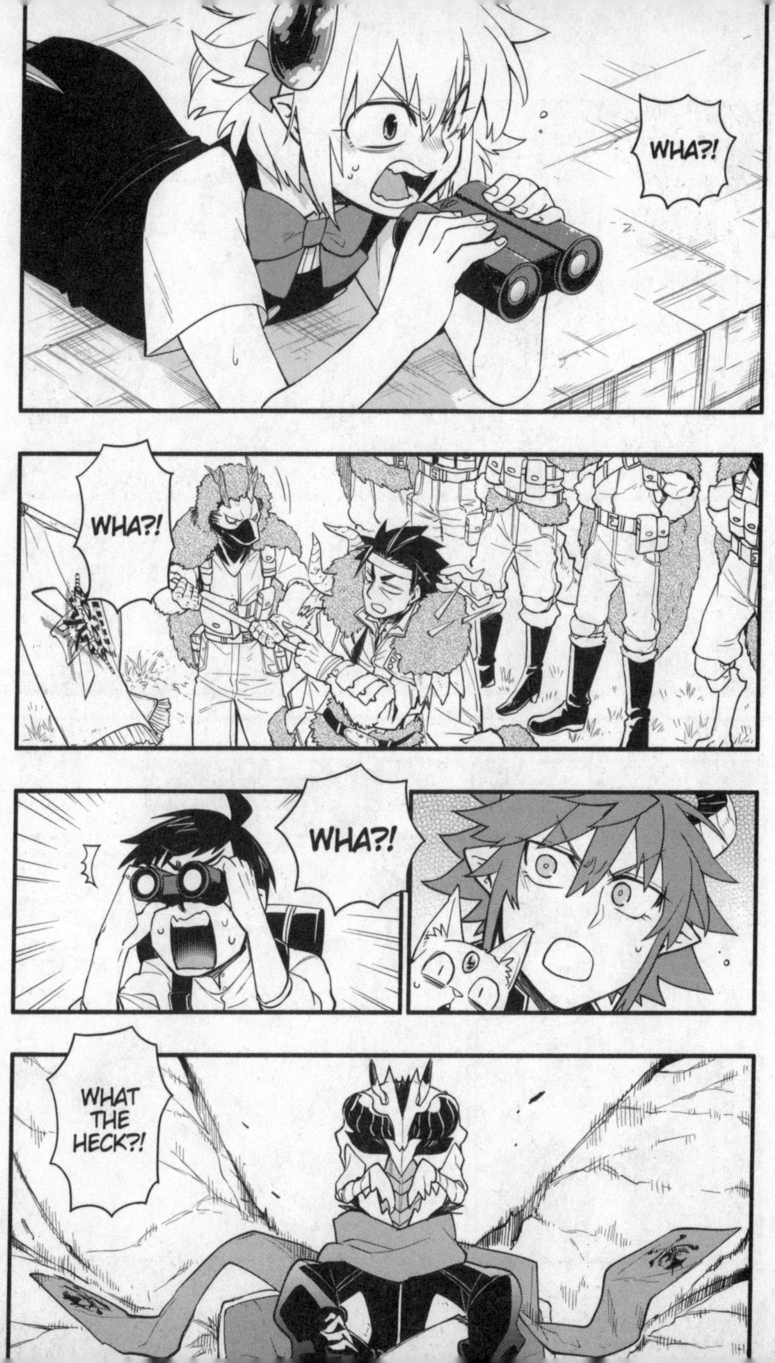
WHA?!
WHA?!
WHA?!
WHAT THE HECK?!

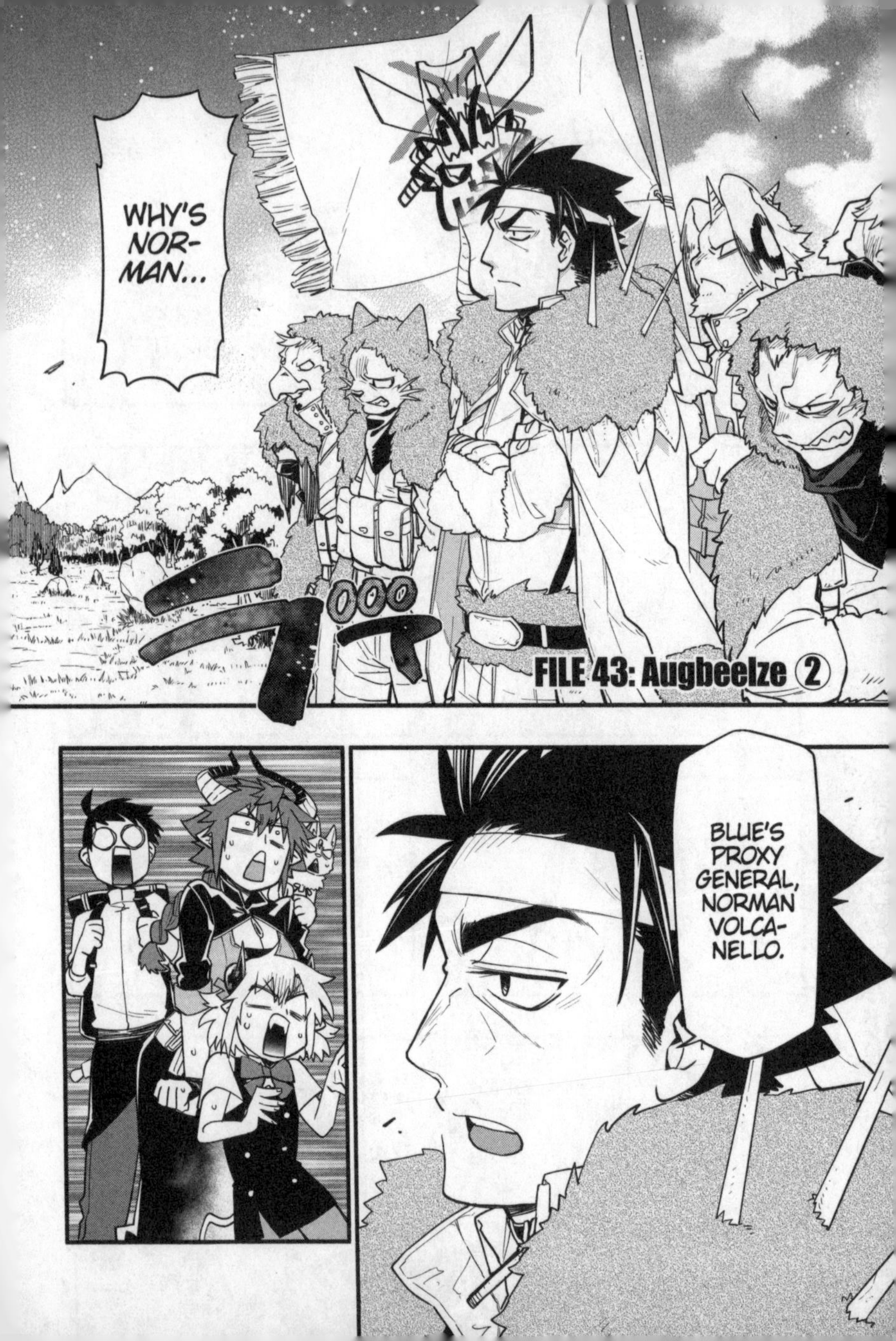
WHY'S NOR-MAN...
FILE 43: Augbeelze ②
BLUE'S PROXY GENERAL, NORMAN VOLCA-NELLO.

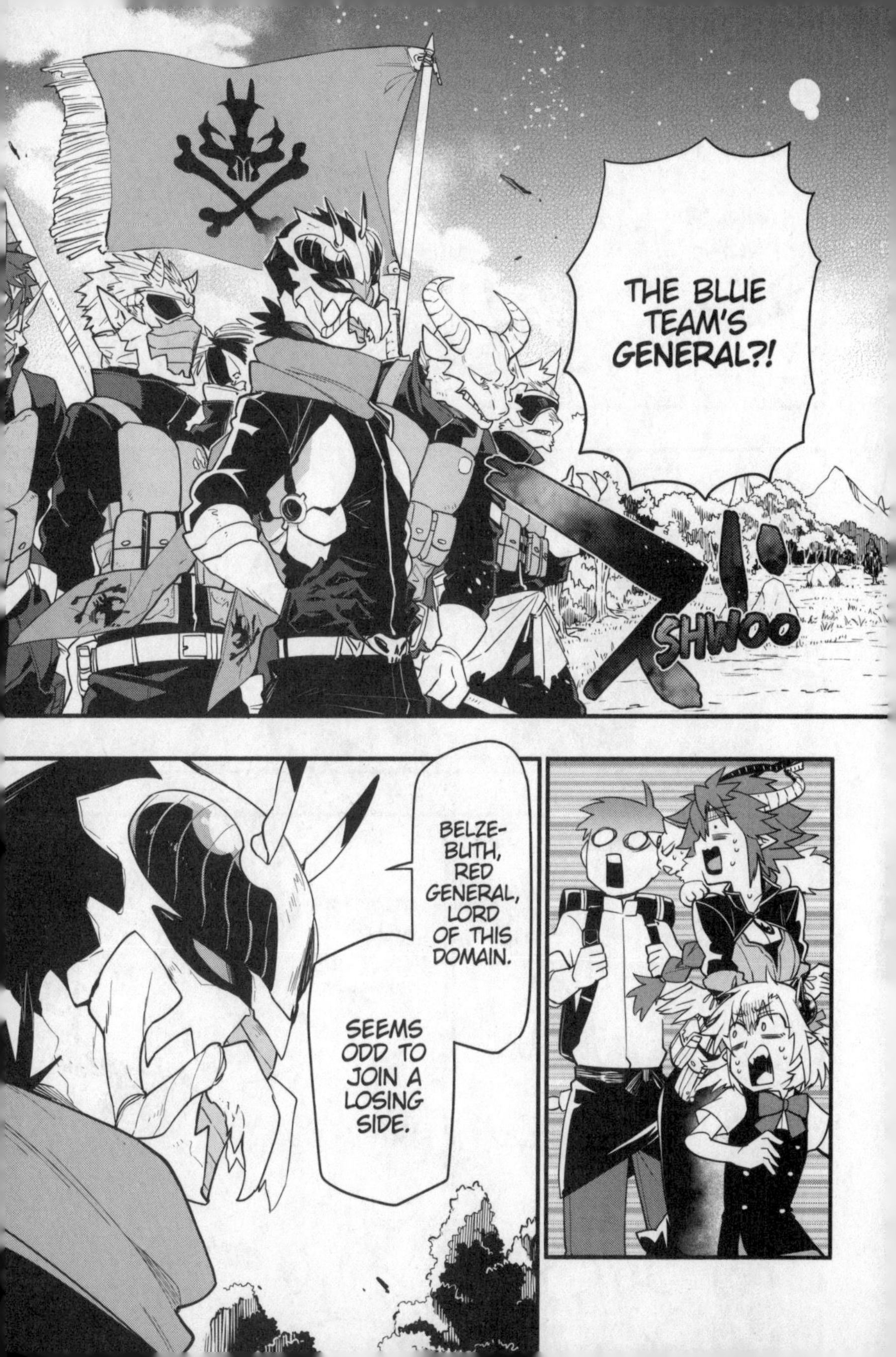
THE BLUE TEAM'S GENERAL?!
SHWOO
BELZE-BUTH, RED GENERAL, LORD OF THIS DOMAIN.
SEEMS ODD TO JOIN A LOSING SIDE.

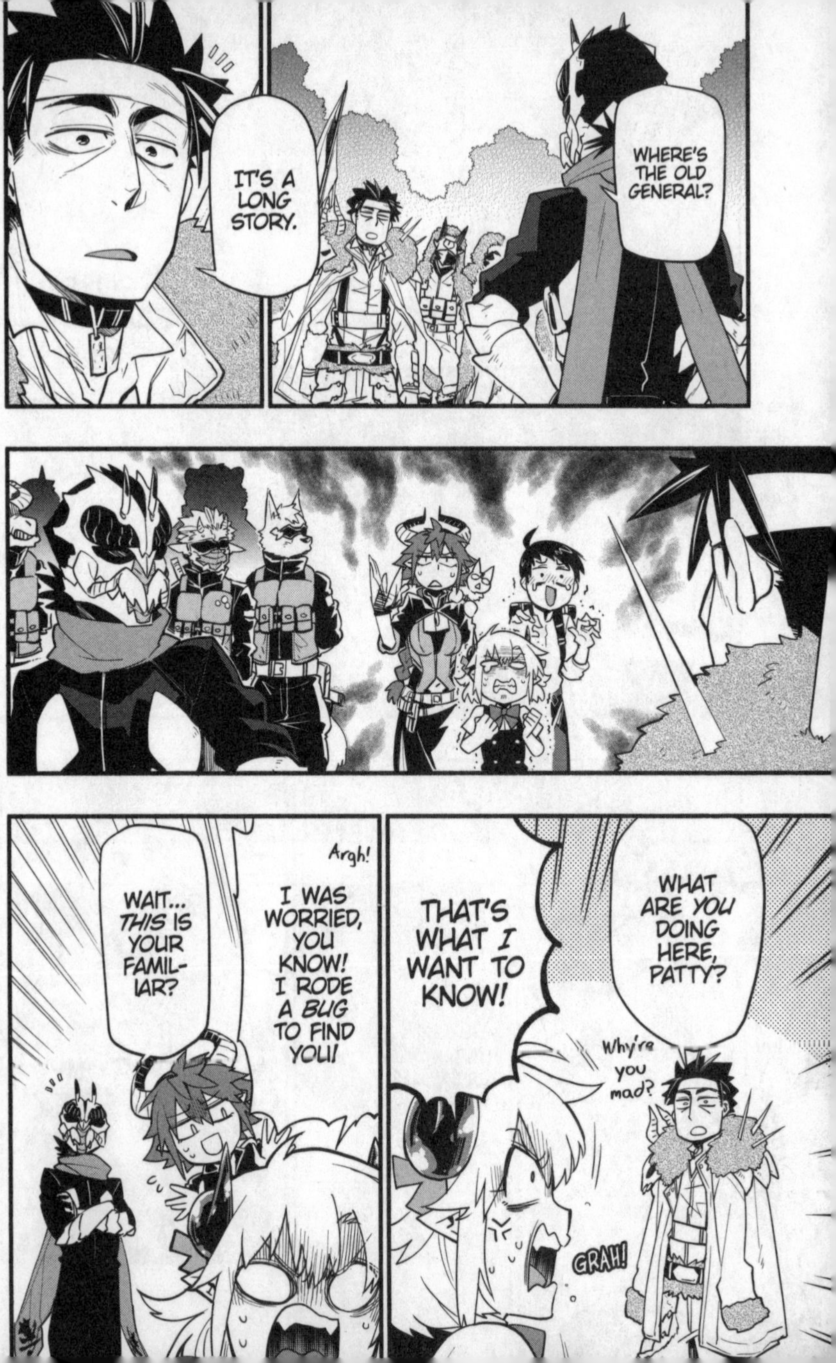
WHERE'S THE OLD GENERAL?
IT'S A LONG STORY.
WHAT ARE *YOU* DOING HERE, PATTY?
Why're you mad?
THAT'S WHAT *I* WANT TO KNOW!
GRAH!
Argh!
I WAS WORRIED, YOU KNOW! I RODE A *BUG* TO FIND YOU!
WAIT... *THIS* IS YOUR FAMIL-IAR?

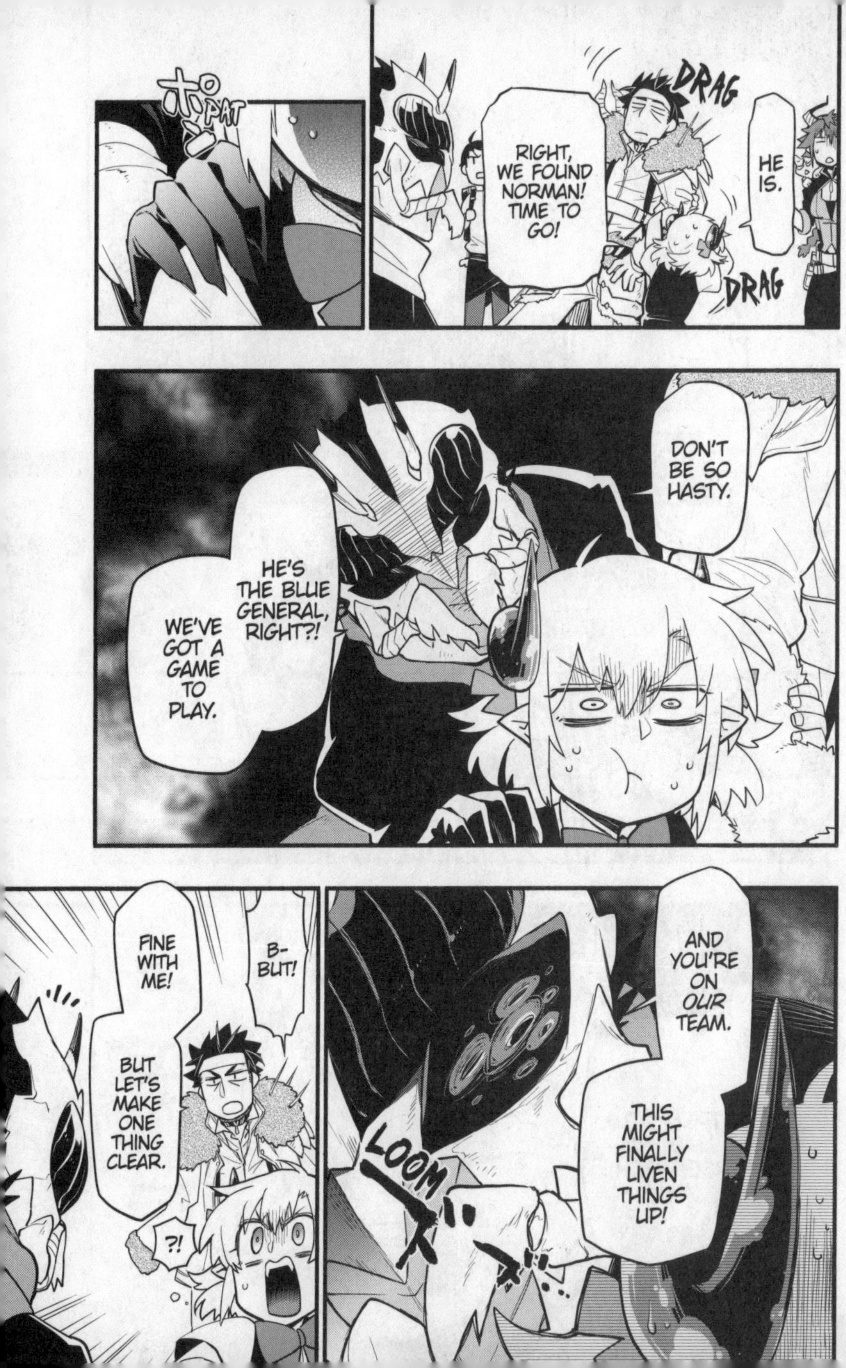
HE IS.
DRAG
DRAG
RIGHT, WE FOUND NORMAN! TIME TO GO!
ポ PAT
DON'T BE SO HASTY.
HE'S THE BLUE GENERAL, RIGHT?!
WE'VE GOT A GAME TO PLAY.
AND YOU'RE ON OUR TEAM.
THIS MIGHT FINALLY LIVEN THINGS UP!
LOOM
B-BUT!
FINE WITH ME!
BUT LET'S MAKE ONE THING CLEAR.
?!

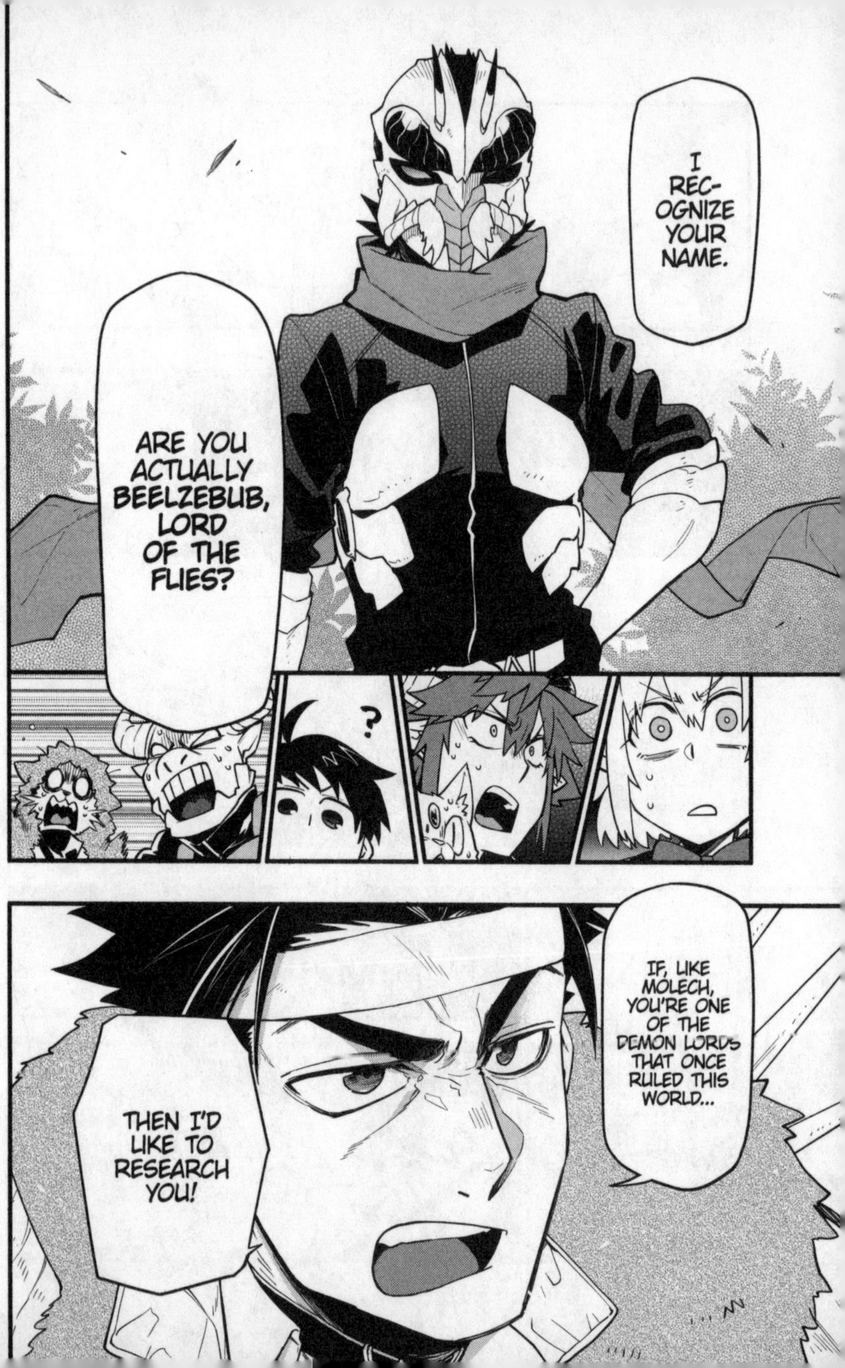
I RECOGNIZE YOUR NAME.
ARE YOU ACTUALLY BEELZEBUB, LORD OF THE FLIES?
?
IF, LIKE MOLECH, YOU'RE ONE OF THE DEMON LORDS THAT ONCE RULED THIS WORLD...
THEN I'D LIKE TO RESEARCH YOU!

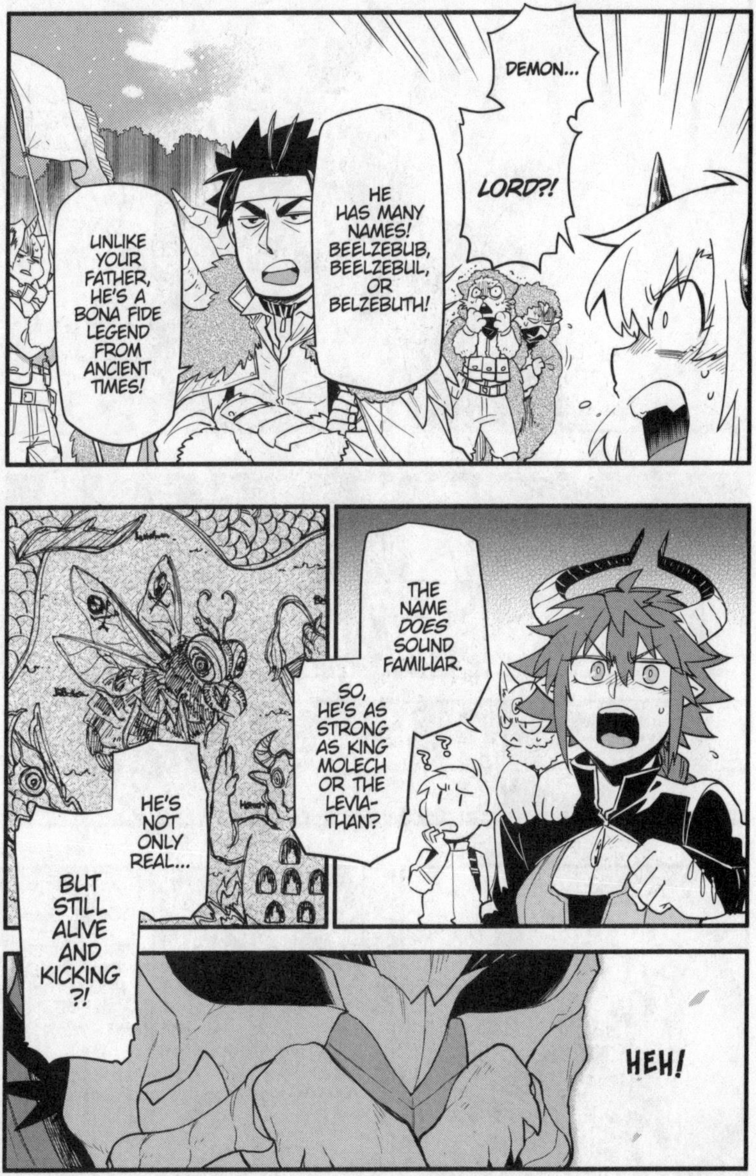
DEMON...
LORD?!
HE HAS MANY NAMES! BEELZEBUB, BEELZEBUL, OR BELZEBUTH!
UNLIKE YOUR FATHER, HE'S A BONA FIDE LEGEND FROM ANCIENT TIMES!
THE NAME *DOES* SOUND FAMILIAR.
SO, HE'S AS STRONG AS KING MOLECH OR THE LEVIA-THAN?
HE'S NOT ONLY REAL...
BUT STILL ALIVE AND KICKING?!
HEH!

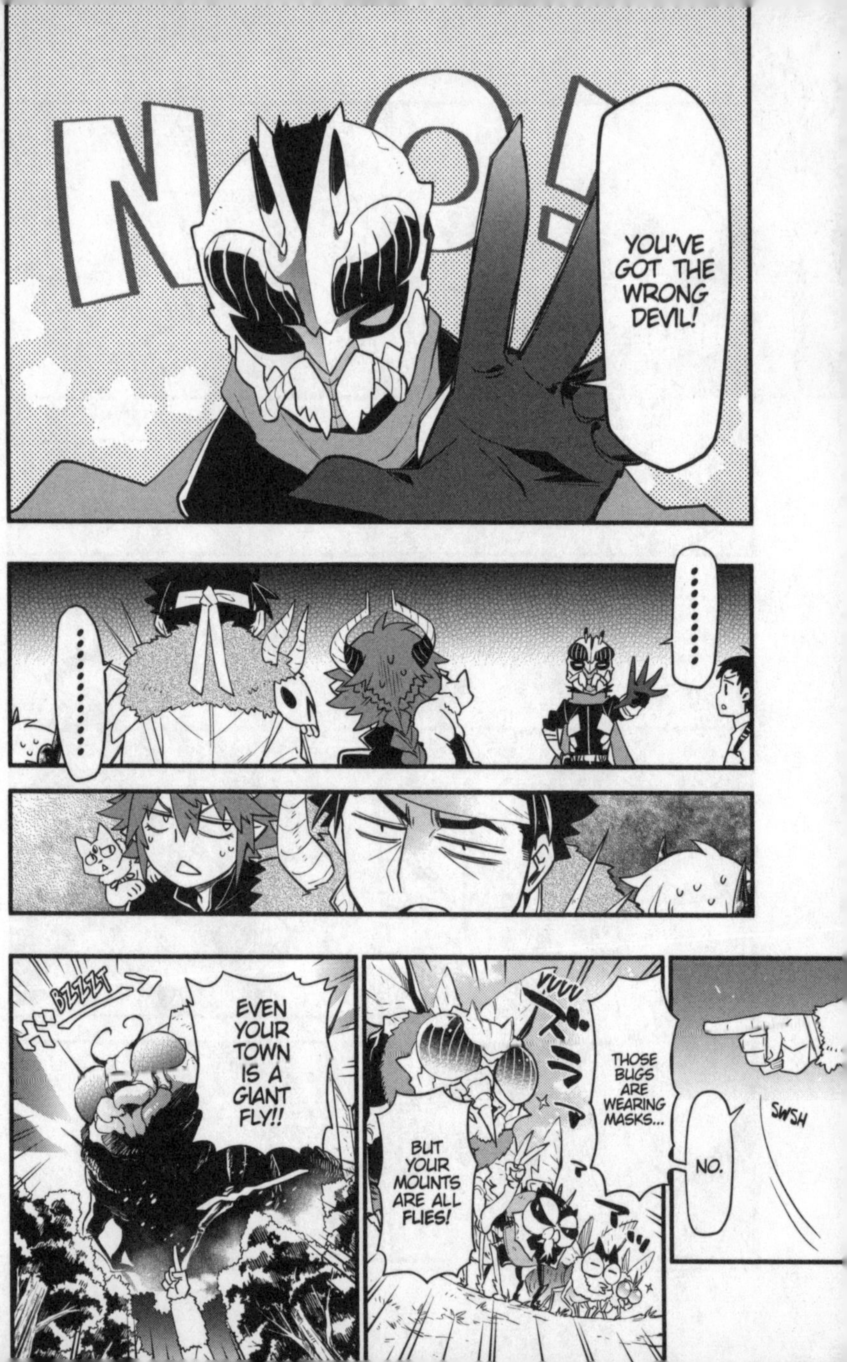

NO!
YOU'VE GOT THE WRONG DEVIL!
....
....
SWSH
NO.
THOSE BUGS ARE WEARING MASKS...
BUT YOUR MOUNTS ARE ALL FLIES!
EVEN YOUR TOWN IS A GIANT FLY!!
BZZZZT

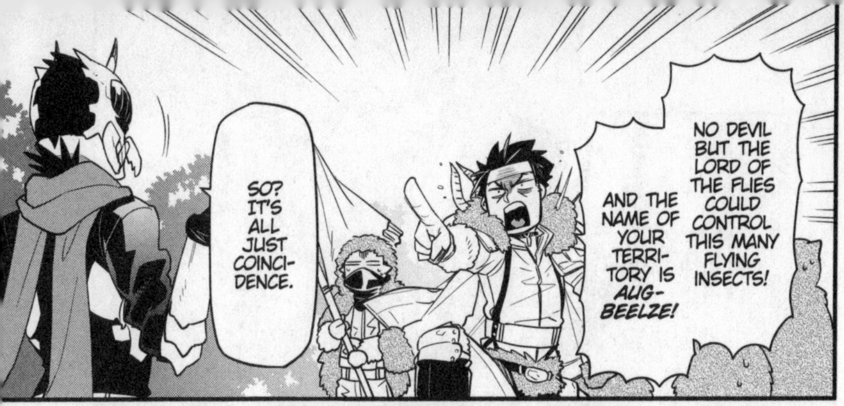
NO DEVIL BUT THE LORD OF THE FLIES COULD CONTROL THIS MANY FLYING INSECTS!
AND THE NAME OF YOUR TERRITORY IS AUGBEELZE!
SO? IT'S ALL JUST COINCIDENCE.

※Norman's theory is that the territories are named after Demon Lords.

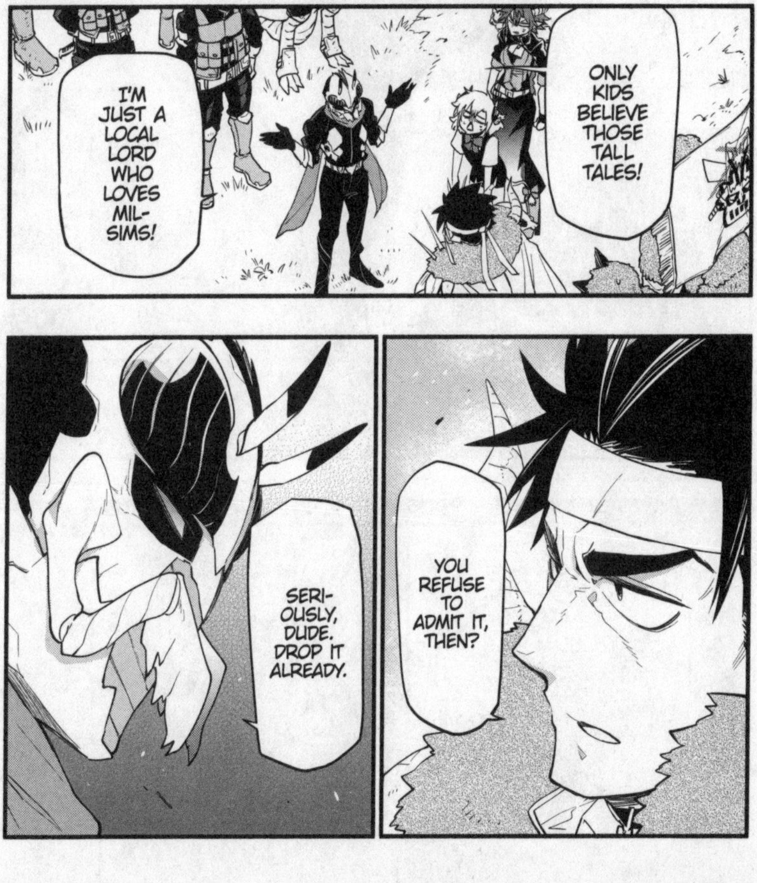
ONLY KIDS BELIEVE THOSE TALL TALES!
I'M JUST A LOCAL LORD WHO LOVES MIL-SIMS!
YOU REFUSE TO ADMIT IT, THEN?
SERIOUSLY, DUDE. DROP IT ALREADY.

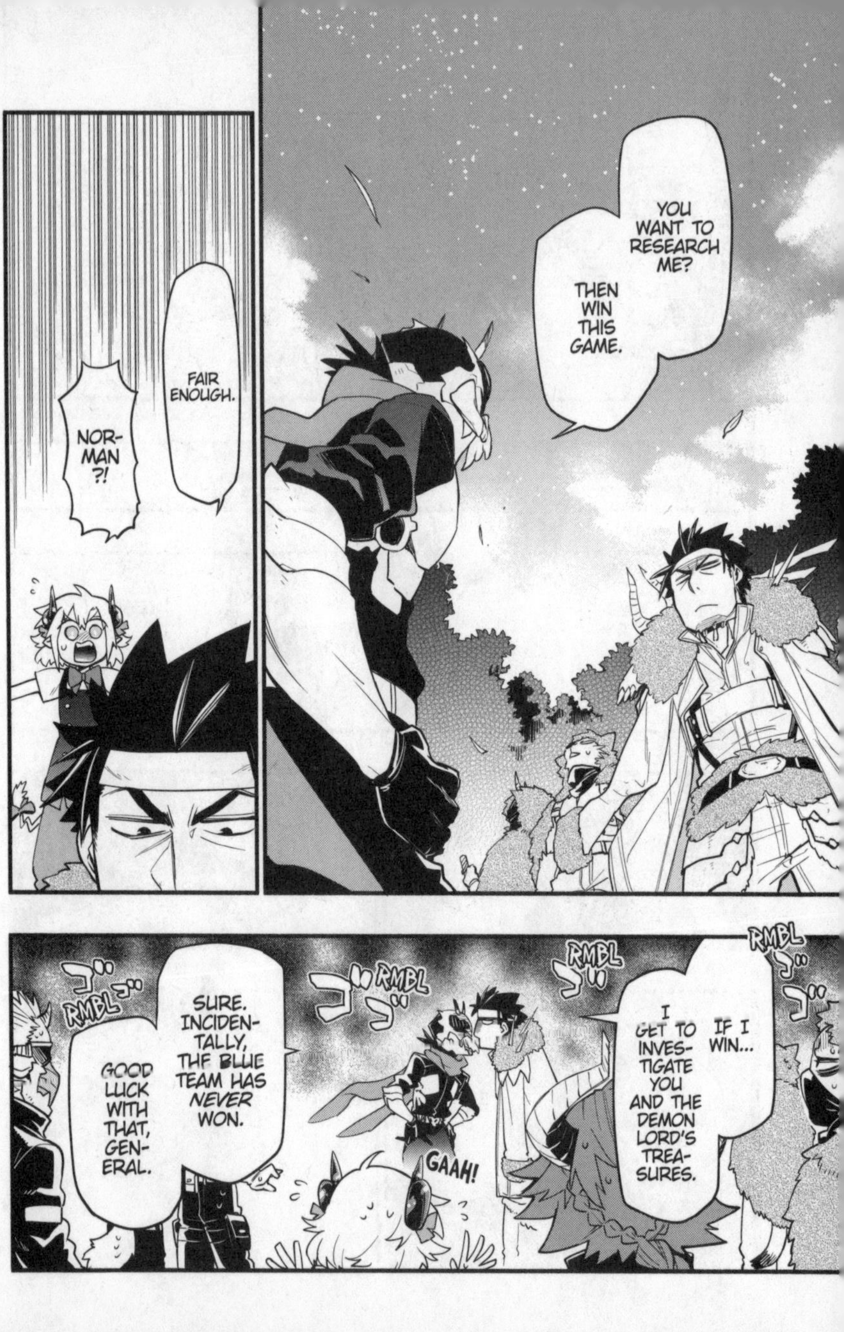
YOU WANT TO RESEARCH ME?
THEN WIN THIS GAME.
FAIR ENOUGH.
NOR-MAN?!
RMBL
IF I WIN...
I GET TO INVESTIGATE YOU AND THE DEMON LORD'S TREASURES.
RMBL
RMBL
GAAH!
SURE. INCIDENTALLY, THE BLUE TEAM HAS *NEVER* WON.
GOOD LUCK WITH THAT, GENERAL.
RMBL

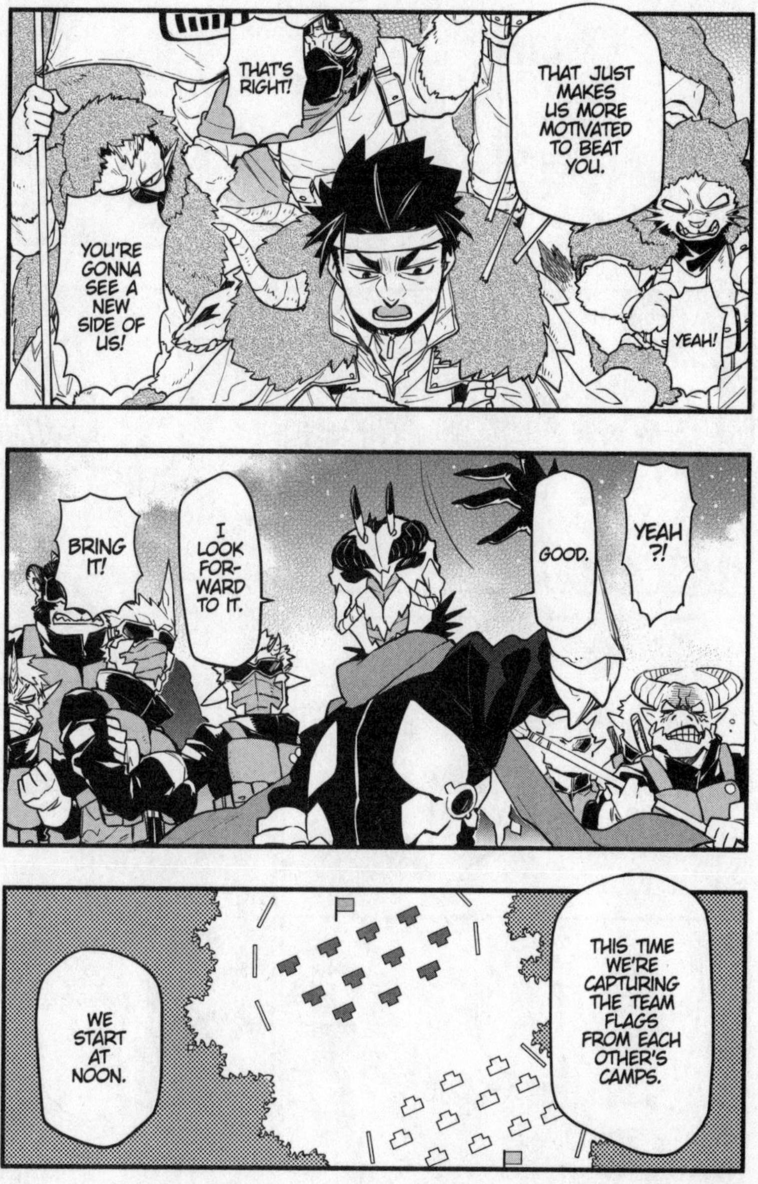
THAT JUST MAKES US MORE MOTIVATED TO BEAT YOU.
THAT'S RIGHT!
YEAH!
YOU'RE GONNA SEE A NEW SIDE OF US!
YEAH ?!
GOOD.
I LOOK FOR-WARD TO IT.
BRING IT!
THIS TIME WE'RE CAPTURING THE TEAM FLAGS FROM EACH OTHER'S CAMPS.
WE START AT NOON.

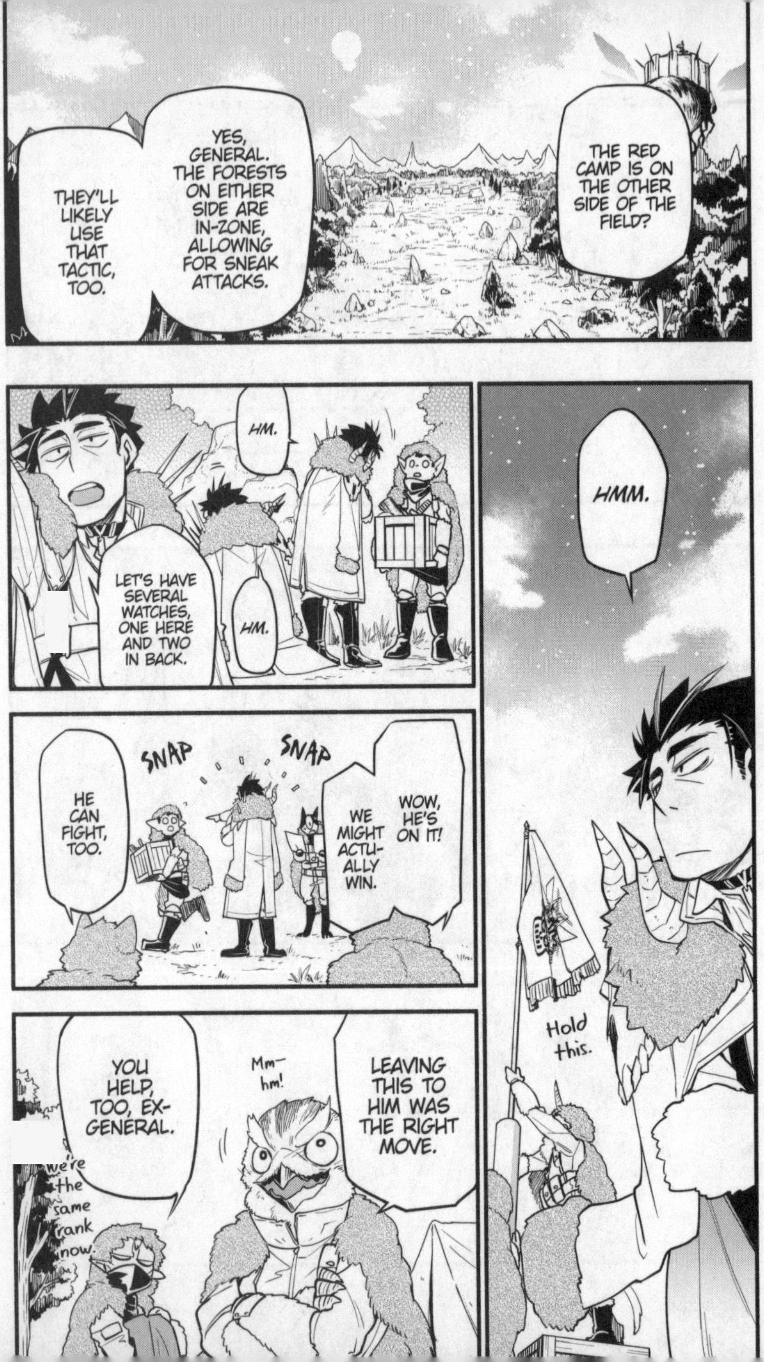
THE RED CAMP IS ON THE OTHER SIDE OF THE FIELD?
YES, GENERAL. THE FORESTS ON EITHER SIDE ARE IN-ZONE, ALLOWING FOR SNEAK ATTACKS.
THEY'LL LIKELY USE THAT TACTIC, TOO.
HMM.
Hold this.
HM.
HM.
LET'S HAVE SEVERAL WATCHES, ONE HERE AND TWO IN BACK.
SNAP
SNAP
WOW, HE'S ON IT!
WE MIGHT ACTUALLY WIN.
HE CAN FIGHT, TOO.
LEAVING THIS TO HIM WAS THE RIGHT MOVE.
Mm-hm!
YOU HELP, TOO, EX-GENERAL.
We're the same rank now.

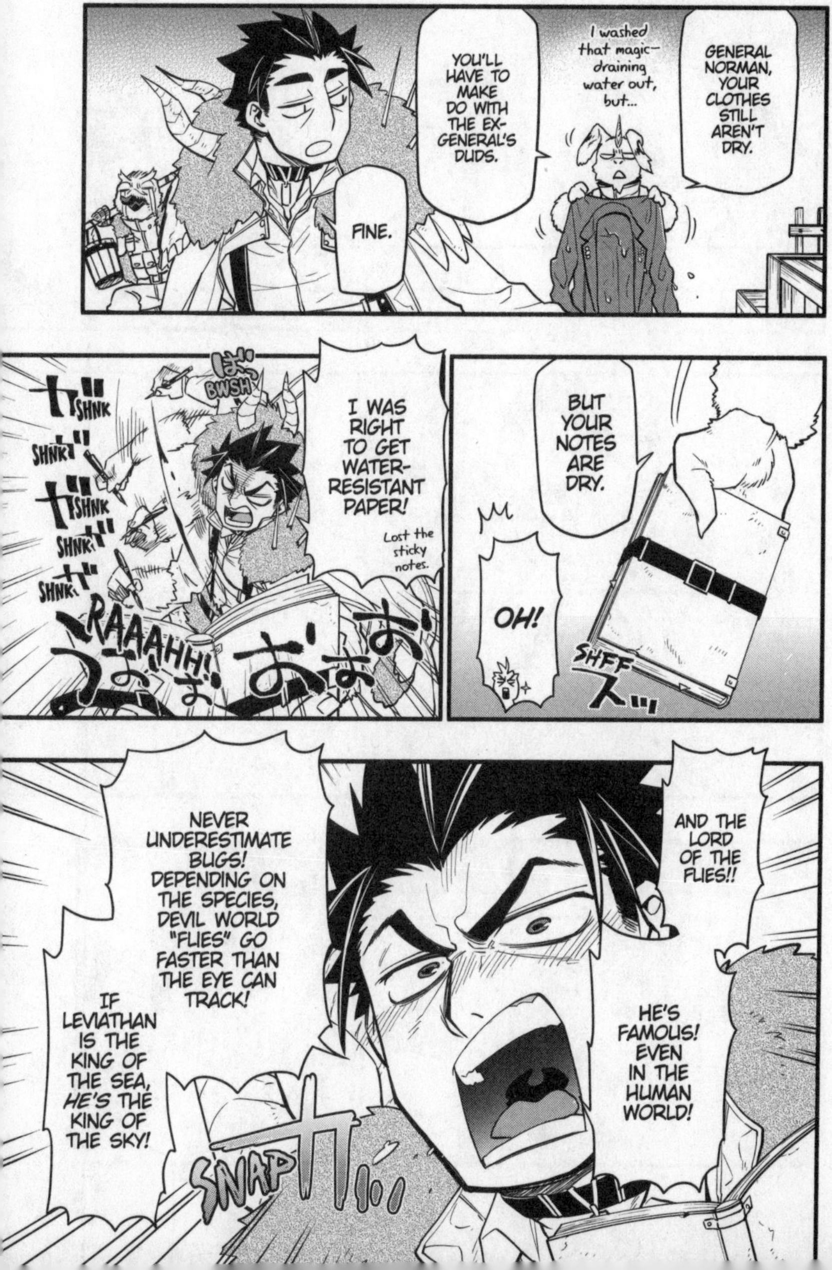
GENERAL NORMAN, YOUR CLOTHES STILL AREN'T DRY.
I washed that magic-draining water out, but...
YOU'LL HAVE TO MAKE DO WITH THE EX-GENERAL'S DUDS.
FINE.
BUT YOUR NOTES ARE DRY.
OH!
SHFF
I WAS RIGHT TO GET WATER-RESISTANT PAPER!
Lost the sticky notes.
BWSH
SHNK
SHNK
SHNK
SHNK
SHNK
RAAAHH!
AND THE LORD OF THE FLIES!!
HE'S FAMOUS! EVEN IN THE HUMAN WORLD!
NEVER UNDERESTIMATE BUGS! DEPENDING ON THE SPECIES, DEVIL WORLD "FLIES" GO FASTER THAN THE EYE CAN TRACK!
IF LEVIATHAN IS THE KING OF THE SEA, *HE'S* THE KING OF THE SKY!
SNAP

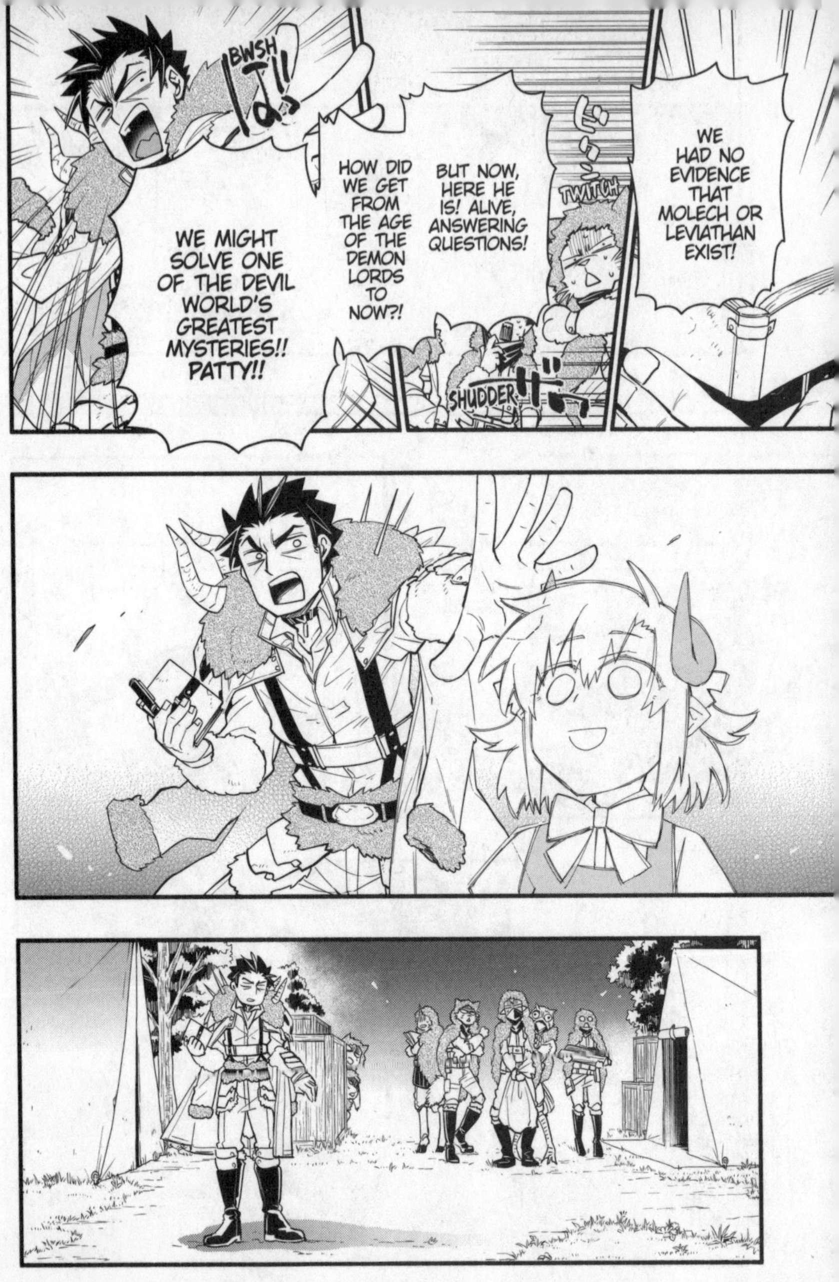
WE HAD NO EVIDENCE THAT MOLECH OR LEVIATHAN EXIST!
TWITCH
BUT NOW, HERE HE IS! ALIVE, ANSWERING QUESTIONS!
HOW DID WE GET FROM THE AGE OF THE DEMON LORDS TO NOW?!
SHUDDER
BWSH
WE MIGHT SOLVE ONE OF THE DEVIL WORLD'S GREATEST MYSTERIES!! PATTY!!

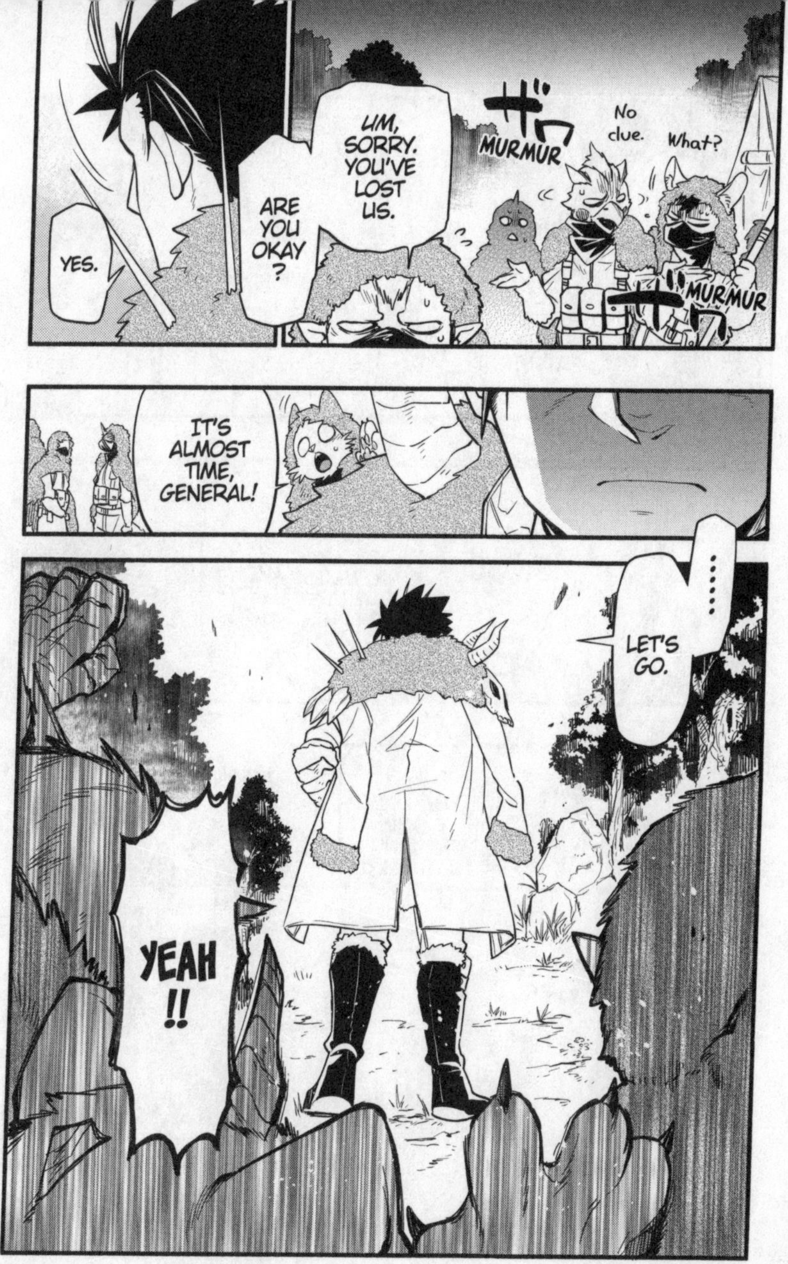
MURMUR
ザワ
What?
No clue.
MURMUR
ザワ
UM, SORRY. YOU'VE LOST US.
ARE YOU OKAY?
YES.
IT'S ALMOST TIME, GENERAL!
......
LET'S GO.
YEAH!!

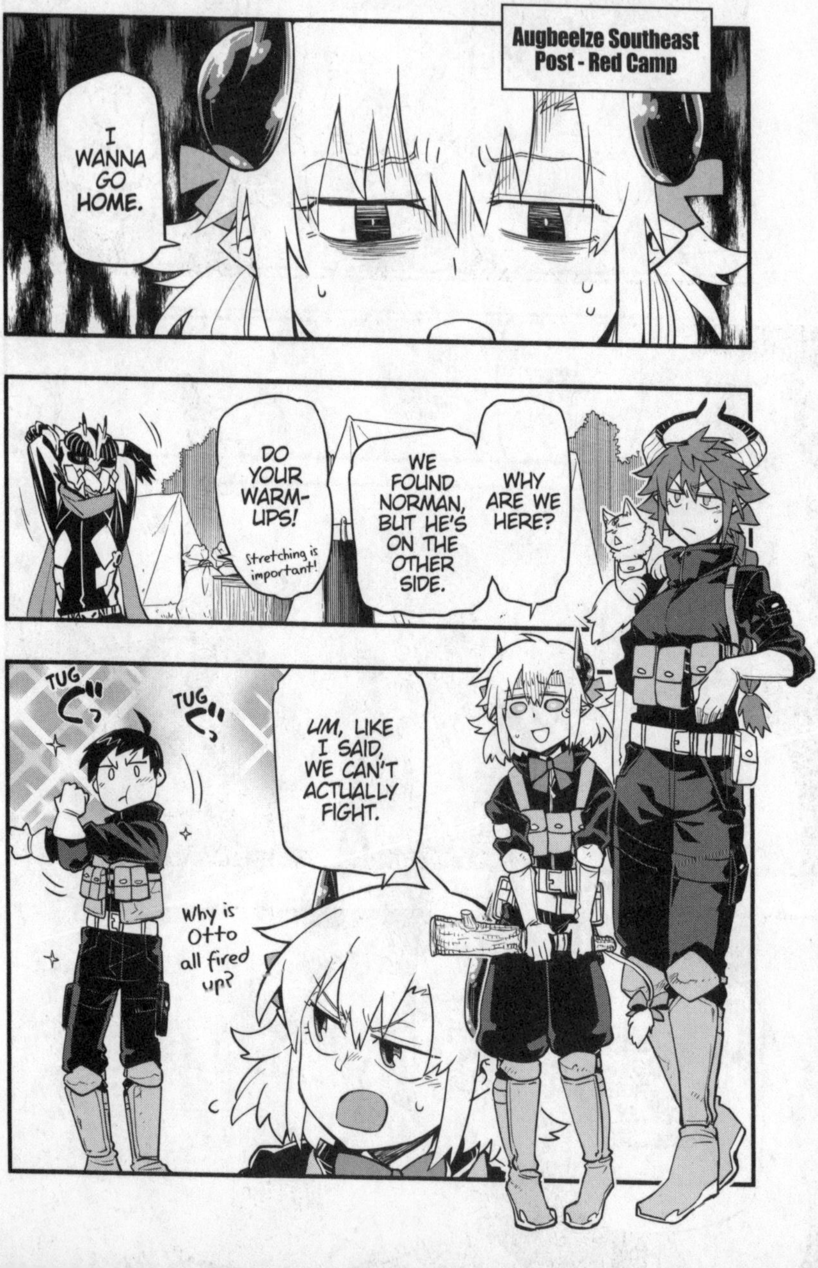
Augbeelze Southeast Post - Red Camp
I WANNA GO HOME.
WHY ARE WE HERE?
WE FOUND NORMAN, BUT HE'S ON THE OTHER SIDE.
DO YOUR WARM-UPS!
Stretching is important!
TUG
TUG
UM, LIKE I SAID, WE CAN'T ACTUALLY FIGHT.
Why is Otto all fired up?

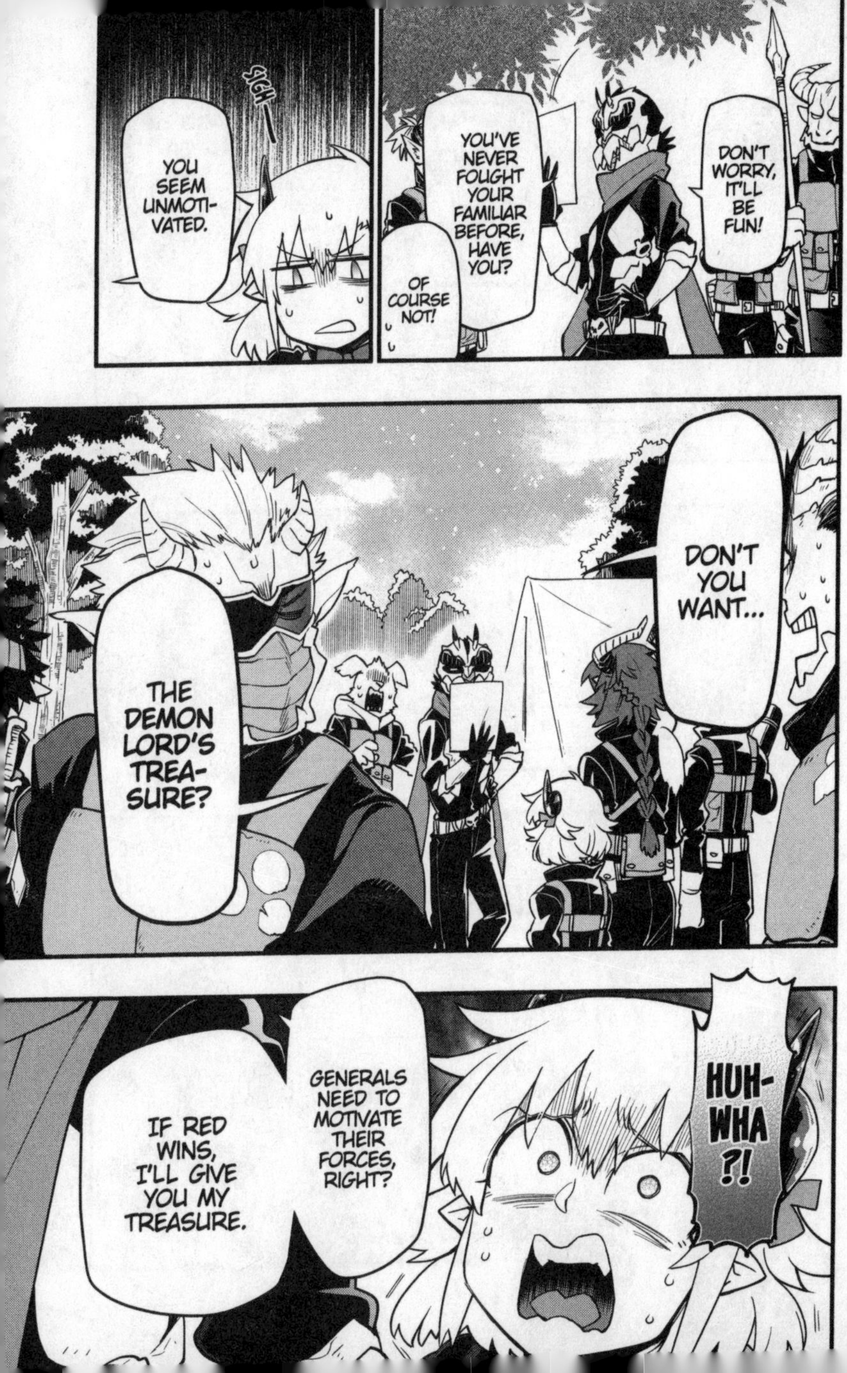
DON'T WORRY, IT'LL BE FUN!
YOU'VE NEVER FOUGHT YOUR FAMILIAR BEFORE, HAVE YOU?
OF COURSE NOT!
SIGH—
YOU SEEM UNMOTI-VATED.
DON'T YOU WANT...
THE DEMON LORD'S TREA-SURE?
GENERALS NEED TO MOTIVATE THEIR FORCES, RIGHT?
IF RED WINS, I'LL GIVE YOU MY TREASURE.
HUH-WHA?!

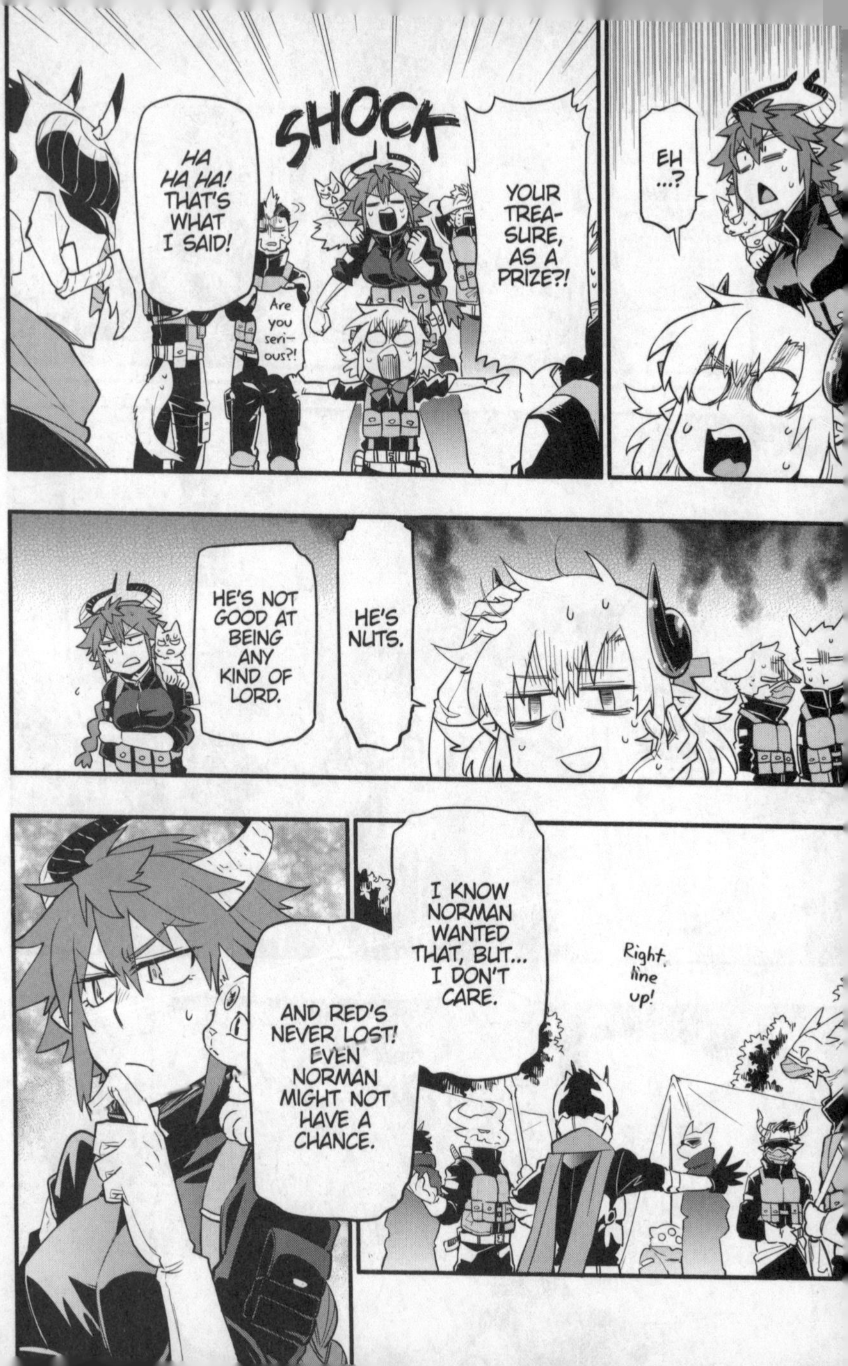
EH ...?
YOUR TREASURE, AS A PRIZE?!
SHOCK
Are you serious?!
HA HA HA! THAT'S WHAT I SAID!
HE'S NUTS.
HE'S NOT GOOD AT BEING ANY KIND OF LORD.
Right, line up!
I KNOW NORMAN WANTED THAT, BUT... I DON'T CARE.
AND RED'S NEVER LOST! EVEN NORMAN MIGHT NOT HAVE A CHANCE.

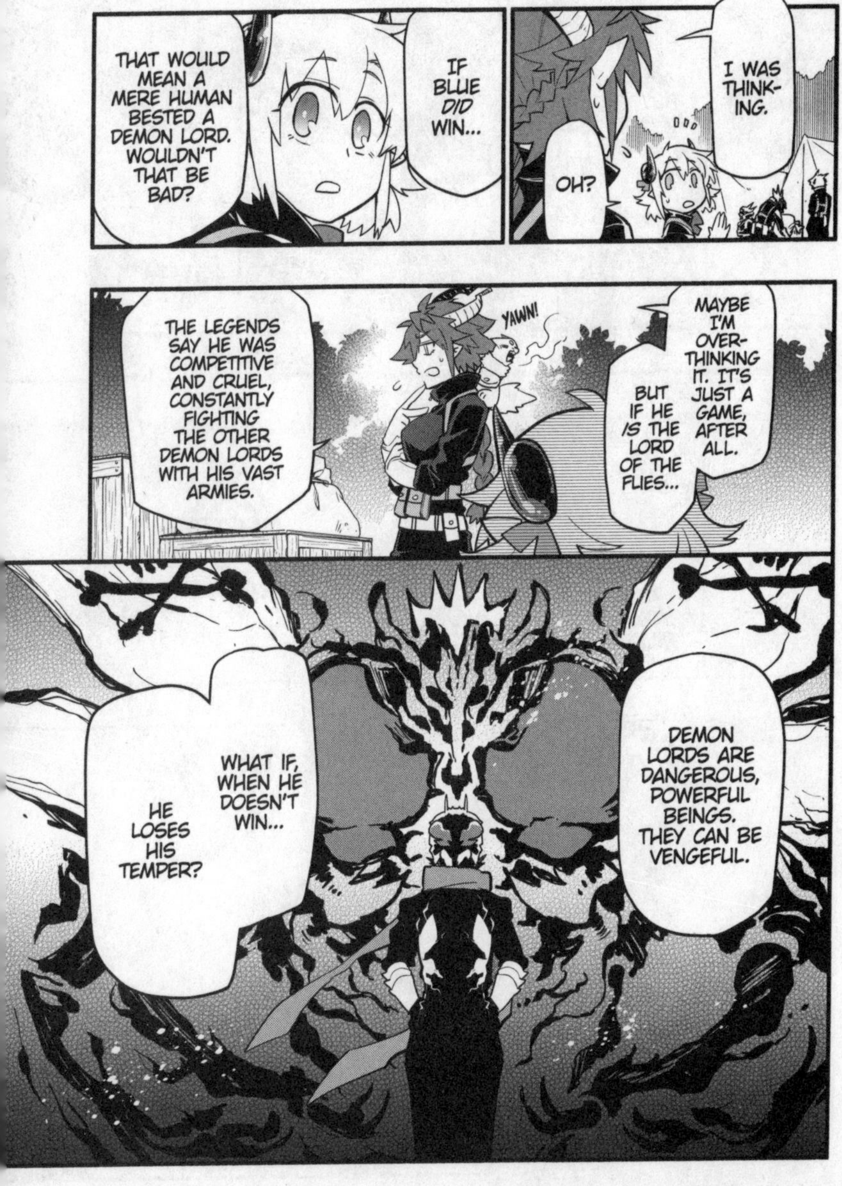
I WAS THINKING.
OH?
IF BLUE DID WIN...
THAT WOULD MEAN A MERE HUMAN BESTED A DEMON LORD. WOULDN'T THAT BE BAD?
MAYBE I'M OVERTHINKING IT. IT'S JUST A GAME, AFTER ALL.
BUT IF HE IS THE LORD OF THE FLIES...
YAWN!
THE LEGENDS SAY HE WAS COMPETITIVE AND CRUEL, CONSTANTLY FIGHTING THE OTHER DEMON LORDS WITH HIS VAST ARMIES.
DEMON LORDS ARE DANGEROUS, POWERFUL BEINGS. THEY CAN BE VENGEFUL.
WHAT IF, WHEN HE DOESN'T WIN...
HE LOSES HIS TEMPER?

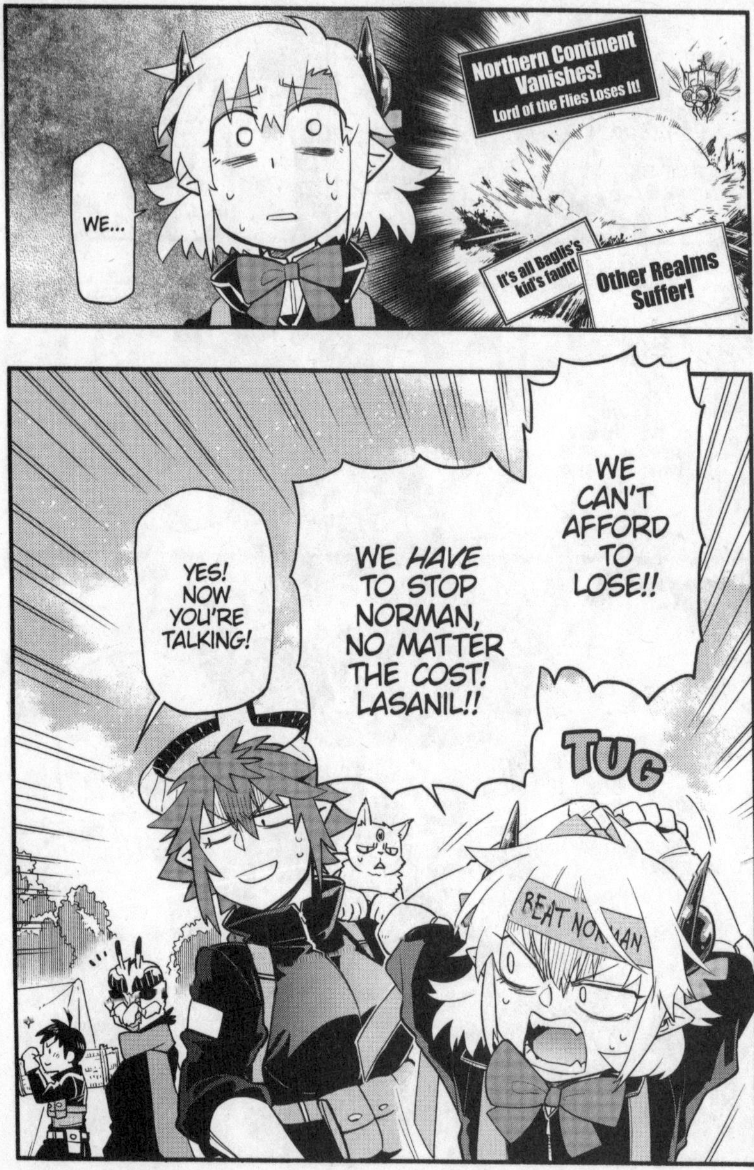
Northern Continent Vanishes!
Lord of the Flies Loses It!
Other Realms Suffer!
It's all Baglis's kid's fault!
WE...
WE CAN'T AFFORD TO LOSE!!
WE HAVE TO STOP NORMAN, NO MATTER THE COST! LASANIL!!
TUG
YES! NOW YOU'RE TALKING!

Sorry For My Familiar

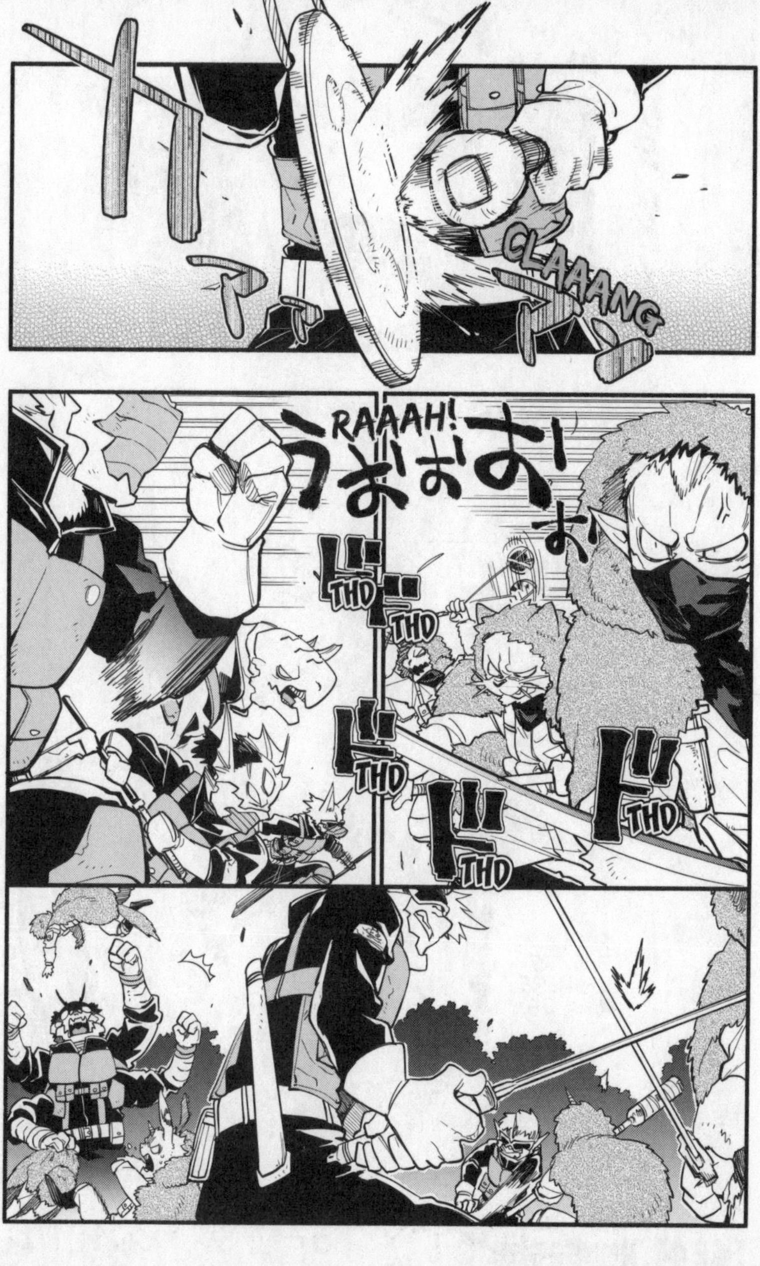
CLAAAANG
RAAAH!
THD
THD
THD
THD
THD

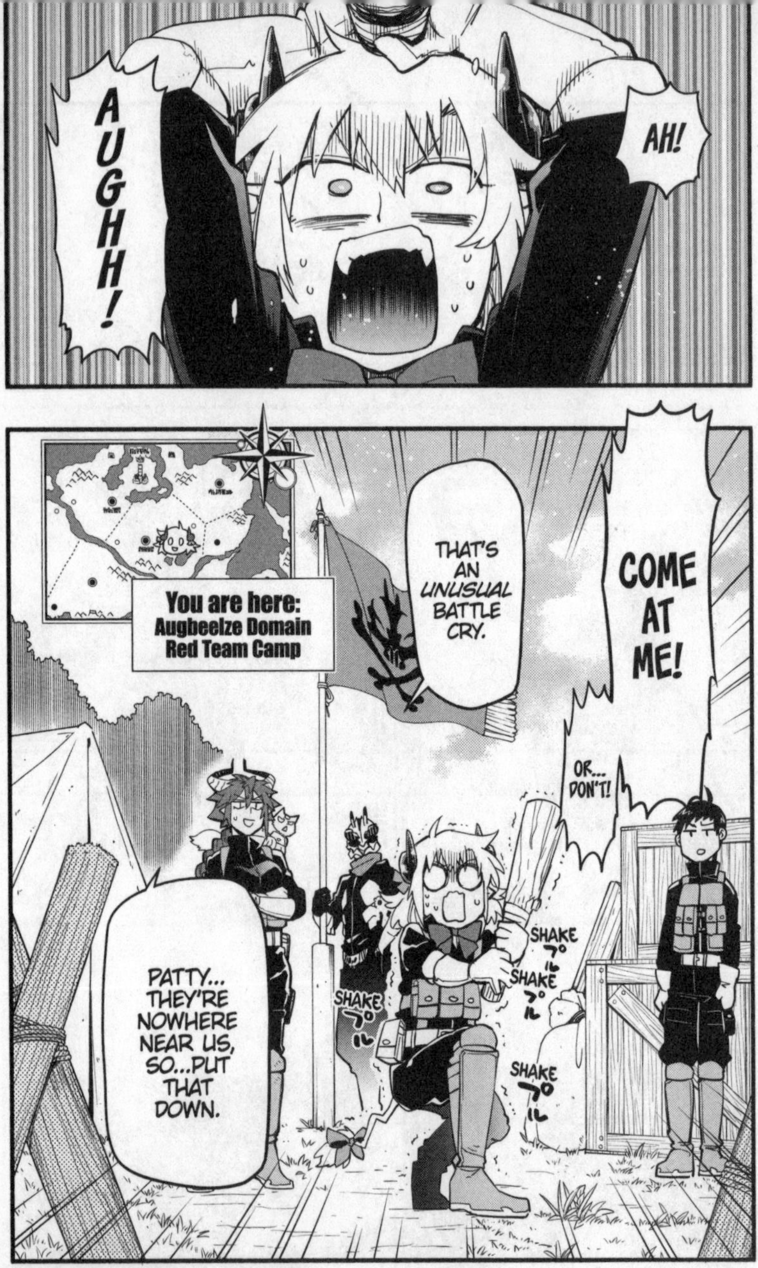
AH!
AUGHH!
COME AT ME!
THAT'S AN UNUSUAL BATTLE CRY.
You are here: Augbeelze Domain Red Team Camp
OR... DON'T!
SHAKE
SHAKE
SHAKE
SHAKE
PATTY... THEY'RE NOWHERE NEAR US, SO...PUT THAT DOWN.

FILE 44: Augbeelze ③

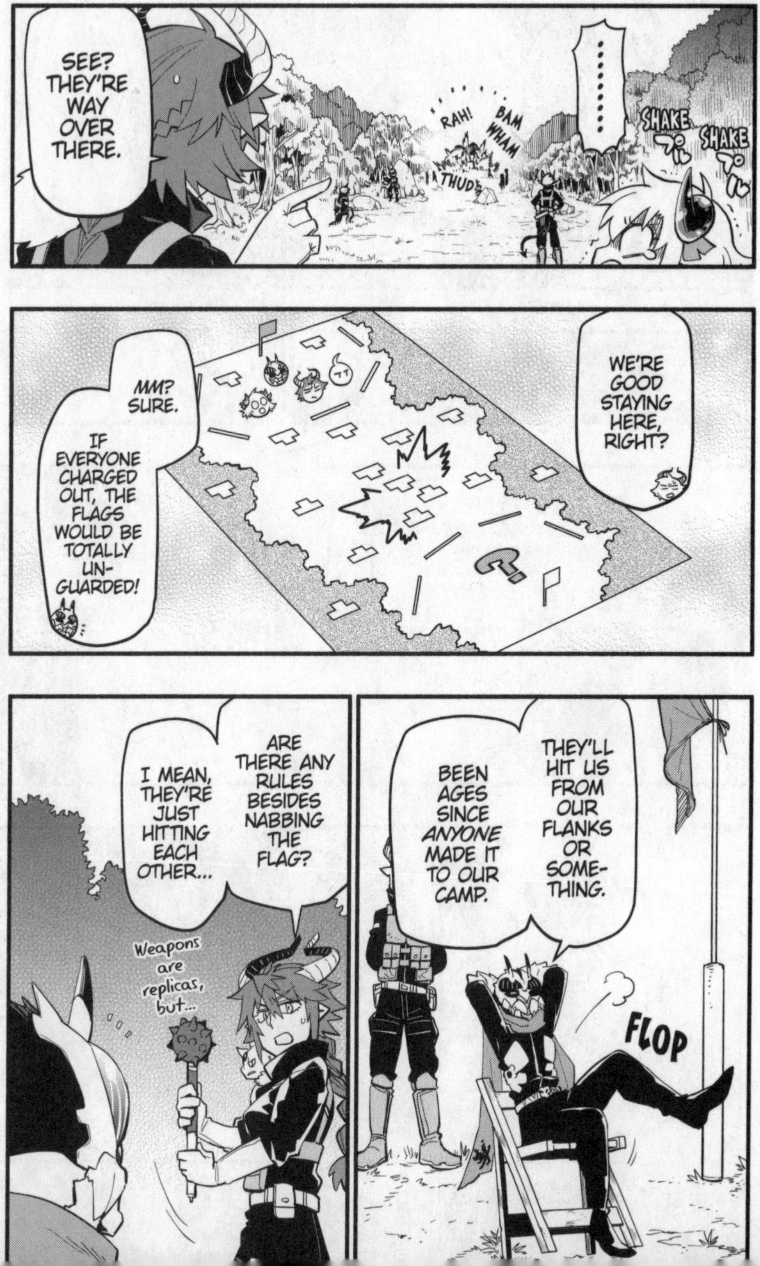
......
SHAKE
SHAKE
BAM WHAM
RAH!
THUD
SEE? THEY'RE WAY OVER THERE.
WE'RE GOOD STAYING HERE, RIGHT?
MM? SURE.
IF EVERYONE CHARGED OUT, THE FLAGS WOULD BE TOTALLY UN-GUARDED!
THEY'LL HIT US FROM OUR FLANKS OR SOME-THING.
BEEN AGES SINCE *ANYONE* MADE IT TO OUR CAMP.
FLOP
ARE THERE ANY RULES BESIDES NABBING THE FLAG?
I MEAN, THEY'RE JUST HITTING EACH OTHER...
Weapons are replicas, but...

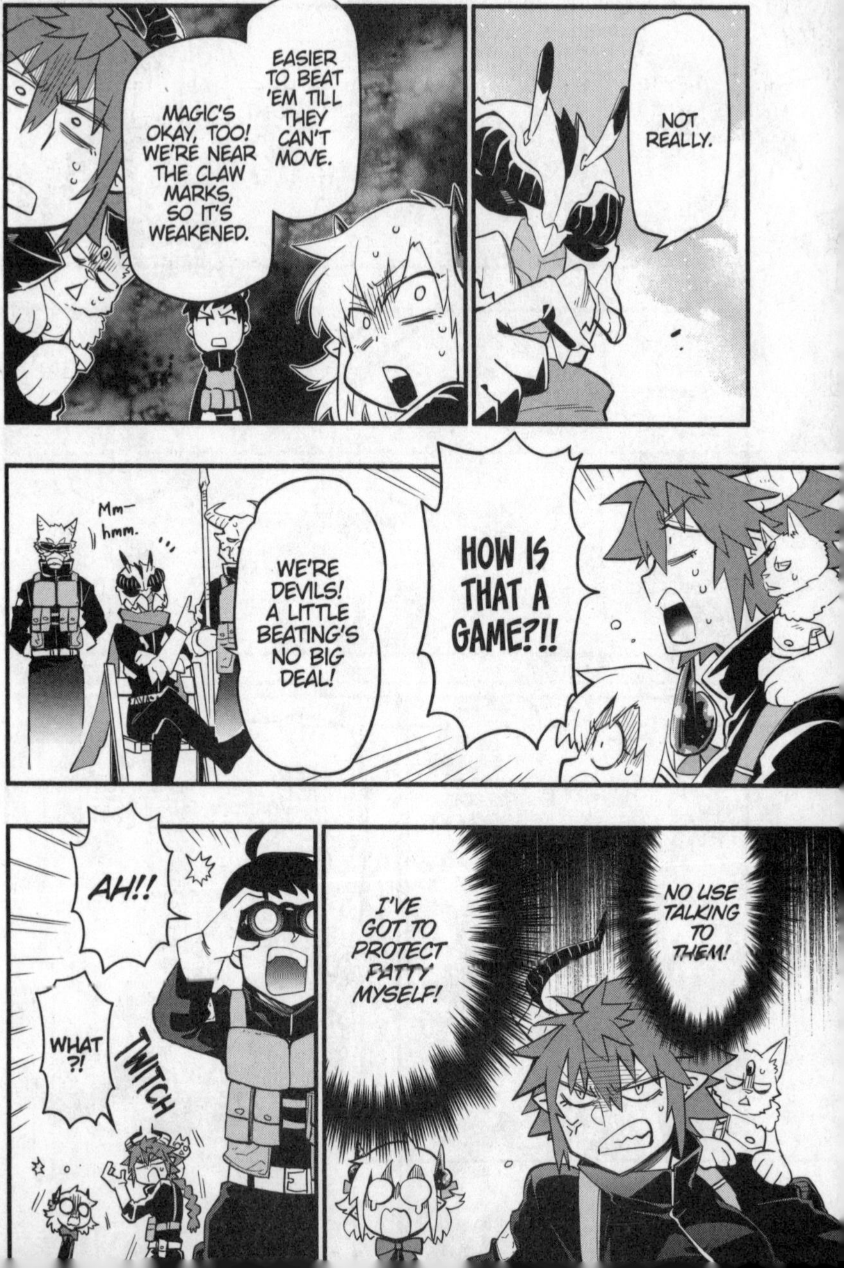
NOT REALLY.
EASIER TO BEAT 'EM TILL THEY CAN'T MOVE.
MAGIC'S OKAY, TOO! WE'RE NEAR THE CLAW MARKS, SO IT'S WEAKENED.
HOW IS THAT A GAME?!!
WE'RE DEVILS! A LITTLE BEATING'S NO BIG DEAL!
Mm-hmm.
NO USE TALKING TO THEM!
I'VE GOT TO PROTECT FATTY MYSELF!
AH!!
WHAT?!
TWITCH

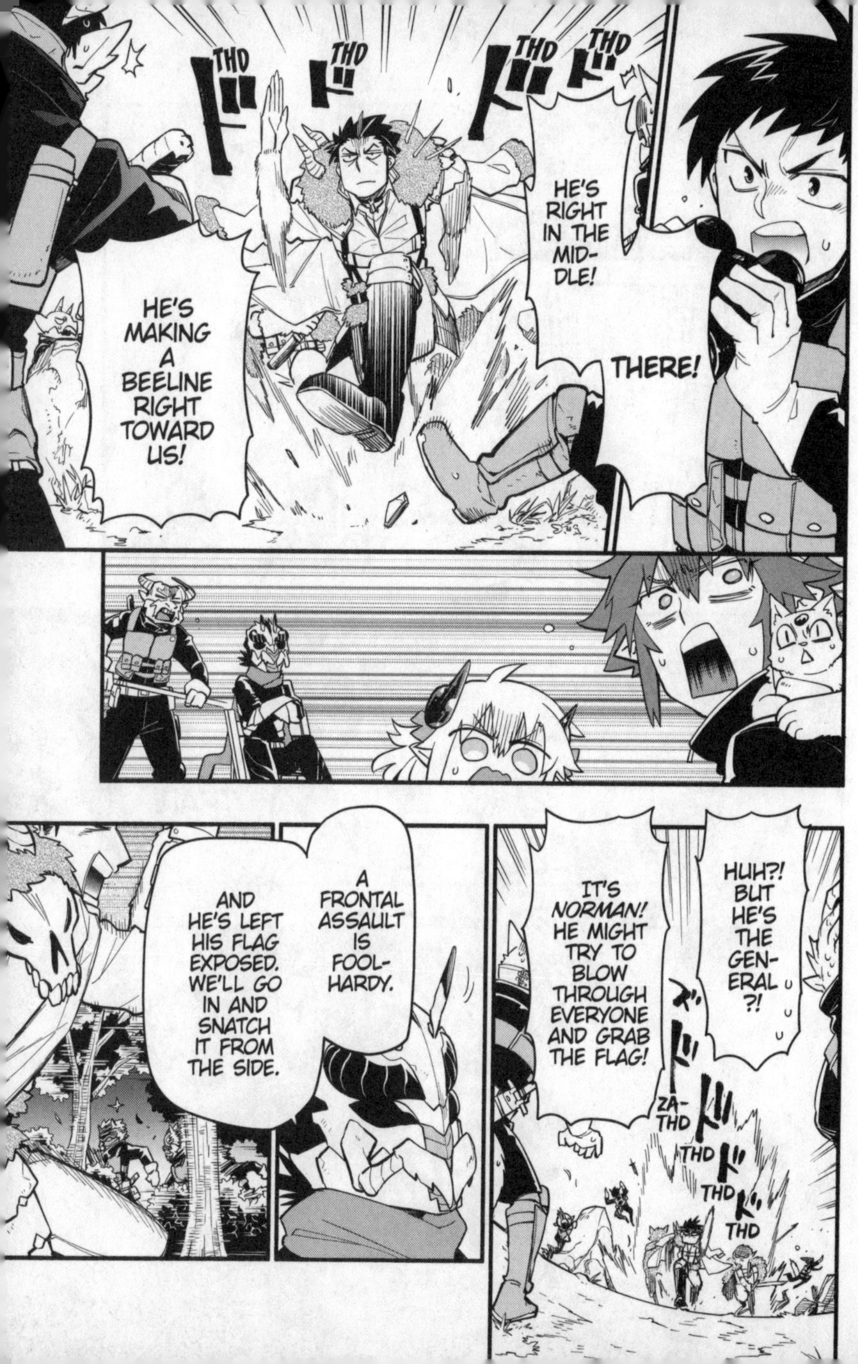
THD
THD
THD
THD
THERE!
HE'S RIGHT IN THE MIDDLE!
HE'S MAKING A BEELINE RIGHT TOWARD US!
HUH?! BUT HE'S THE GENERAL?!
IT'S NORMAN! HE MIGHT TRY TO BLOW THROUGH EVERYONE AND GRAB THE FLAG!
ZA-THD
THD
THD
THD
A FRONTAL ASSAULT IS FOOLHARDY.
AND HE'S LEFT HIS FLAG EXPOSED. WE'LL GO IN AND SNATCH IT FROM THE SIDE.

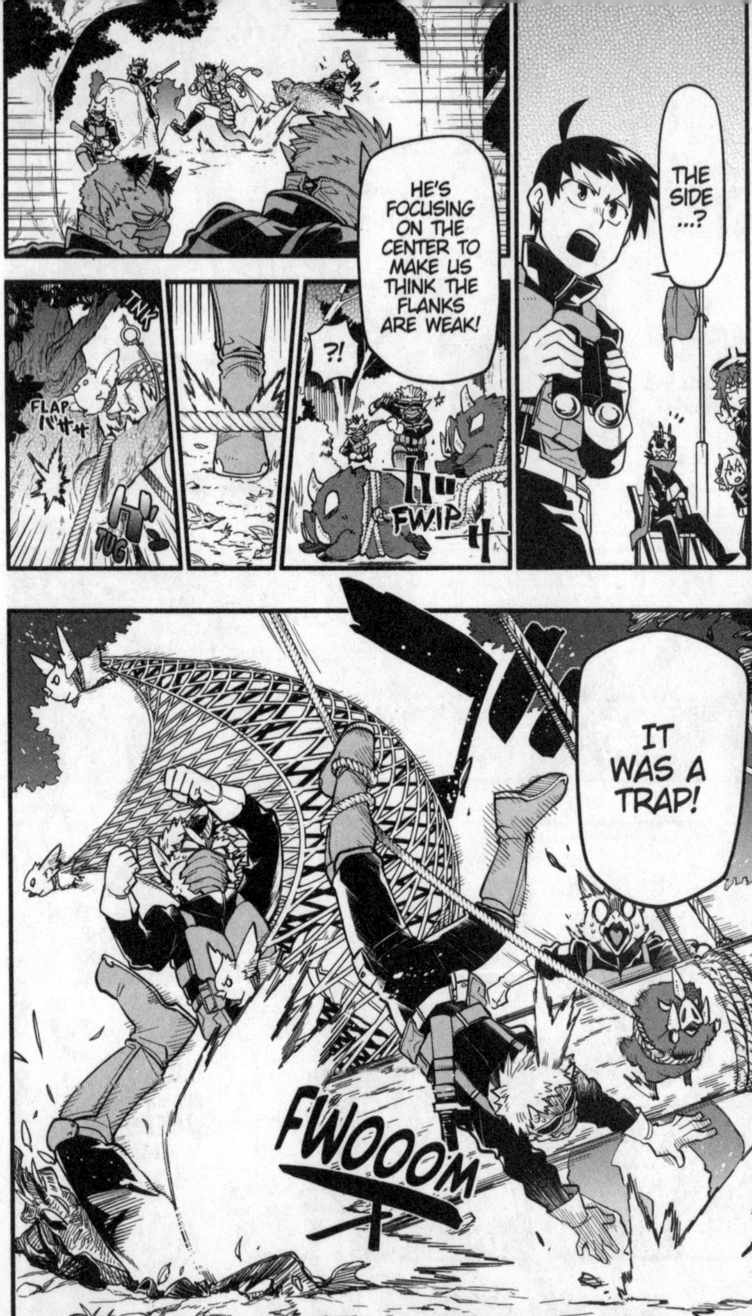
THE SIDE ...?
HE'S FOCUSING ON THE CENTER TO MAKE US THINK THE FLANKS ARE WEAK!
?!
FWIP
TNK
FLAP バサッ
TUG
IT WAS A TRAP!
FWOOOM

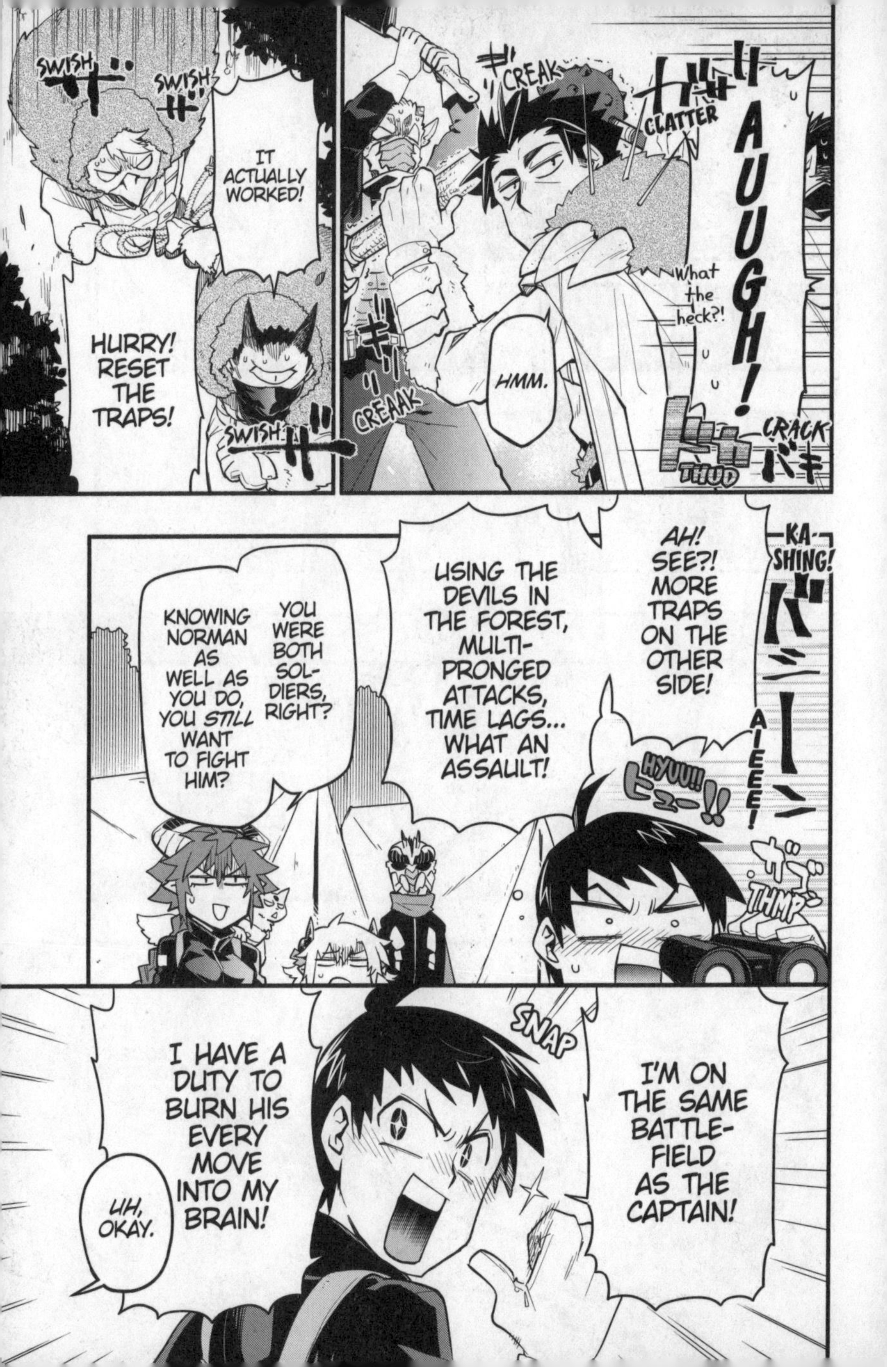
CREAK
CLATTER
AUUGH!
What the heck?!
HMM.
CREAAK
CRACK
THUD
SWISH
SWISH
IT ACTUALLY WORKED!
HURRY! RESET THE TRAPS!
SWISH
KA-SHING!
AH! SEE?! MORE TRAPS ON THE OTHER SIDE!
AIEEE!
HYUU!!
THMP
USING THE DEVILS IN THE FOREST, MULTI-PRONGED ATTACKS, TIME LAGS... WHAT AN ASSAULT!
YOU WERE BOTH SOL-DIERS, RIGHT?
KNOWING NORMAN AS WELL AS YOU DO, YOU STILL WANT TO FIGHT HIM?
SNAP
I'M ON THE SAME BATTLE-FIELD AS THE CAPTAIN!
I HAVE A DUTY TO BURN HIS EVERY MOVE INTO MY BRAIN!
UH, OKAY.

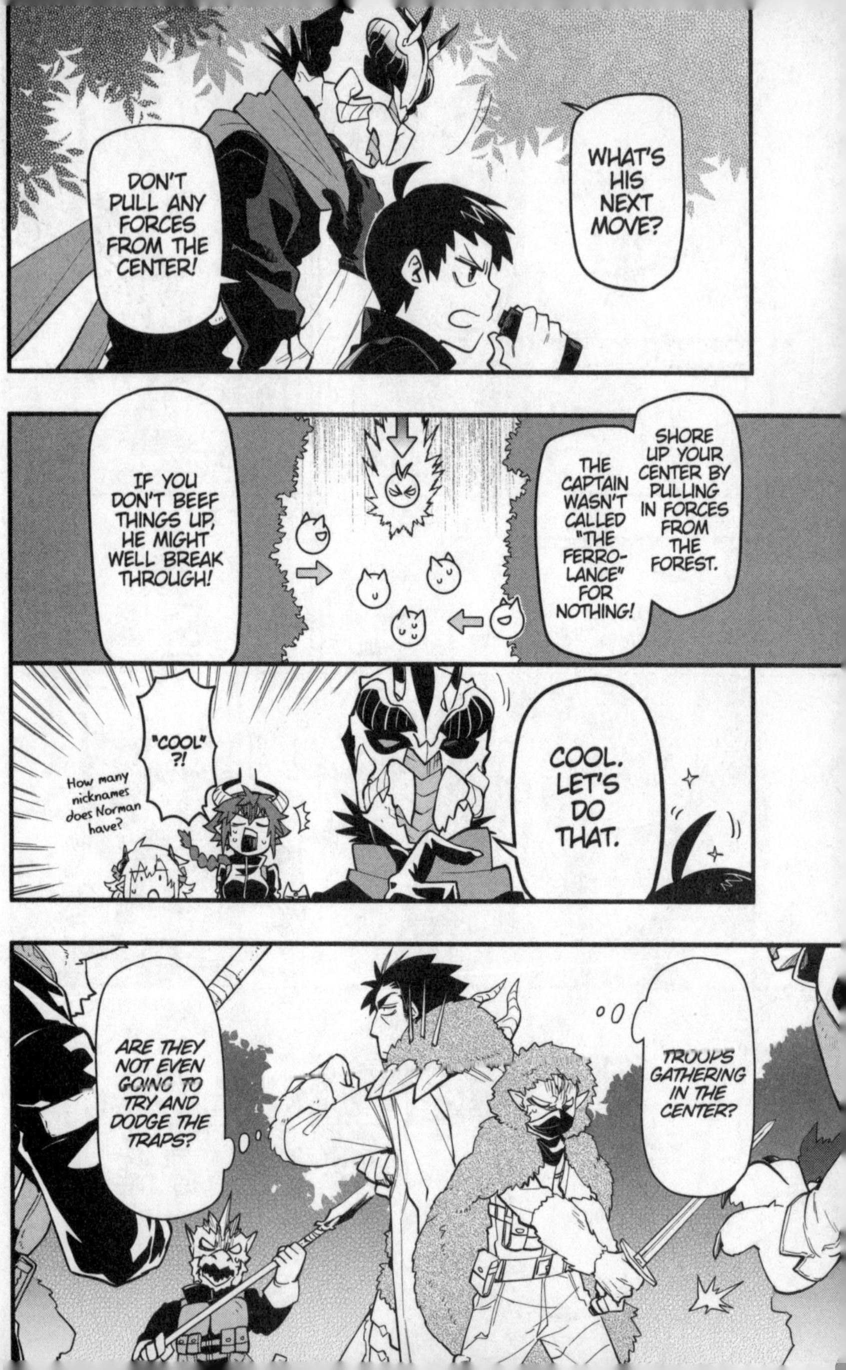
WHAT'S HIS NEXT MOVE?
DON'T PULL ANY FORCES FROM THE CENTER!
SHORE UP YOUR CENTER BY PULLING IN FORCES FROM THE FOREST.
THE CAPTAIN WASN'T CALLED "THE FERRO-LANCE" FOR NOTHING!
IF YOU DON'T BEEF THINGS UP, HE MIGHT WELL BREAK THROUGH!
COOL. LET'S DO THAT.
"COOL"?!
How many nicknames does Norman have?
TROOPS GATHERING IN THE CENTER?
ARE THEY NOT EVEN GOING TO TRY AND DODGE THE TRAPS?

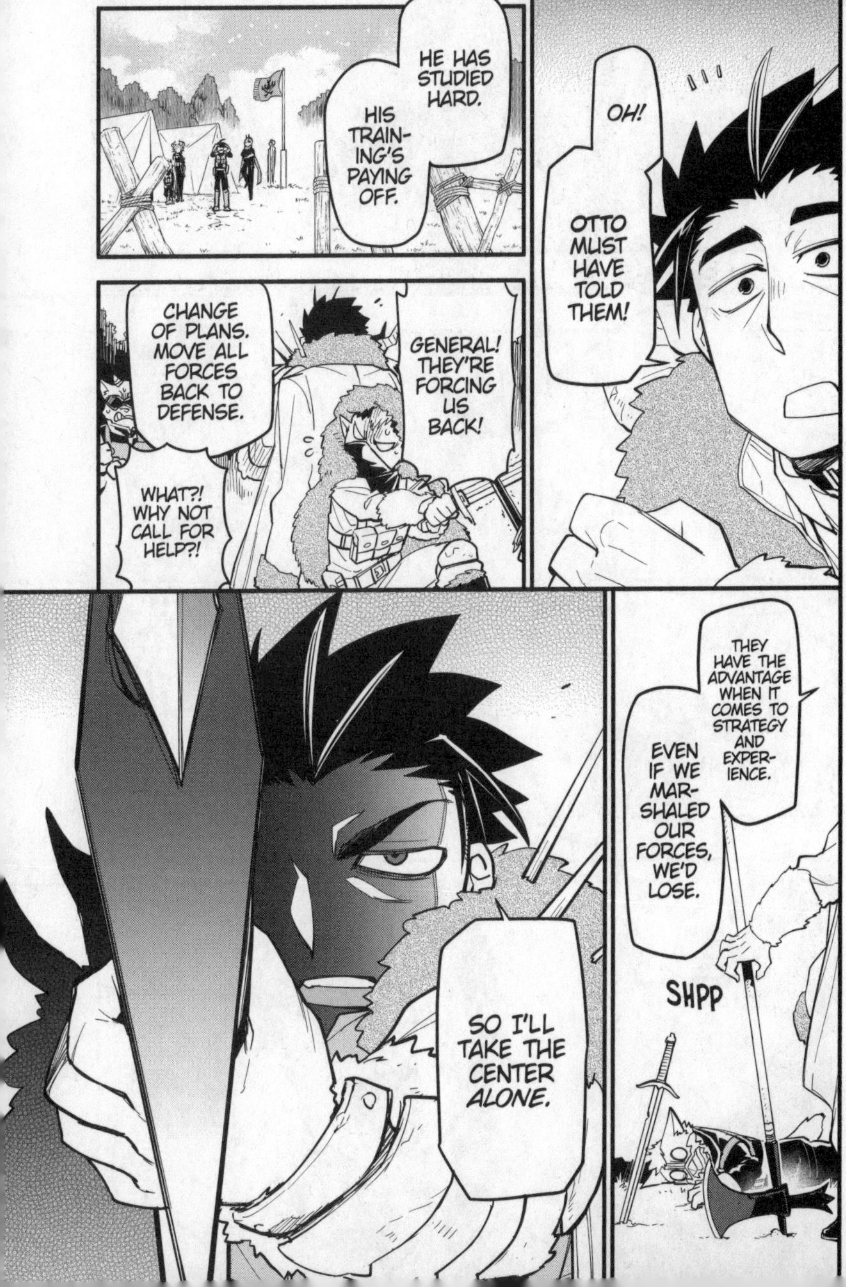
OH!
OTTO MUST HAVE TOLD THEM!
HE HAS STUDIED HARD.
HIS TRAINING'S PAYING OFF.
GENERAL! THEY'RE FORCING US BACK!
CHANGE OF PLANS. MOVE ALL FORCES BACK TO DEFENSE.
WHAT?! WHY NOT CALL FOR HELP?!
THEY HAVE THE ADVANTAGE WHEN IT COMES TO STRATEGY AND EXPERIENCE.
EVEN IF WE MARSHALED OUR FORCES, WE'D LOSE.
SHPP
SO I'LL TAKE THE CENTER ALONE.

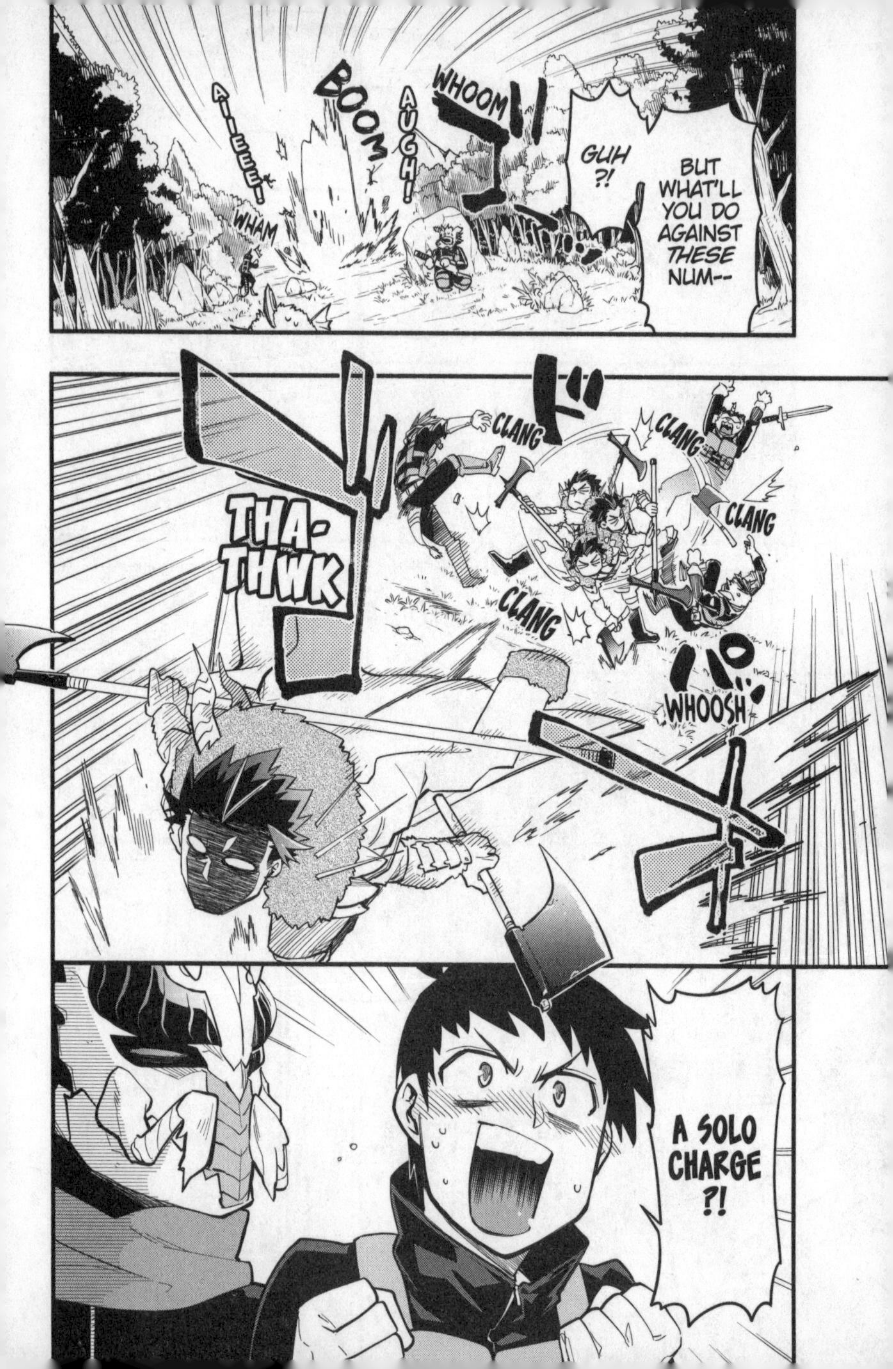
BUT WHAT'LL YOU DO AGAINST THESE NUM--
GUH ?!
WHOOM
AUGH!
BOOM
AIIEEEE!
WHAM
CLANG
CLANG
CLANG
CLANG
THA-THWK
WHOOSH
A SOLO CHARGE ?!

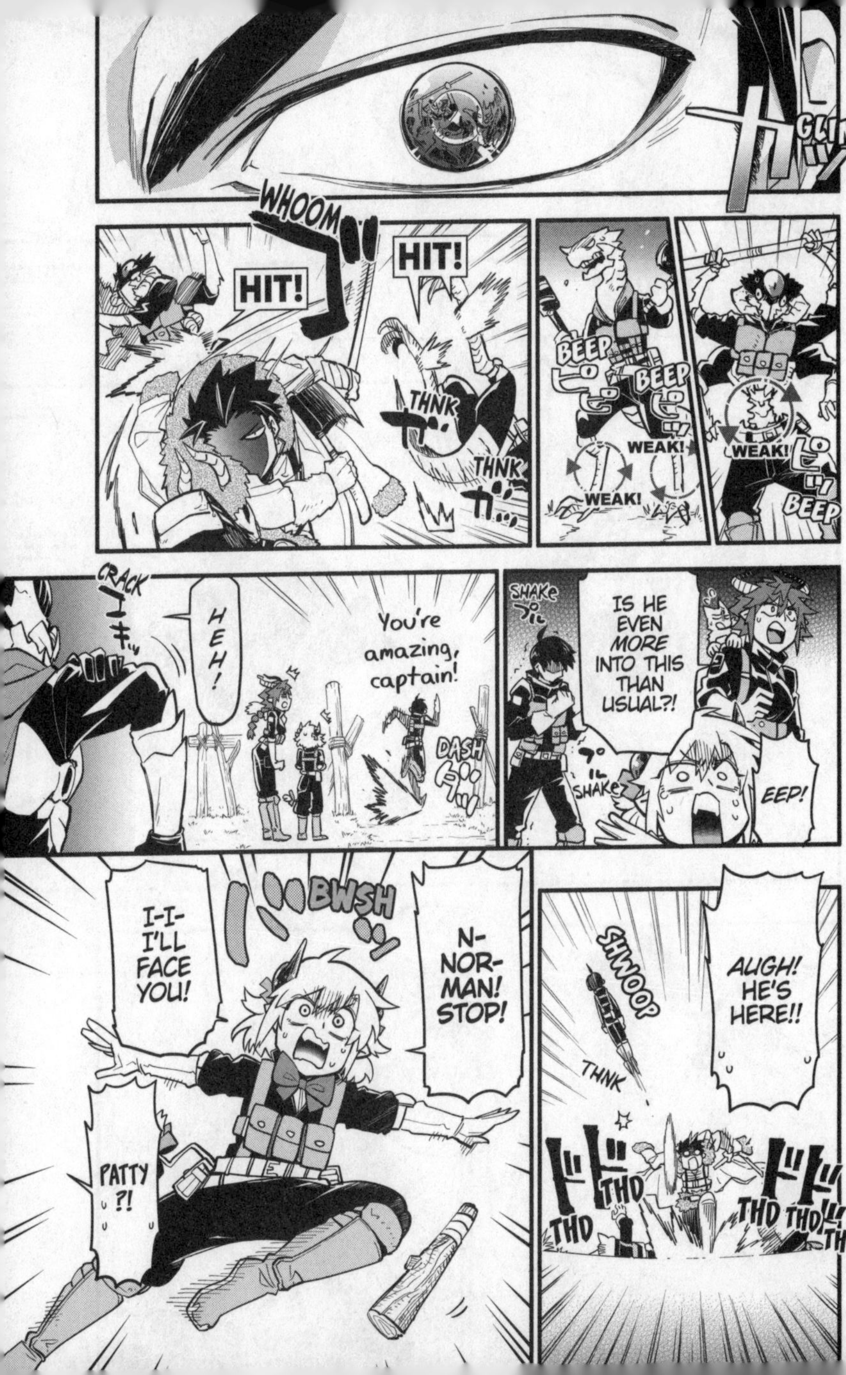
GLINT
WHOOM
HIT!
HIT!
THNK
THNK
BEEP
BEEP
WEAK!
WEAK!
WEAK!
BEEP
SHAKE
IS HE EVEN MORE INTO THIS THAN USUAL?!
SHAKE
EEP!
CRACK
HEH!
You're amazing, captain!
DASH
AUGH! HE'S HERE!!
SHWOOP
THNK
THD
THD
THD THD THD
THD
N-NOR-MAN! STOP!
BWSH
I-I-I'LL FACE YOU!
PATTY?!

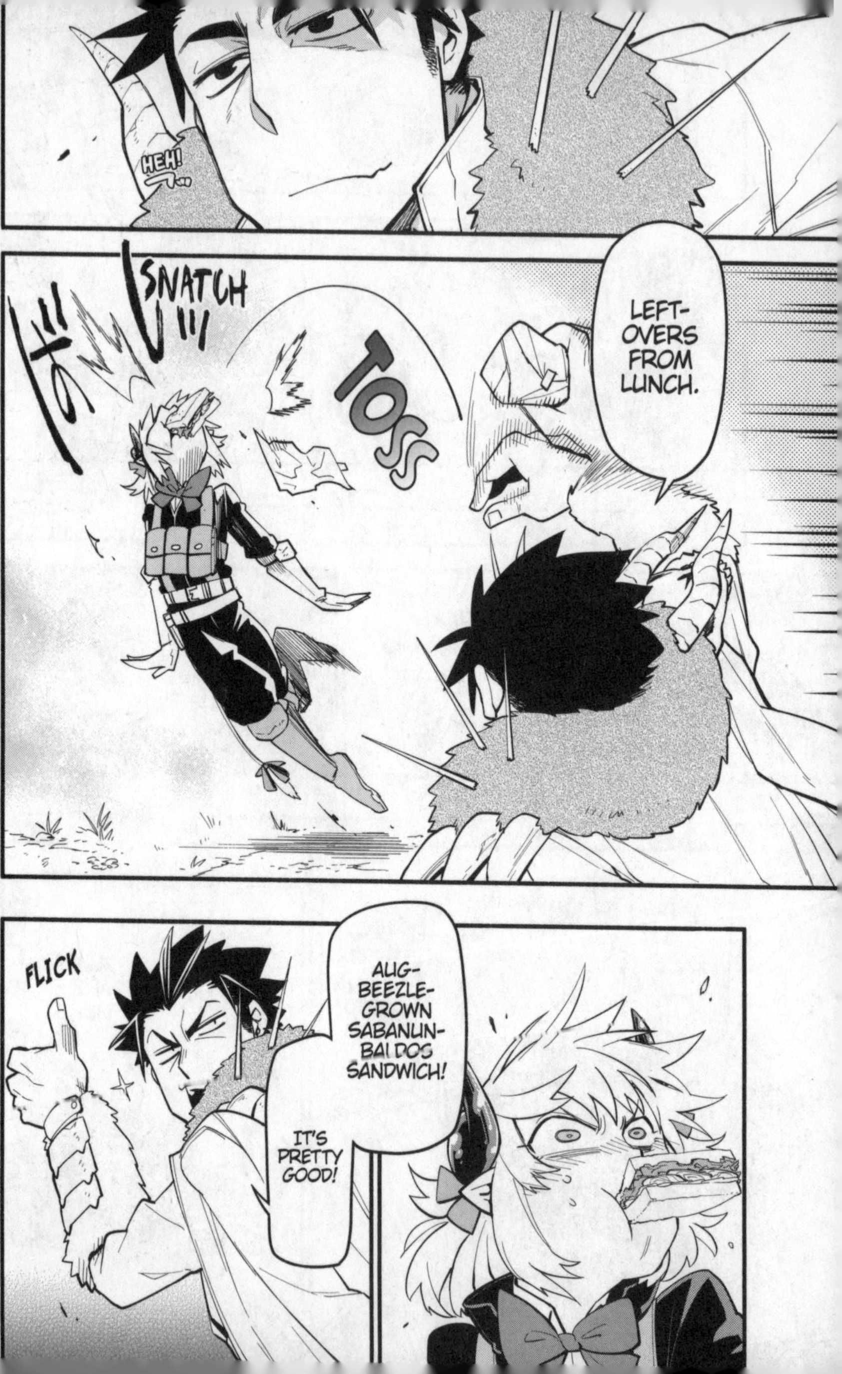
HEH!
LEFT-OVERS FROM LUNCH.
TOSS
SNATCH
AUG-BEEZLE-GROWN SABANUNBAI DOS SANDWICH!
IT'S PRETTY GOOD!
FLICK

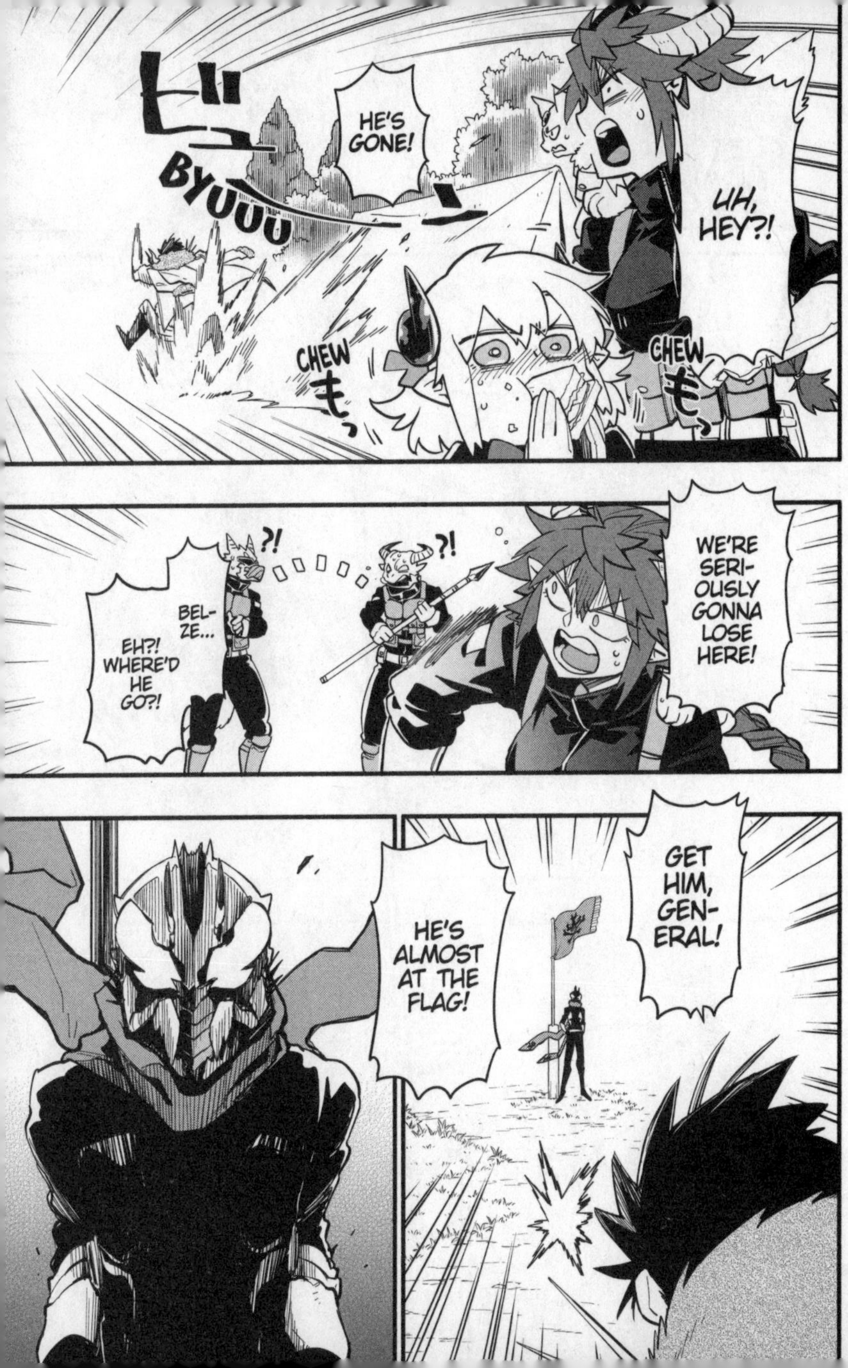
UH, HEY?!
HE'S GONE!
BYUUU
CHEW
CHEW
WE'RE SERI-OUSLY GONNA LOSE HERE!
?!
?!
BELZE...
EH?! WHERE'D HE GO?!
GET HIM, GEN-ERAL!
HE'S ALMOST AT THE FLAG!

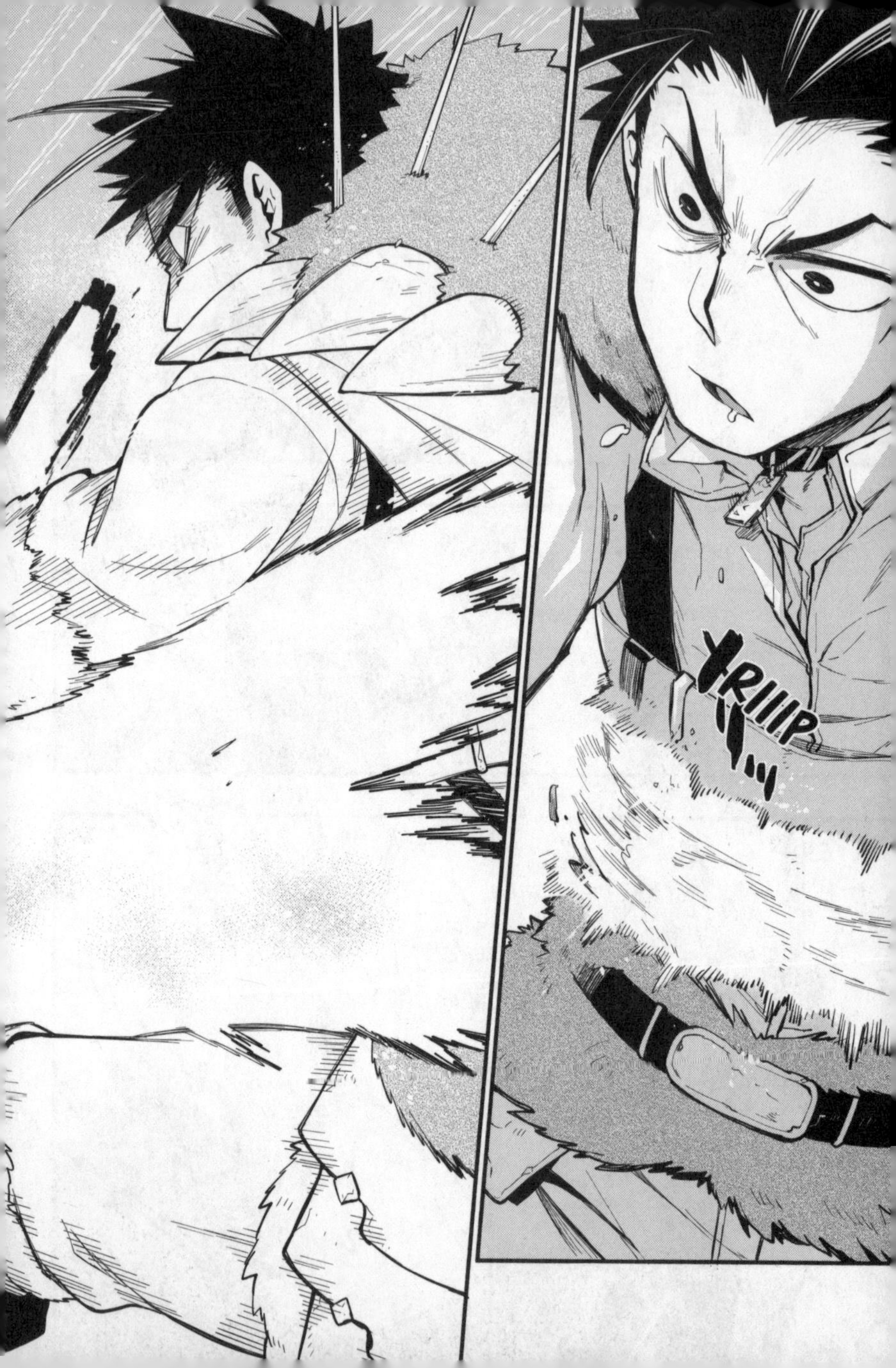
RIIIP

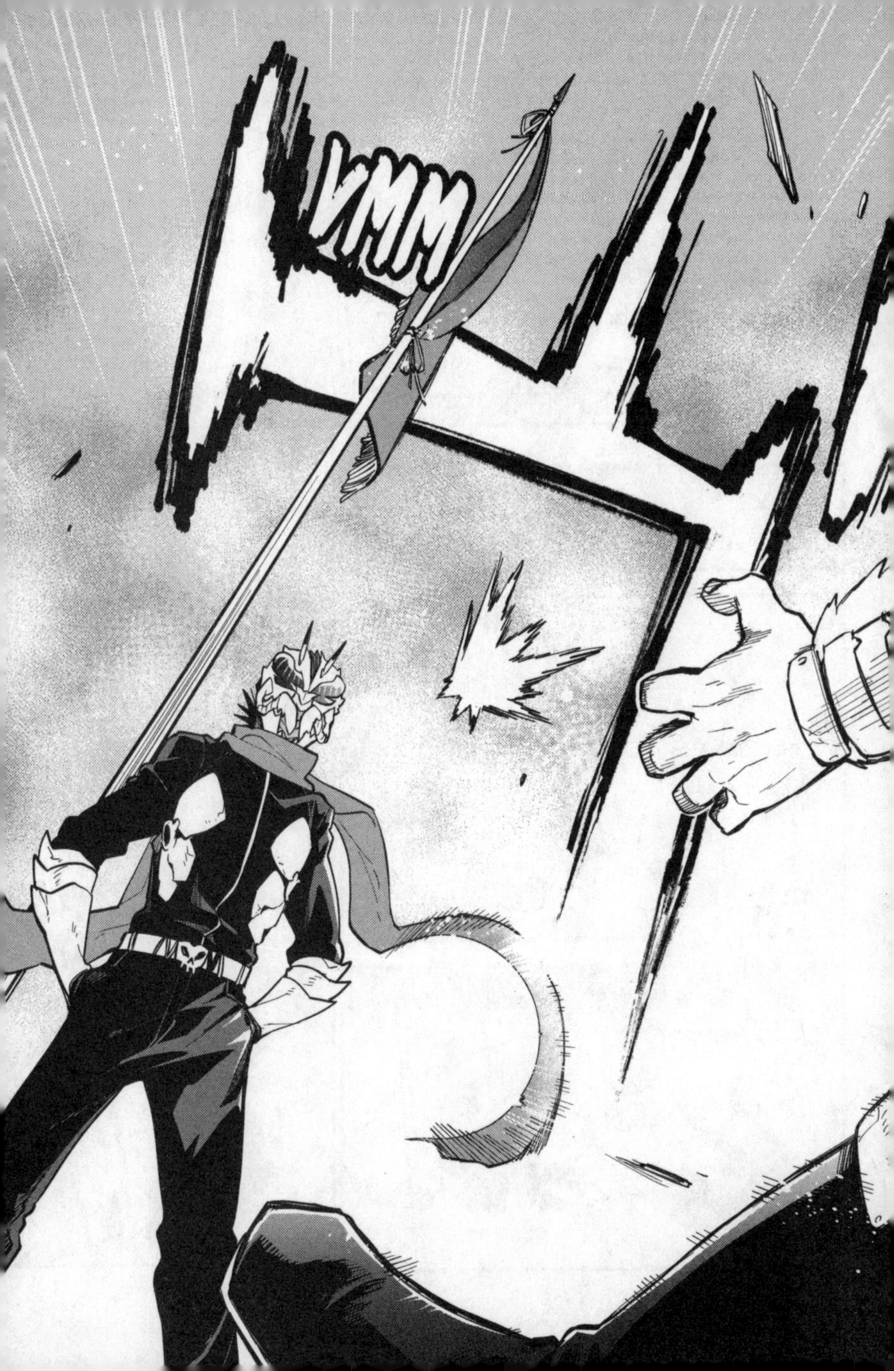
HMMM

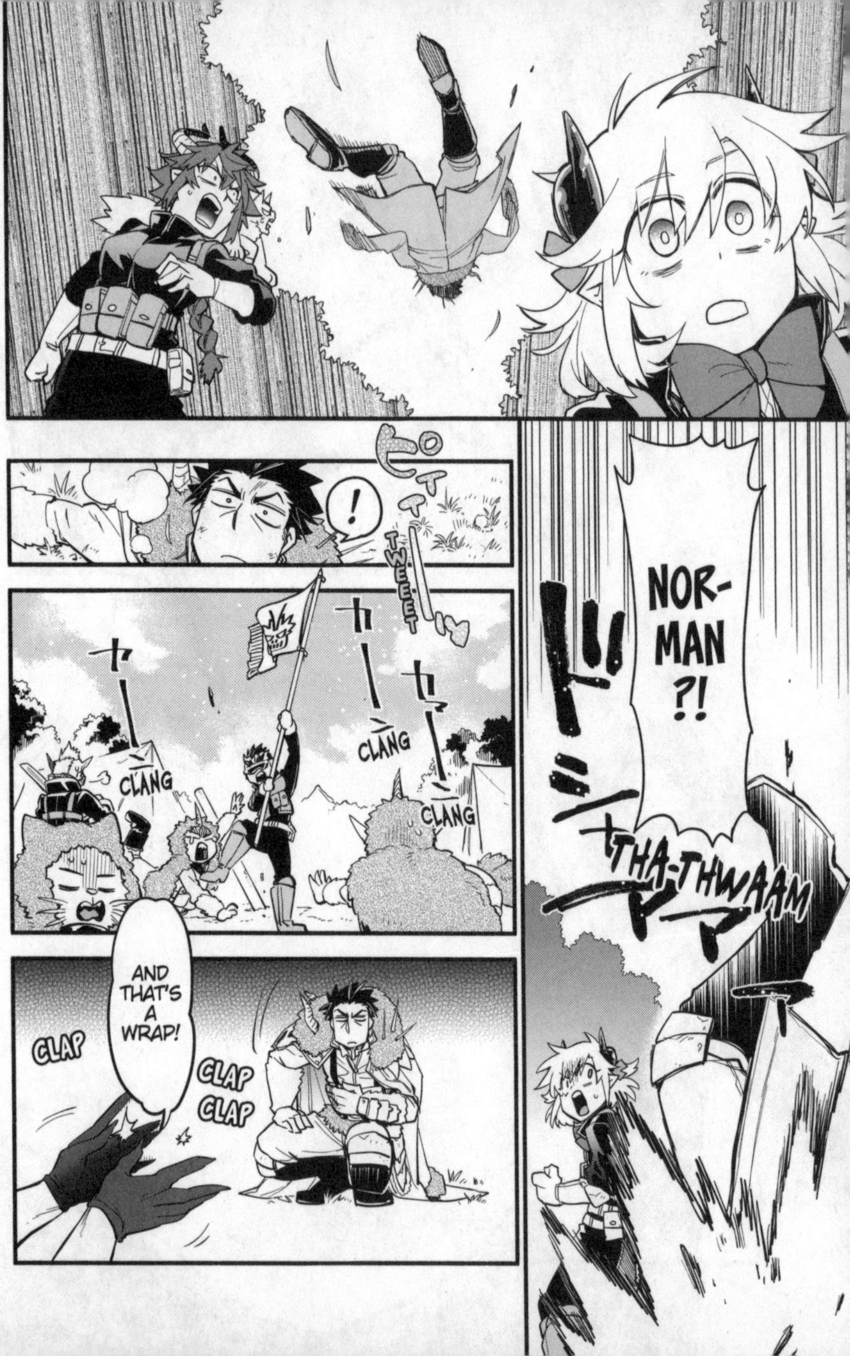

NOR-MAN?!
THA-THWAAM
!
TWEEEET
CLANG
CLANG
CLANG
AND THAT'S A WRAP!
CLAP
CLAP CLAP

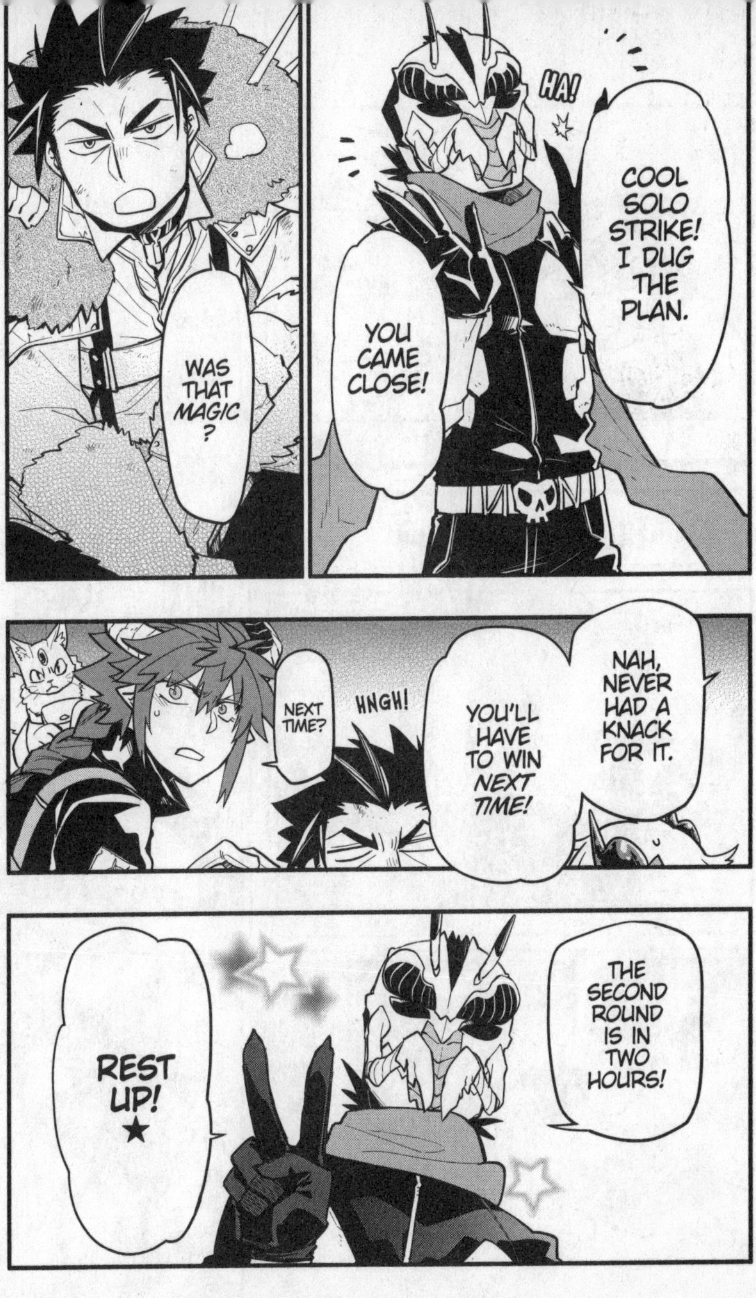
HA!
COOL SOLO STRIKE! I DUG THE PLAN.
YOU CAME CLOSE!
WAS THAT MAGIC?
NAH, NEVER HAD A KNACK FOR IT.
YOU'LL HAVE TO WIN NEXT TIME!
HNGH!
NEXT TIME?
THE SECOND ROUND IS IN TWO HOURS!
REST UP! ★

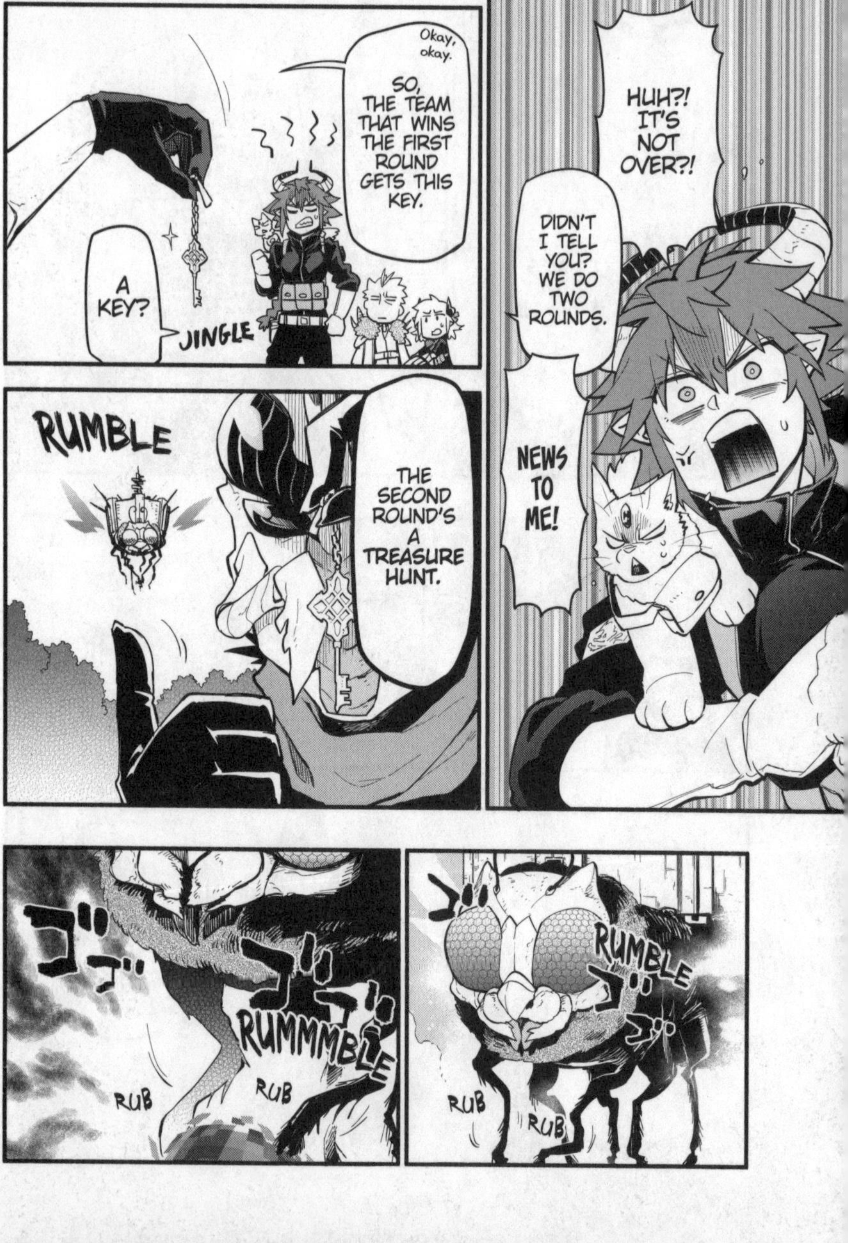
HUH?! IT'S NOT OVER?!
DIDN'T I TELL YOU? WE DO TWO ROUNDS.
NEWS TO ME!
Okay, okay.
SO, THE TEAM THAT WINS THE FIRST ROUND GETS THIS KEY.
A KEY?
JINGLE
RUMBLE
THE SECOND ROUND'S A TREASURE HUNT.
RUMBLE
RUB
RUB
RUMMMBLE
RUB
RUB

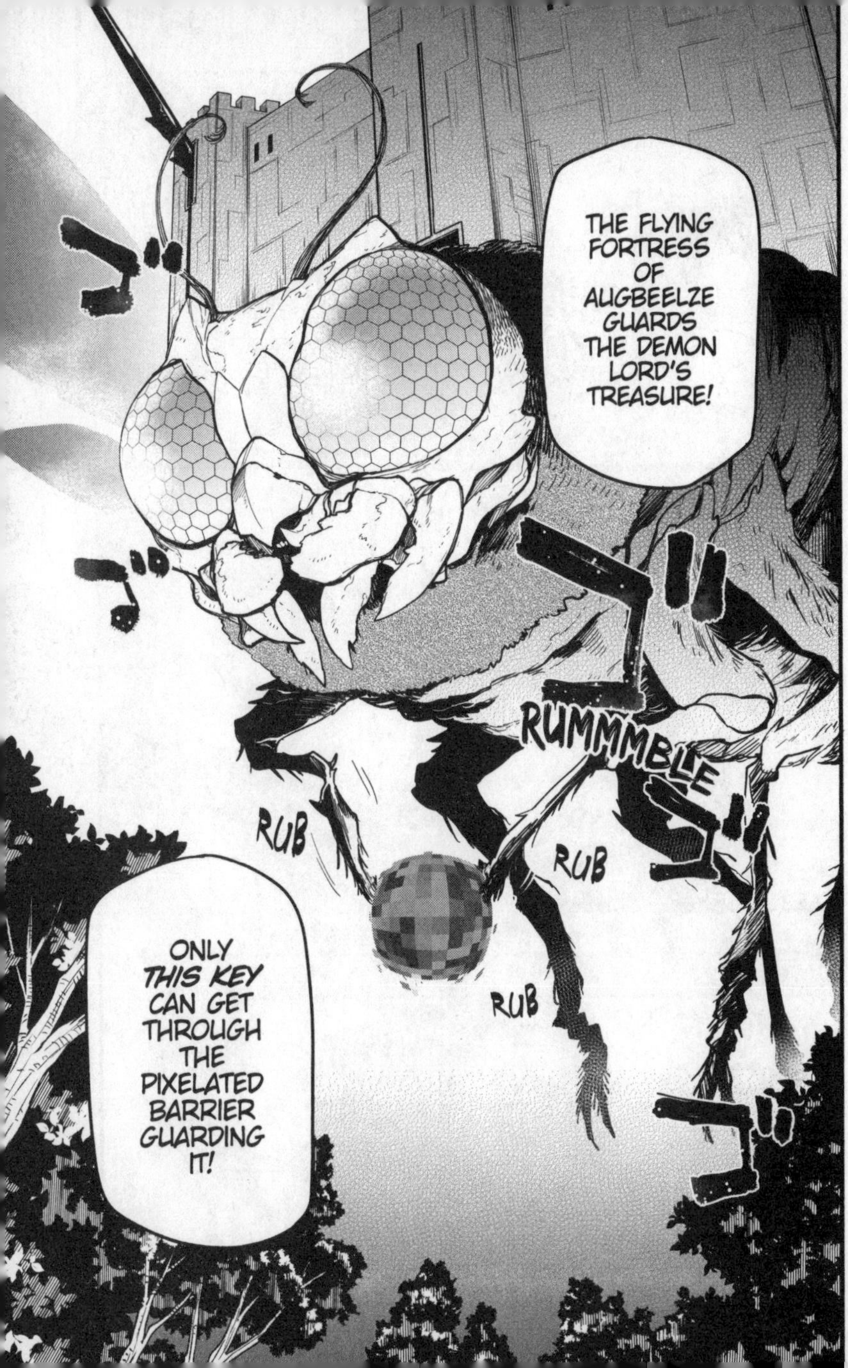
THE FLYING FORTRESS OF AUGBEELZE GUARDS THE DEMON LORD'S TREASURE!
RUMMMBLE
RUB
RUB
RUB
ONLY *THIS KEY* CAN GET THROUGH THE PIXELATED BARRIER GUARDING IT!

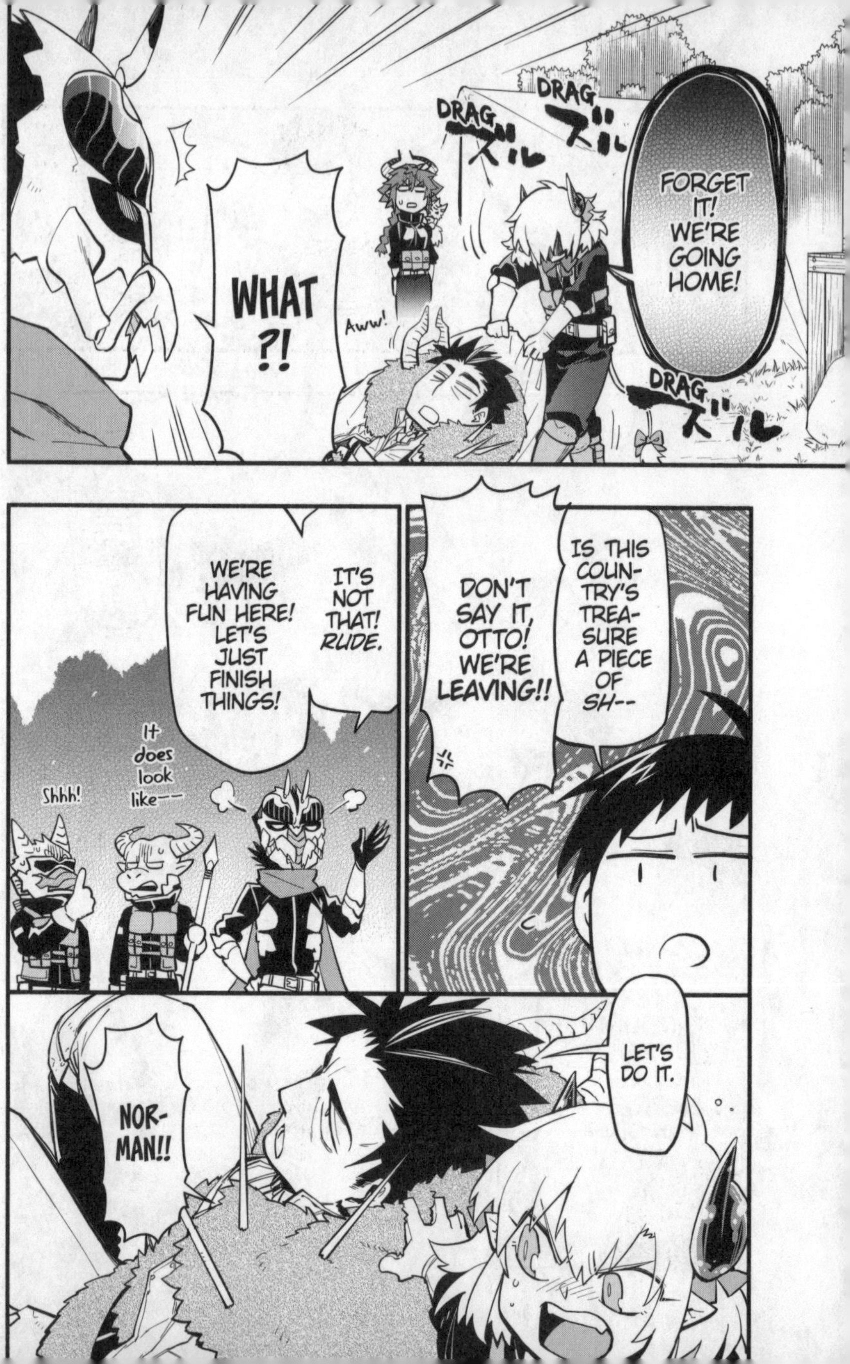
DRAG ズル
DRAG ズル
FORGET IT! WE'RE GOING HOME!
DRAG ズル
WHAT?!
Aww!
IS THIS COUN-TRY'S TREA-SURE A PIECE OF SH--
DON'T SAY IT, OTTO! WE'RE LEAVING!!
IT'S NOT THAT! RUDE.
WE'RE HAVING FUN HERE! LET'S JUST FINISH THINGS!
It does look like--
Shhh!
LET'S DO IT.
NOR-MAN!!

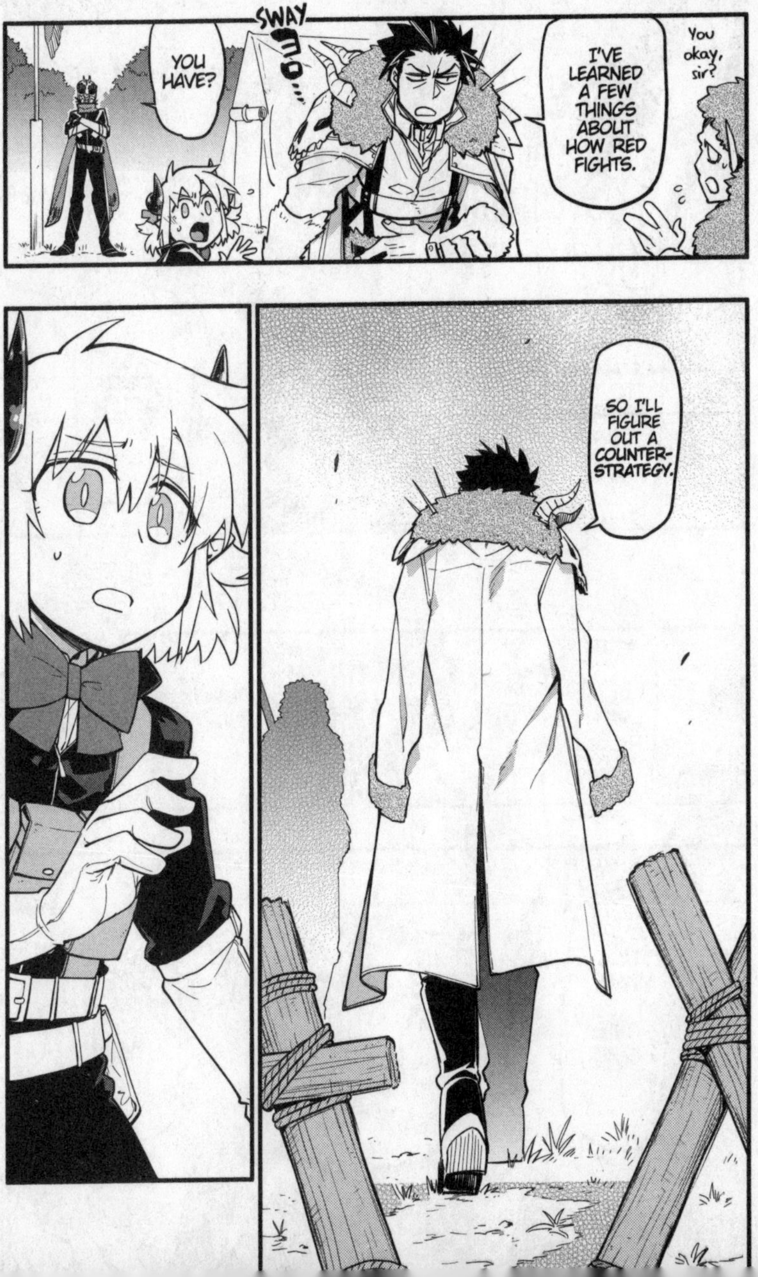
You okay, sir?
I'VE LEARNED A FEW THINGS ABOUT HOW RED FIGHTS.
SWAY
YOU HAVE?
SO I'LL FIGURE OUT A COUNTER-STRATEGY.

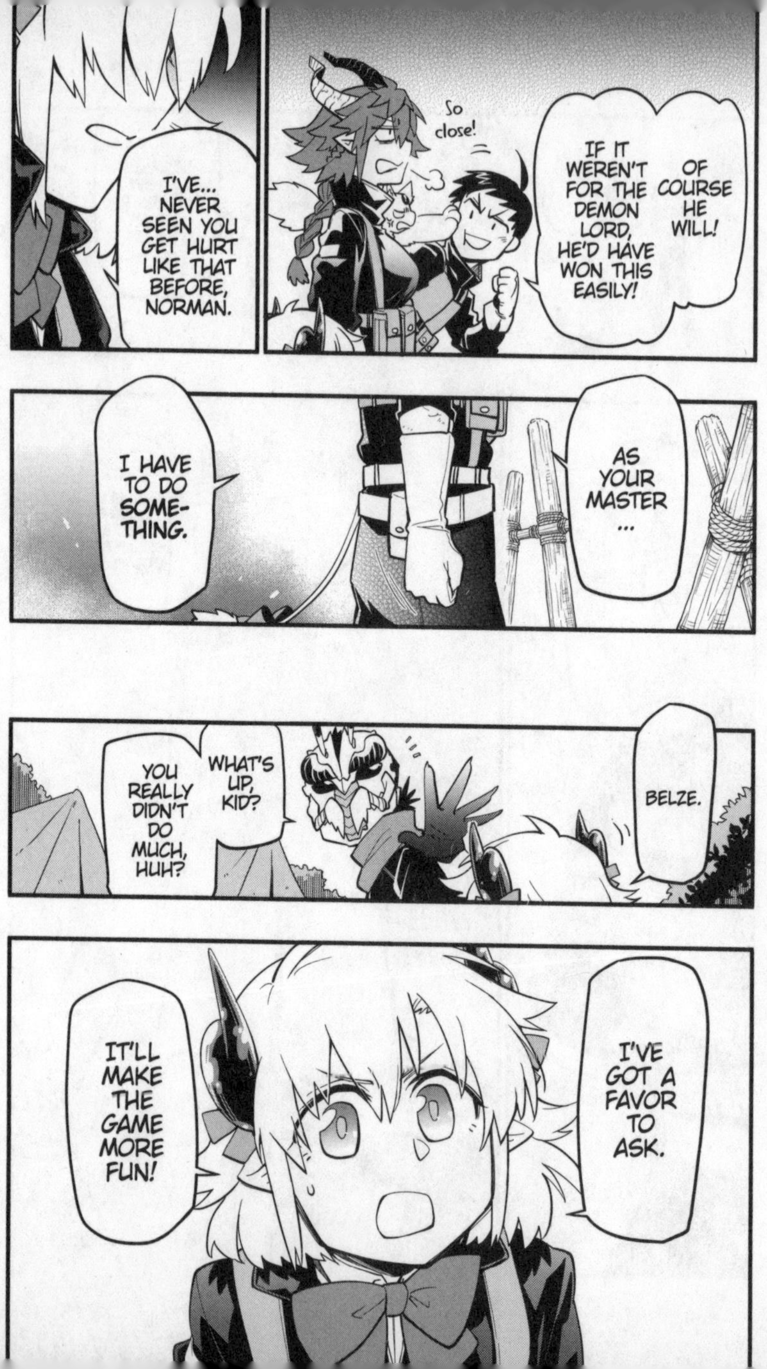
OF COURSE HE WILL!
IF IT WEREN'T FOR THE DEMON LORD, HE'D HAVE WON THIS EASILY!
So close!
I'VE... NEVER SEEN YOU GET HURT LIKE THAT BEFORE, NORMAN.
AS YOUR MASTER...
I HAVE TO DO SOME-THING.
BELZE.
WHAT'S UP, KID?
YOU REALLY DIDN'T DO MUCH, HUH?
I'VE GOT A FAVOR TO ASK.
IT'LL MAKE THE GAME MORE FUN!

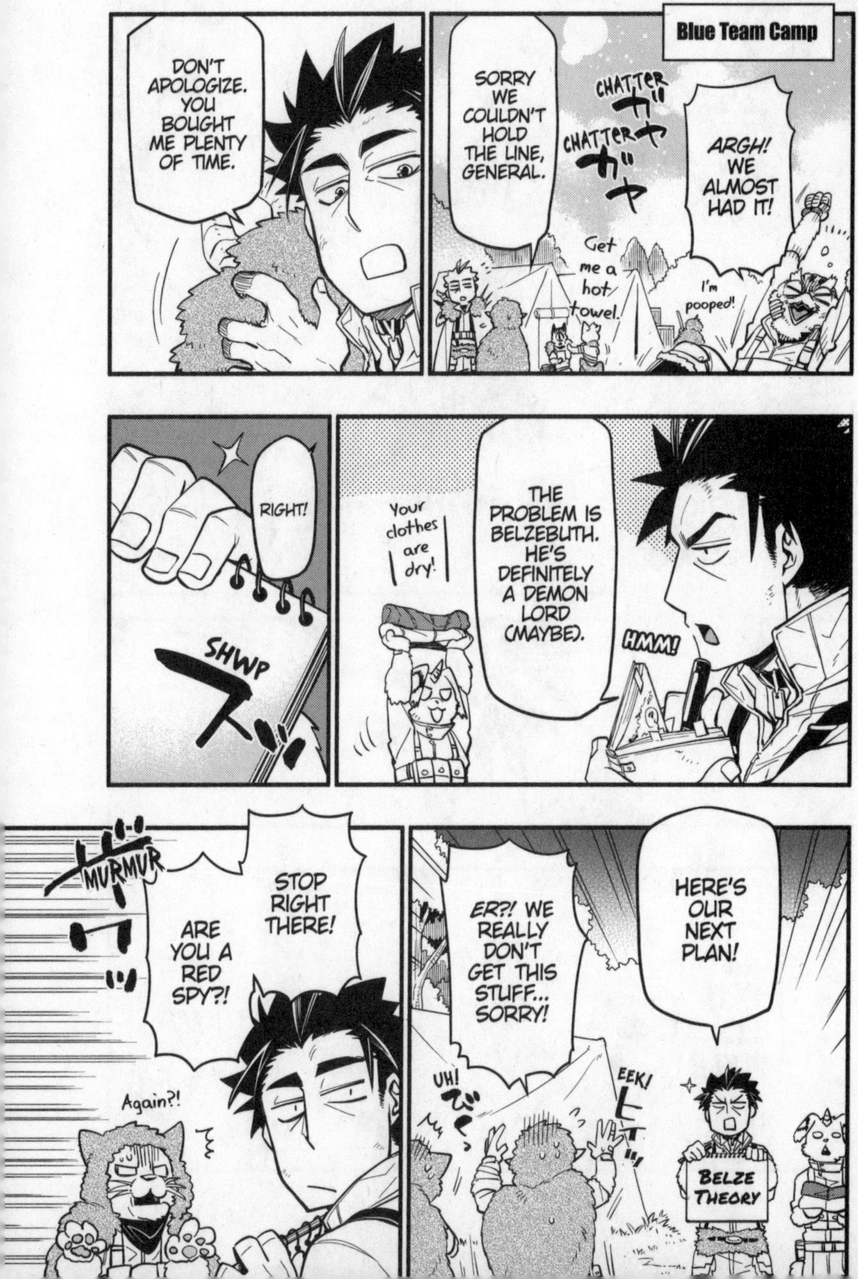
Blue Team Camp
ARGH! WE ALMOST HAD IT!
I'm pooped!
CHATTER
CHATTER
Get me a hot towel.
SORRY WE COULDN'T HOLD THE LINE, GENERAL.
DON'T APOLOGIZE. YOU BOUGHT ME PLENTY OF TIME.
THE PROBLEM IS BELZEBUTH. HE'S DEFINITELY A DEMON LORD (MAYBE).
HMM!
Your clothes are dry!
RIGHT!
SHWP
HERE'S OUR NEXT PLAN!
BELZE THEORY
EEK!
UH!
ER?! WE REALLY DON'T GET THIS STUFF... SORRY!
STOP RIGHT THERE!
ARE YOU A RED SPY?!
MURMUR
Again?!

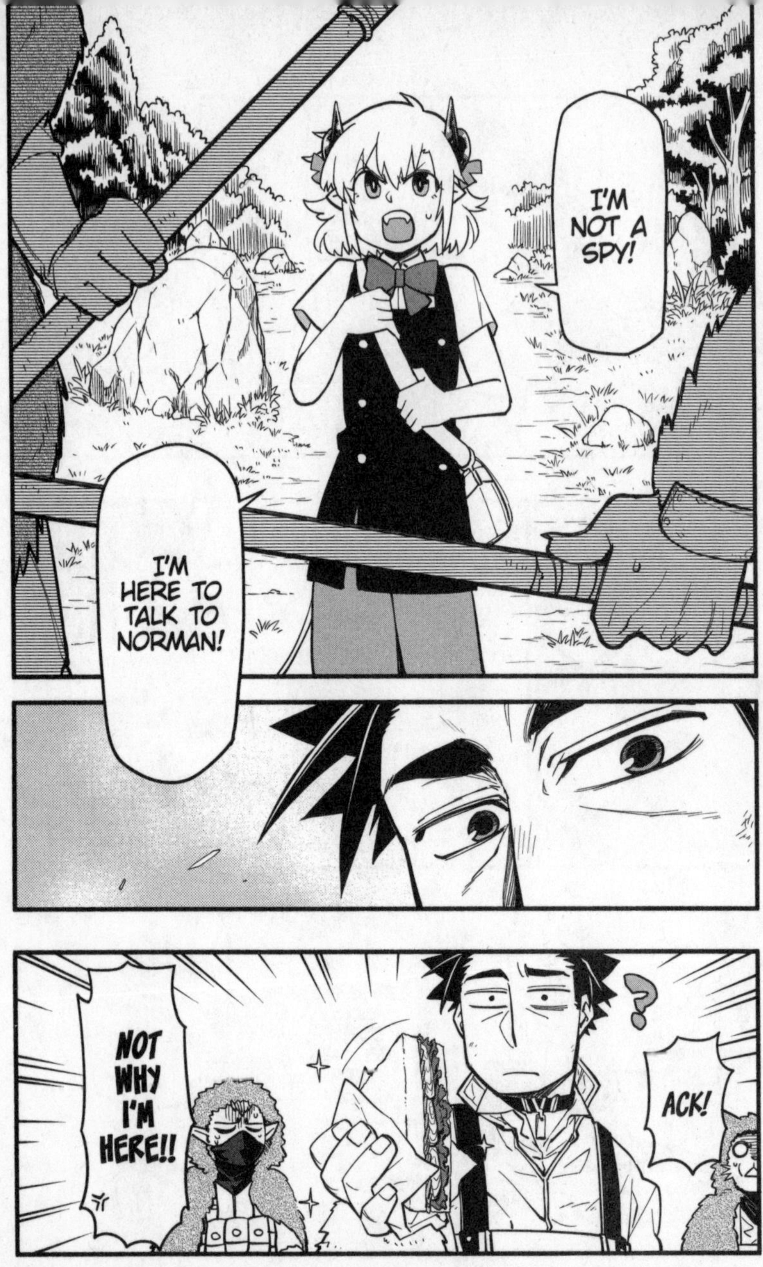
I'M NOT A SPY!
I'M HERE TO TALK TO NORMAN!
ACK!
NOT WHY I'M HERE!!

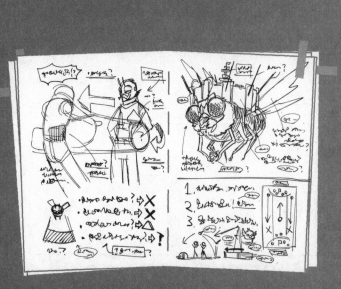

Sorry For My Familiar

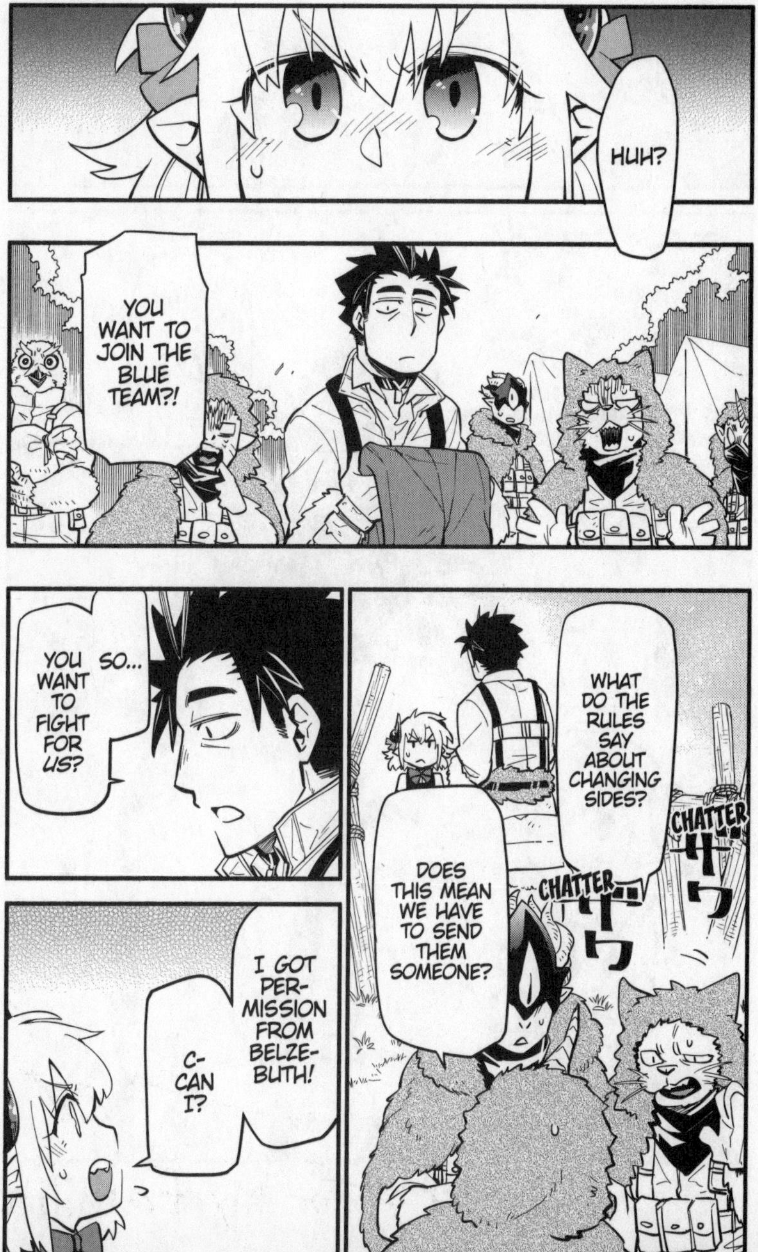
HUH?
YOU WANT TO JOIN THE BLUE TEAM?!
WHAT DO THE RULES SAY ABOUT CHANGING SIDES?
CHATTER ザワ
CHATTER ザワ
DOES THIS MEAN WE HAVE TO SEND THEM SOMEONE?
SO... YOU WANT TO FIGHT FOR US?
I GOT PERMISSION FROM BELZEBUTH!
C-CAN I?

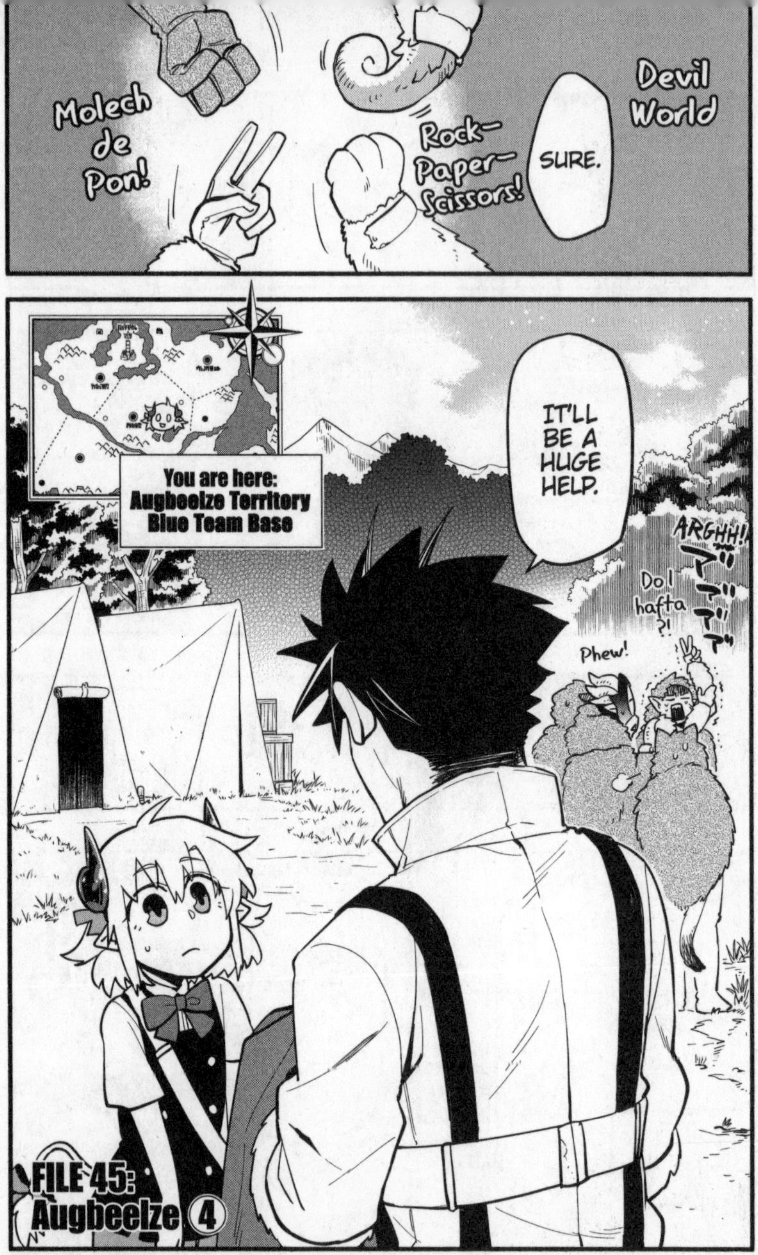
Devil World
SURE.
Rock-Paper-Scissors!
Molech de Pon!
You are here: Augbeelze Territory Blue Team Base
IT'LL BE A HUGE HELP.
ARGHH!
Do I hafta?!
Phew!
FILE 45: Augbeelze 4

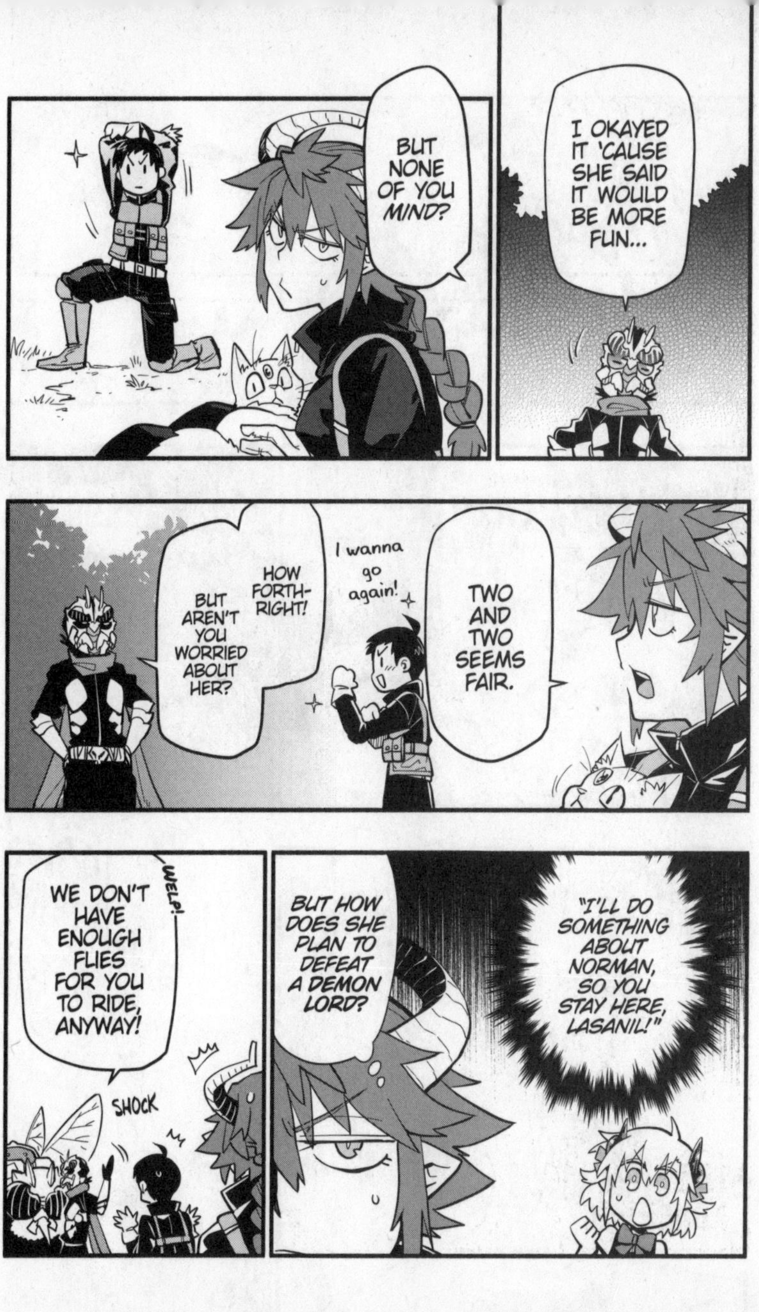
BUT NONE OF YOU MIND?
I OKAYED IT 'CAUSE SHE SAID IT WOULD BE MORE FUN...
BUT AREN'T YOU WORRIED ABOUT HER?
HOW FORTH-RIGHT!
I wanna go again!
TWO AND TWO SEEMS FAIR.
WE DON'T HAVE ENOUGH FLIES FOR YOU TO RIDE, ANYWAY!
WELP!
SHOCK
BUT HOW DOES SHE PLAN TO DEFEAT A DEMON LORD?
"I'LL DO SOMETHING ABOUT NORMAN, SO YOU STAY HERE, LASANIL!"

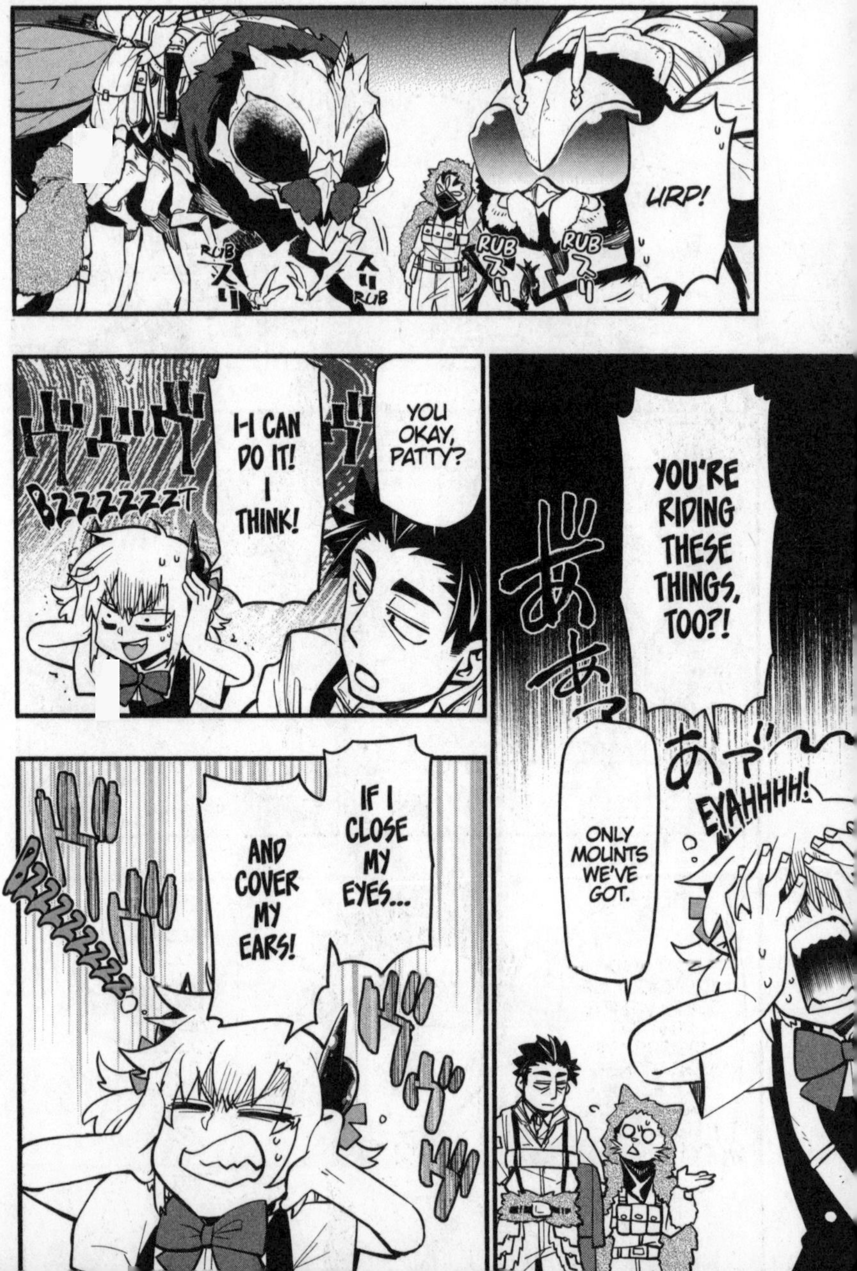
URP!
RUB
RUB
RUB
RUB
YOU'RE RIDING THESE THINGS, TOO?!
EYAHHHH!
ONLY MOUNTS WE'VE GOT.
YOU OKAY, PATTY?
I-I CAN DO IT! I THINK!
BZZZZZZZT
IF I CLOSE MY EYES...
AND COVER MY EARS!

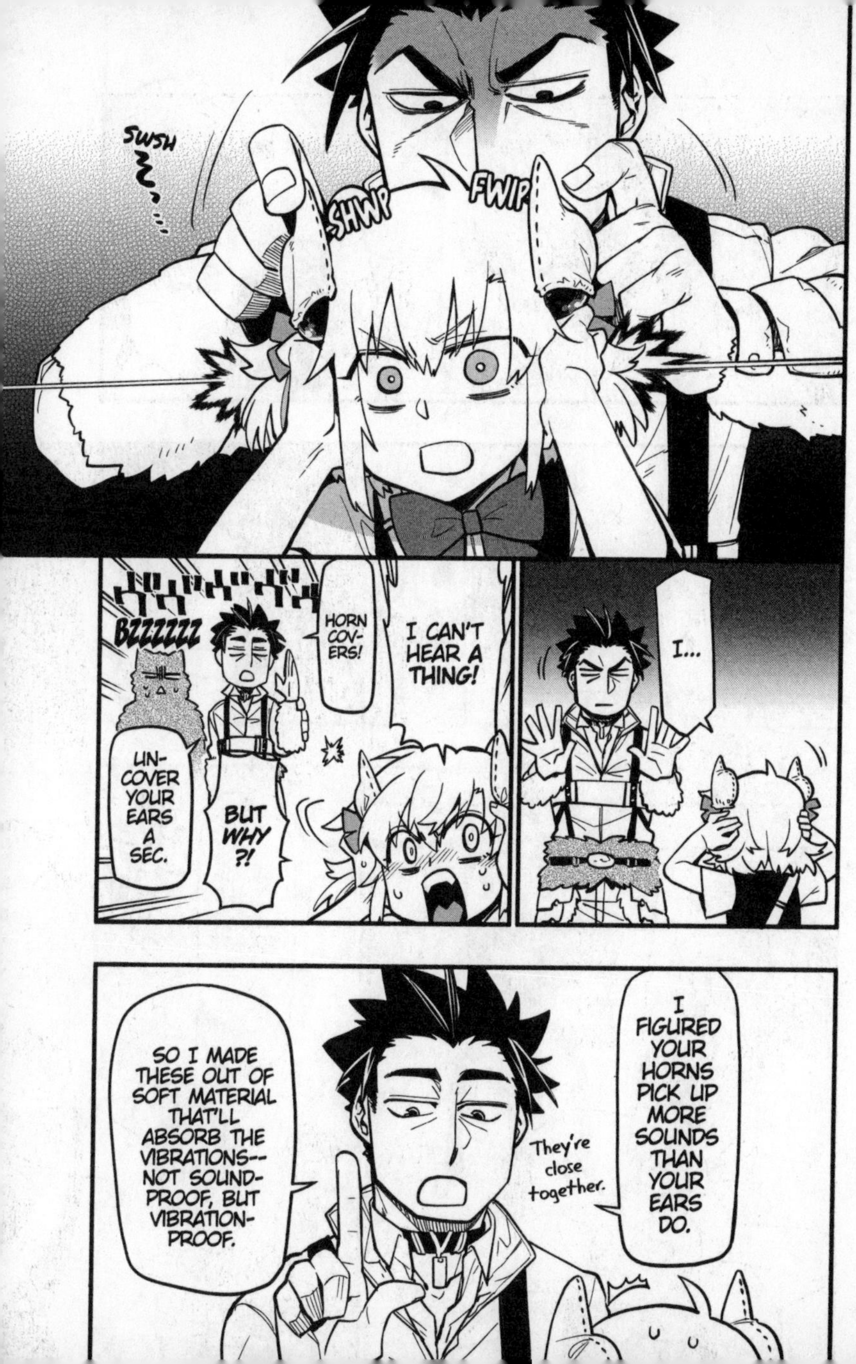
FWIP
SHWP
SWSH
I...
I CAN'T HEAR A THING!
HORN COV-ERS!
BZZZZZZ
UN-COVER YOUR EARS A SEC.
BUT WHY?!
I FIGURED YOUR HORNS PICK UP MORE SOUNDS THAN YOUR EARS DO.
They're close together.
SO I MADE THESE OUT OF SOFT MATERIAL THAT'LL ABSORB THE VIBRATIONS--NOT SOUND-PROOF, BUT VIBRATION-PROOF.

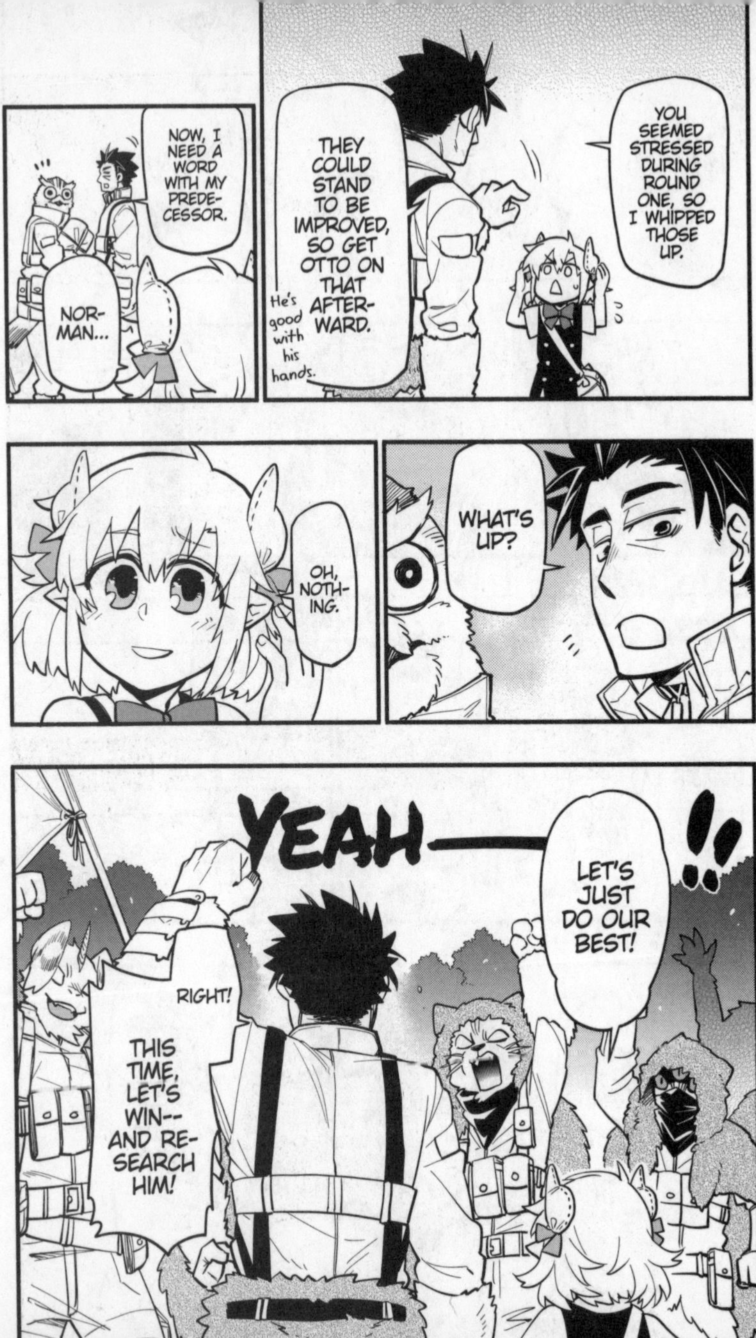
YOU SEEMED STRESSED DURING ROUND ONE, SO I WHIPPED THOSE UP.
THEY COULD STAND TO BE IMPROVED, SO GET OTTO ON THAT AFTERWARD.
He's good with his hands.
NOW, I NEED A WORD WITH MY PREDECESSOR.
NORMAN...
WHAT'S UP?
OH, NOTHING.
LET'S JUST DO OUR BEST!
YEAH——!!
RIGHT!
THIS TIME, LET'S WIN-- AND RESEARCH HIM!

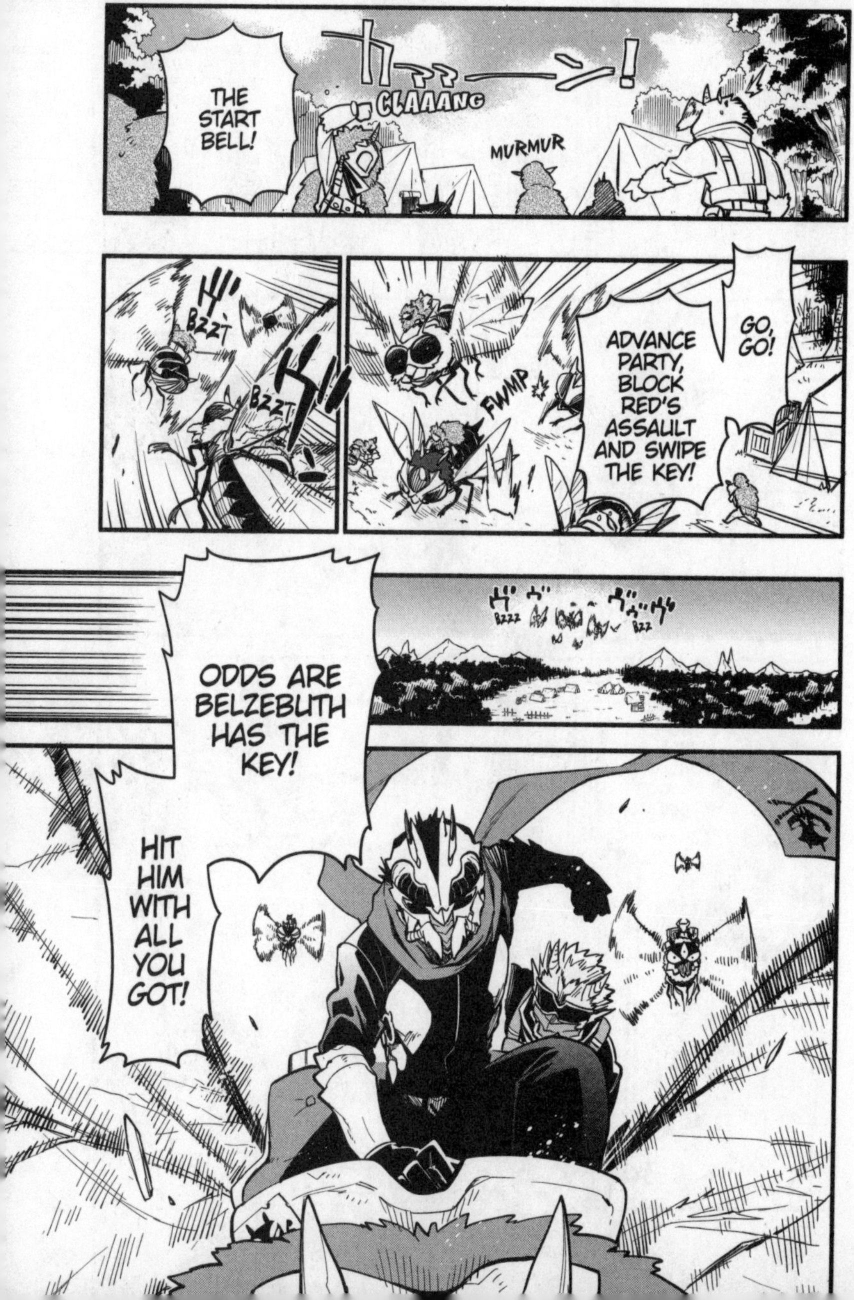
THE START BELL!
CLAAANG
MURMUR
BZZT
BZZT
FWUMP
ADVANCE PARTY, BLOCK RED'S ASSAULT AND SWIPE THE KEY!
GO, GO!
BZZZ
BZZ
ODDS ARE BELZEBUTH HAS THE KEY!
HIT HIM WITH ALL YOU GOT!

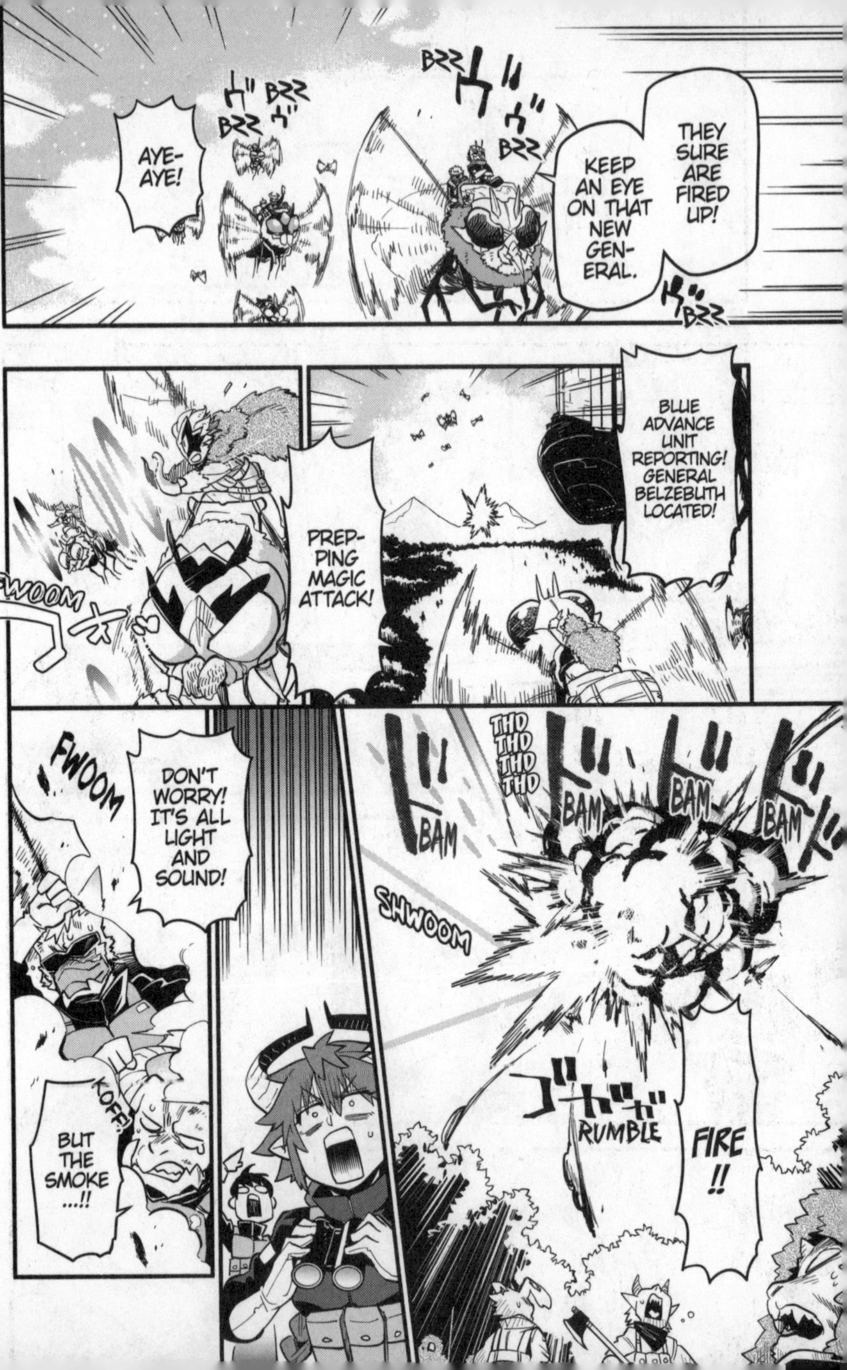
BZZ
THEY SURE ARE FIRED UP!
KEEP AN EYE ON THAT NEW GEN-ERAL.
BZZ
BZZ
BZZ
AYE-AYE!
BZZ
BLUE ADVANCE UNIT REPORTING! GENERAL BELZEBUTH LOCATED!
PREP-PING MAGIC ATTACK!
FWOOM
THD THD THD THD
BAM
BAM
BAM
BAM
SHWOOM
RUMBLE
FIRE!!
FWOOM
DON'T WORRY! IT'S ALL LIGHT AND SOUND!
KOFF
BUT THE SMOKE ...!!

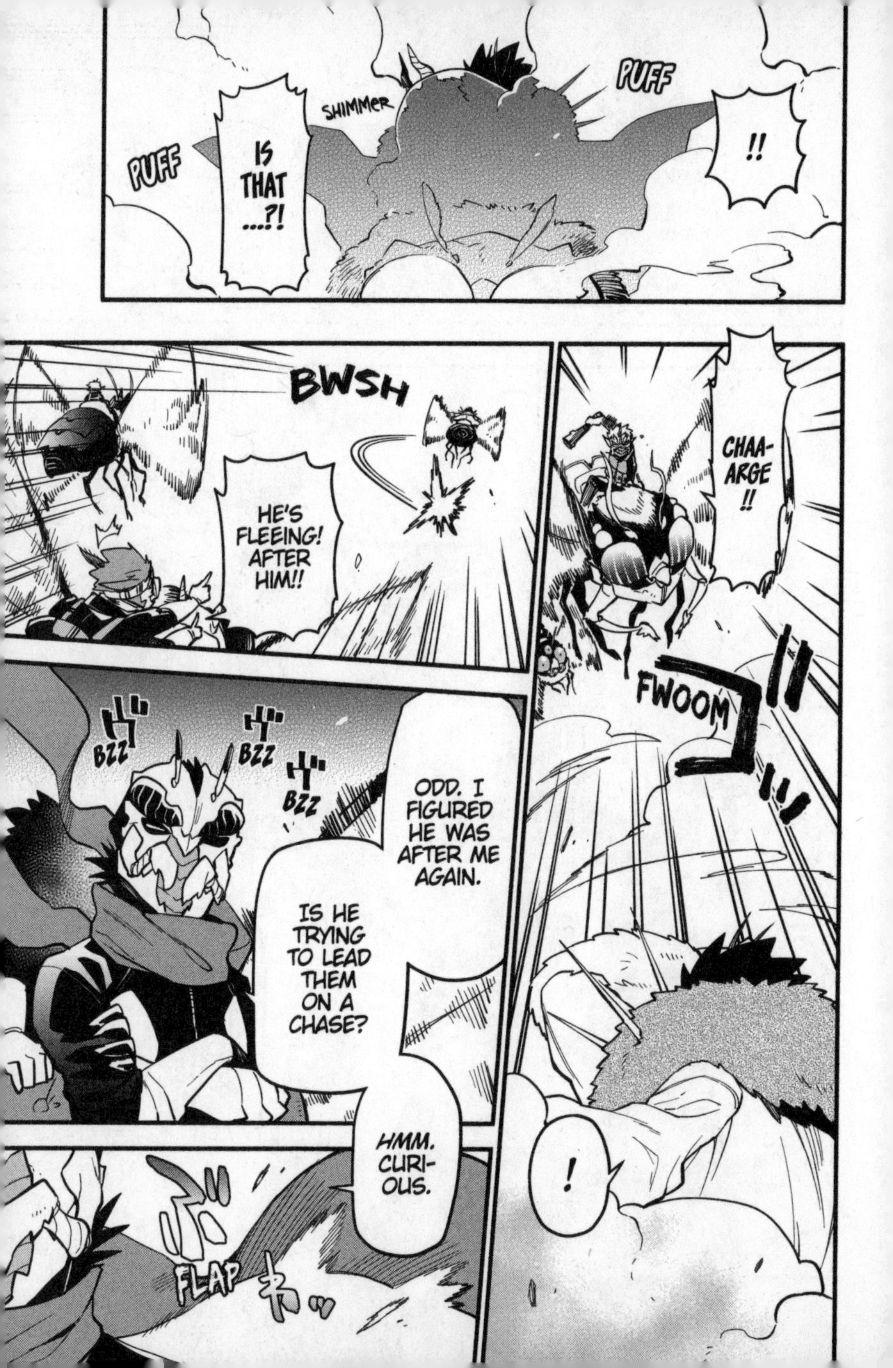
PUFF
!!
SHIMMER
IS THAT ...?!
PUFF
CHAA-ARGE!!
FWOOM
BWSH
HE'S FLEEING! AFTER HIM!!
BZZ
BZZ
BZZ
ODD. I FIGURED HE WAS AFTER ME AGAIN.
IS HE TRYING TO LEAD THEM ON A CHASE?
!
HMM. CURIOUS.
FLAP

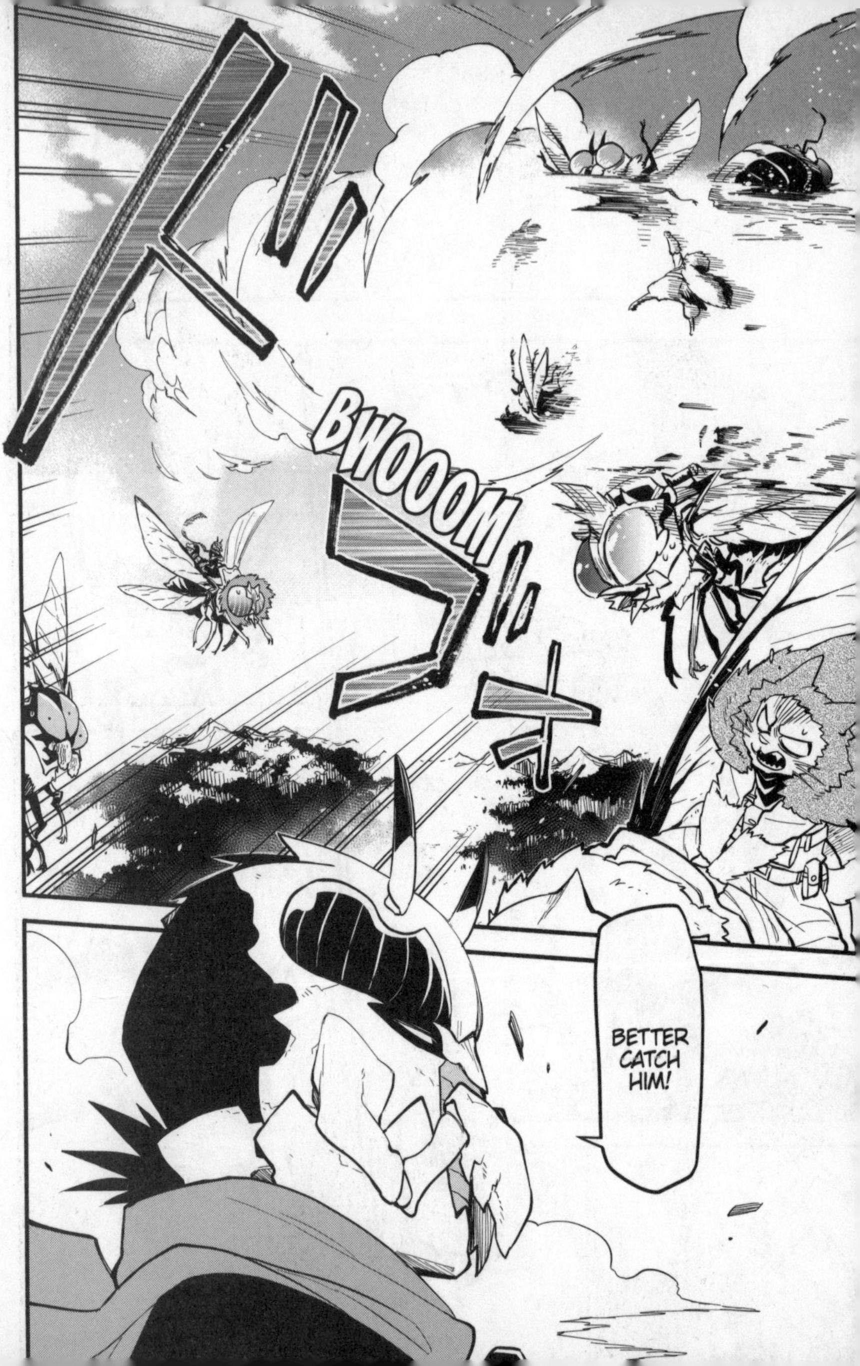
BWOOOM
BETTER CATCH HIM!

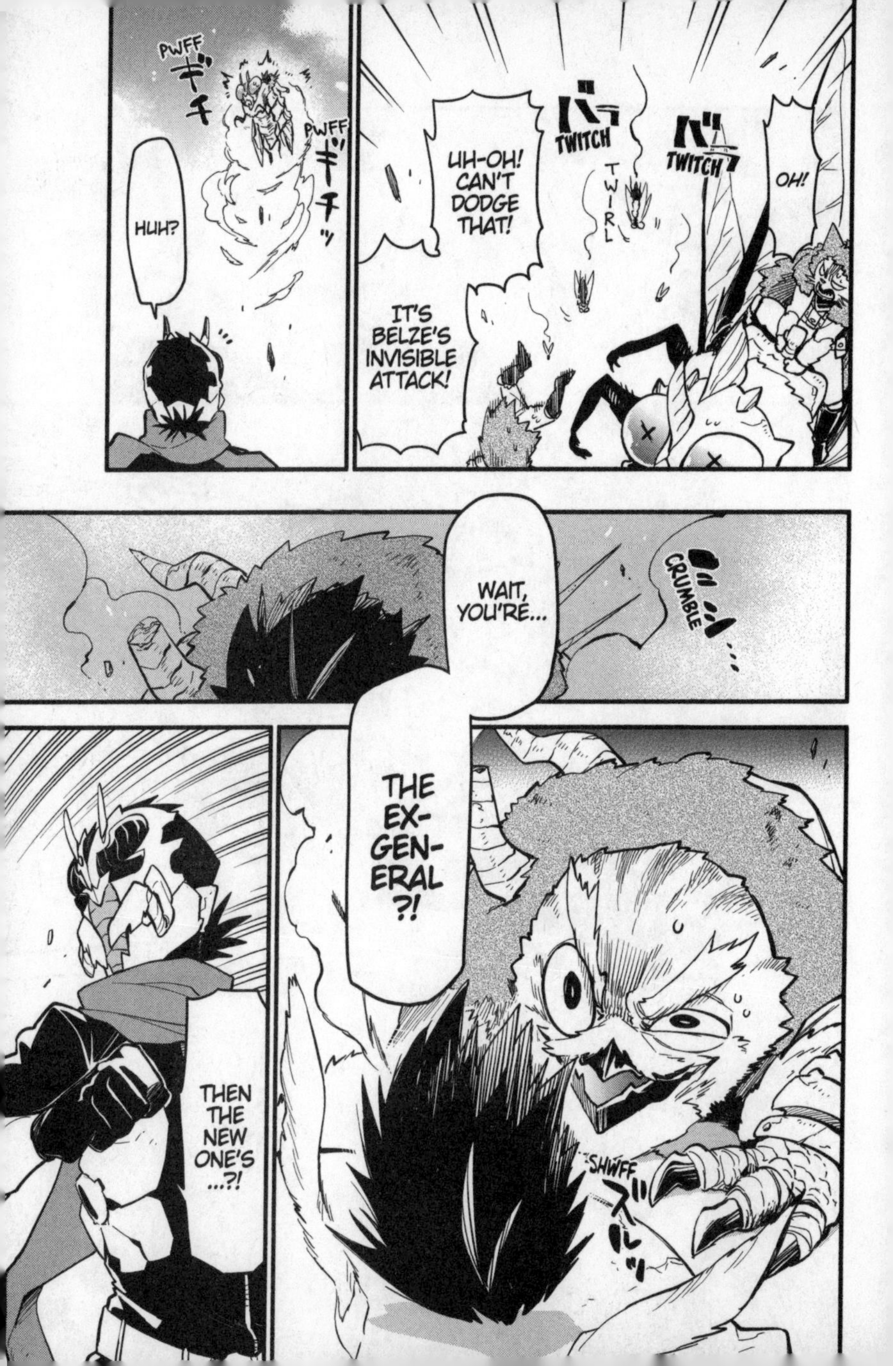
OH!
TWITCH
TWITCH
TWIRL
UH-OH! CAN'T DODGE THAT!
IT'S BELZE'S INVISIBLE ATTACK!
PWFF
PWFF
HUH?
CRUMBLE
WAIT, YOU'RE...
THE EX-GENERAL?!
SHWFF
THEN THE NEW ONE'S ...?!

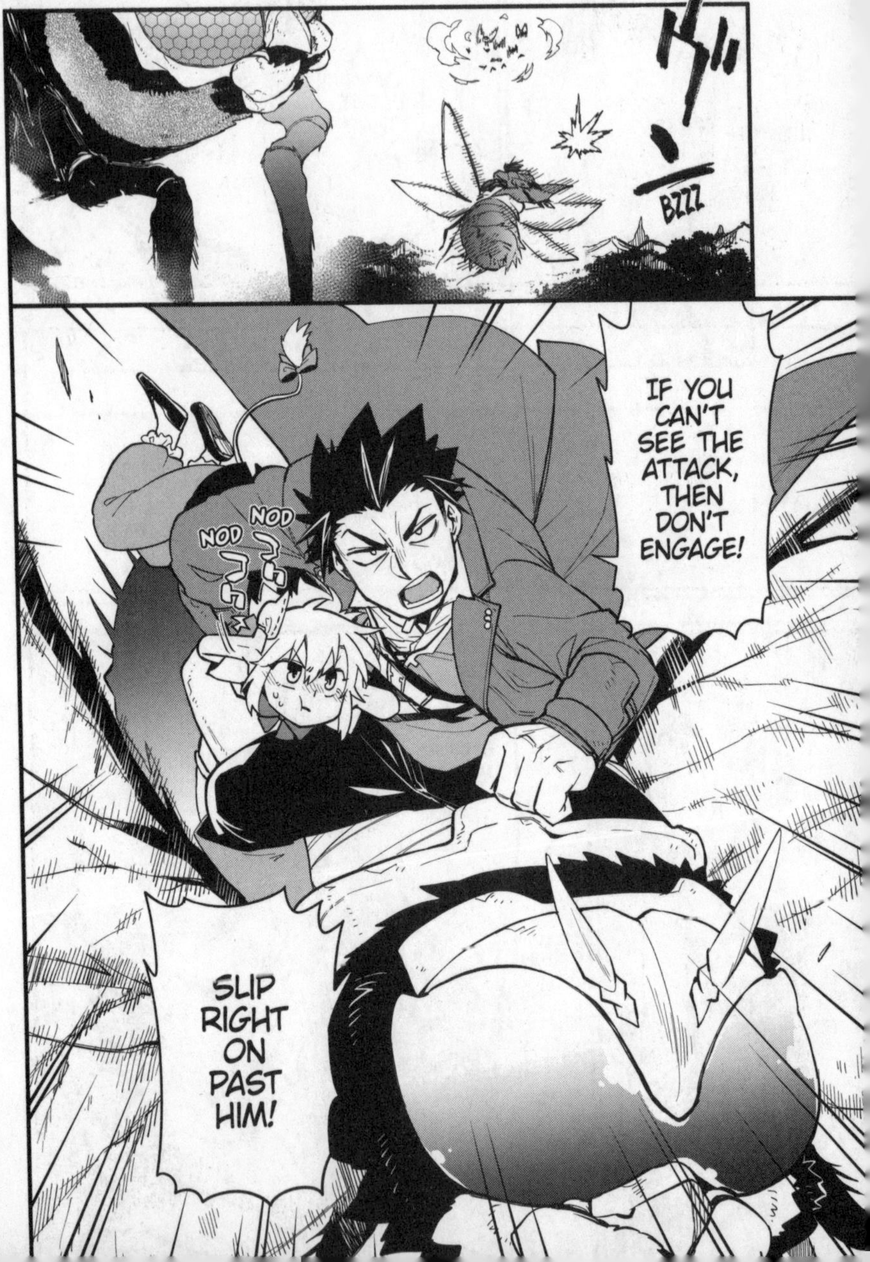
BZZZ
NOD
NOD
IF YOU CAN'T SEE THE ATTACK, THEN DON'T ENGAGE!
SLIP RIGHT ON PAST HIM!

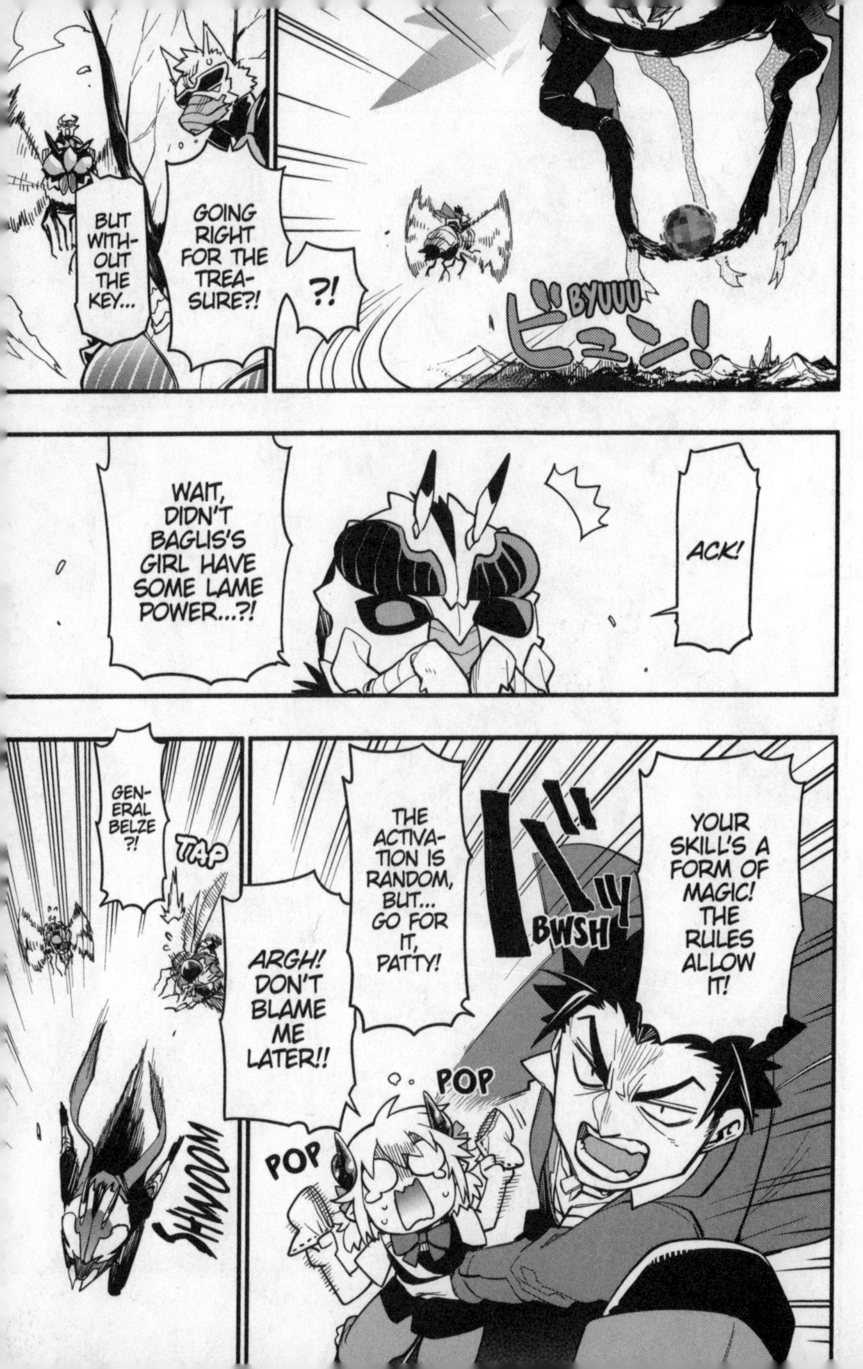
BYUUU
ビュン！
?!
GOING RIGHT FOR THE TREA-SURE?!
BUT WITH-OUT THE KEY...
ACK!
WAIT, DIDN'T BAGLIS'S GIRL HAVE SOME LAME POWER...?!
YOUR SKILL'S A FORM OF MAGIC! THE RULES ALLOW IT!
BWSH
THE ACTIVA-TION IS RANDOM, BUT... GO FOR IT, PATTY!
ARGH! DON'T BLAME ME LATER!!
POP
POP
TAP
GEN-ERAL BELZE ?!
SHWOOM

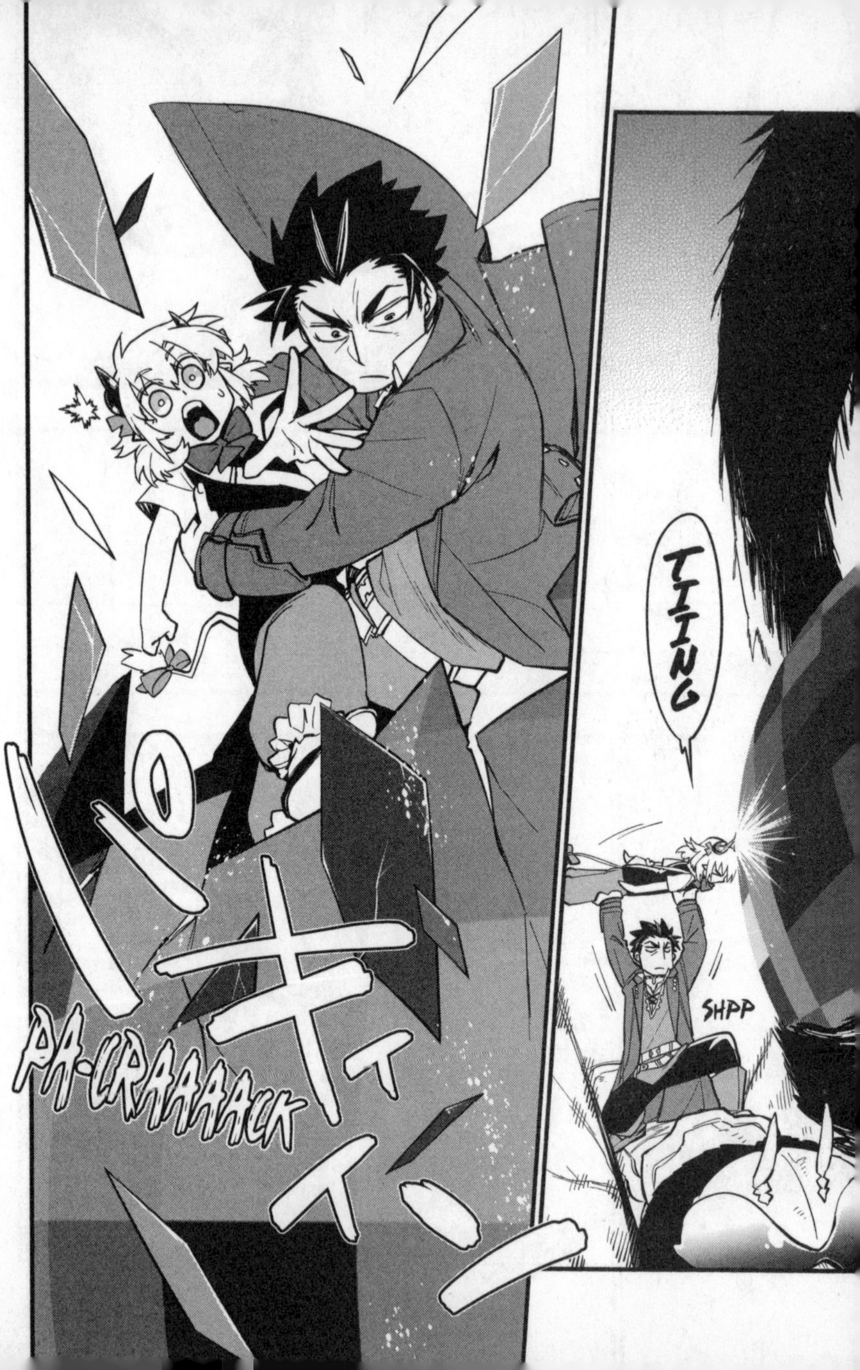
TIING
SHPP
PA-CRAAAACK

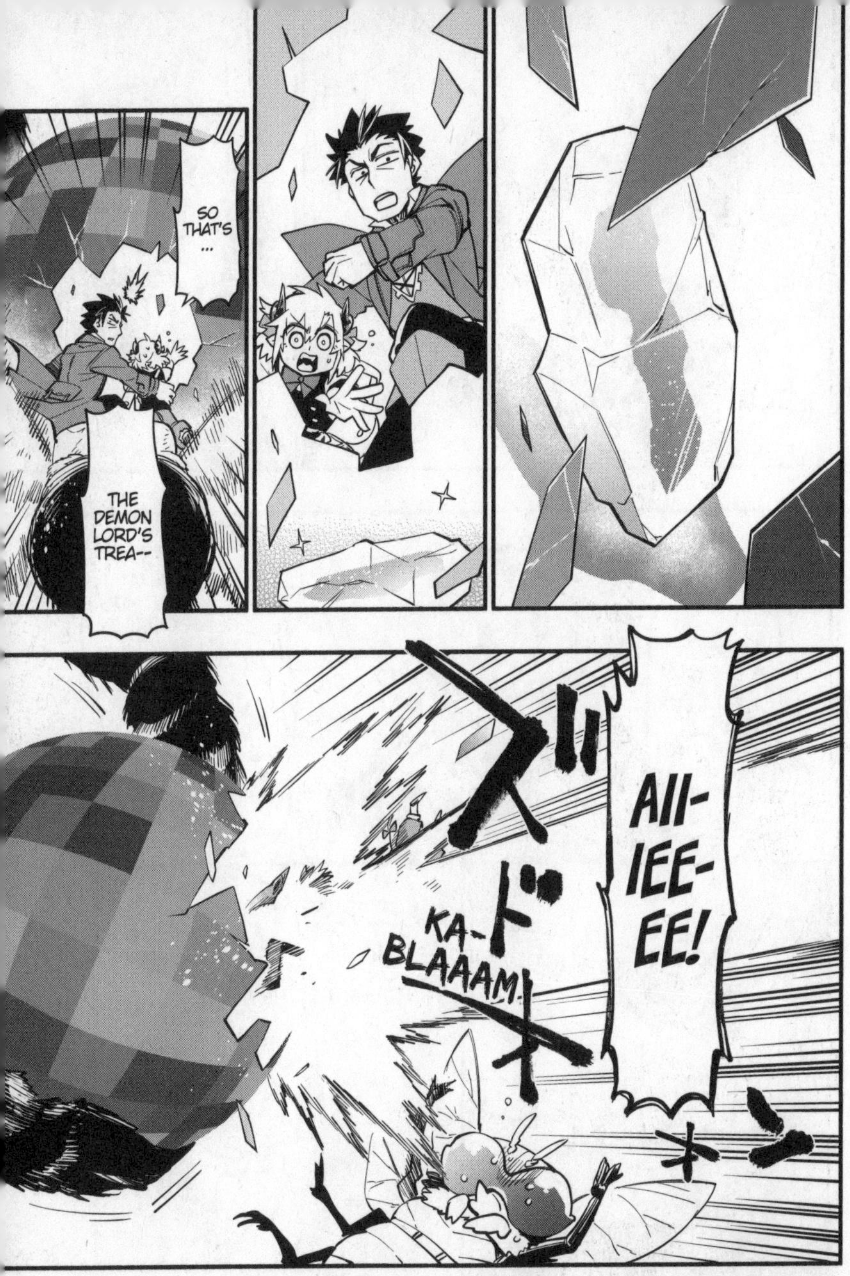
SO THAT'S ...
THE DEMON LORD'S TREA--
AII-IEE-EE!
KA-BLAAAM

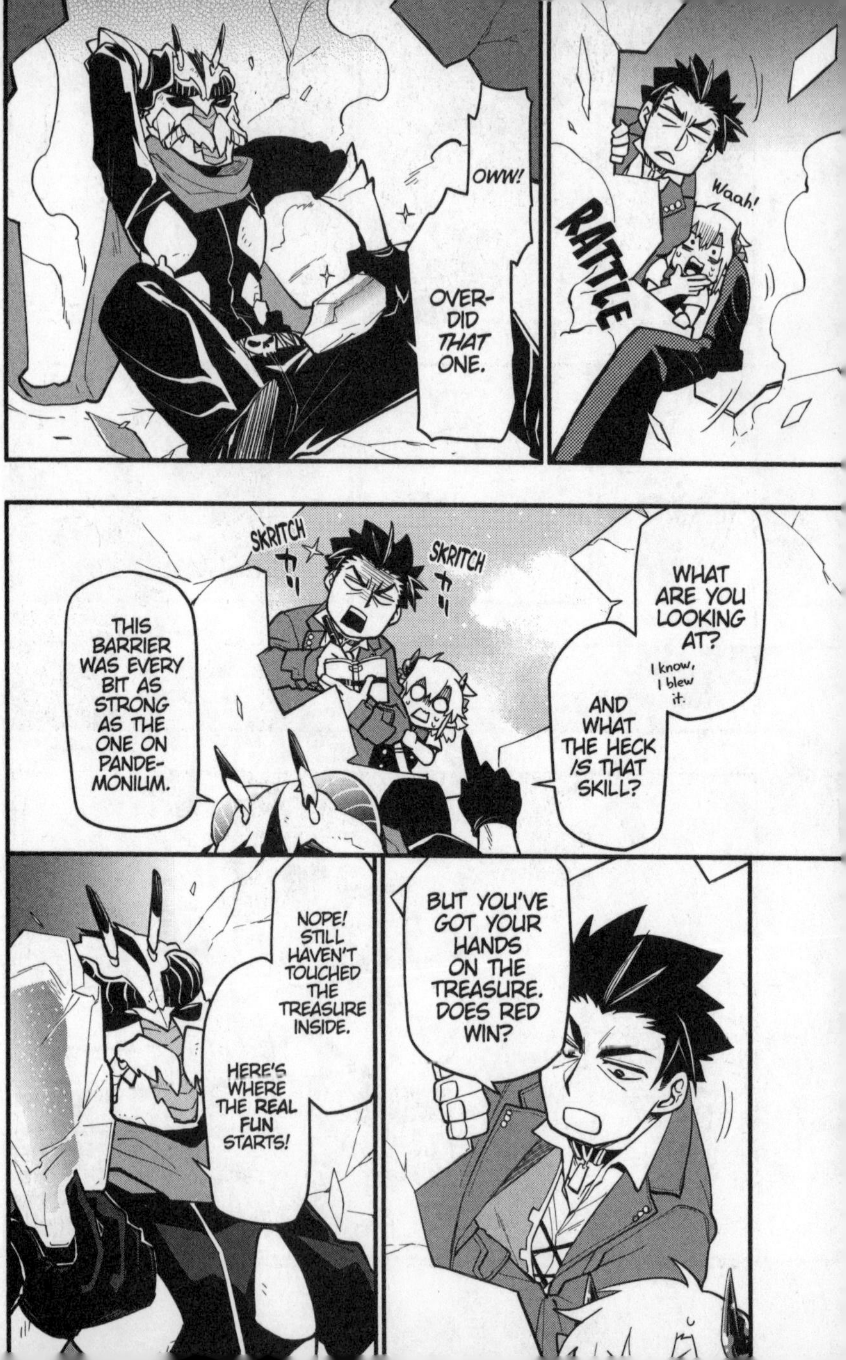
RATTLE
Waah!
OWW!
OVERDID THAT ONE.
WHAT ARE YOU LOOKING AT?
I know, I blew it.
AND WHAT THE HECK IS THAT SKILL?
SKRITCH
SKRITCH
THIS BARRIER WAS EVERY BIT AS STRONG AS THE ONE ON PANDEMONIUM.
BUT YOU'VE GOT YOUR HANDS ON THE TREASURE. DOES RED WIN?
NOPE! STILL HAVEN'T TOUCHED THE TREASURE INSIDE.
HERE'S WHERE THE REAL FUN STARTS!

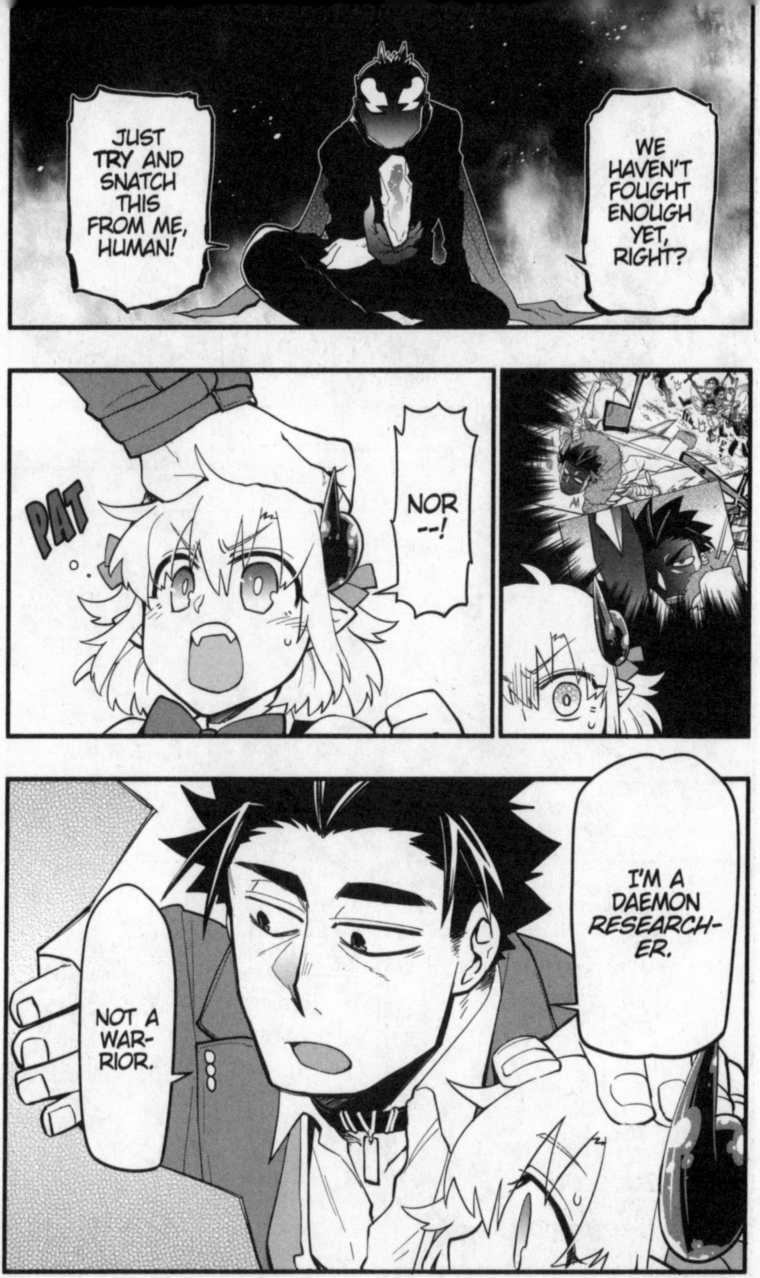
WE HAVEN'T FOUGHT ENOUGH YET, RIGHT?
JUST TRY AND SNATCH THIS FROM ME, HUMAN!
NOR--!
PAT
I'M A DAEMON RESEARCHER.
NOT A WARRIOR.

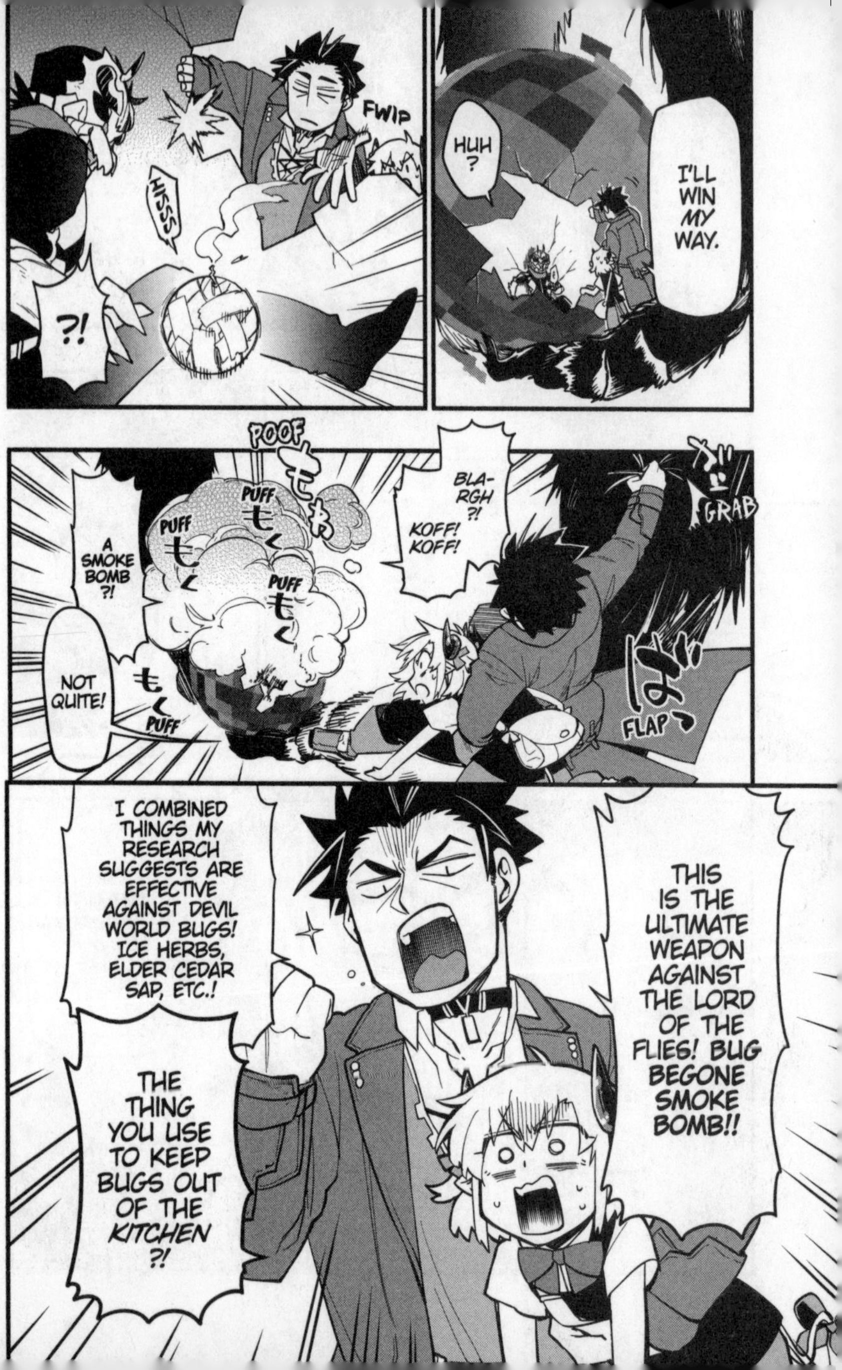
I'LL WIN MY WAY.
HUH?
FWIP
HISSS
?!
BLARGH?! KOFF! KOFF!
POOF
もわ
PUFF
もく
PUFF
もく
A SMOKE BOMB?!
PUFF
もく
もく
PUFF
NOT QUITE!
GRAB
ばっ
FLAP
THIS IS THE ULTIMATE WEAPON AGAINST THE LORD OF THE FLIES! BUG BEGONE SMOKE BOMB!!
I COMBINED THINGS MY RESEARCH SUGGESTS ARE EFFECTIVE AGAINST DEVIL WORLD BUGS! ICE HERBS, ELDER CEDAR SAP, ETC.!
THE THING YOU USE TO KEEP BUGS OUT OF THE *KITCHEN*?!

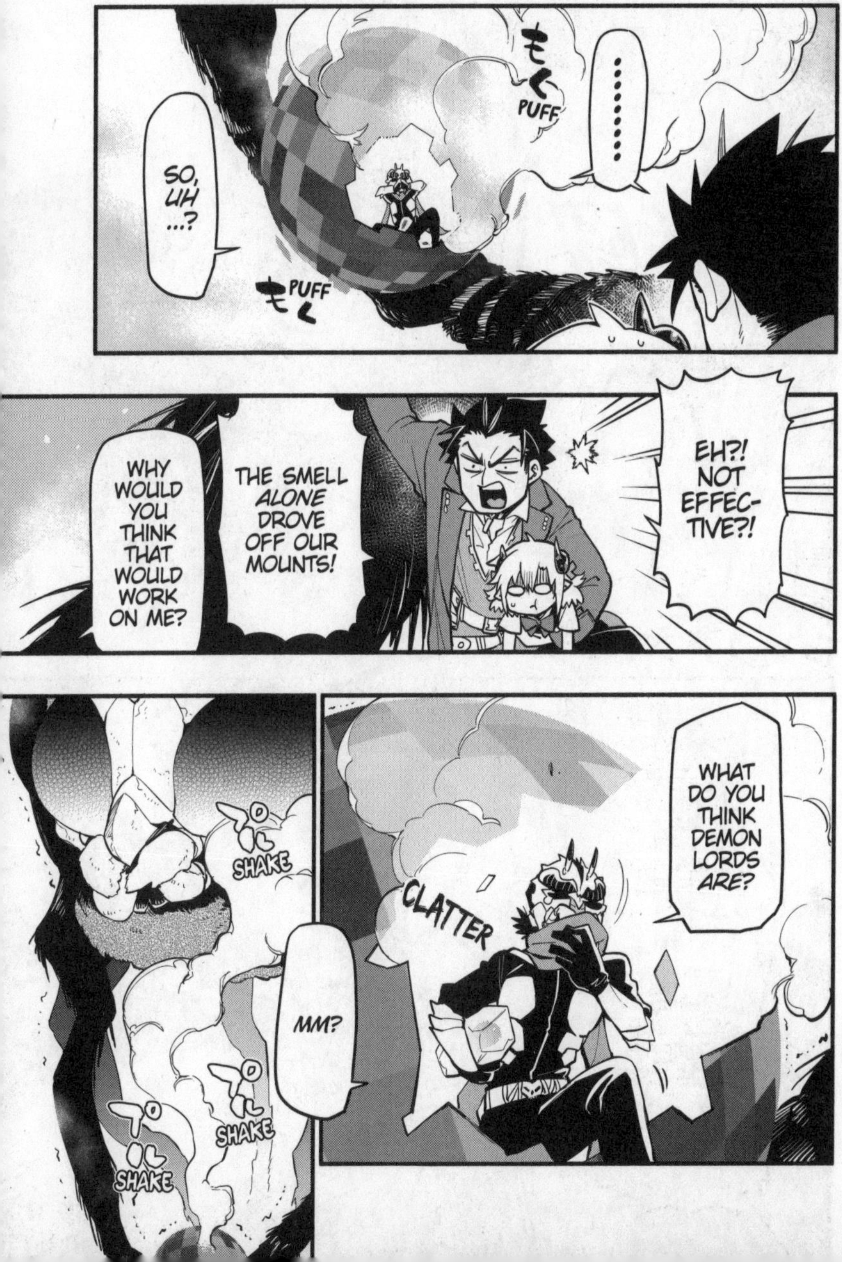

……
もく
PUFF
SO, UH ...?
もく
PUFF
EH?! NOT EFFEC-TIVE?!
THE SMELL ALONE DROVE OFF OUR MOUNTS!
WHY WOULD YOU THINK THAT WOULD WORK ON ME?
WHAT DO YOU THINK DEMON LORDS ARE?
CLATTER
MM?
SHAKE
SHAKE
SHAKE

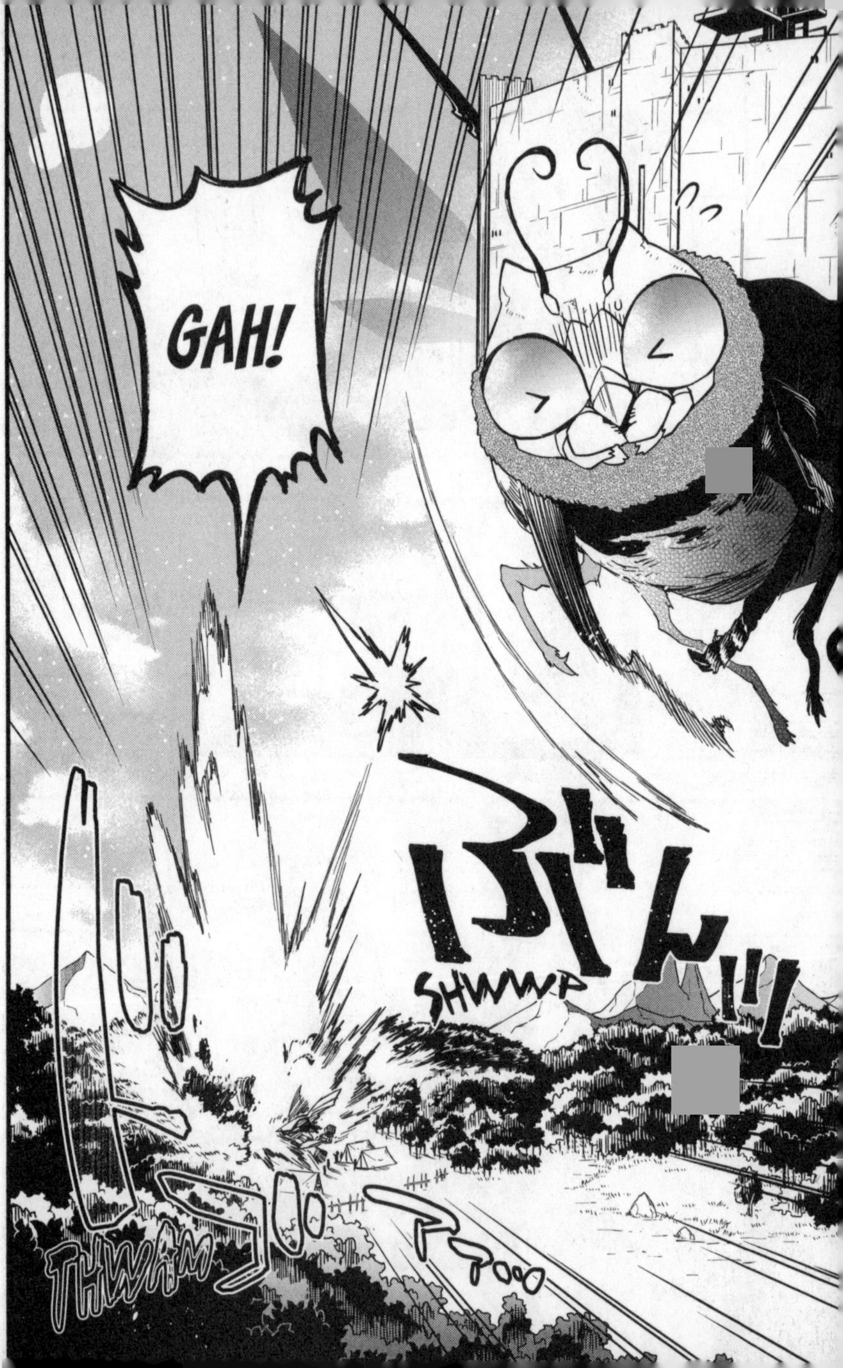
GAH!
SHWWP
THWAM

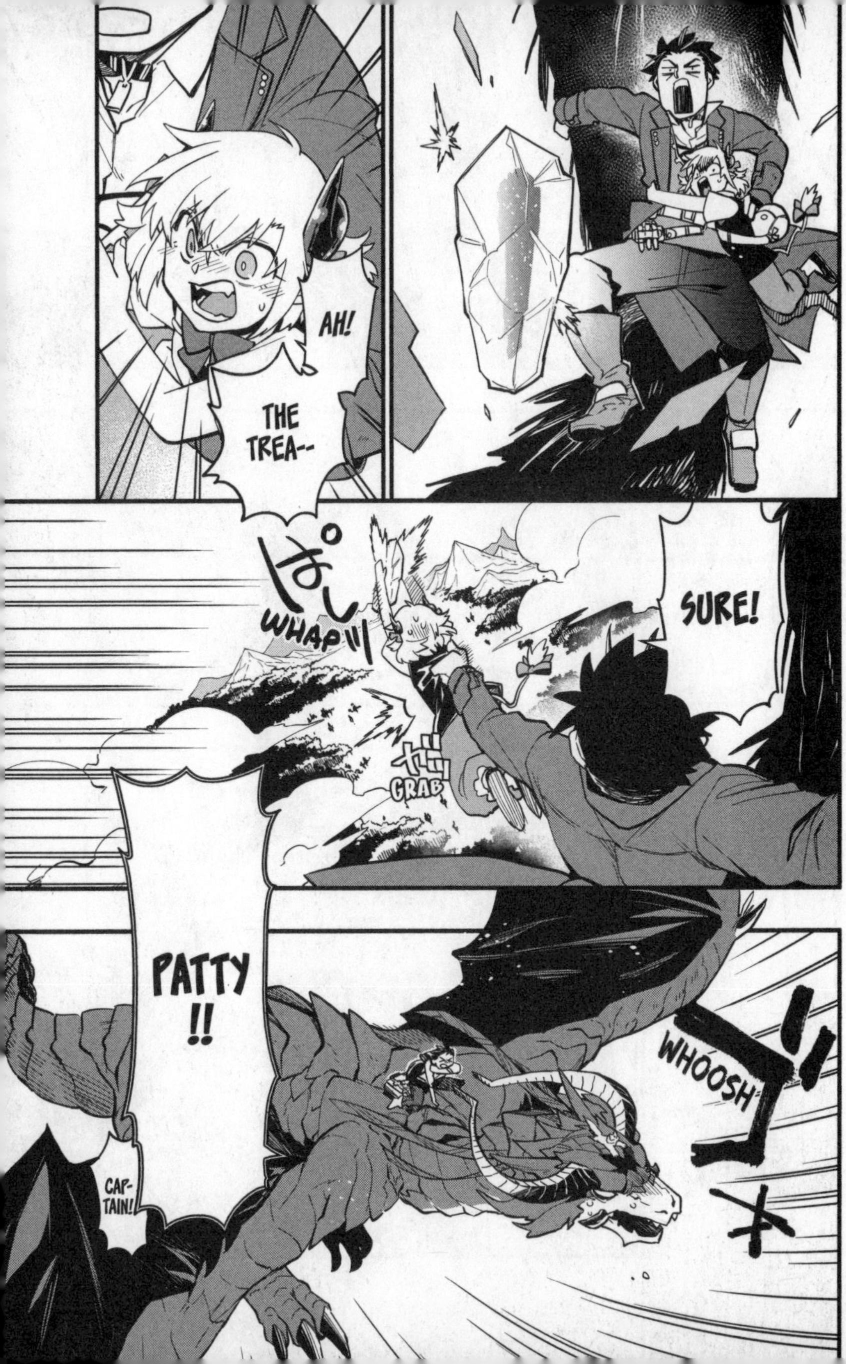

AH!
THE TREA--
ぱし
WHAP!!
SURE!
ガッ
GRAB
PATTY !!
WHOOSH
CAP-TAIN!

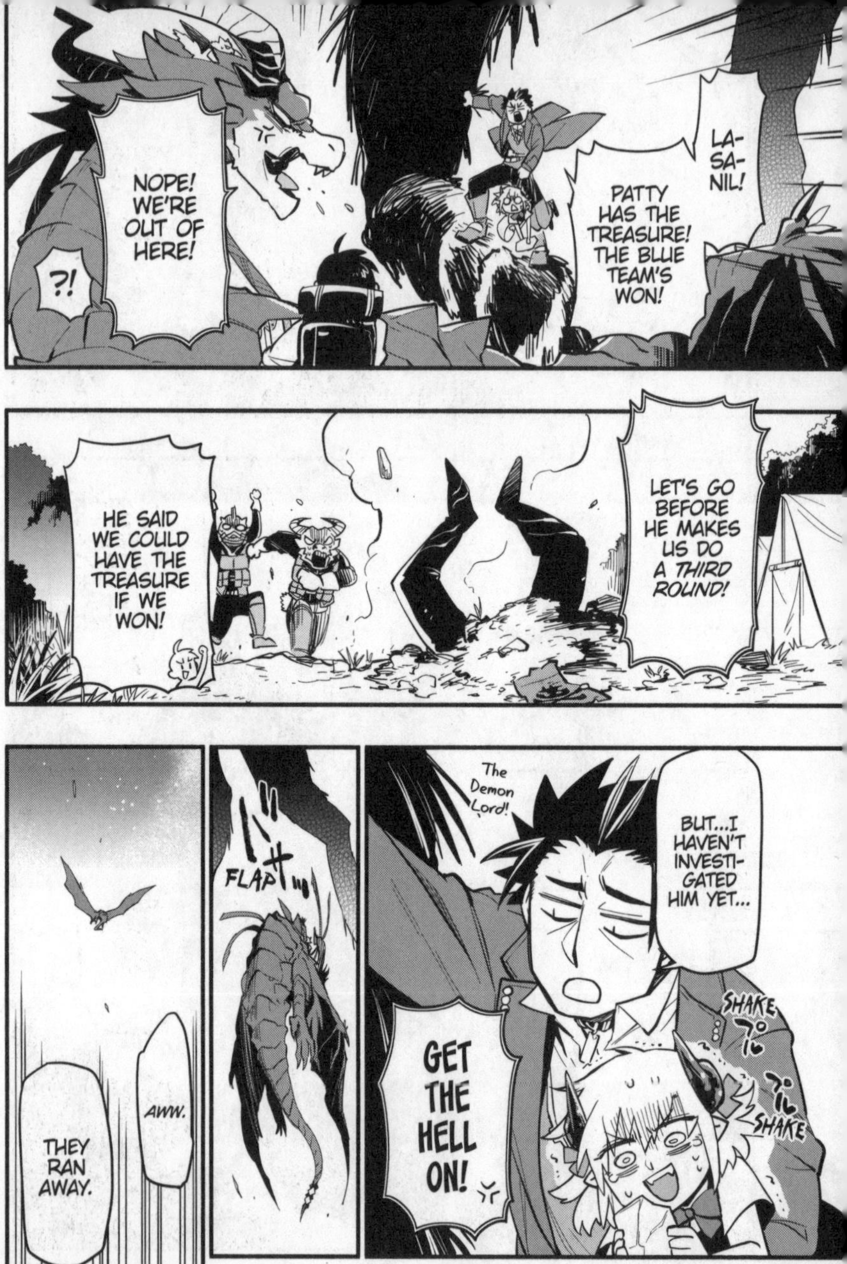
LA-SA-NIL!
PATTY HAS THE TREASURE! THE BLUE TEAM'S WON!
NOPE! WE'RE OUT OF HERE!
?!
LET'S GO BEFORE HE MAKES US DO A *THIRD ROUND!*
HE SAID WE COULD HAVE THE TREASURE IF WE WON!
The Demon Lord!
BUT...I HAVEN'T INVESTI-GATED HIM YET...
SHAKE
SHAKE
GET THE HELL ON!
FLAP
AWW.
THEY RAN AWAY.

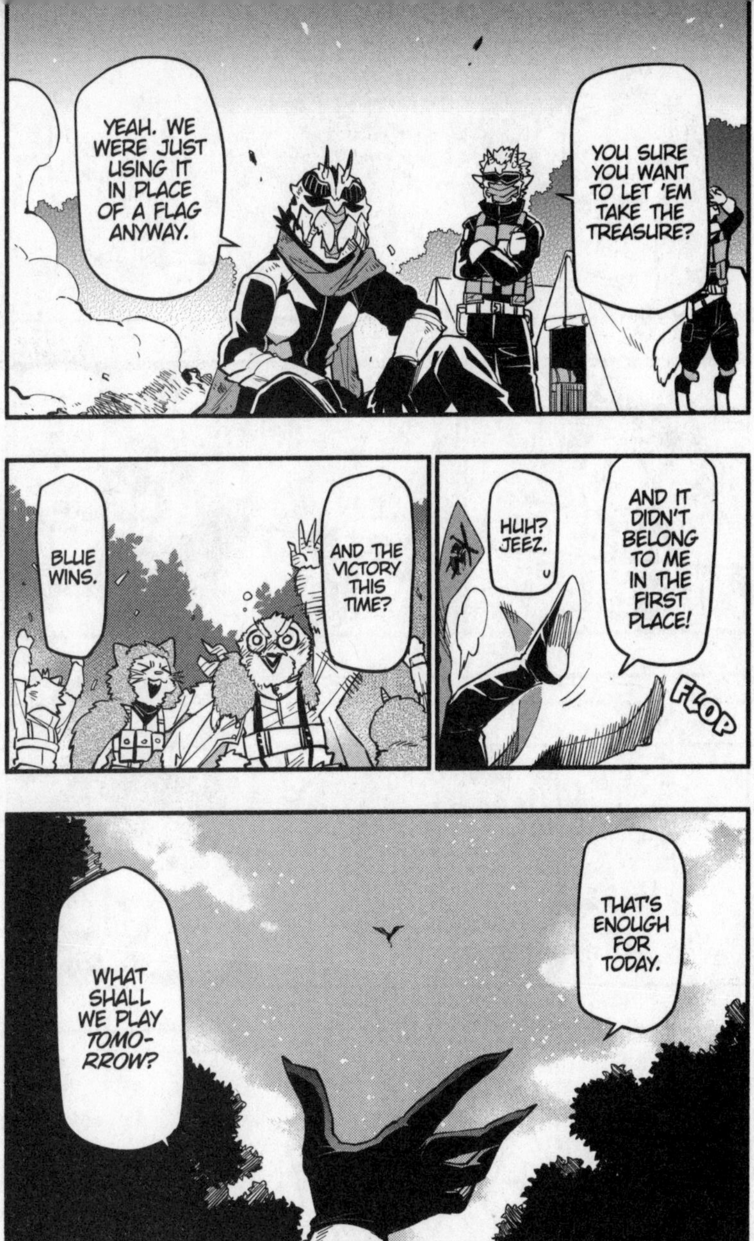
YOU SURE YOU WANT TO LET 'EM TAKE THE TREASURE?
YEAH. WE WERE JUST USING IT IN PLACE OF A FLAG ANYWAY.
AND IT DIDN'T BELONG TO ME IN THE FIRST PLACE!
FLOP
HUH? JEEZ.
AND THE VICTORY THIS TIME?
BLUE WINS.
THAT'S ENOUGH FOR TODAY.
WHAT SHALL WE PLAY TOMO-RROW?

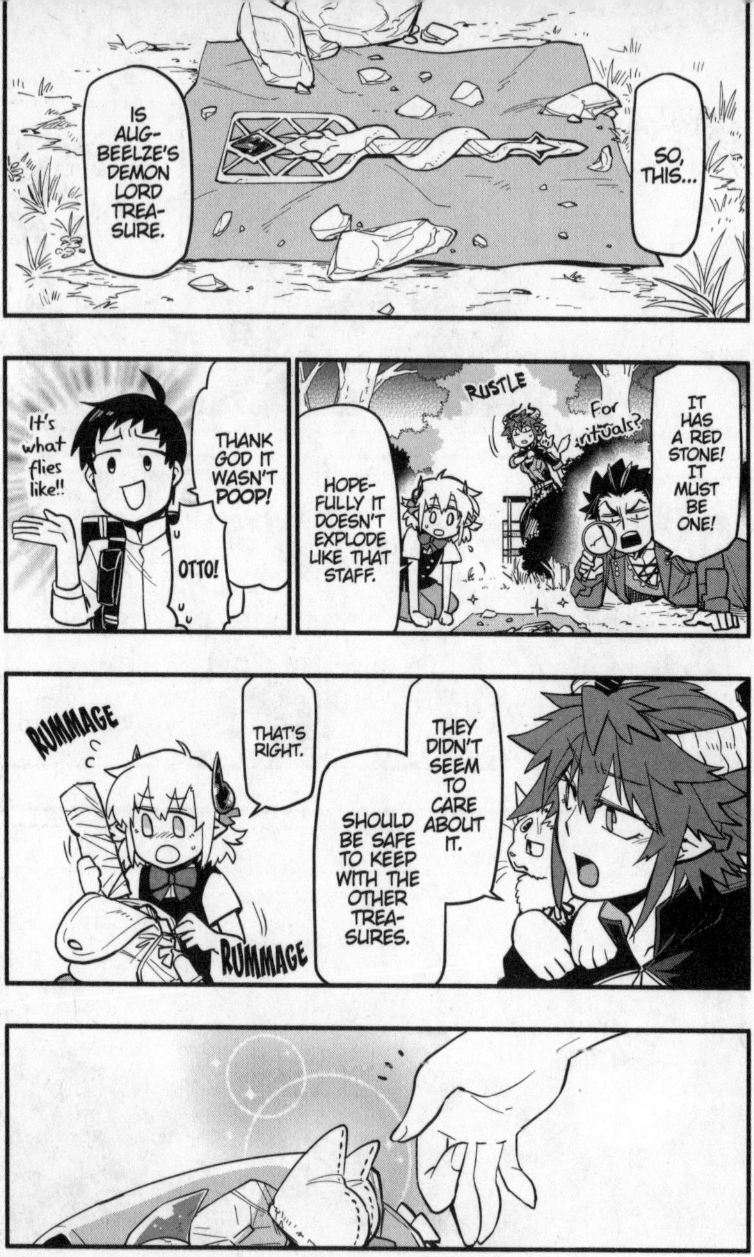
SO, THIS...
IS AUGBEELZE'S DEMON LORD TREASURE.
IT HAS A RED STONE! IT MUST BE ONE!
RUSTLE
For rituals?
HOPEFULLY IT DOESN'T EXPLODE LIKE THAT STAFF.
THANK GOD IT WASN'T POOP!
OTTO!
It's what flies like!!
THEY DIDN'T SEEM TO CARE ABOUT IT.
SHOULD BE SAFE TO KEEP WITH THE OTHER TREASURES.
THAT'S RIGHT.
RUMMAGE
RUMMAGE

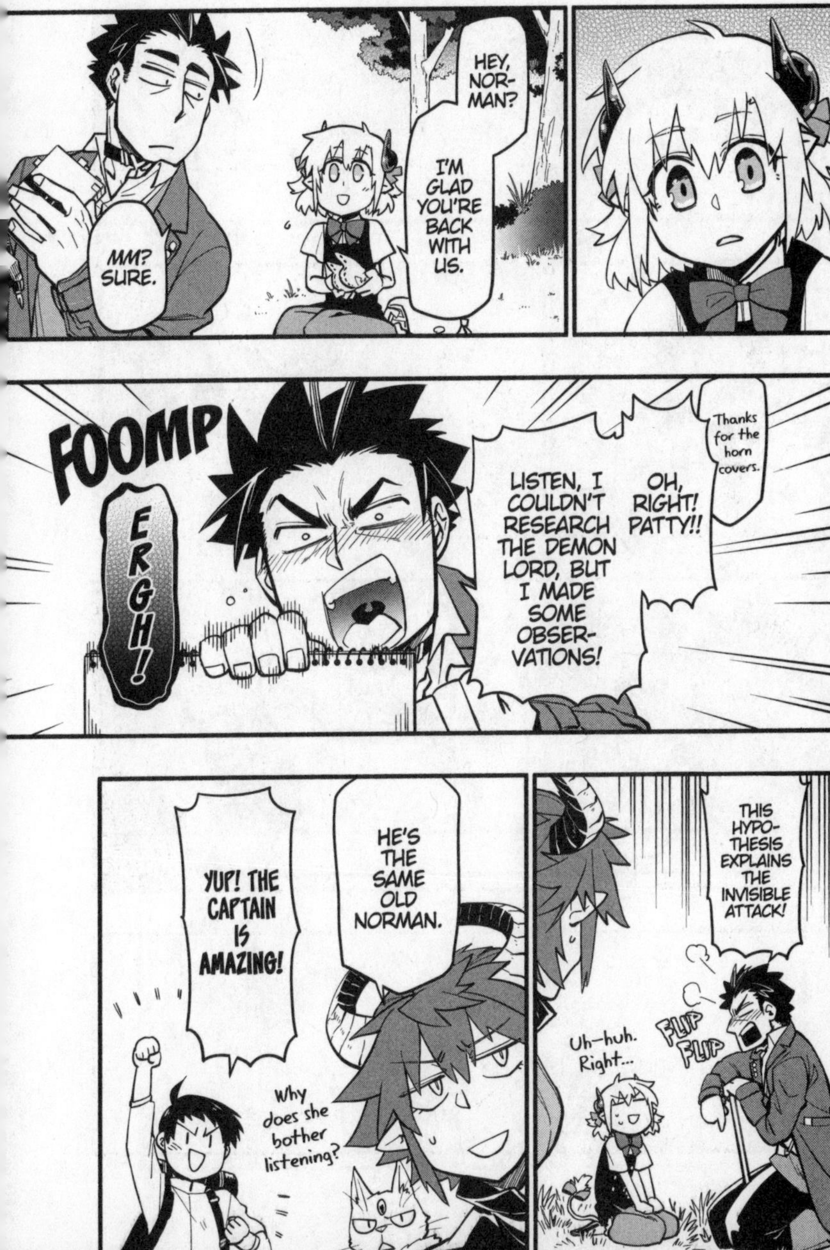
HEY, NOR-MAN?
I'M GLAD YOU'RE BACK WITH US.
MM? SURE.
Thanks for the horn covers.
OH, RIGHT! PATTY!!
LISTEN, I COULDN'T RESEARCH THE DEMON LORD, BUT I MADE SOME OBSER-VATIONS!
FOOMP
ERGH!
THIS HYPO-THESIS EXPLAINS THE INVISIBLE ATTACK!
FLIP FLIP
Uh-huh. Right...
HE'S THE SAME OLD NORMAN.
YUP! THE CAPTAIN IS AMAZING!
Why does she bother listening?

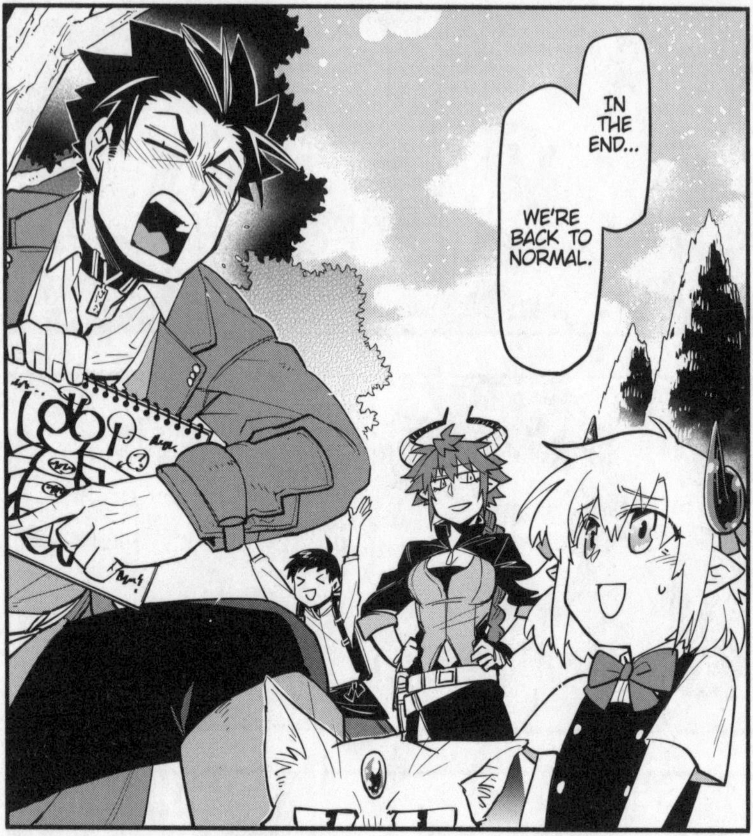
IN THE END...
WE'RE BACK TO NORMAL.

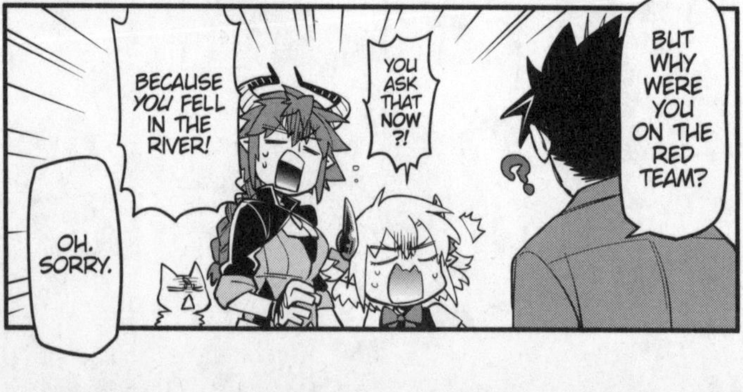
BUT WHY WERE YOU ON THE RED TEAM?
YOU ASK THAT NOW?!
BECAUSE *YOU* FELL IN THE RIVER!
OH. SORRY.

Sorry For My Familiar

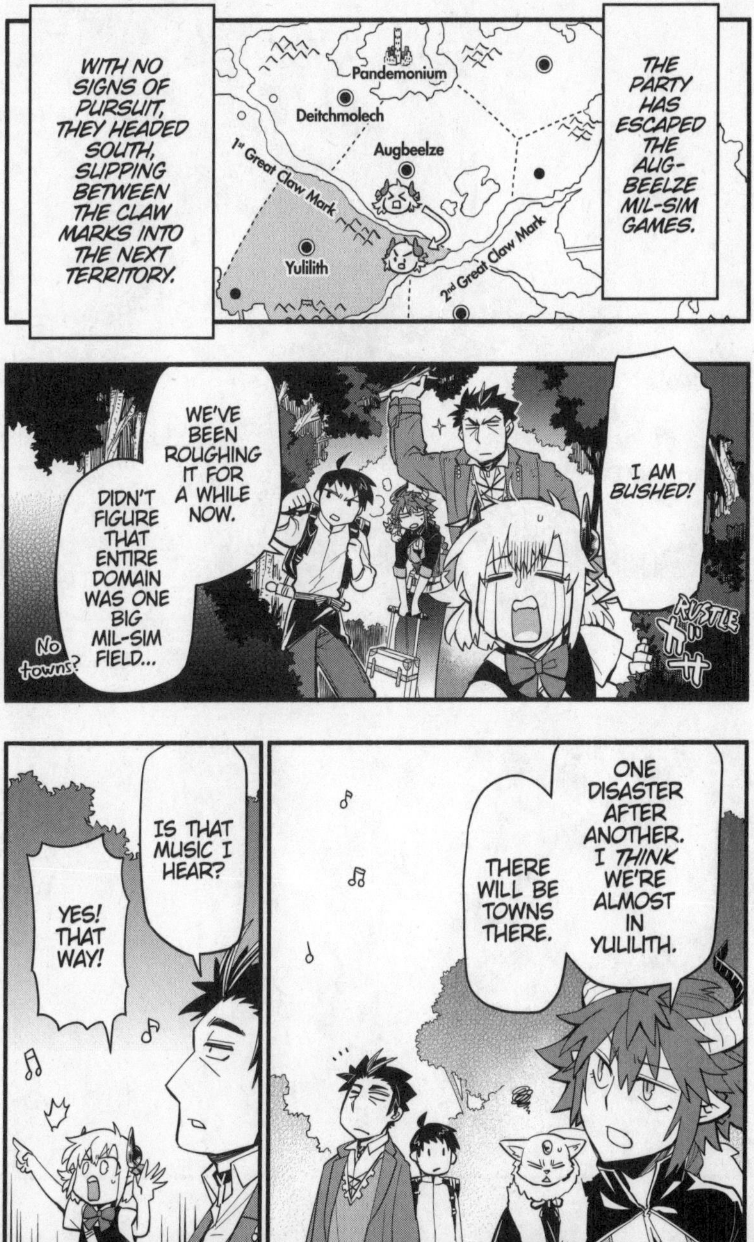

THE PARTY HAS ESCAPED THE AUG-BEELZE MIL-SIM GAMES.
WITH NO SIGNS OF PURSUIT, THEY HEADED SOUTH, SLIPPING BETWEEN THE CLAW MARKS INTO THE NEXT TERRITORY.
Pandemonium
Deitchmolech
Augbeelze
1st Great Claw Mark
2nd Great Claw Mark
Yulilith
I AM BUSHED!
WE'VE BEEN ROUGHING IT FOR A WHILE NOW.
DIDN'T FIGURE THAT ENTIRE DOMAIN WAS ONE BIG MIL-SIM FIELD...
No towns?
RUSTLE
ONE DISASTER AFTER ANOTHER. I THINK WE'RE ALMOST IN YULILITH.
THERE WILL BE TOWNS THERE.
IS THAT MUSIC I HEAR?
YES! THAT WAY!

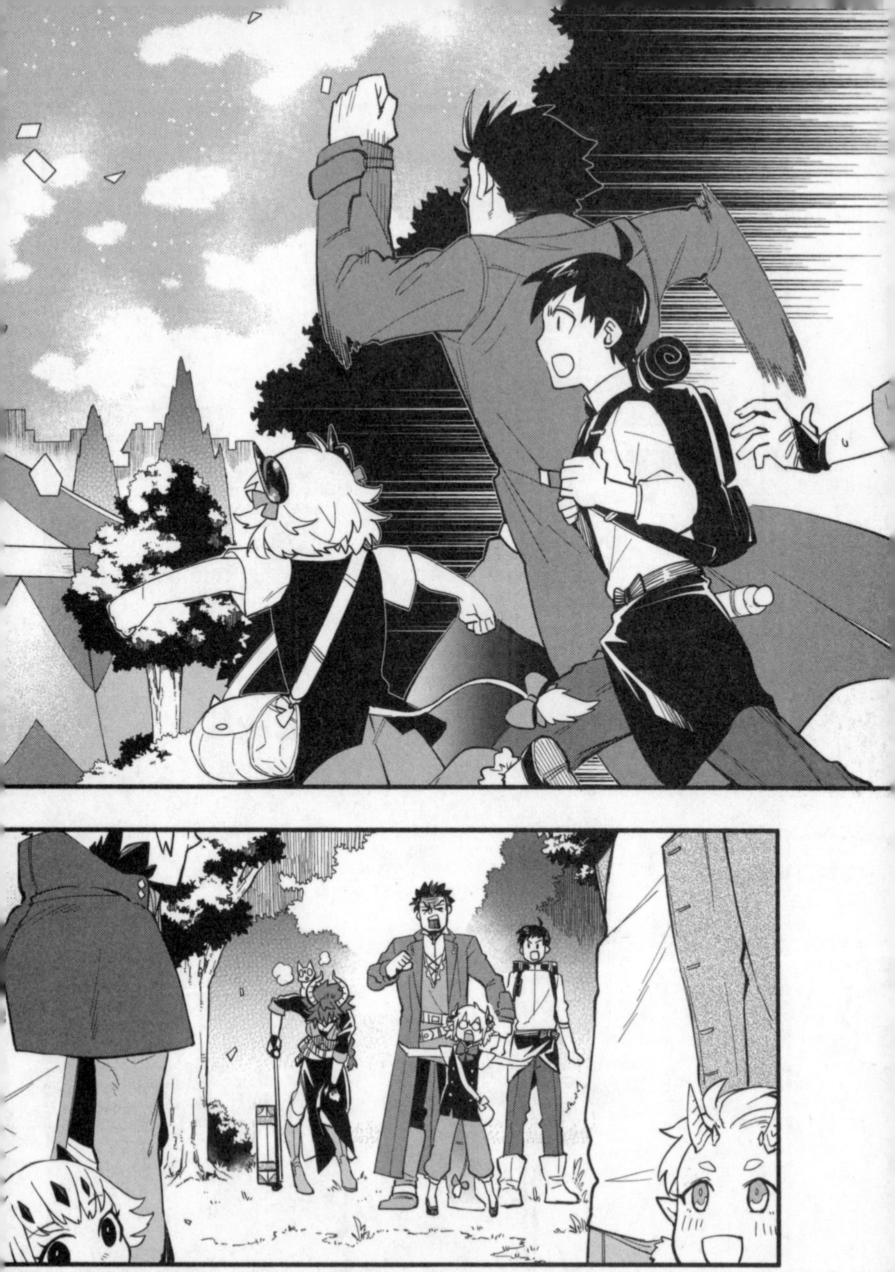

FILE 46: Charchax

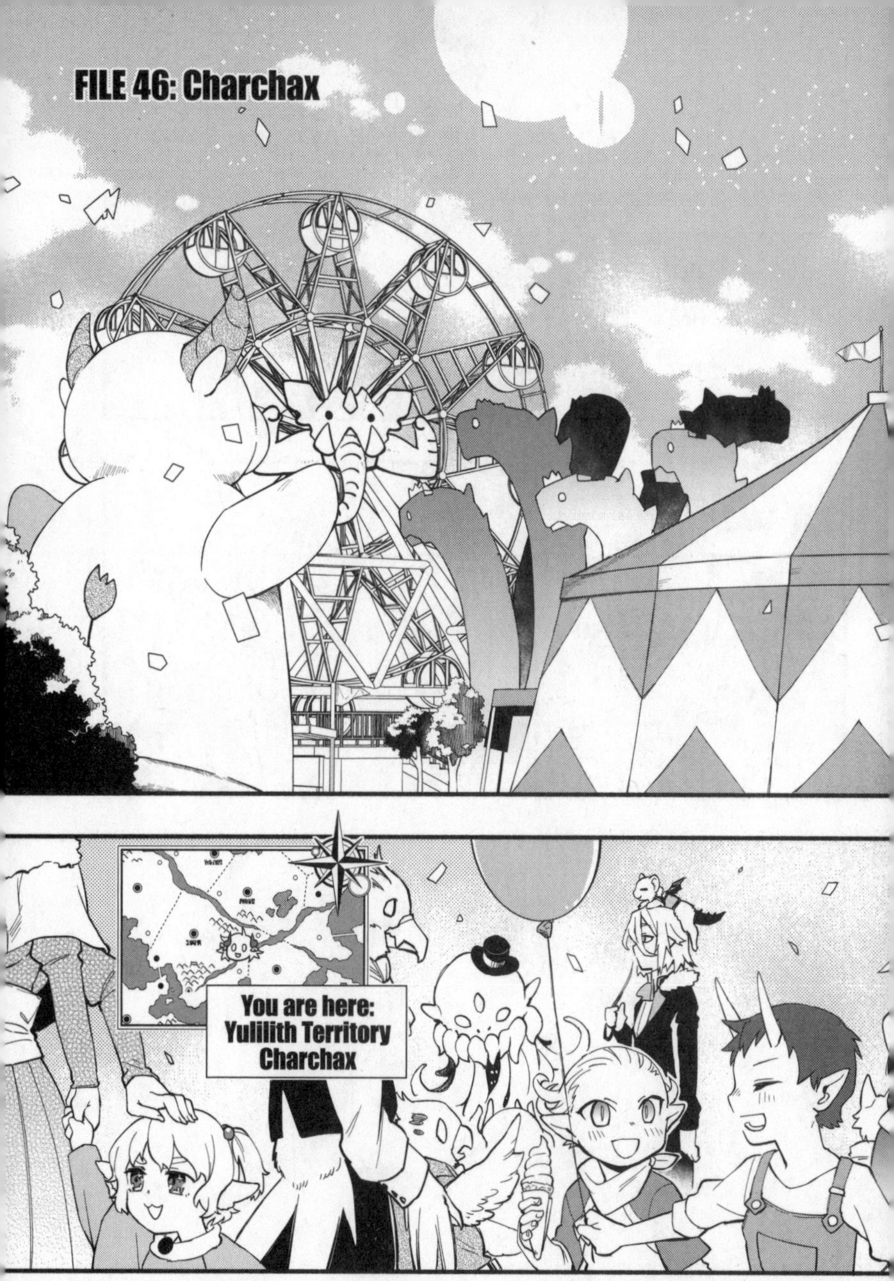
You are here:
Yulilith Territory
Charchax

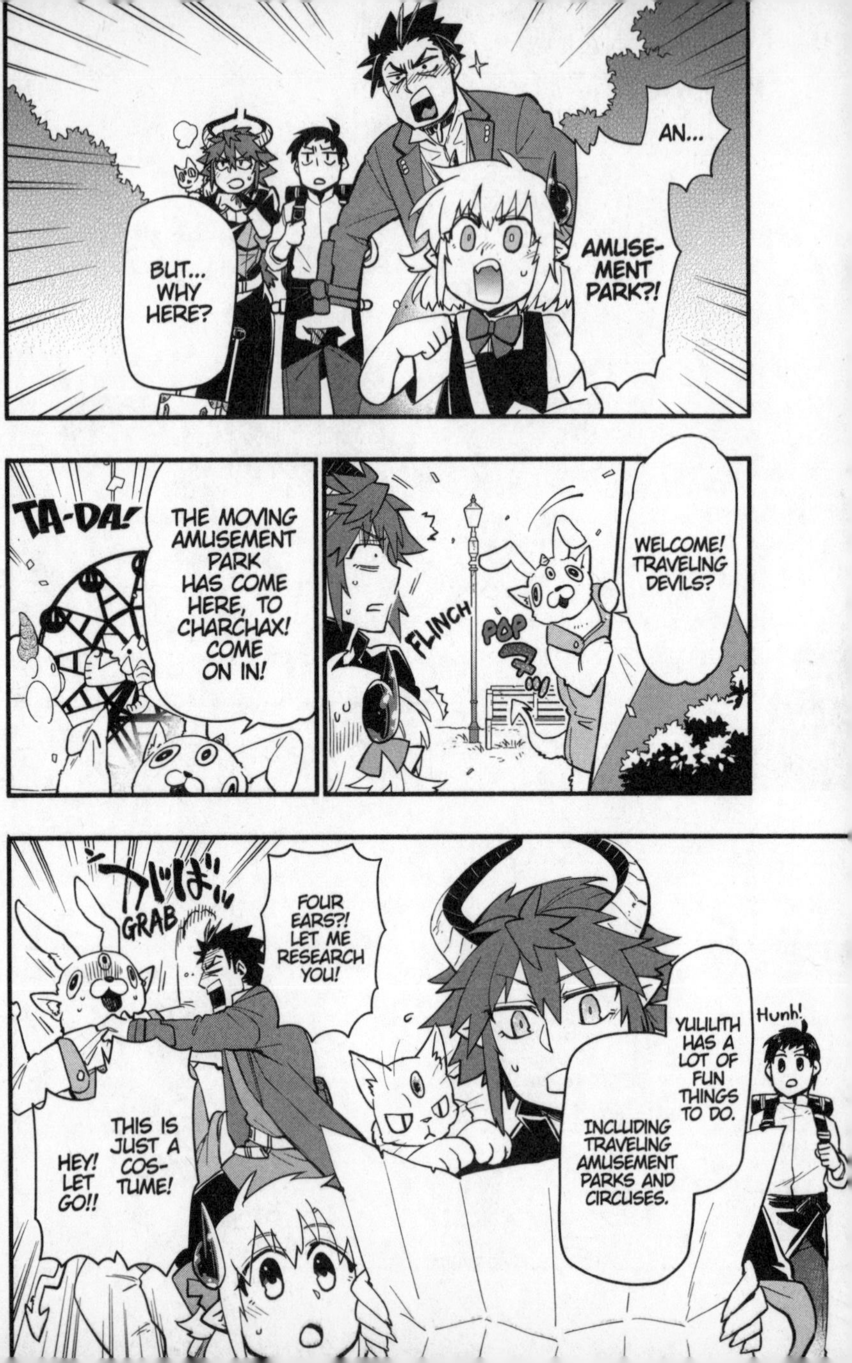
AN... AMUSEMENT PARK?!
BUT... WHY HERE?
WELCOME! TRAVELING DEVILS?
FLINCH
POP
TA-DA!
THE MOVING AMUSEMENT PARK HAS COME HERE, TO CHARCHAX! COME ON IN!
GRAB
FOUR EARS?! LET ME RESEARCH YOU!
Hunh!
YULILITH HAS A LOT OF FUN THINGS TO DO.
INCLUDING TRAVELING AMUSEMENT PARKS AND CIRCUSES.
THIS IS JUST A COS-TUME!
HEY! LET GO!!

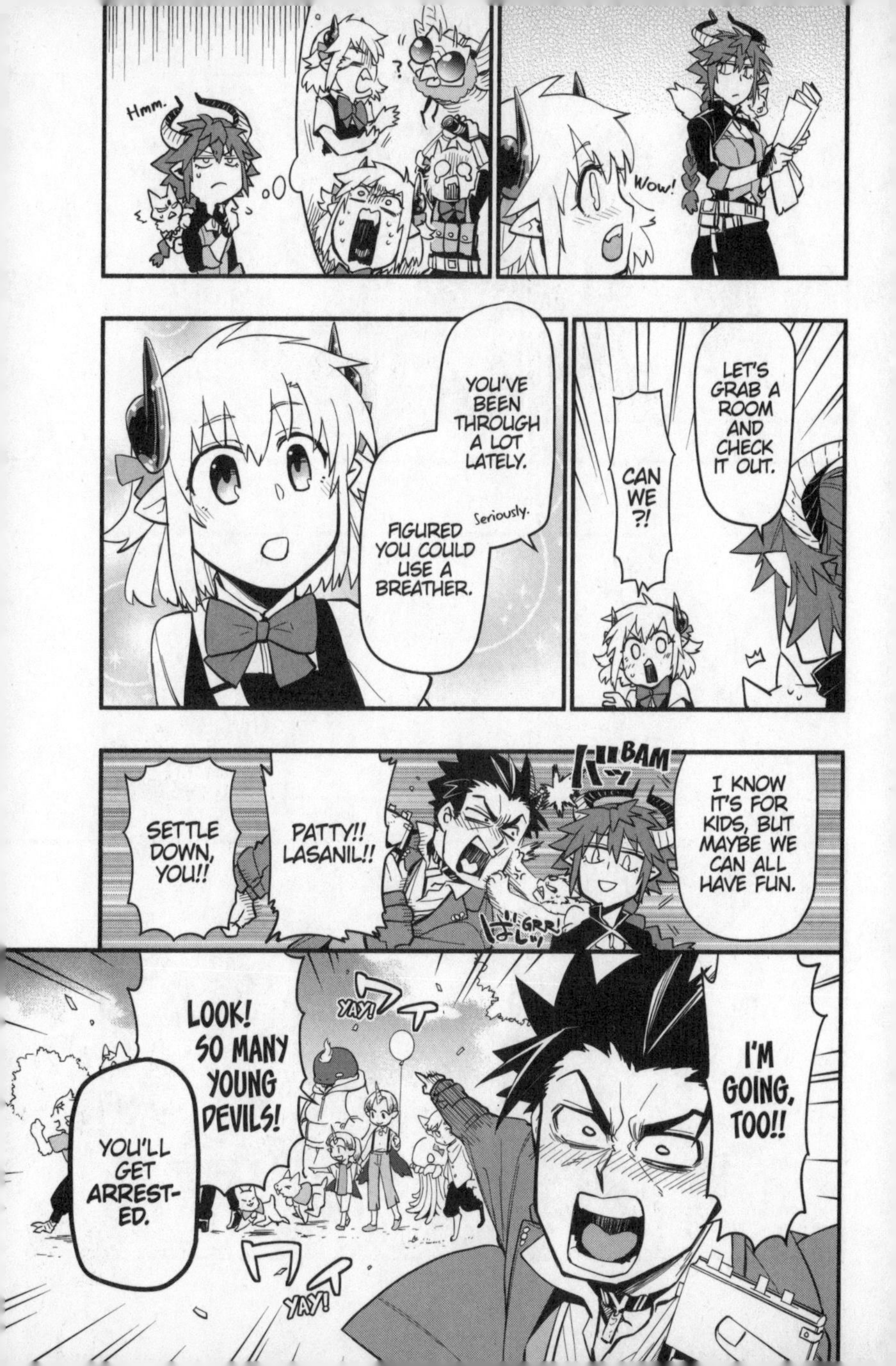
Wow!
?
Hmm.
LET'S GRAB A ROOM AND CHECK IT OUT.
CAN WE ?!
YOU'VE BEEN THROUGH A LOT LATELY.
Seriously.
FIGURED YOU COULD USE A BREATHER.
I KNOW IT'S FOR KIDS, BUT MAYBE WE CAN ALL HAVE FUN.
BAM
GRR!
PATTY!! LASANIL!!
SETTLE DOWN, YOU!!
I'M GOING, TOO!!
YAY!
LOOK! SO MANY YOUNG DEVILS!
YOU'LL GET ARREST-ED.
YAY!

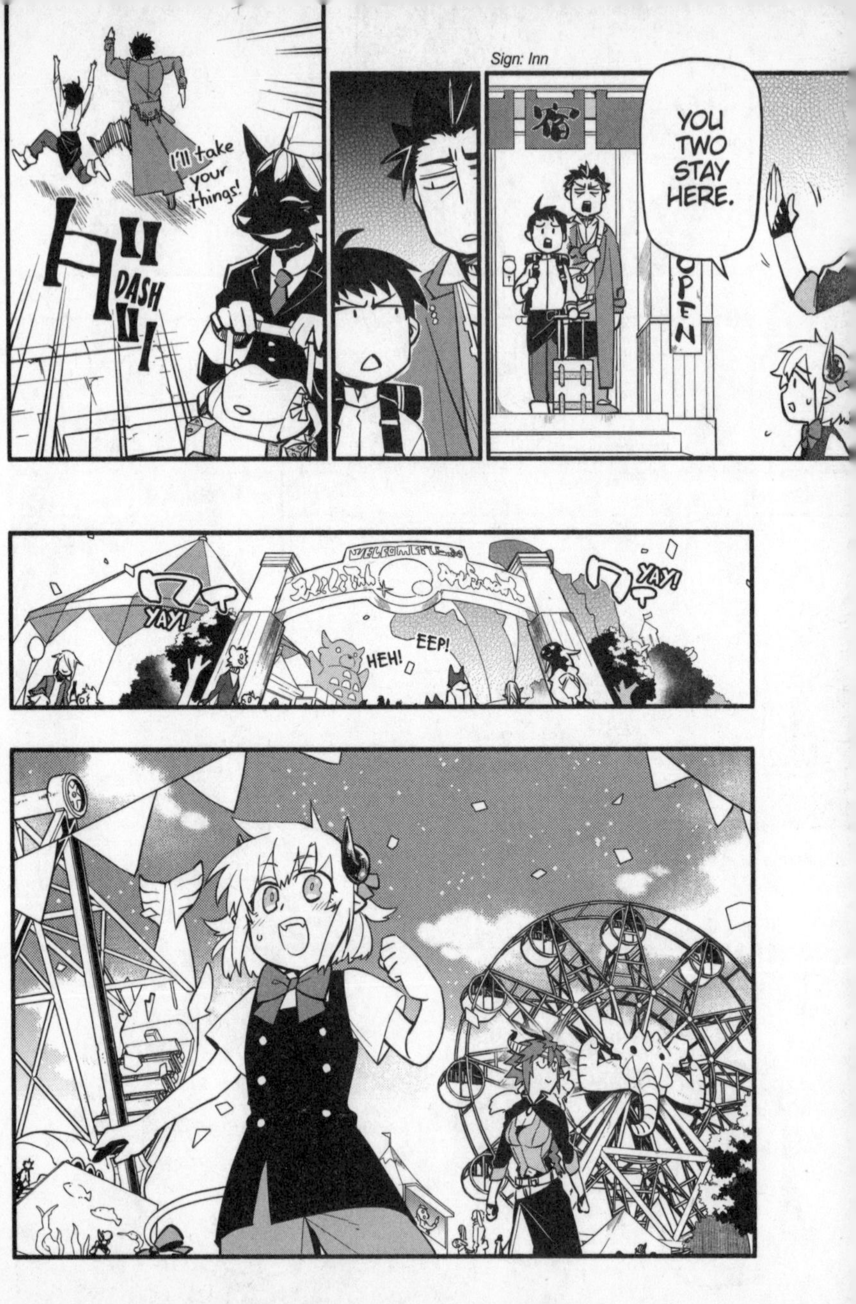
YOU TWO STAY HERE.
Sign: Inn
OPEN
I'll take your things!
DASH
YAY!
EEP!
HEH!
YAY!

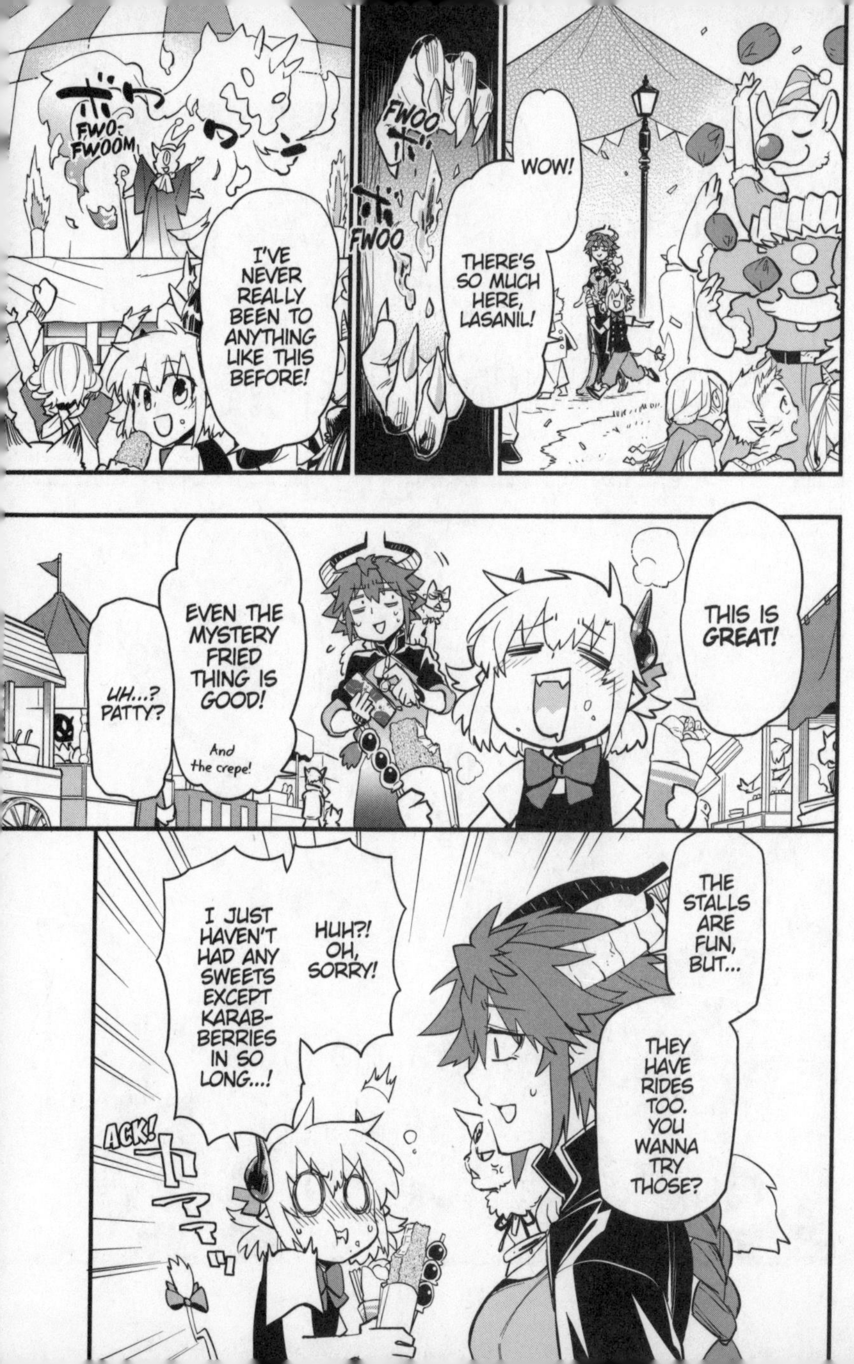
WOW!
THERE'S SO MUCH HERE, LASANIL!
FWOO
FWOO
I'VE NEVER REALLY BEEN TO ANYTHING LIKE THIS BEFORE!
FWO-FWOOM
THIS IS GREAT!
EVEN THE MYSTERY FRIED THING IS GOOD!
And the crepe!
UH...? PATTY?
THE STALLS ARE FUN, BUT...
THEY HAVE RIDES TOO. YOU WANNA TRY THOSE?
HUH?! OH, SORRY!
I JUST HAVEN'T HAD ANY SWEETS EXCEPT KARAB-BERRIES IN SO LONG...!
ACK!

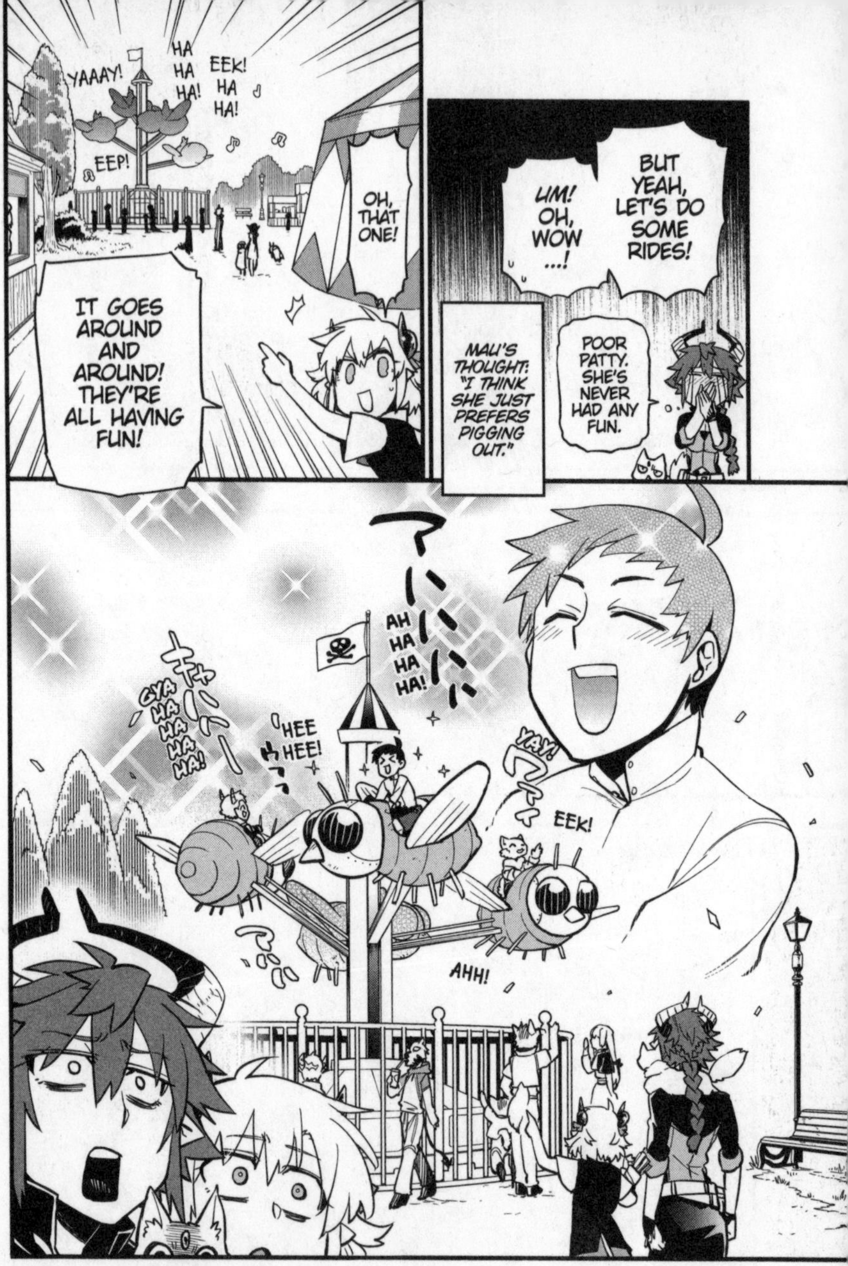

EEK! HA HA!
HA HA HA!
YAAAY!
EEP!
OH, THAT ONE!
IT GOES AROUND AND AROUND! THEY'RE ALL HAVING FUN!
BUT YEAH, LET'S DO SOME RIDES!
UM! OH, WOW ...!
POOR PATTY. SHE'S NEVER HAD ANY FUN.
MAU'S THOUGHT: "I THINK SHE JUST PREFERS PIGGING OUT."
AH HA HA HA!
YAY!
EEK!
HEE HEE!
GYA HA HA HA HA!
AHH!

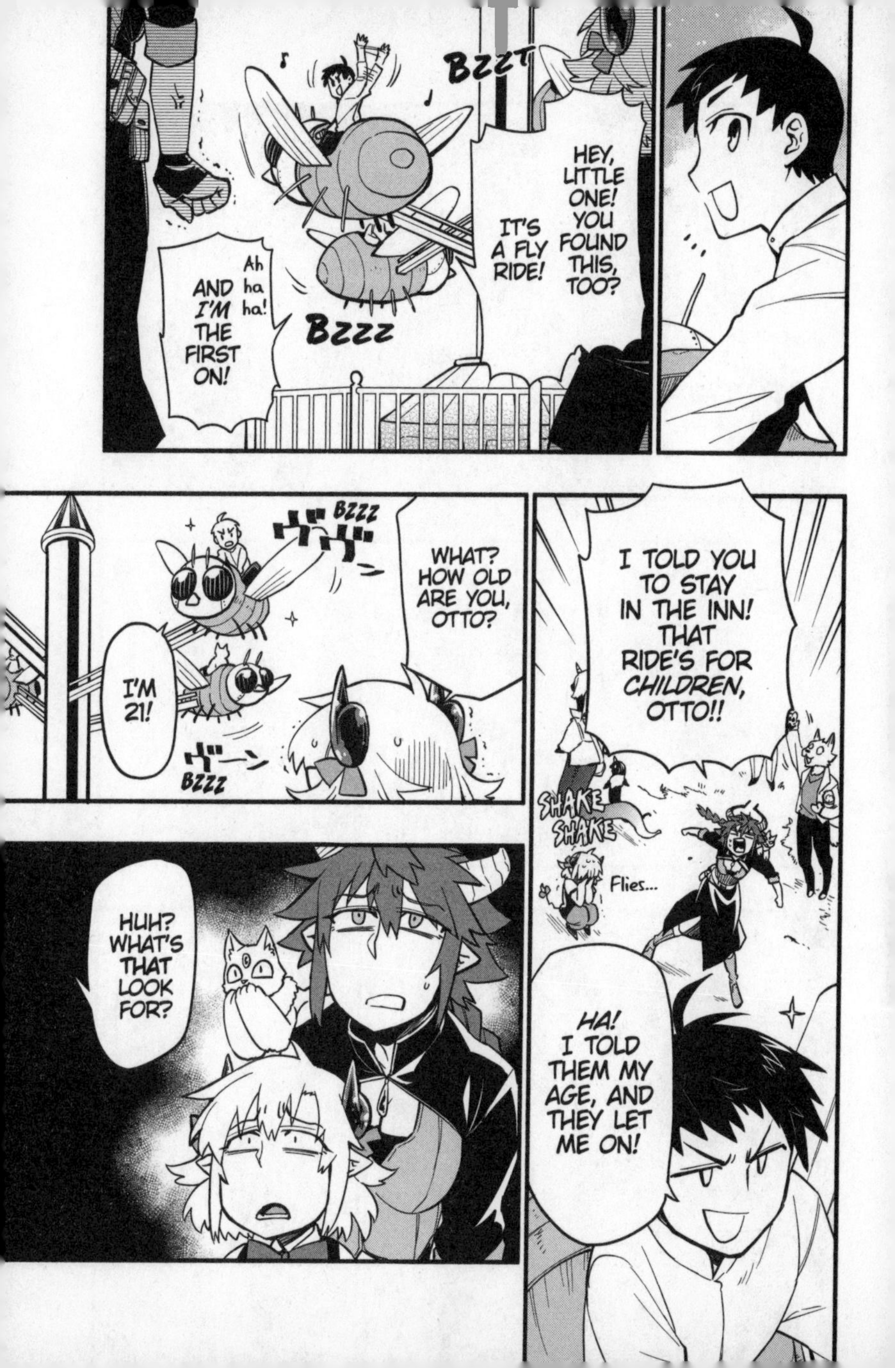
HEY, LITTLE ONE! YOU FOUND THIS, TOO?
IT'S A FLY RIDE!
BZZT
Ah ha ha!
AND I'M THE FIRST ON!
BZZZ
I TOLD YOU TO STAY IN THE INN! THAT RIDE'S FOR CHILDREN, OTTO!!
SHAKE SHAKE
Flies...
WHAT? HOW OLD ARE YOU, OTTO?
BZZZ
I'M 21!
BZZZ
HA! I TOLD THEM MY AGE, AND THEY LET ME ON!
HUH? WHAT'S THAT LOOK FOR?

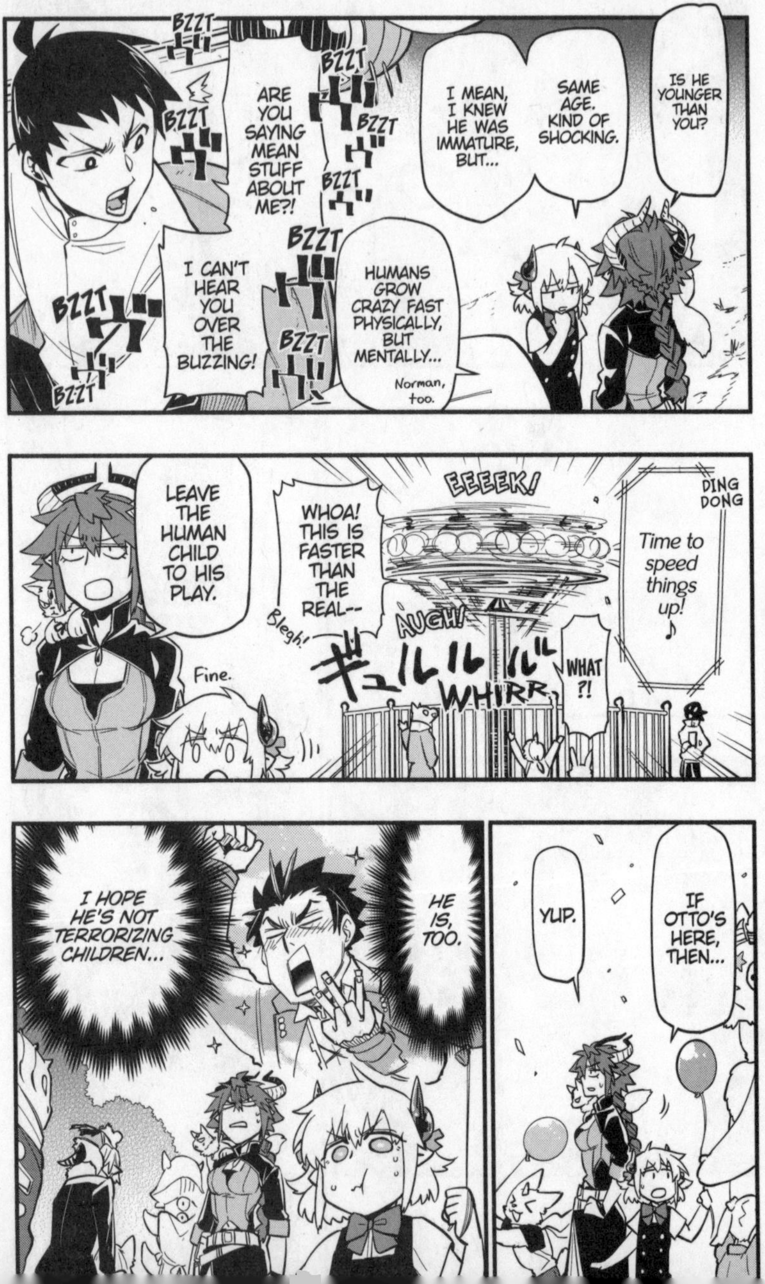

IS HE YOUNGER THAN YOU?
SAME AGE. KIND OF SHOCKING.
I MEAN, I KNEW HE WAS IMMATURE, BUT...
HUMANS GROW CRAZY FAST PHYSICALLY, BUT MENTALLY...
Norman, too.
ARE YOU SAYING MEAN STUFF ABOUT ME?!
I CAN'T HEAR YOU OVER THE BUZZING!
BZZT BZZT BZZT BZZT BZZT BZZT BZZT BZZT BZZT
DING DONG
Time to speed things up! ♪
WHAT?!
EEEEK!
WHOA! THIS IS FASTER THAN THE REAL--
AUGH!
Blegh!
WHIRR
LEAVE THE HUMAN CHILD TO HIS PLAY.
Fine.
IF OTTO'S HERE, THEN...
YUP.
HE IS, TOO.
I HOPE HE'S NOT TERRORIZING CHILDREN...

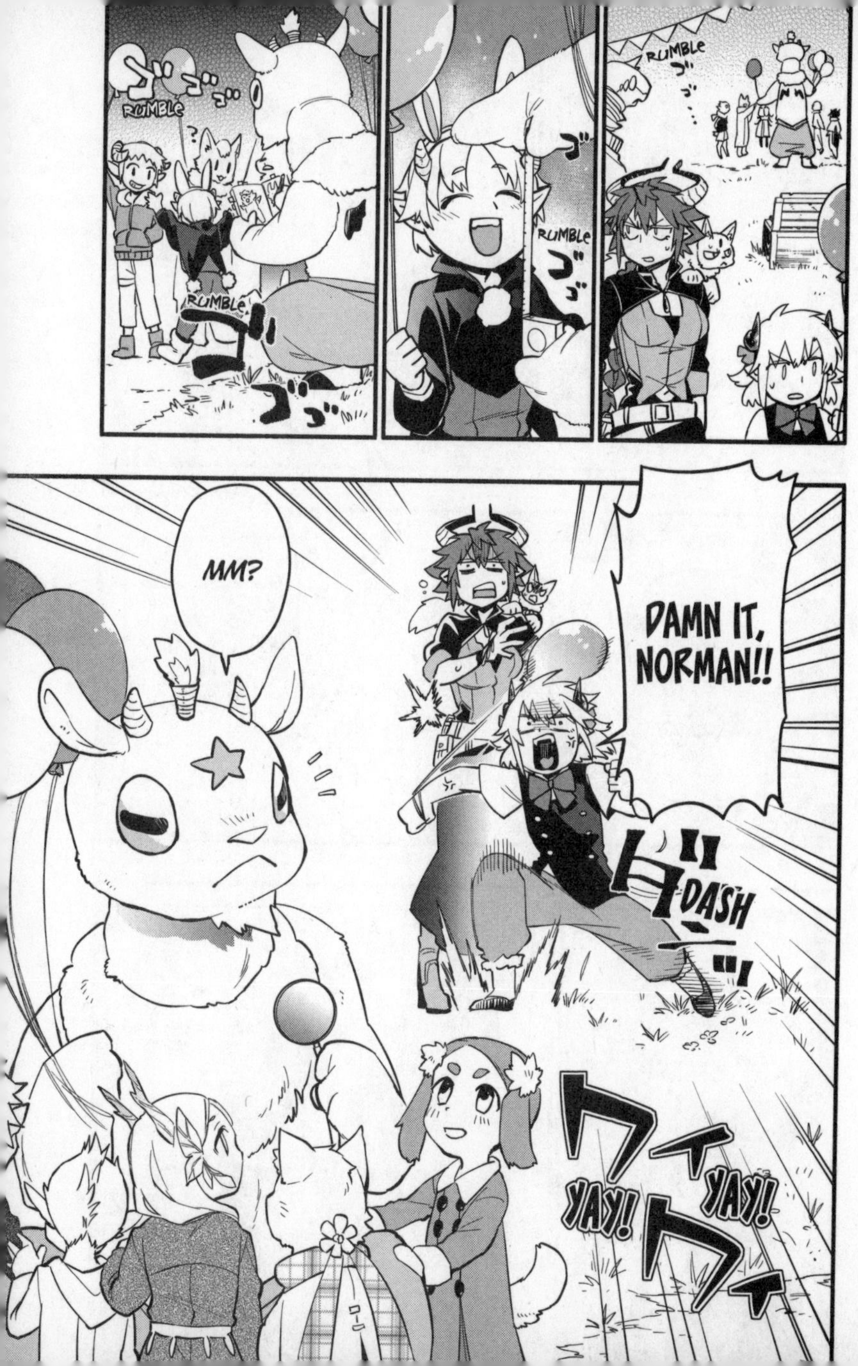

ゴゴゴ
RUMBLE
ゴゴ
RUMBLE
ゴゴ
ゴ
RUMBLE
ゴ
RUMBLE
ゴゴ
RUMBLE
ゴ...
MM?
DAMN IT, NORMAN!!
DASH
YAY!
YAY!

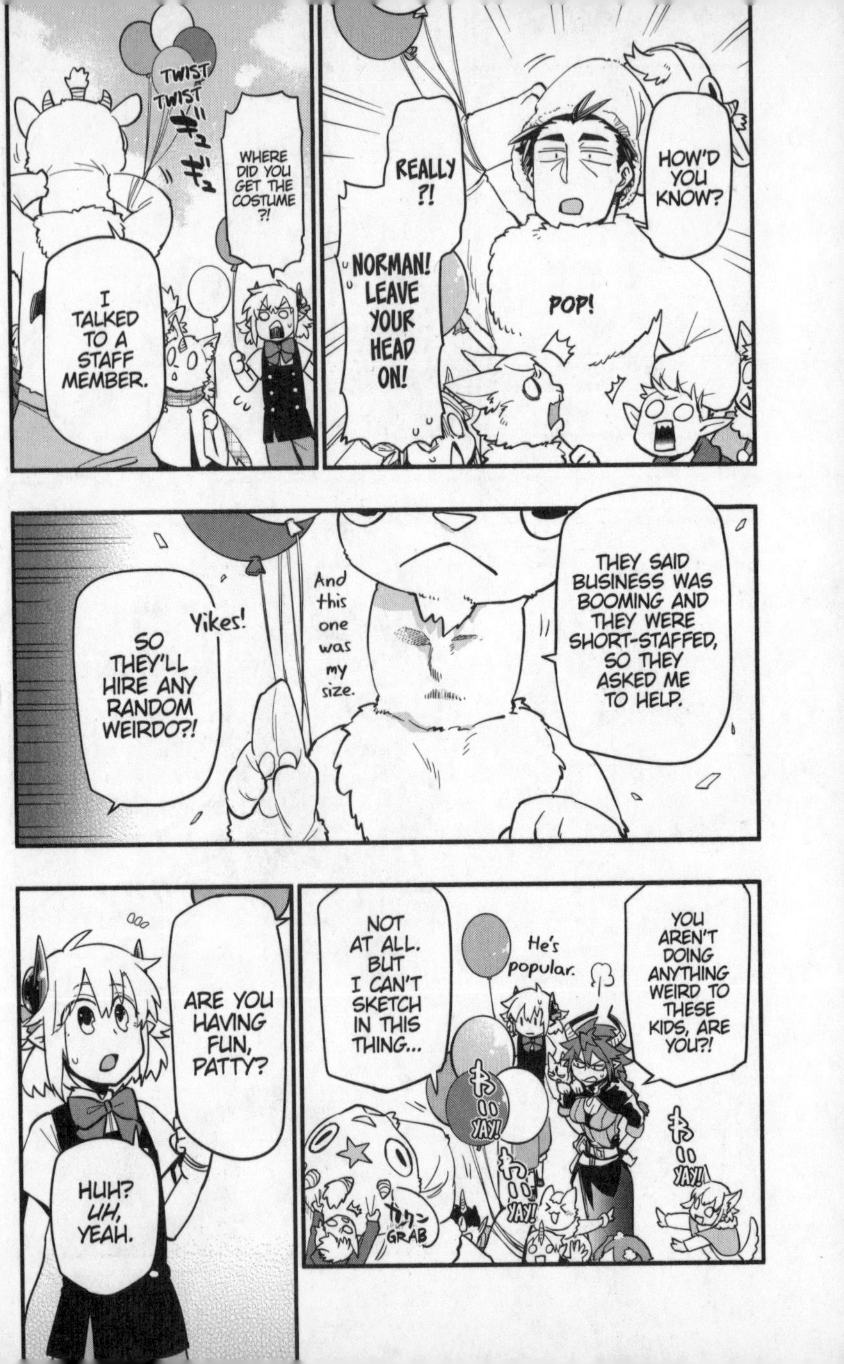
HOW'D YOU KNOW?
POP!
REALLY ?!
NORMAN! LEAVE YOUR HEAD ON!
WHERE DID YOU GET THE COSTUME ?!
TWIST TWIST
I TALKED TO A STAFF MEMBER.
THEY SAID BUSINESS WAS BOOMING AND THEY WERE SHORT-STAFFED, SO THEY ASKED ME TO HELP.
And this one was my size.
Yikes!
SO THEY'LL HIRE ANY RANDOM WEIRDO?!
YOU AREN'T DOING ANYTHING WEIRD TO THESE KIDS, ARE YOU?!
NOT AT ALL. BUT I CAN'T SKETCH IN THIS THING...
He's popular.
YAY!
YAY!
YAY!
GRAB
ARE YOU HAVING FUN, PATTY?
HUH? UH, YEAH.

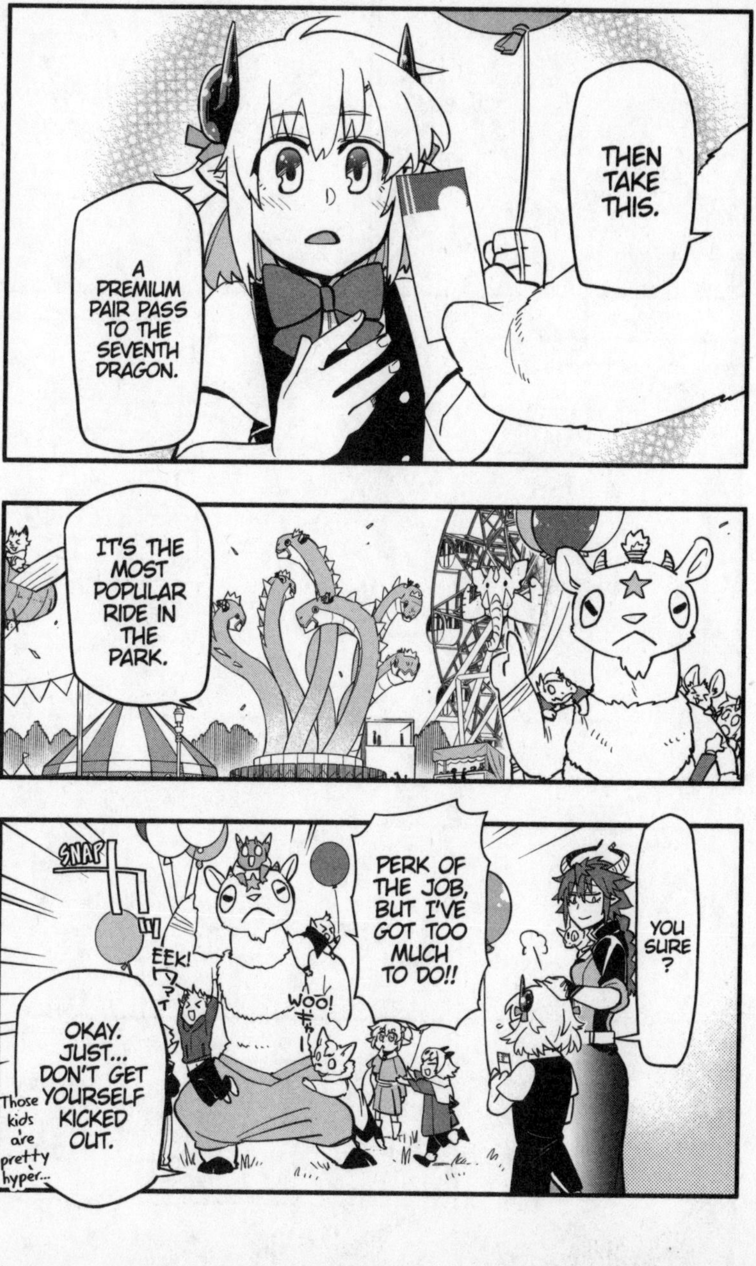
THEN TAKE THIS.
A PREMIUM PAIR PASS TO THE SEVENTH DRAGON.
IT'S THE MOST POPULAR RIDE IN THE PARK.
YOU SURE?
PERK OF THE JOB, BUT I'VE GOT TOO MUCH TO DO!!
SNAP
EEK!
WOO!
OKAY. JUST... DON'T GET YOURSELF KICKED OUT.
Those kids are pretty hyper...

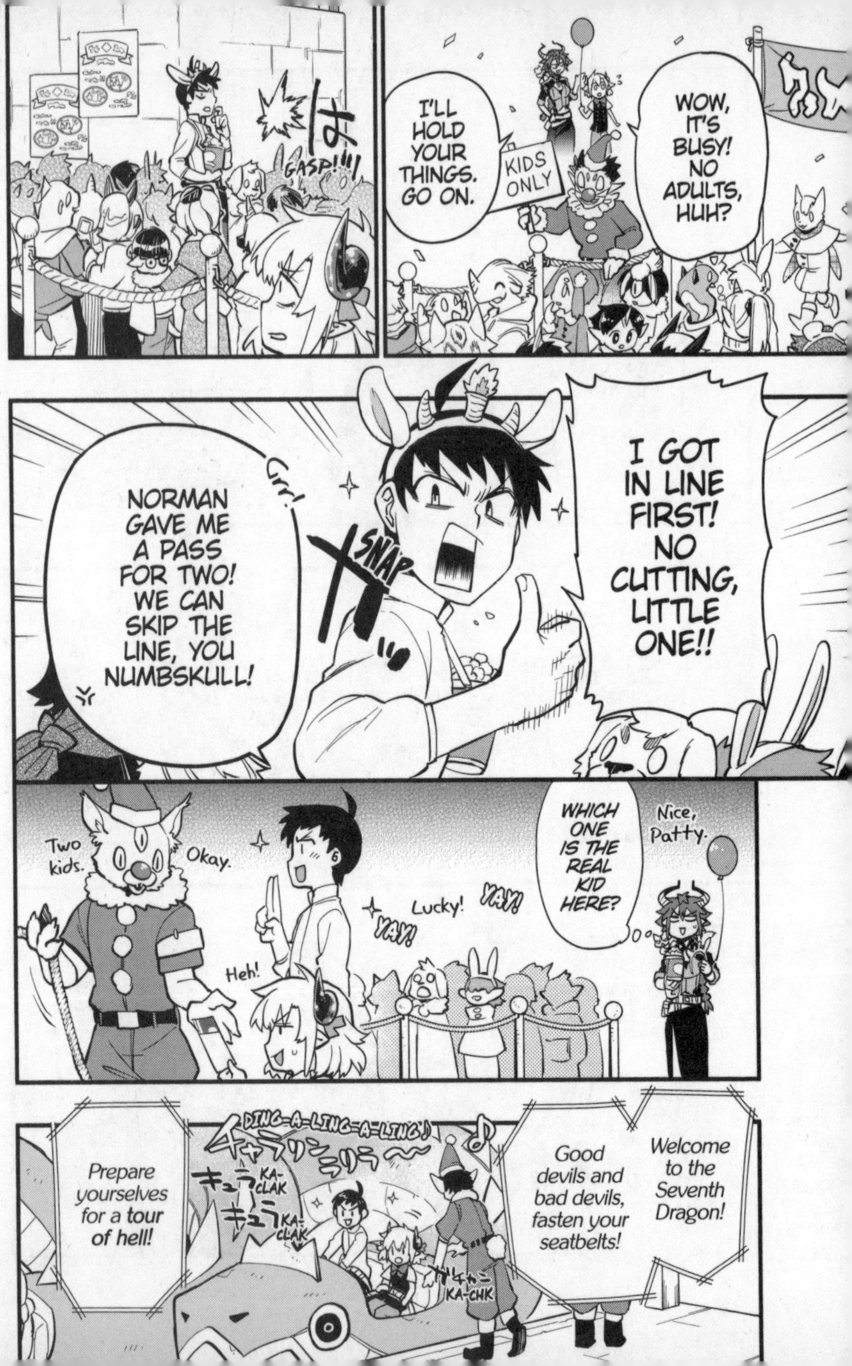
WOW, IT'S BUSY! NO ADULTS, HUH?
KIDS ONLY
I'LL HOLD YOUR THINGS. GO ON.
GASP!!!
I GOT IN LINE FIRST! NO CUTTING, LITTLE ONE!!
Grr!
SNAP
NORMAN GAVE ME A PASS FOR TWO! WE CAN SKIP THE LINE, YOU NUMBSKULL!
Nice, Patty.
WHICH ONE IS THE REAL KID HERE?
YAY!
Lucky!
YAY!
Okay.
Two kids.
Heh!
Welcome to the Seventh Dragon!
Good devils and bad devils, fasten your seatbelts!
DING-A-LING-A-LING
KA-CLAK
KA-CLAK
KA-CHK
Prepare yourselves for a tour of hell!

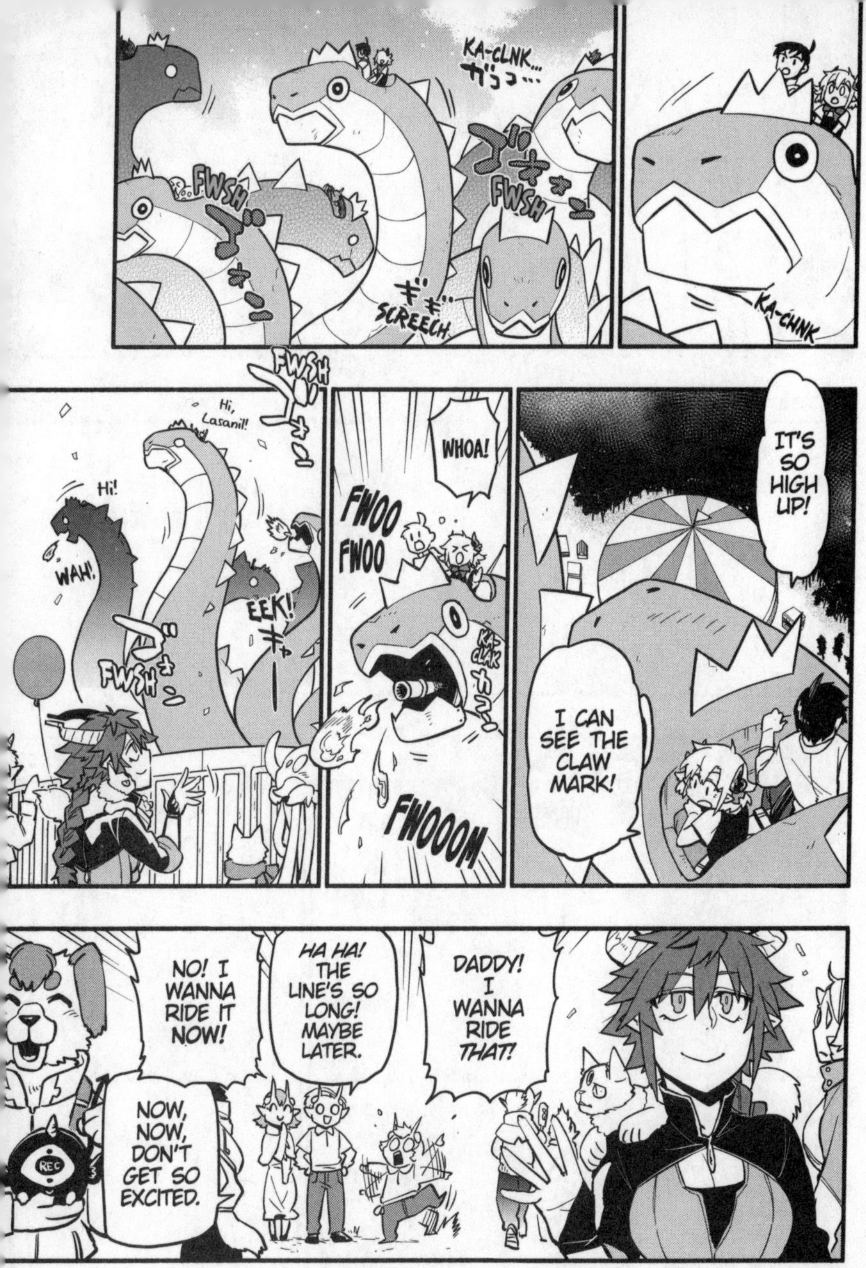
KA-CHNK
KA-CLNK...
FWSH
FWSH
SCREECH
IT'S SO HIGH UP!
I CAN SEE THE CLAW MARK!
WHOA!
FWOO FWOO
KA-CLAK
FWOOOM
FWSH
Hi, Lasanil!
Hi!
WAH!
EEK!
FWSH
DADDY! I WANNA RIDE THAT!
HA HA! THE LINE'S SO LONG! MAYBE LATER.
NO! I WANNA RIDE IT NOW!
NOW, NOW, DON'T GET SO EXCITED.
REC

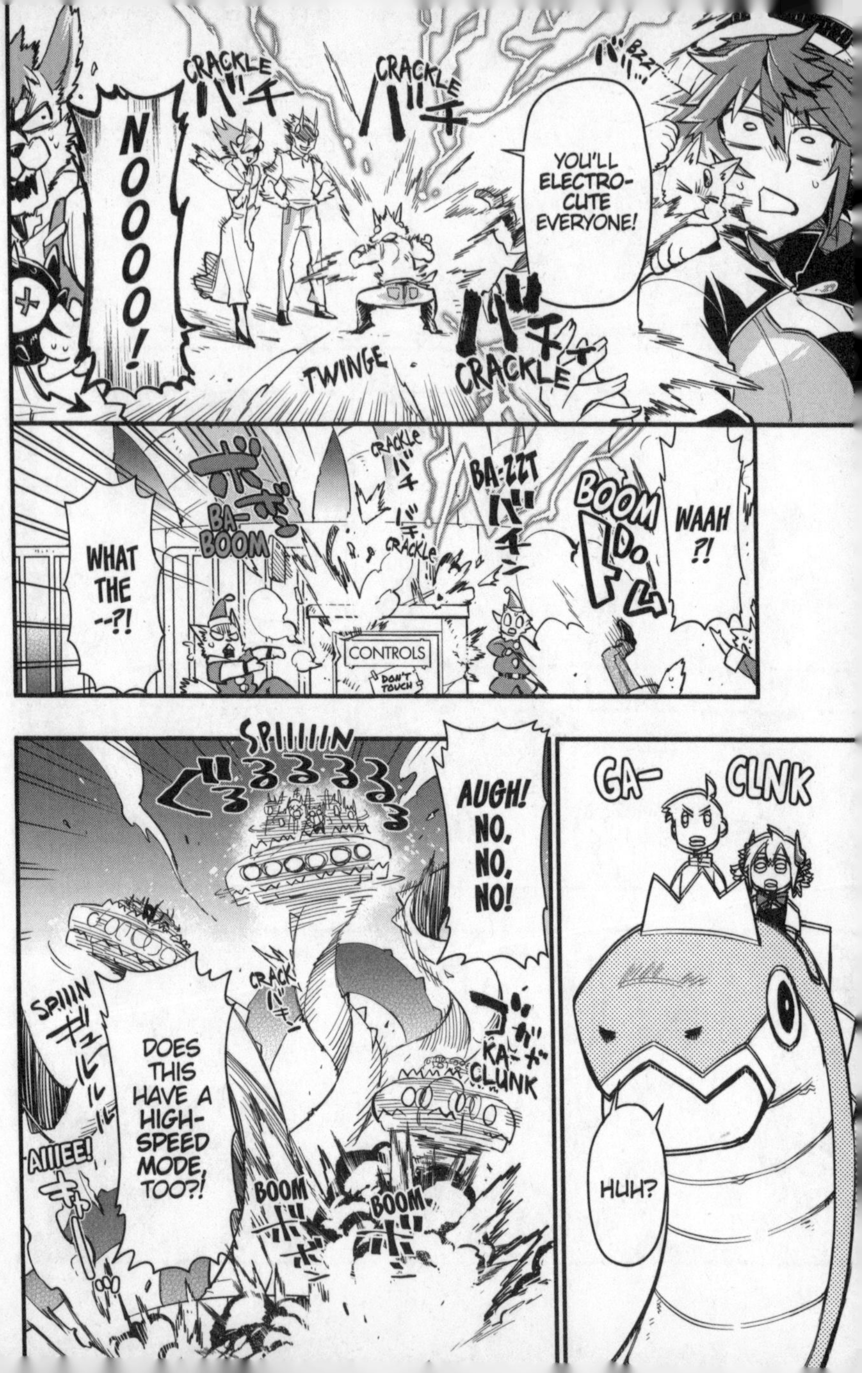
BZZT
YOU'LL ELECTROCUTE EVERYONE!
CRACKLE バチ
CRACKLE バチ
NOOOOO!
TWINGE
CRACKLE
WAAH?!
BOOM
BA-ZZT
CRACKLE バチ
CRACKLE バチ
BA-BOOM
WHAT THE --?!
CONTROLS
DON'T TOUCH
GA- CLNK
HUH?
SPIIIIN
AUGH! NO. NO. NO!
CRACK
KA-CLUNK
DOES THIS HAVE A HIGH-SPEED MODE, TOO?!
SPIIIN
AIIIEE!
BOOM
BOOM

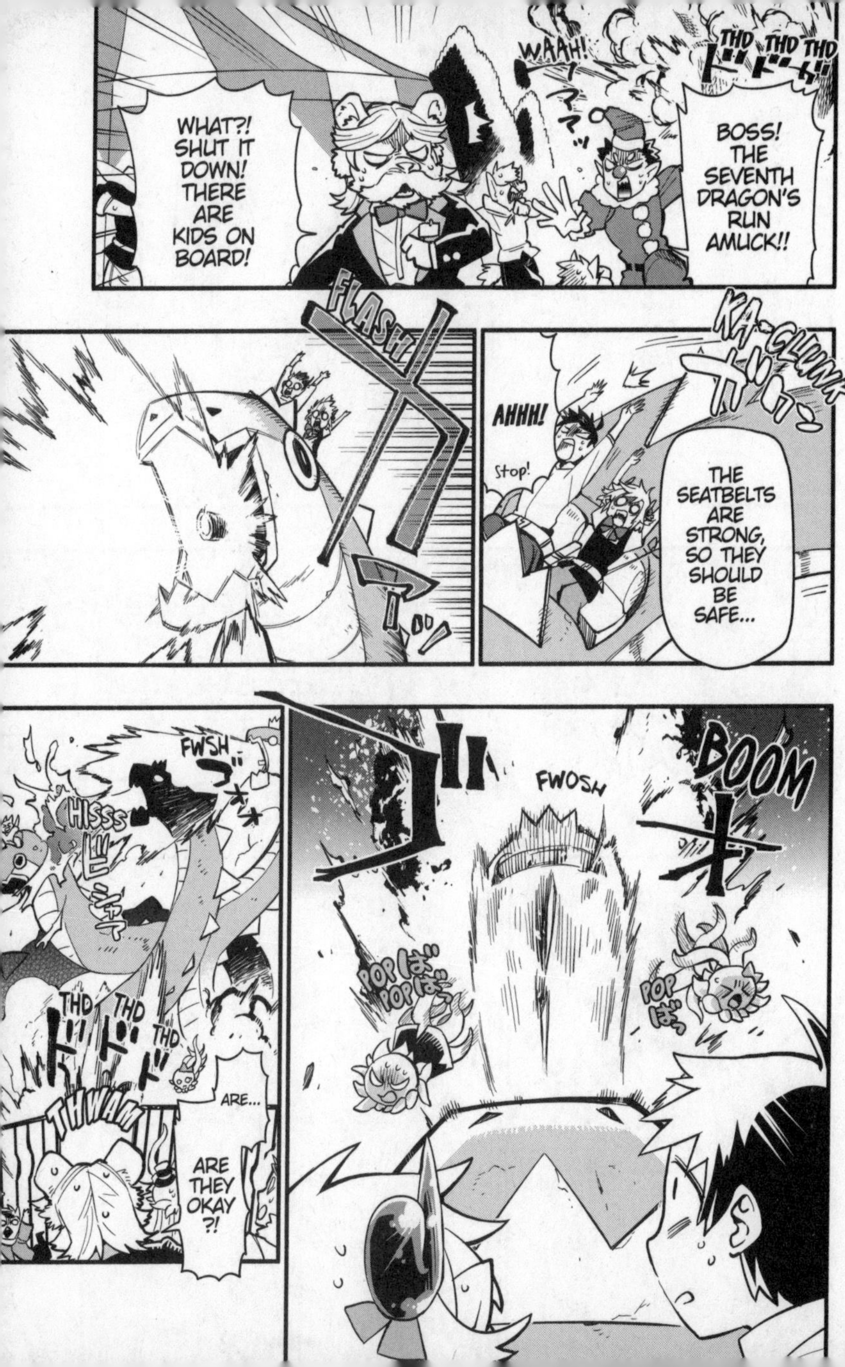
THD THD THD
WAAH!
BOSS! THE SEVENTH DRAGON'S RUN AMUCK!!
WHAT?! SHUT IT DOWN! THERE ARE KIDS ON BOARD!
KA-GLUNK
AHHH!
Stop!
THE SEATBELTS ARE STRONG, SO THEY SHOULD BE SAFE...
FLASH
BOOM
FWOSH
POP
POP POP
FWSH
HISSS
THD THD THD
THWAM
ARE...
ARE THEY OKAY?!

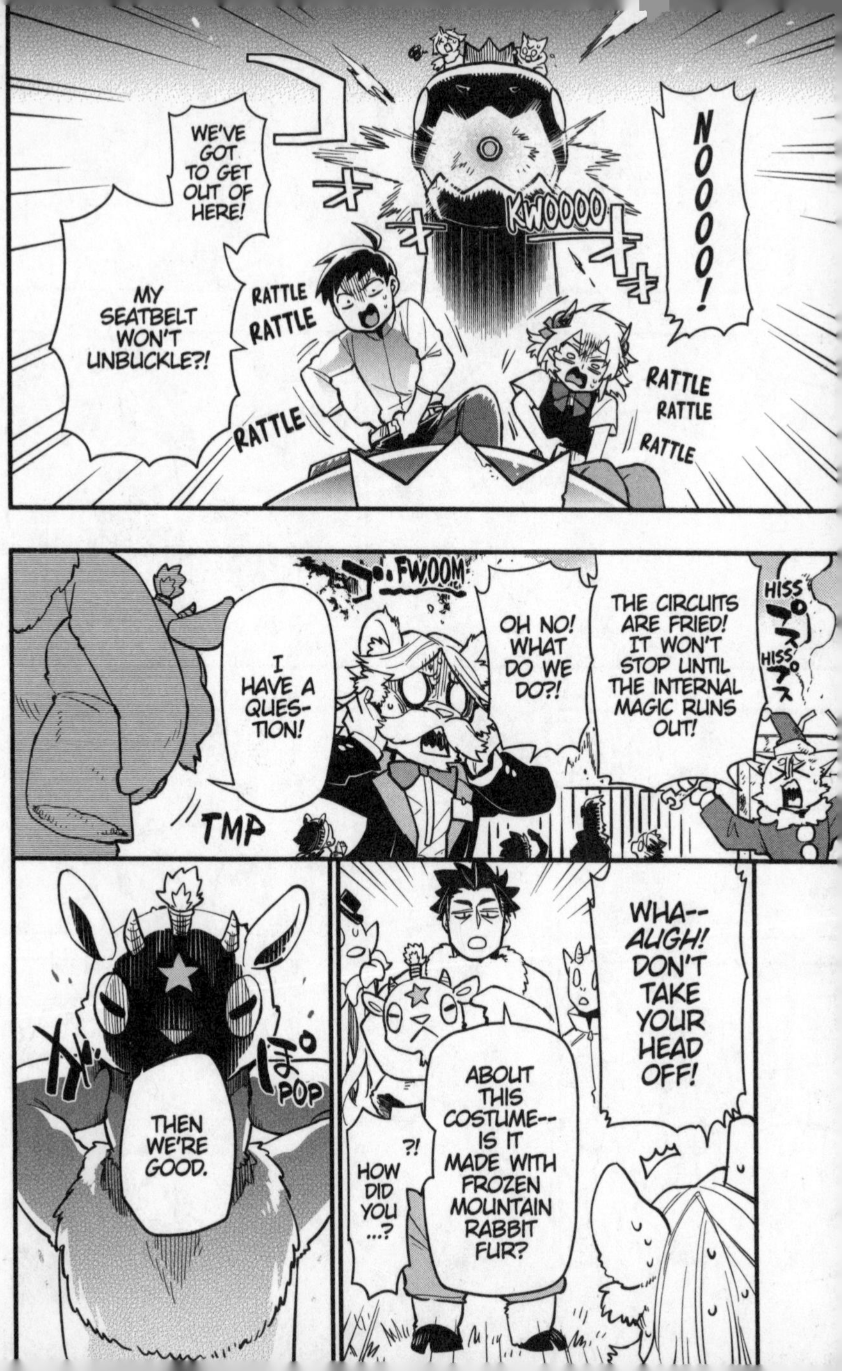
NOOOOO!
KWOOOO
WE'VE GOT TO GET OUT OF HERE!
RATTLE RATTLE RATTLE
MY SEATBELT WON'T UNBUCKLE?!
RATTLE RATTLE
RATTLE
HISS HISS
THE CIRCUITS ARE FRIED! IT WON'T STOP UNTIL THE INTERNAL MAGIC RUNS OUT!
OH NO! WHAT DO WE DO?!
FWOOM
I HAVE A QUES-TION!
TMP
WHA-- AUGH! DON'T TAKE YOUR HEAD OFF!
ABOUT THIS COSTUME-- IS IT MADE WITH FROZEN MOUNTAIN RABBIT FUR?
?!
HOW DID YOU ...?
POP
THEN WE'RE GOOD.

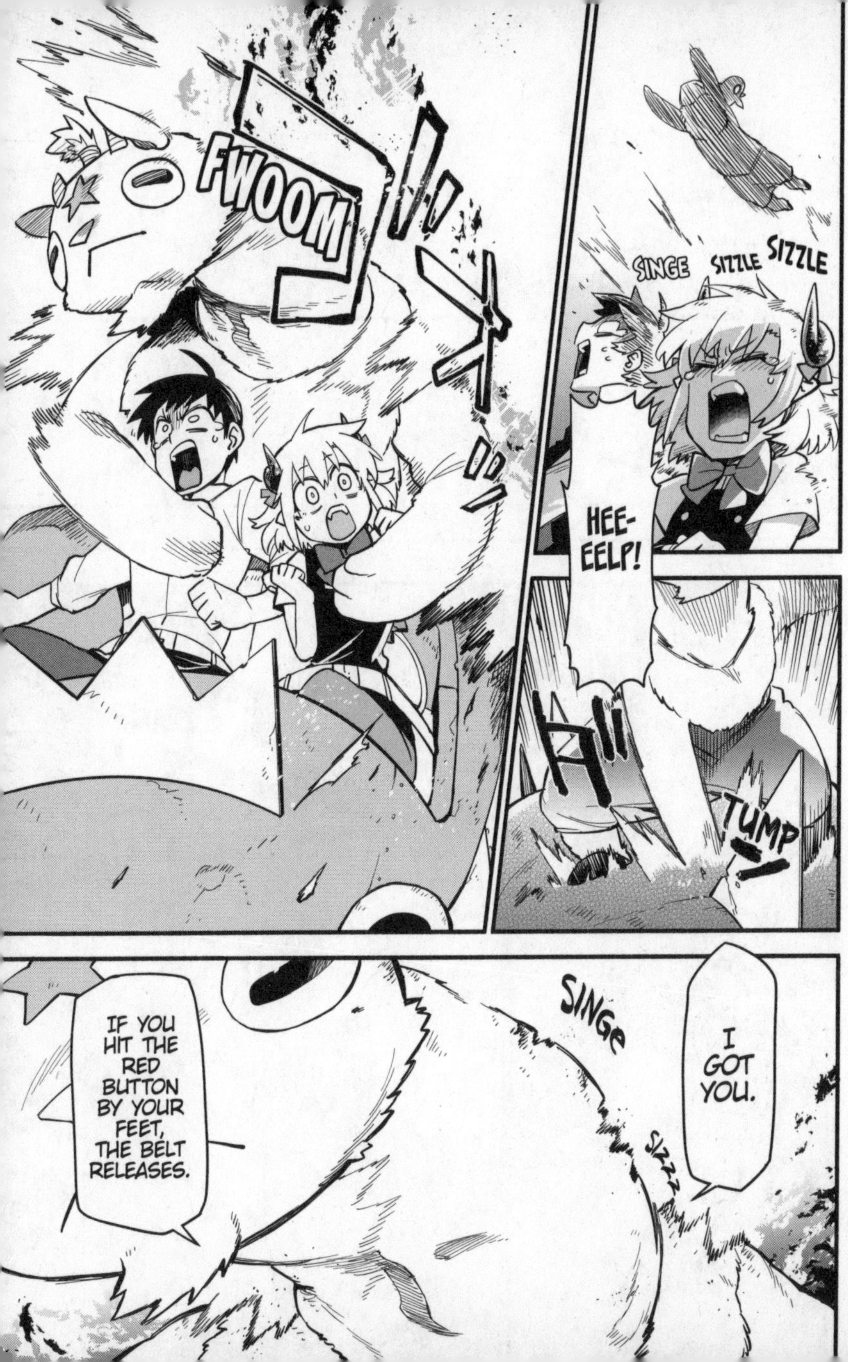
SINGE
SIZZLE
SIZZLE
HEE-EELP!
TUMP
FWOOM
SINGe
I GOT YOU.
SIZZZ
IF YOU HIT THE RED BUTTON BY YOUR FEET, THE BELT RELEASES.

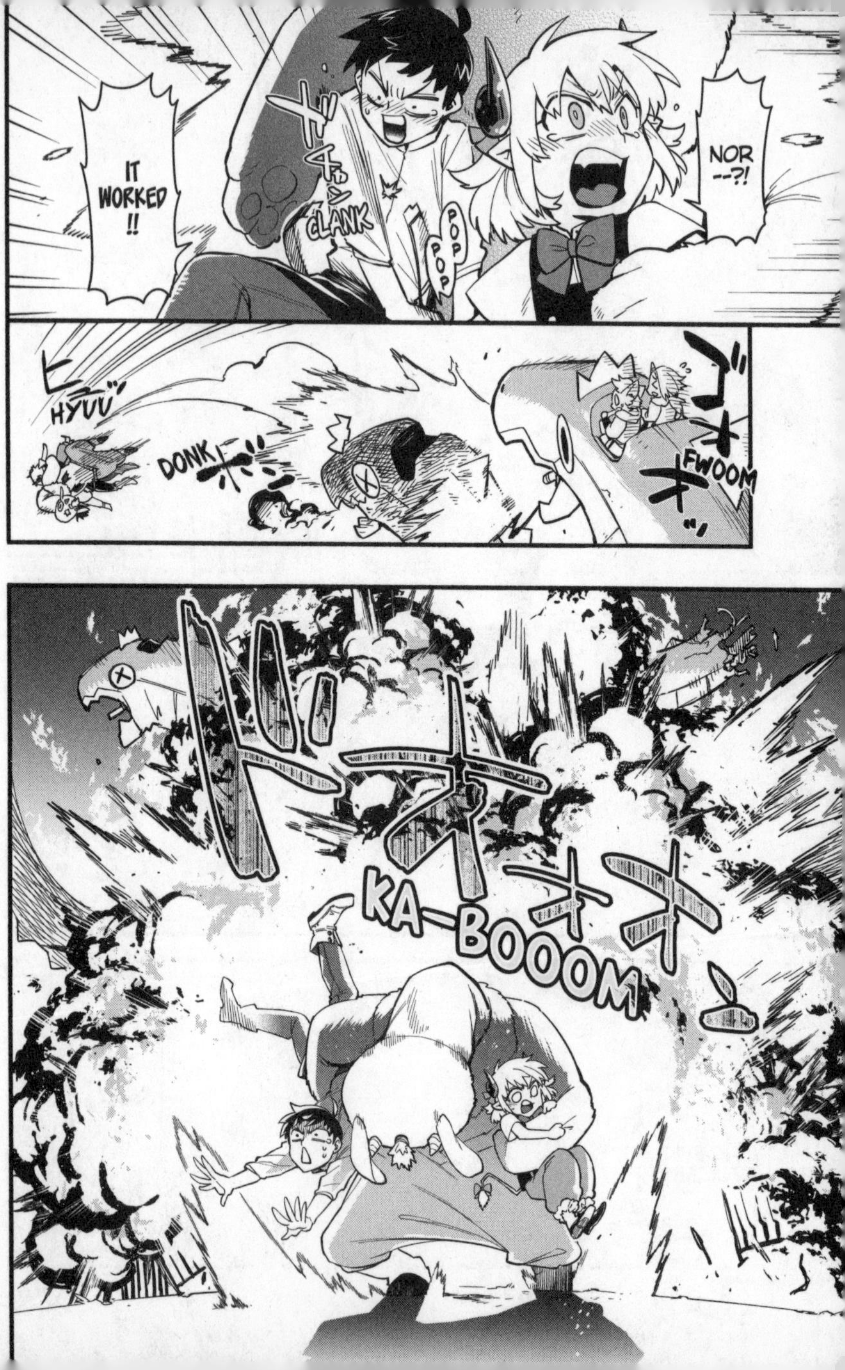
NOR--?!
IT WORKED!!
CLANK
POP POP
FWOOM
DONK
HYUU
KA-BOOOM

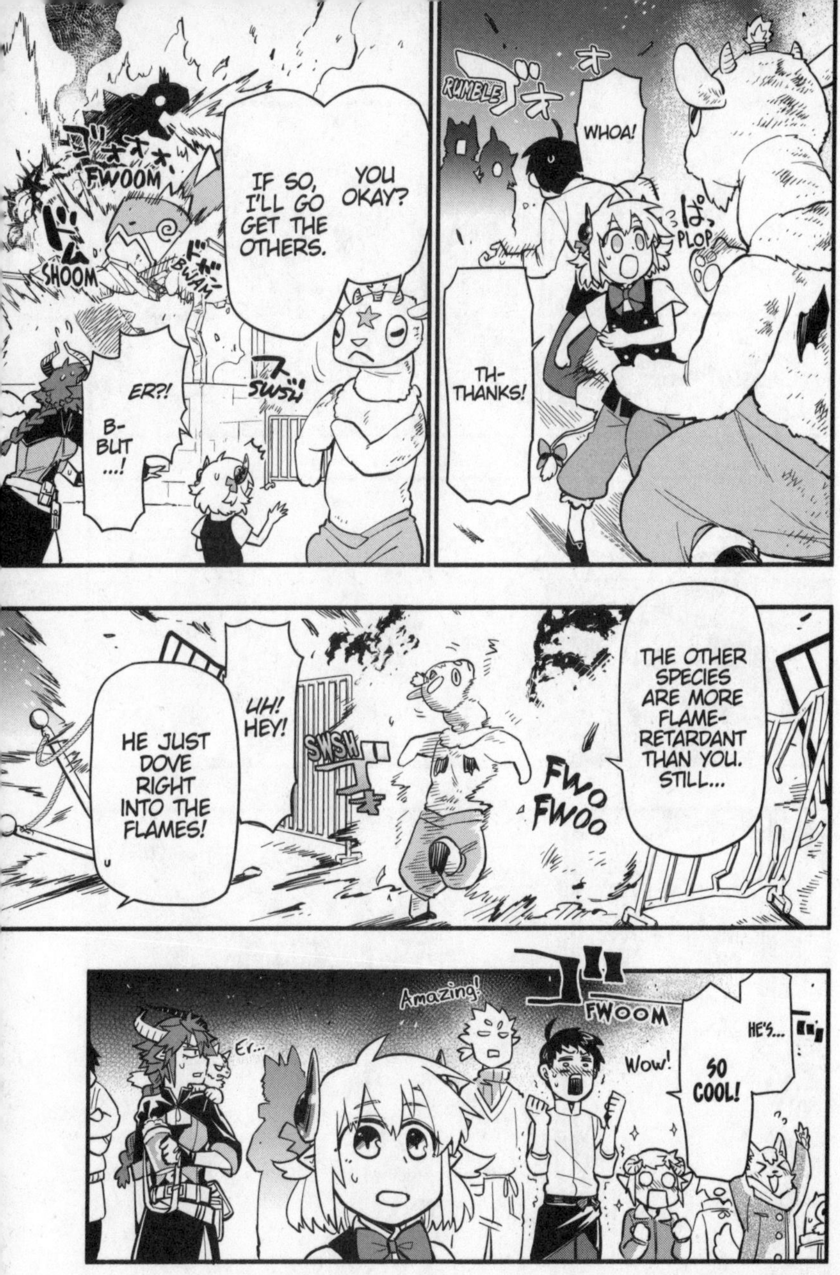
RUMBLE
WHOA!
TH-THANKS!
PLOP
FWOOM
SHOOM
BWAM
YOU OKAY?
IF SO, I'LL GO GET THE OTHERS.
SWSH
ER?!
B-BUT ...!
THE OTHER SPECIES ARE MORE FLAME-RETARDANT THAN YOU. STILL...
FWOO FWOO
SWSH
UH! HEY!
HE JUST DOVE RIGHT INTO THE FLAMES!
FWOOM
HE'S...
SO COOL!
Wow!
Amazing!
Er...

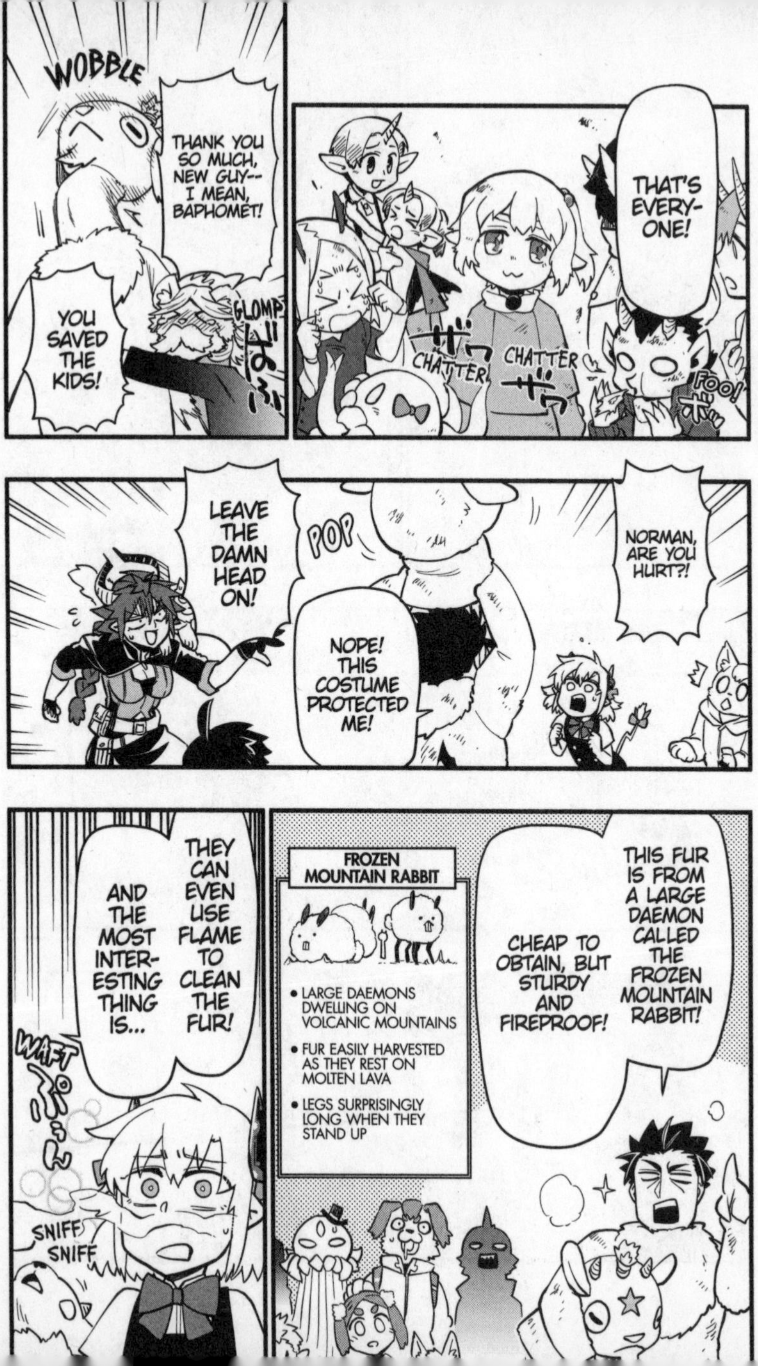
THAT'S EVERY-ONE!
CHATTER
CHATTER
FOO!
WOBBLE
THANK YOU SO MUCH, NEW GUY-- I MEAN, BAPHOMET!
YOU SAVED THE KIDS!
GLOMP
NORMAN, ARE YOU HURT?!
NOPE! THIS COSTUME PROTECTED ME!
POP
LEAVE THE DAMN HEAD ON!
THIS FUR IS FROM A LARGE DAEMON CALLED THE FROZEN MOUNTAIN RABBIT!
CHEAP TO OBTAIN, BUT STURDY AND FIREPROOF!
FROZEN MOUNTAIN RABBIT
• LARGE DAEMONS DWELLING ON VOLCANIC MOUNTAINS
• FUR EASILY HARVESTED AS THEY REST ON MOLTEN LAVA
• LEGS SURPRISINGLY LONG WHEN THEY STAND UP
THEY CAN EVEN USE FLAME TO CLEAN THE FUR!
AND THE MOST INTER-ESTING THING IS...
WAFT
SNIFF SNIFF

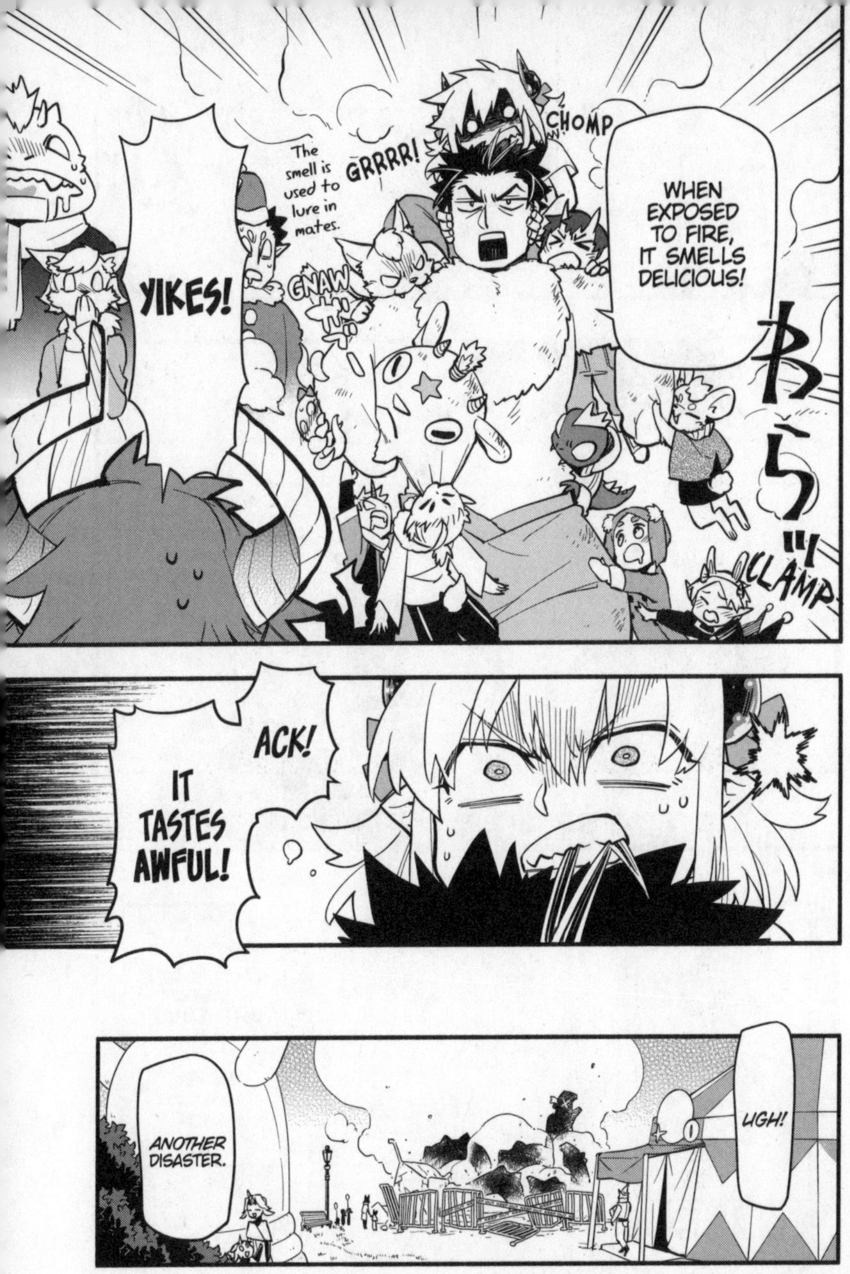
WHEN EXPOSED TO FIRE, IT SMELLS DELICIOUS!
CHOMP
GRRRR!
The smell is used to lure in mates.
GNAW
YIKES!
CLAMP
ACK!
IT TASTES AWFUL!
UGH!
ANOTHER DISASTER.

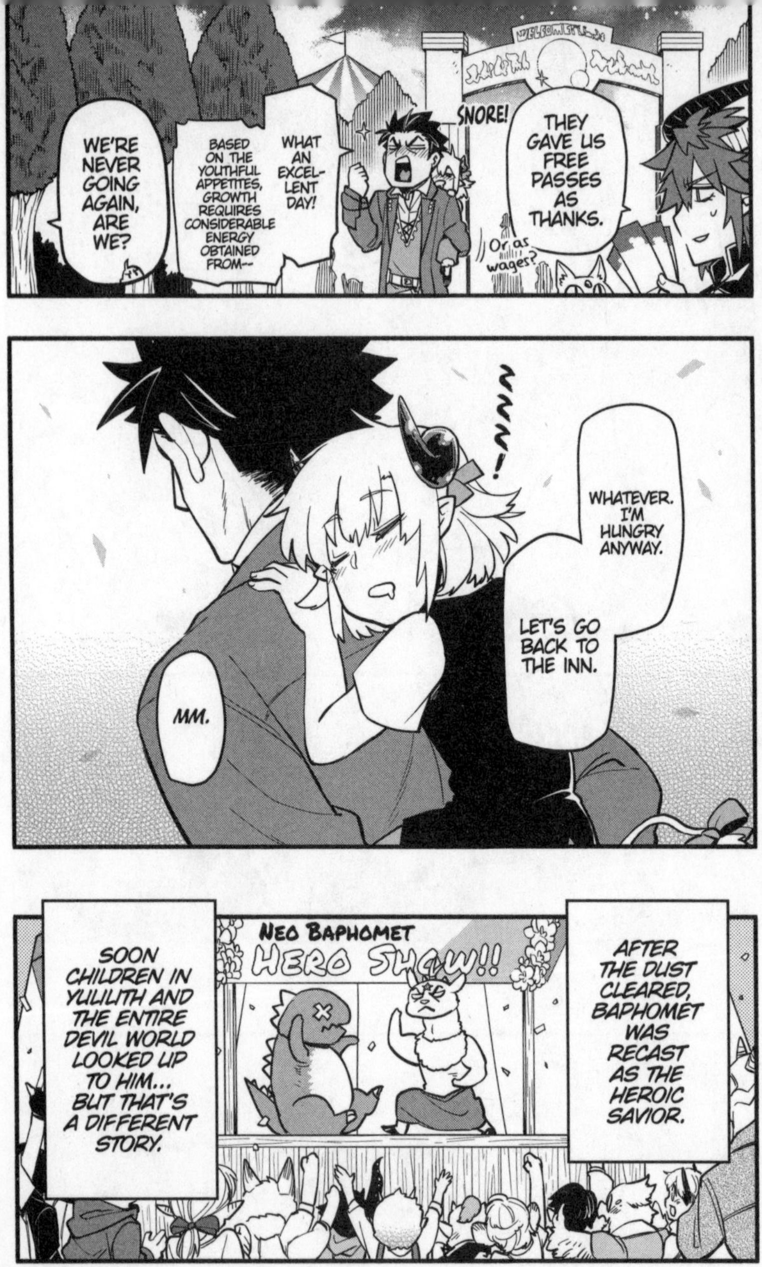
THEY GAVE US FREE PASSES AS THANKS.
Or as wages?
SNORE!
WHAT AN EXCEL-LENT DAY!
BASED ON THE YOUTHFUL APPETITES, GROWTH REQUIRES CONSIDERABLE ENERGY OBTAINED FROM--
WE'RE NEVER GOING AGAIN, ARE WE?
NNNN!
WHATEVER. I'M HUNGRY ANYWAY.
LET'S GO BACK TO THE INN.
MM.
AFTER THE DUST CLEARED, BAPHOMET WAS RECAST AS THE HEROIC SAVIOR.
NEO BAPHOMET
HERO SHOW!!
SOON CHILDREN IN YULILITH AND THE ENTIRE DEVIL WORLD LOOKED UP TO HIM... BUT THAT'S A DIFFERENT STORY.

Sorry For My Familiar

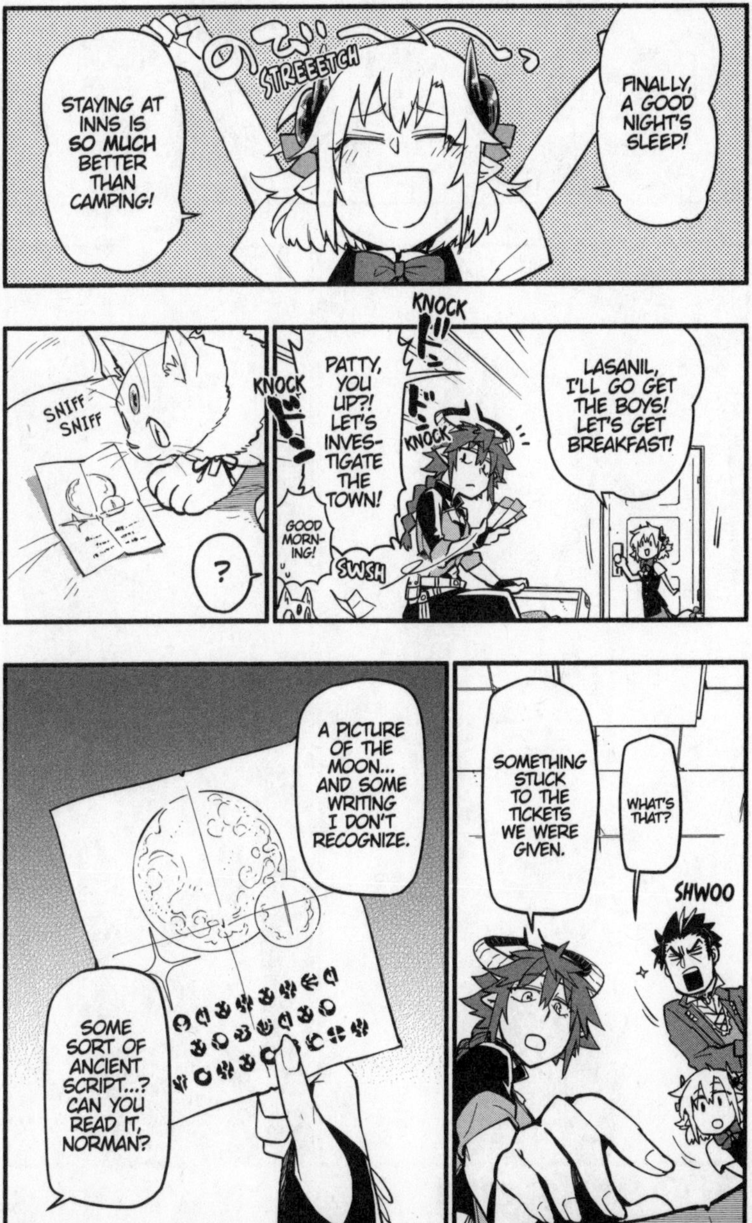
FINALLY, A GOOD NIGHT'S SLEEP!
STREEETCH
STAYING AT INNS IS SO MUCH BETTER THAN CAMPING!
KNOCK
LASANIL, I'LL GO GET THE BOYS! LET'S GET BREAKFAST!
KNOCK
PATTY, YOU UP?! LET'S INVESTIGATE THE TOWN!
KNOCK
GOOD MORNING!
SWSH
SNIFF SNIFF
?
WHAT'S THAT?
SOMETHING STUCK TO THE TICKETS WE WERE GIVEN.
SHWOO
A PICTURE OF THE MOON... AND SOME WRITING I DON'T RECOGNIZE.
SOME SORT OF ANCIENT SCRIPT...? CAN YOU READ IT, NORMAN?

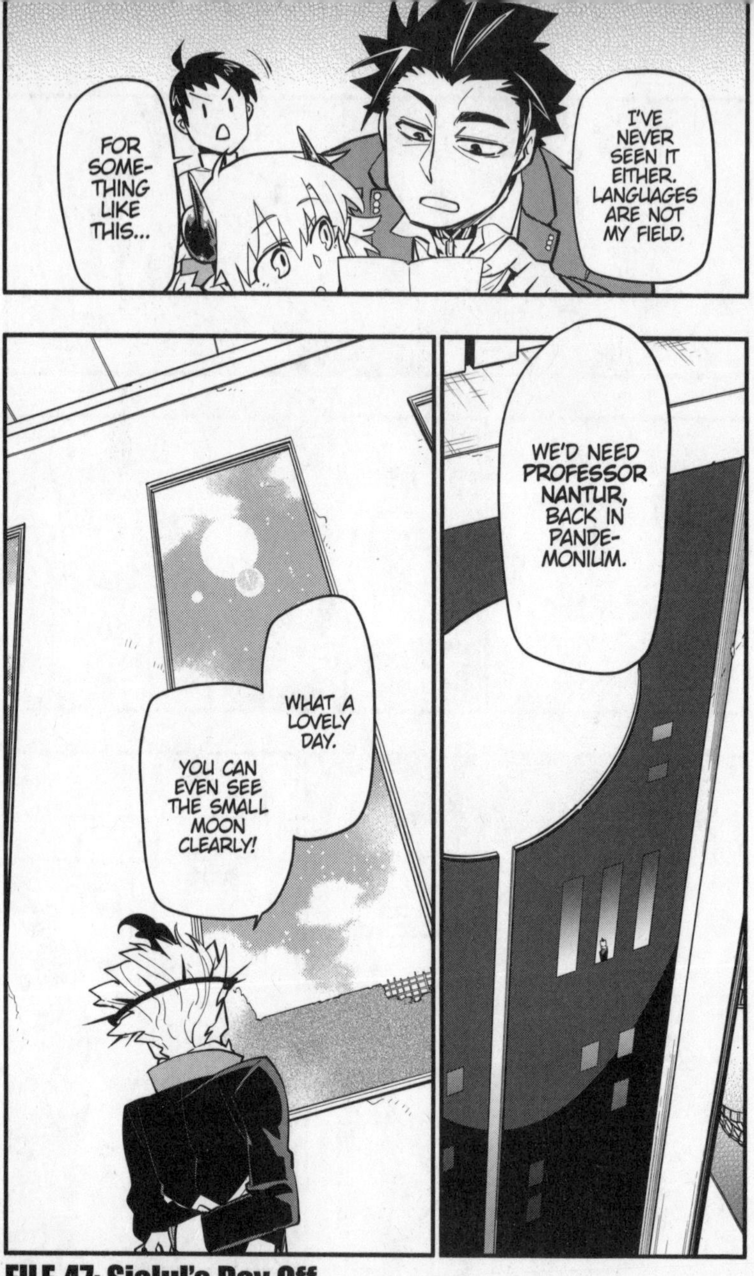
I'VE NEVER SEEN IT EITHER. LANGUAGES ARE NOT MY FIELD.
FOR SOME-THING LIKE THIS...
WE'D NEED PROFESSOR NANTUR, BACK IN PANDE-MONIUM.
WHAT A LOVELY DAY.
YOU CAN EVEN SEE THE SMALL MOON CLEARLY!

FILE 47: Sialul's Day Off

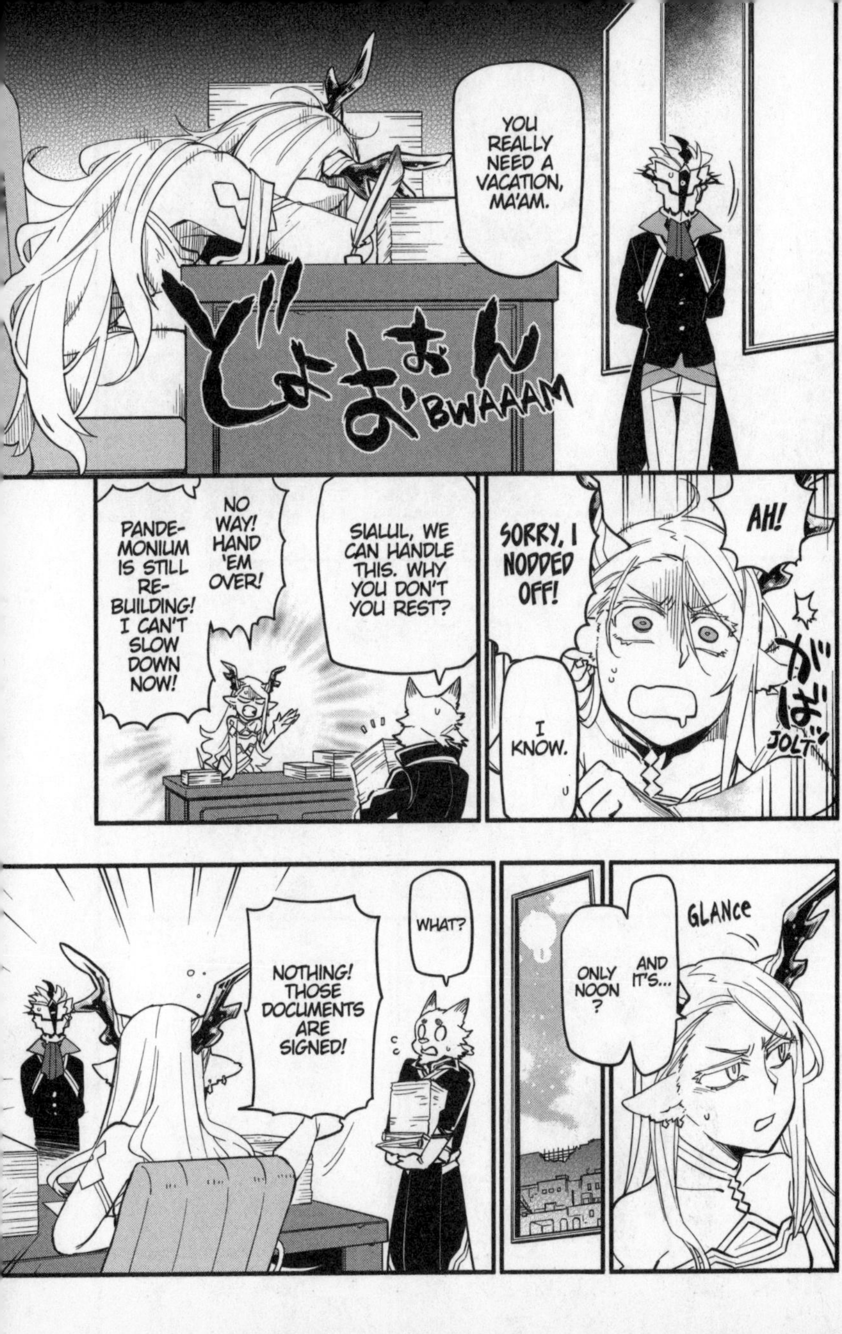
YOU REALLY NEED A VACATION, MA'AM.
BWAAAM
AH!
がばっ
JOLT
SORRY, I NODDED OFF!
I KNOW.
SIALUL, WE CAN HANDLE THIS. WHY YOU DON'T YOU REST?
NO WAY! HAND 'EM OVER!
PANDE-MONIUM IS STILL RE-BUILDING! I CAN'T SLOW DOWN NOW!
GLANCE
AND IT'S...
ONLY NOON?
WHAT?
NOTHING! THOSE DOCUMENTS ARE SIGNED!

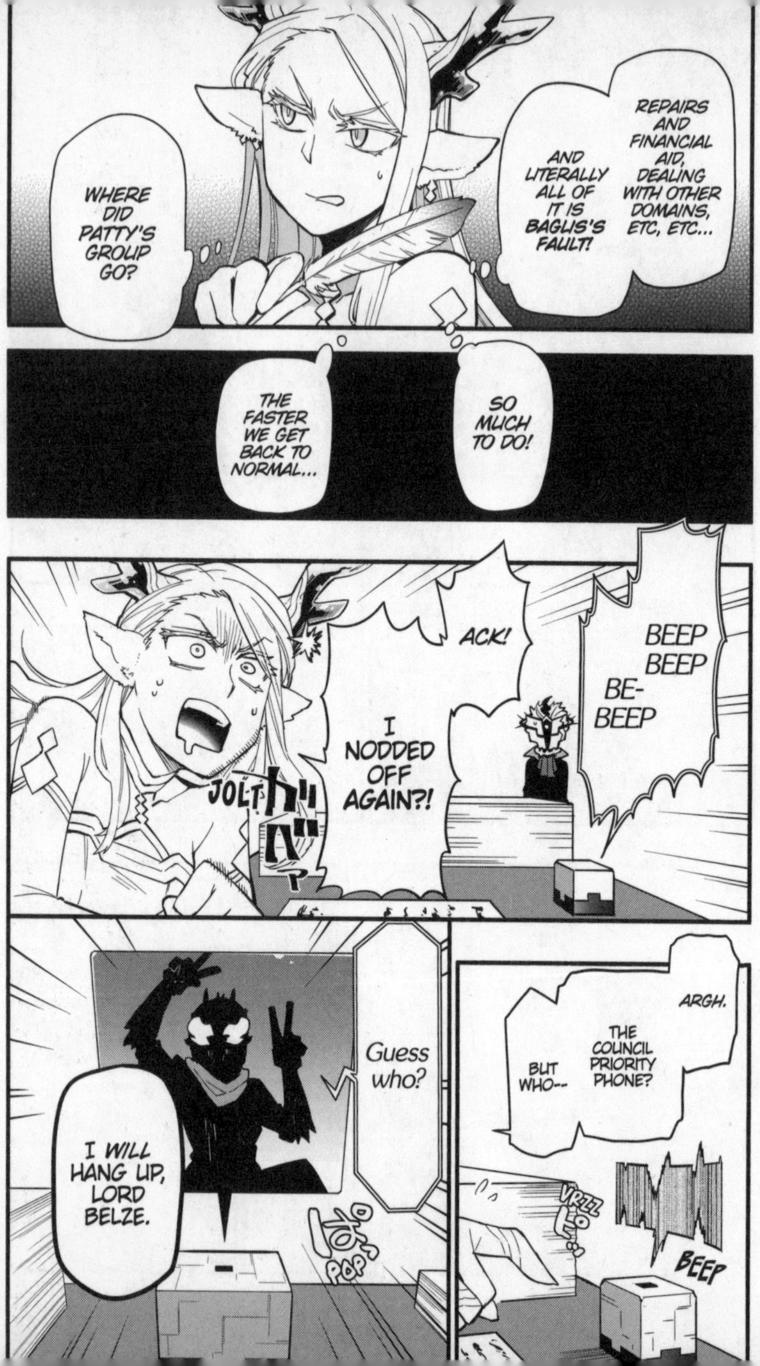
REPAIRS AND FINANCIAL AID, DEALING WITH OTHER DOMAINS, ETC, ETC...
AND LITERALLY ALL OF IT IS BAGUS'S FAULT!
WHERE DID PATTY'S GROUP GO?
SO MUCH TO DO!
THE FASTER WE GET BACK TO NORMAL...
BEEP BEEP BE-BEEP
ACK!
I NODDED OFF AGAIN?!
JOLT
ARGH.
THE COUNCIL PRIORITY PHONE?
BUT WHO--
VRZZ
BEEP
Guess who?
I WILL HANG UP, LORD BELZE.
POP

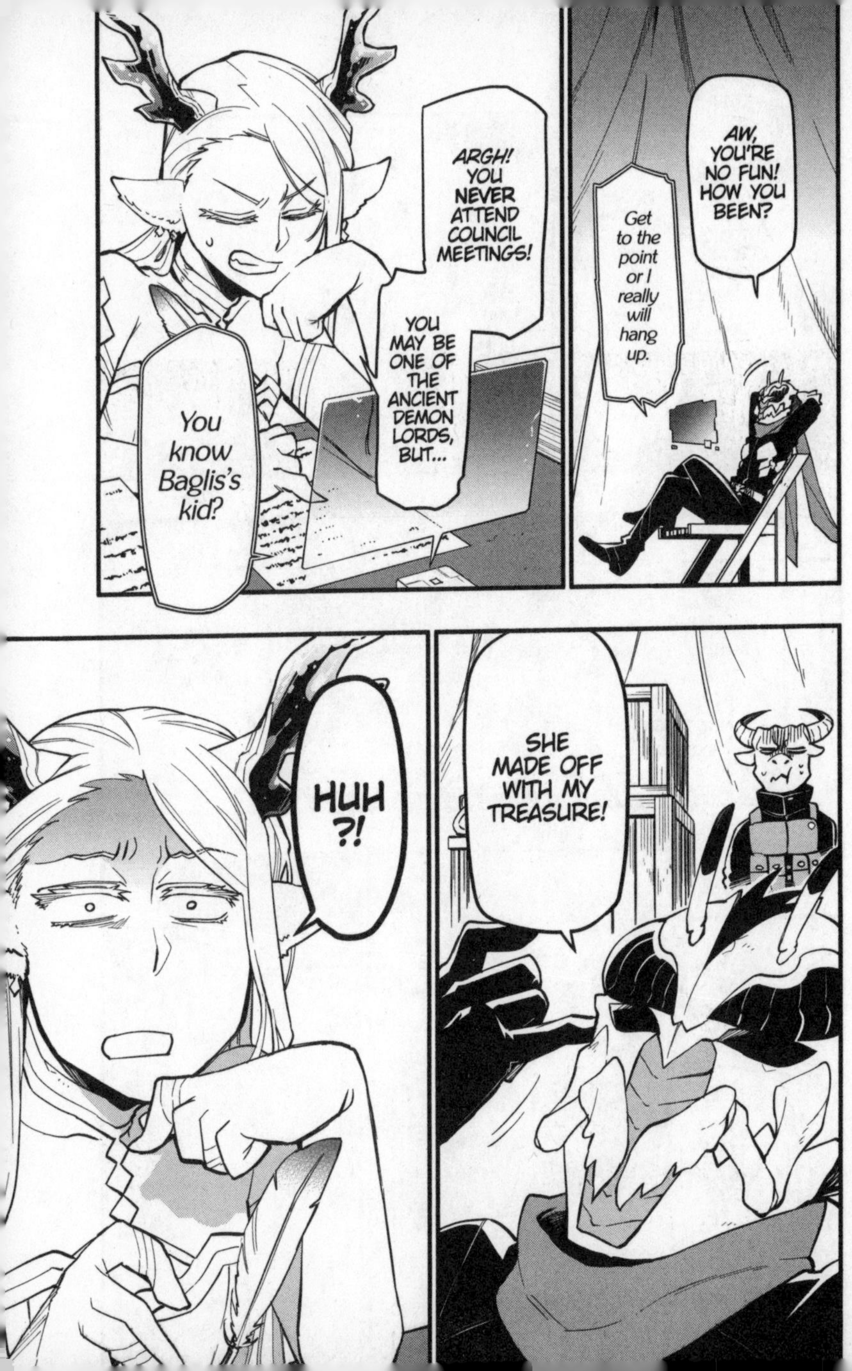
AW, YOU'RE NO FUN! HOW YOU BEEN?
Get to the point or I really will hang up.
ARGH! YOU NEVER ATTEND COUNCIL MEETINGS!
YOU MAY BE ONE OF THE ANCIENT DEMON LORDS, BUT...
You know Baglis's kid?
SHE MADE OFF WITH MY TREASURE!
HUH ?!

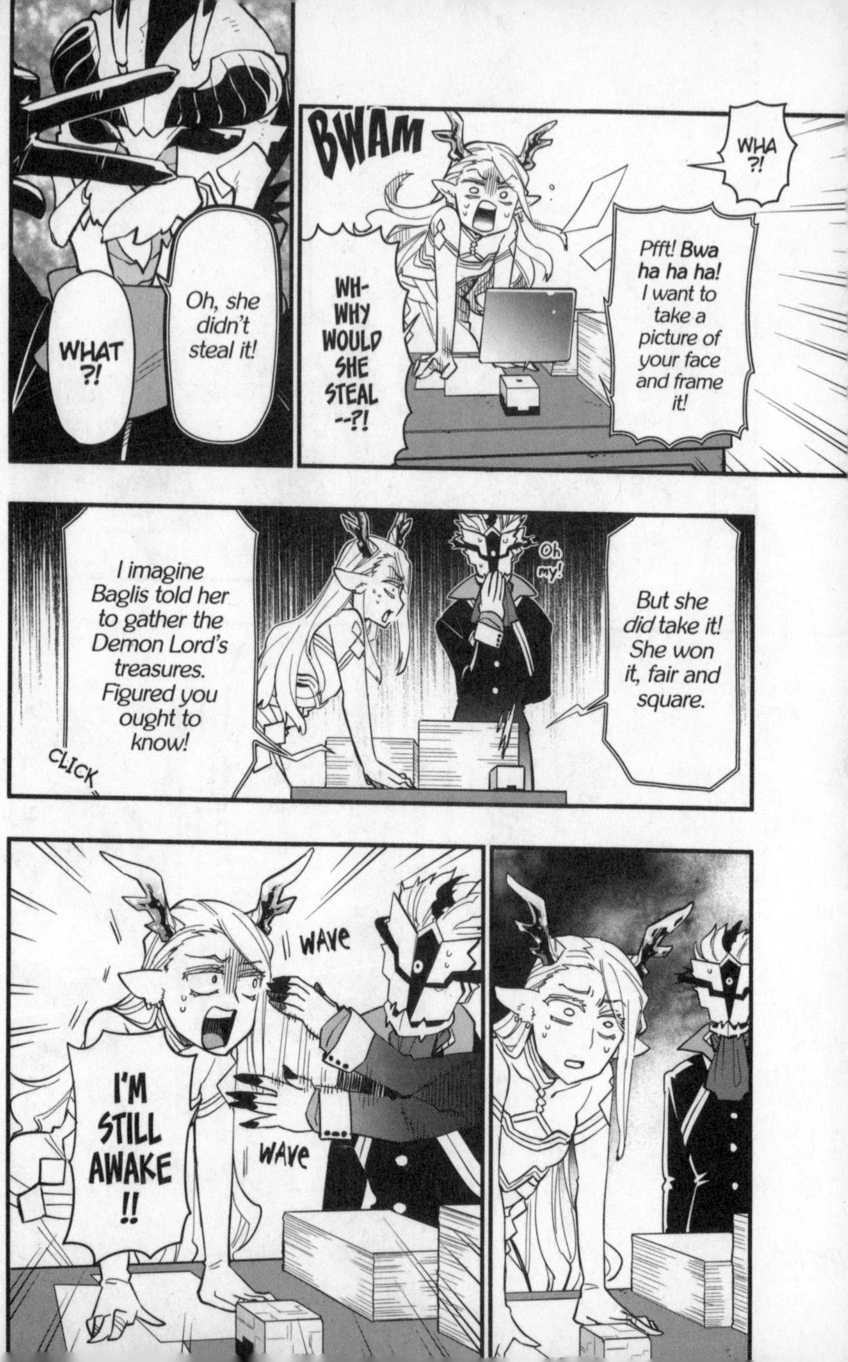
Oh, she didn't steal it!
WHAT ?!
WHA ?!
BWAM
Pfft! Bwa ha ha ha! I want to take a picture of your face and frame it!
WH-WHY WOULD SHE STEAL --?!
But she did take it! She won it, fair and square.
Oh my!
I imagine Baglis told her to gather the Demon Lord's treasures. Figured you ought to know!
CLICK
wave
wave
I'M STILL AWAKE !!

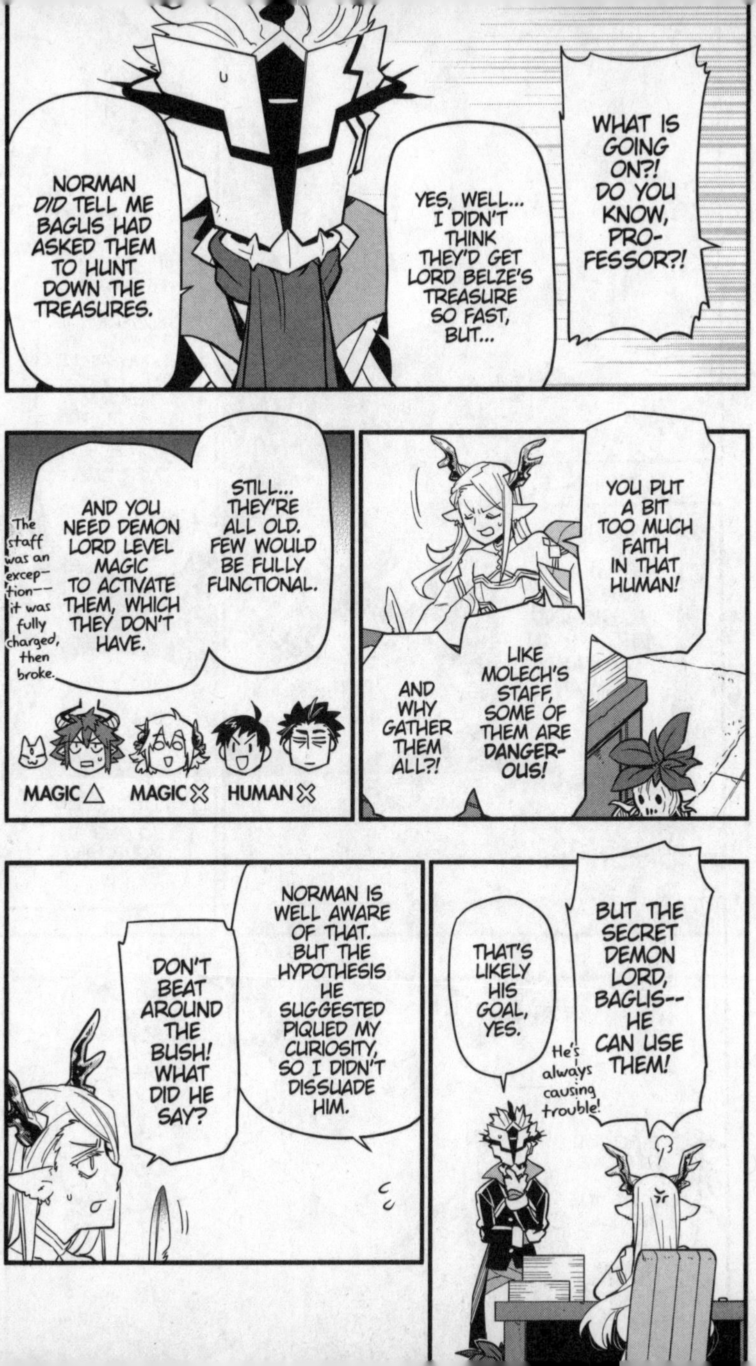
WHAT IS GOING ON?! DO YOU KNOW, PRO-FESSOR?!
YES, WELL... I DIDN'T THINK THEY'D GET LORD BELZE'S TREASURE SO FAST, BUT...
NORMAN *DID* TELL ME BAGLIS HAD ASKED THEM TO HUNT DOWN THE TREASURES.
YOU PUT A BIT TOO MUCH FAITH IN THAT HUMAN!
LIKE MOLECH'S STAFF, SOME OF THEM ARE DANGER-OUS!
AND WHY GATHER THEM ALL?!
STILL... THEY'RE ALL OLD. FEW WOULD BE FULLY FUNCTIONAL.
AND YOU NEED DEMON LORD LEVEL MAGIC TO ACTIVATE THEM, WHICH THEY DON'T HAVE.
The staff was an excep-tion--it was fully charged, then broke.
MAGIC △
MAGIC ✕
HUMAN ✕
BUT THE SECRET DEMON LORD, BAGLIS--HE CAN USE THEM!
THAT'S LIKELY HIS GOAL, YES.
He's always causing trouble!
NORMAN IS WELL AWARE OF THAT. BUT THE HYPOTHESIS HE SUGGESTED PIQUED MY CURIOSITY, SO I DIDN'T DISSUADE HIM.
DON'T BEAT AROUND THE BUSH! WHAT DID HE SAY?

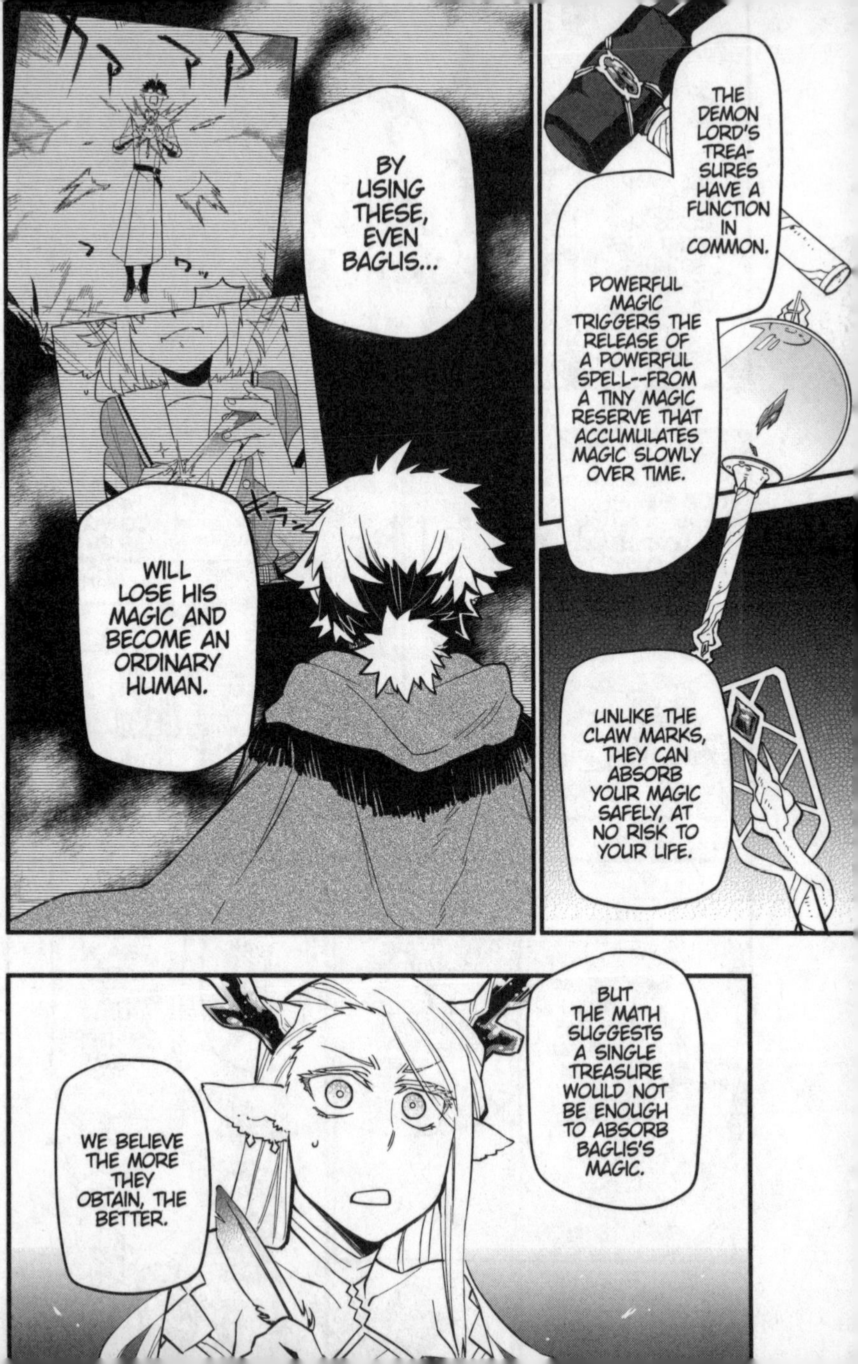
THE DEMON LORD'S TREASURES HAVE A FUNCTION IN COMMON.
POWERFUL MAGIC TRIGGERS THE RELEASE OF A POWERFUL SPELL--FROM A TINY MAGIC RESERVE THAT ACCUMULATES MAGIC SLOWLY OVER TIME.
UNLIKE THE CLAW MARKS, THEY CAN ABSORB YOUR MAGIC SAFELY, AT NO RISK TO YOUR LIFE.
BY USING THESE, EVEN BAGLIS...
WILL LOSE HIS MAGIC AND BECOME AN ORDINARY HUMAN.
BUT THE MATH SUGGESTS A SINGLE TREASURE WOULD NOT BE ENOUGH TO ABSORB BAGLIS'S MAGIC.
WE BELIEVE THE MORE THEY OBTAIN, THE BETTER.

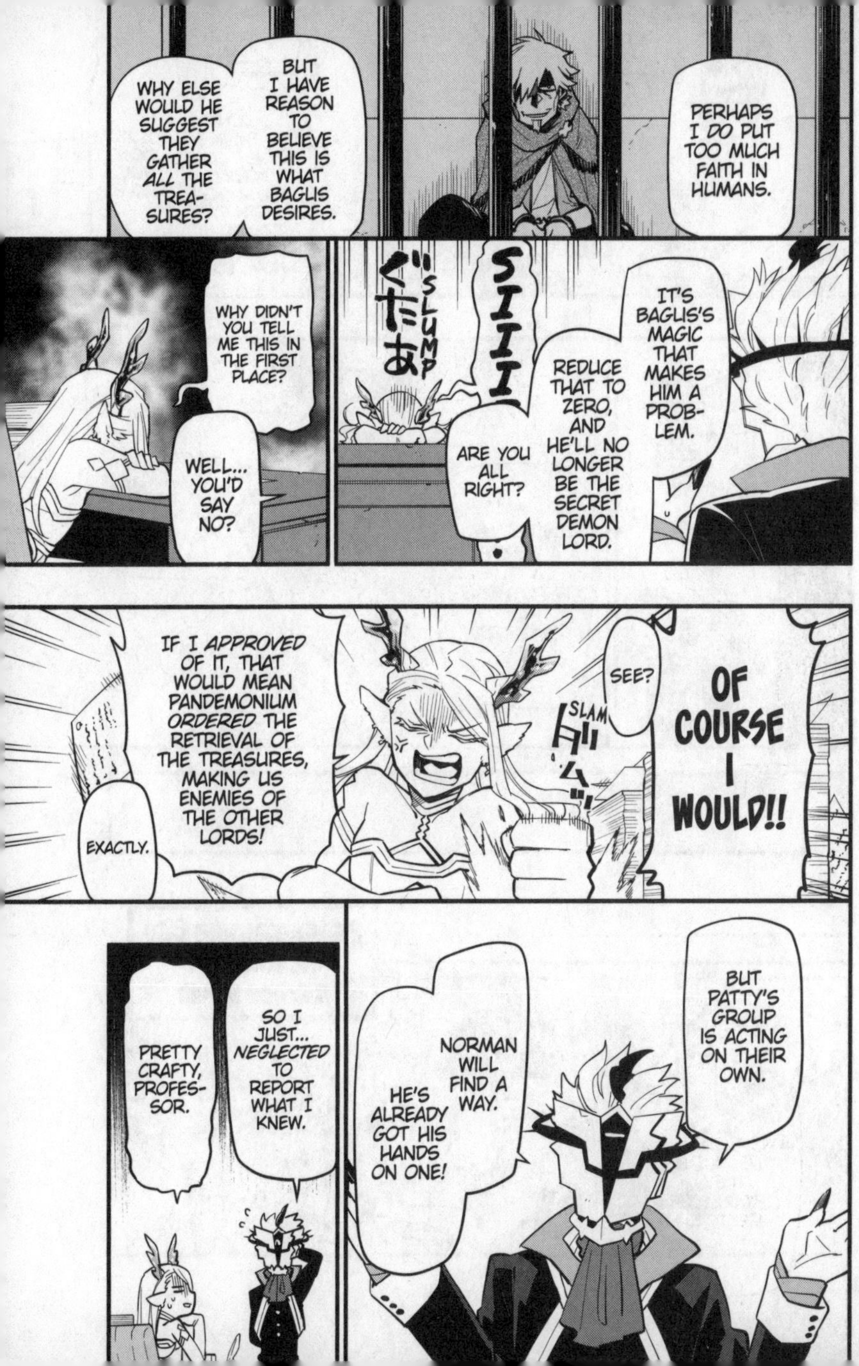
PERHAPS I *DO* PUT TOO MUCH FAITH IN HUMANS.
BUT I HAVE REASON TO BELIEVE THIS IS WHAT BAGLIS DESIRES.
WHY ELSE WOULD HE SUGGEST THEY GATHER *ALL* THE TREASURES?
IT'S BAGLIS'S MAGIC THAT MAKES HIM A PROBLEM.
REDUCE THAT TO ZERO, AND HE'LL NO LONGER BE THE SECRET DEMON LORD.
SIIII—
ぐだあ SLUMP
ARE YOU ALL RIGHT?
WHY DIDN'T YOU TELL ME THIS IN THE FIRST PLACE?
WELL... YOU'D SAY NO?
SEE?
OF COURSE I WOULD!!
SLAM
IF I *APPROVED* OF IT, THAT WOULD MEAN PANDEMONIUM *ORDERED* THE RETRIEVAL OF THE TREASURES, MAKING US ENEMIES OF THE OTHER LORDS!
EXACTLY.
BUT PATTY'S GROUP IS ACTING ON THEIR OWN.
NORMAN WILL FIND A WAY.
HE'S ALREADY GOT HIS HANDS ON ONE!
SO I JUST... *NEGLECTED* TO REPORT WHAT I KNEW.
PRETTY CRAFTY, PROFESSOR.

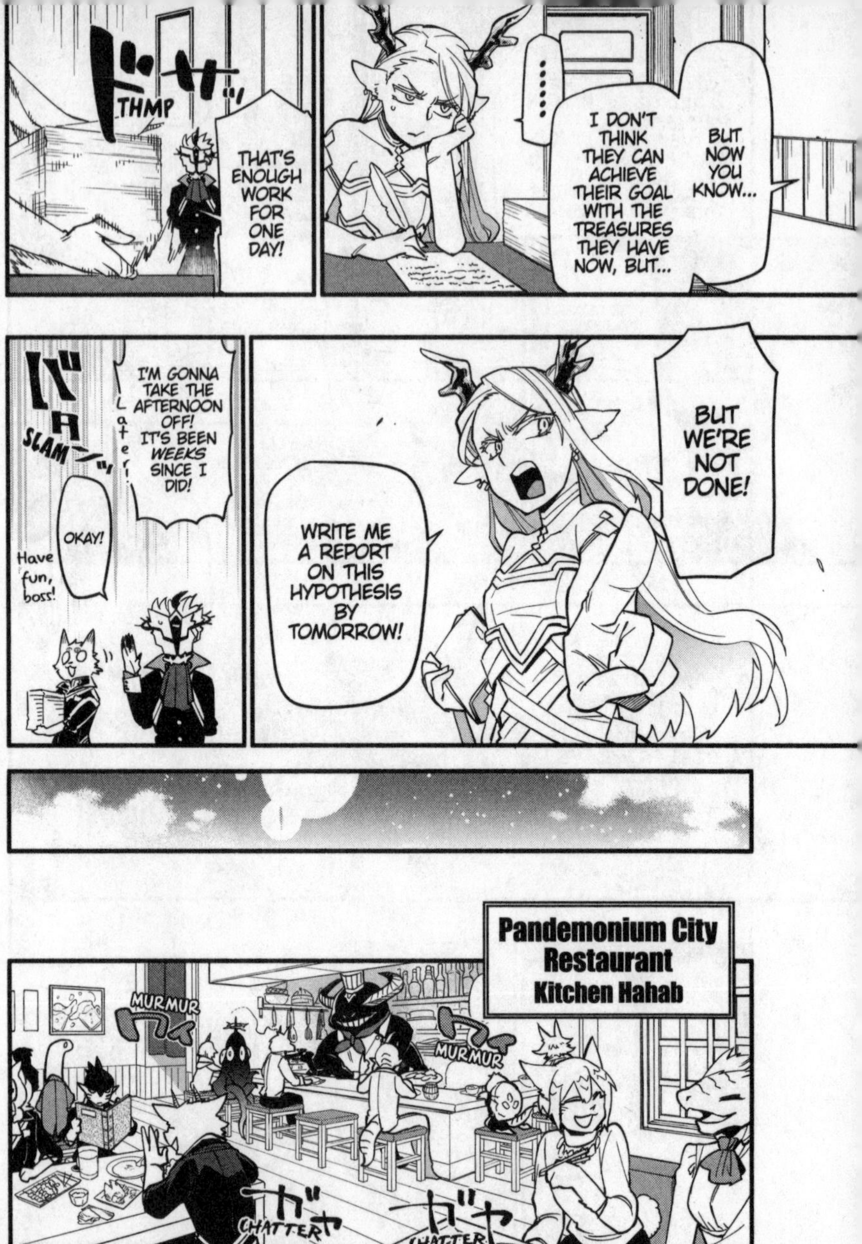
BUT NOW YOU KNOW...
I DON'T THINK THEY CAN ACHIEVE THEIR GOAL WITH THE TREASURES THEY HAVE NOW, BUT...
......
THAT'S ENOUGH WORK FOR ONE DAY!
THMP
BUT WE'RE NOT DONE!
WRITE ME A REPORT ON THIS HYPOTHESIS BY TOMORROW!
I'M GONNA TAKE THE AFTERNOON OFF! IT'S BEEN WEEKS SINCE I DID!
Later!
SLAM
OKAY!
Have fun, boss!
Pandemonium City
Restaurant
Kitchen Hahab
MURMUR
MURMUR
CHATTER
CHATTER

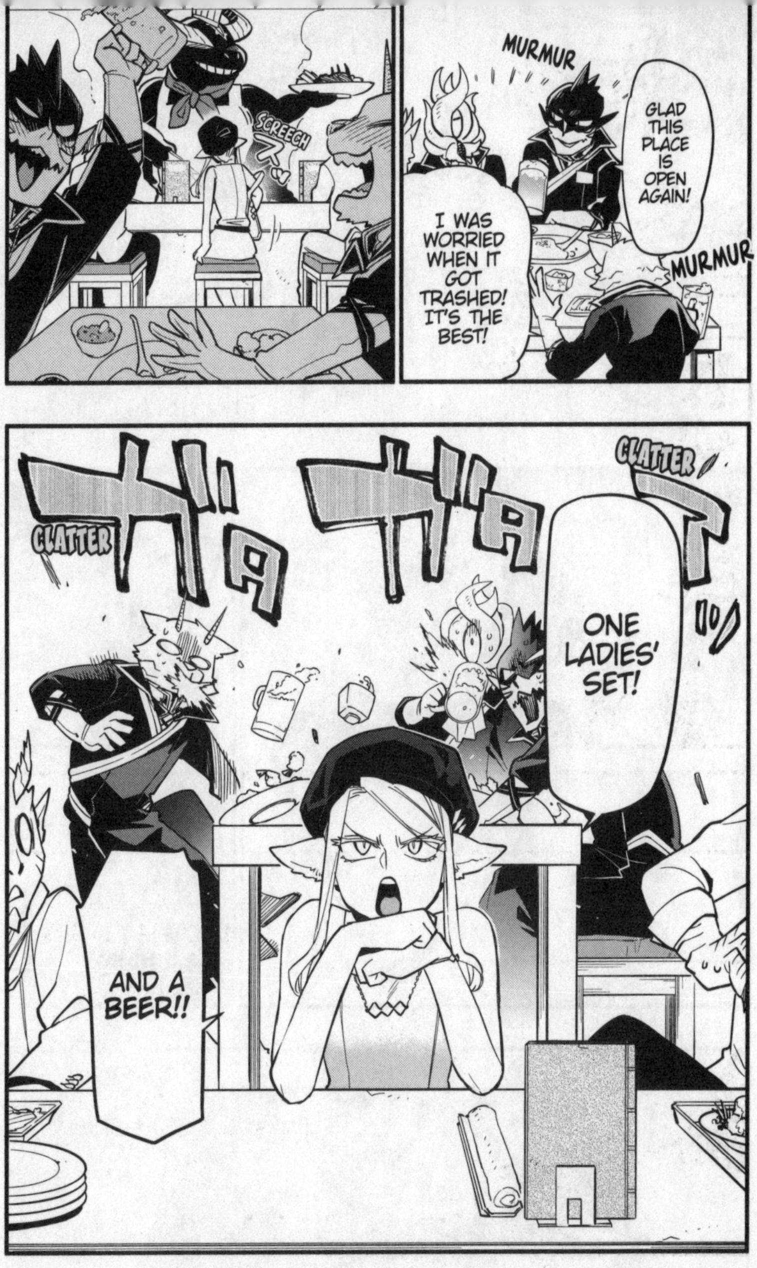
MURMUR
GLAD THIS PLACE IS OPEN AGAIN!
I WAS WORRIED WHEN IT GOT TRASHED! IT'S THE BEST!
MURMUR
SCREECH
CLATTER
CLATTER
ONE LADIES' SET!
AND A BEER!!

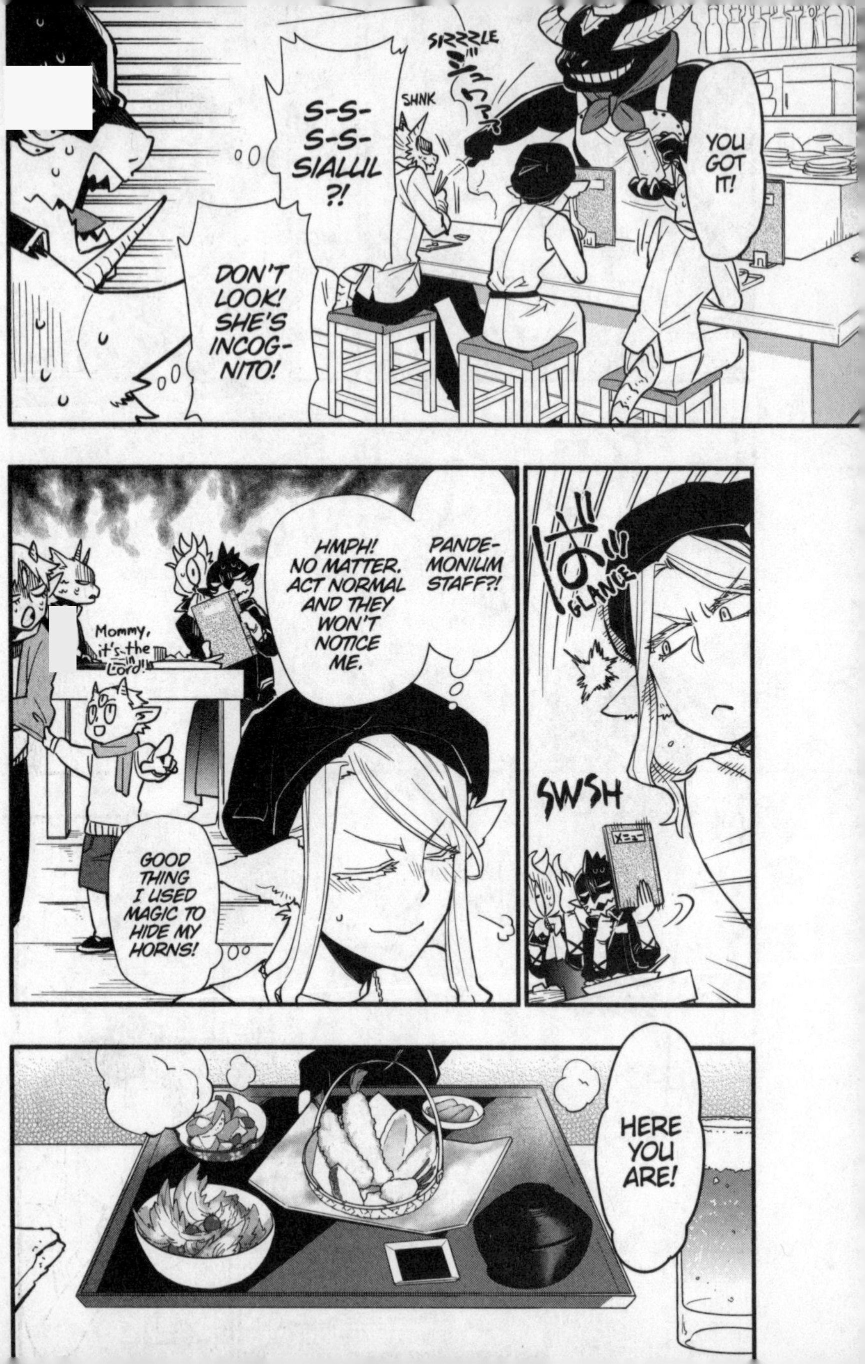
YOU GOT IT!
SIZZLE
SHNK
S-S-S-S-SIALUL?!
DON'T LOOK! SHE'S INCOGNITO!
GLANCE
SWSH
PANDEMONIUM STAFF?!
HMPH! NO MATTER. ACT NORMAL AND THEY WON'T NOTICE ME.
Mommy, it's the Lord!!
GOOD THING I USED MAGIC TO HIDE MY HORNS!
HERE YOU ARE!

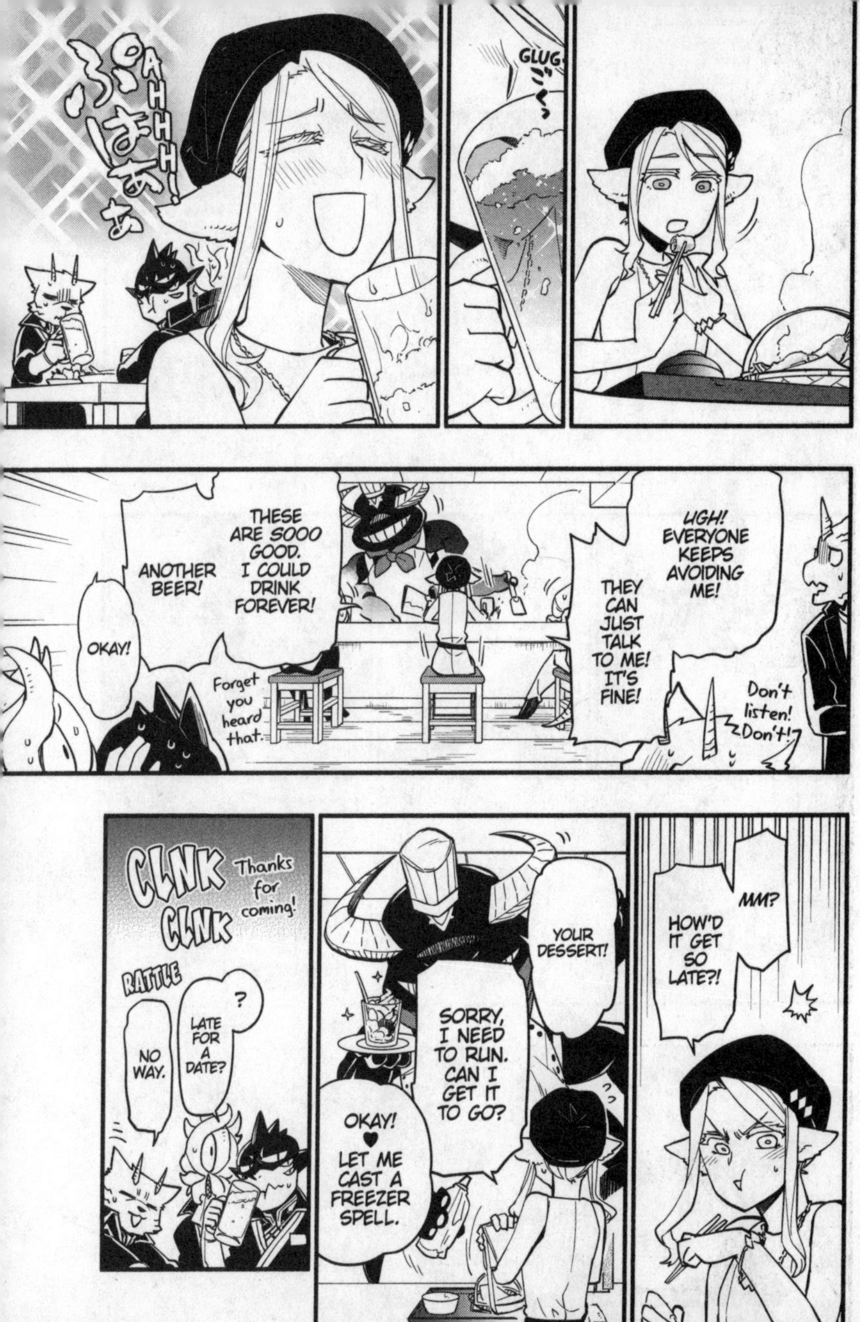
GLUG
ごくっ
AHHHH!
ふはあぁ
UGH! EVERYONE KEEPS AVOIDING ME!
THEY CAN JUST TALK TO ME! IT'S FINE!
Don't listen! Don't!
THESE ARE SOOO GOOD. I COULD DRINK FOREVER!
ANOTHER BEER!
OKAY!
Forget you heard that.
MM?
HOW'D IT GET SO LATE?!
YOUR DESSERT!
SORRY, I NEED TO RUN. CAN I GET IT TO GO?
OKAY! ♥ LET ME CAST A FREEZER SPELL.
CLNK
CLNK
Thanks for coming!
RATTLE
?
LATE FOR A DATE?
NO WAY.

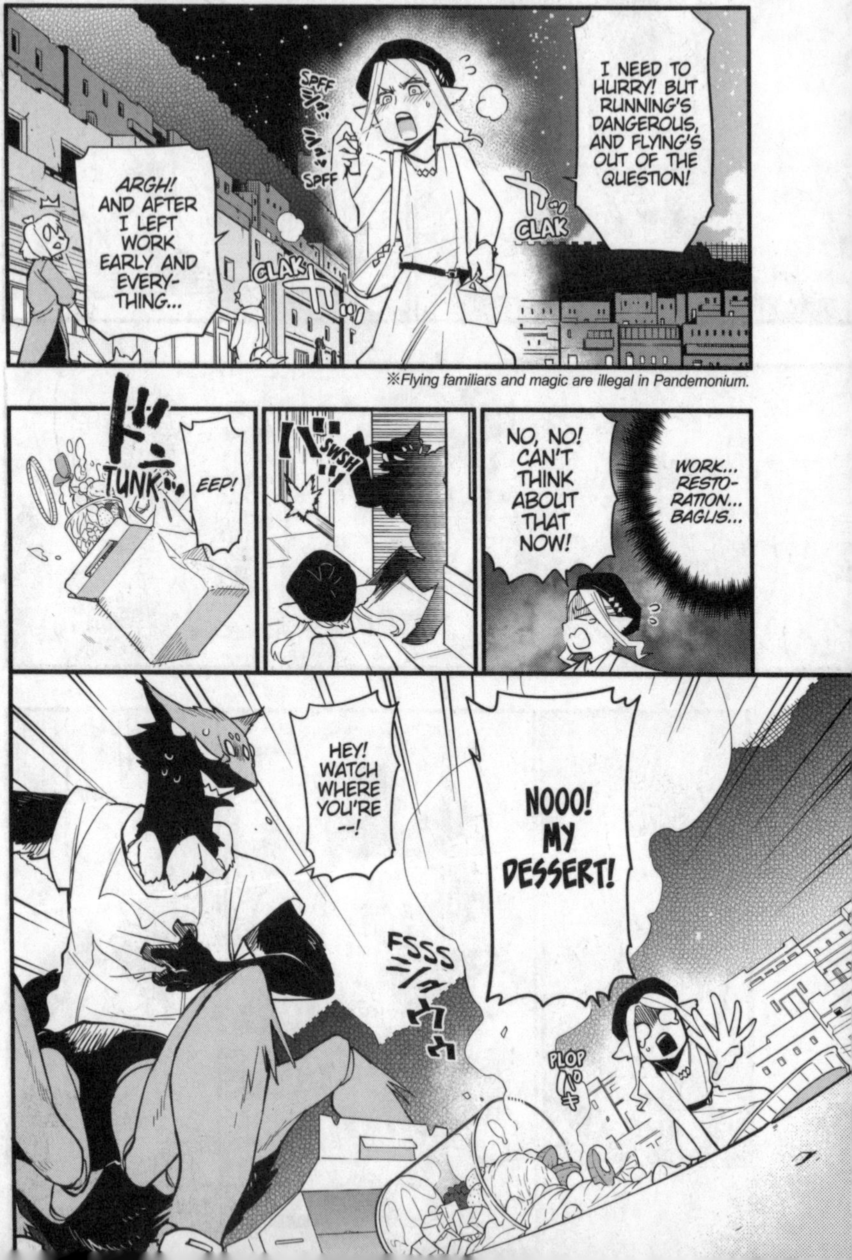
I NEED TO HURRY! BUT RUNNING'S DANGEROUS, AND FLYING'S OUT OF THE QUESTION!
SPFF
SPFF
ARGH! AND AFTER I LEFT WORK EARLY AND EVERY-THING...
CLAK
CLAK
WORK... RESTO-RATION... BAGUS...
NO, NO! CAN'T THINK ABOUT THAT NOW!
SWSH
TUNK
EEP!
NOOO! MY DESSERT!
HEY! WATCH WHERE YOU'RE --!
FSSS
PLOP
※Flying familiars and magic are illegal in Pandemonium.

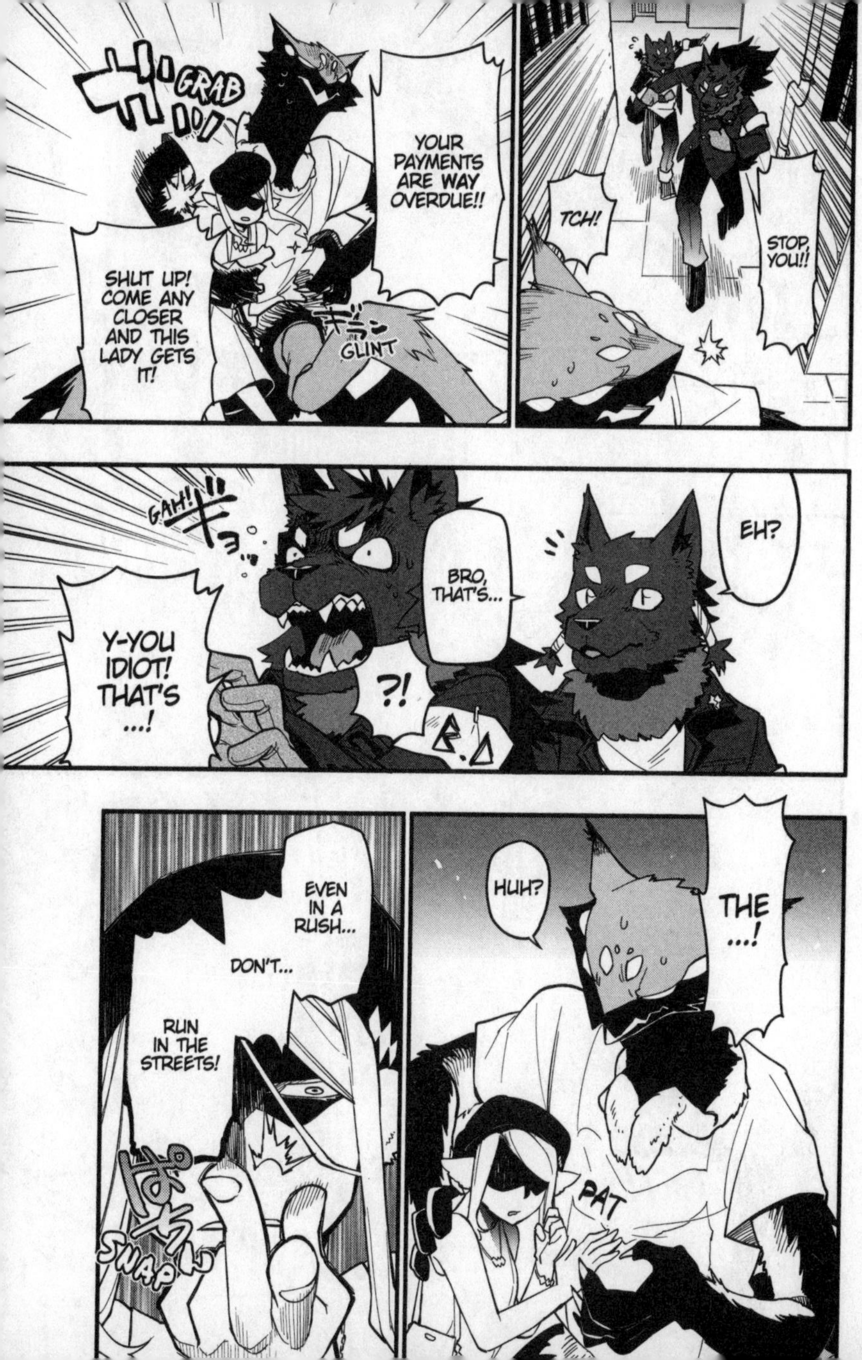
STOP, YOU!!
TCH!
YOUR PAYMENTS ARE WAY OVERDUE!!
GRAB
SHUT UP! COME ANY CLOSER AND THIS LADY GETS IT!
GLINT
EH?
BRO, THAT'S...
?!
Y-YOU IDIOT! THAT'S ...!
GAH!
THE ...!
HUH?
PAT
EVEN IN A RUSH...
DON'T...
RUN IN THE STREETS!
SNAP

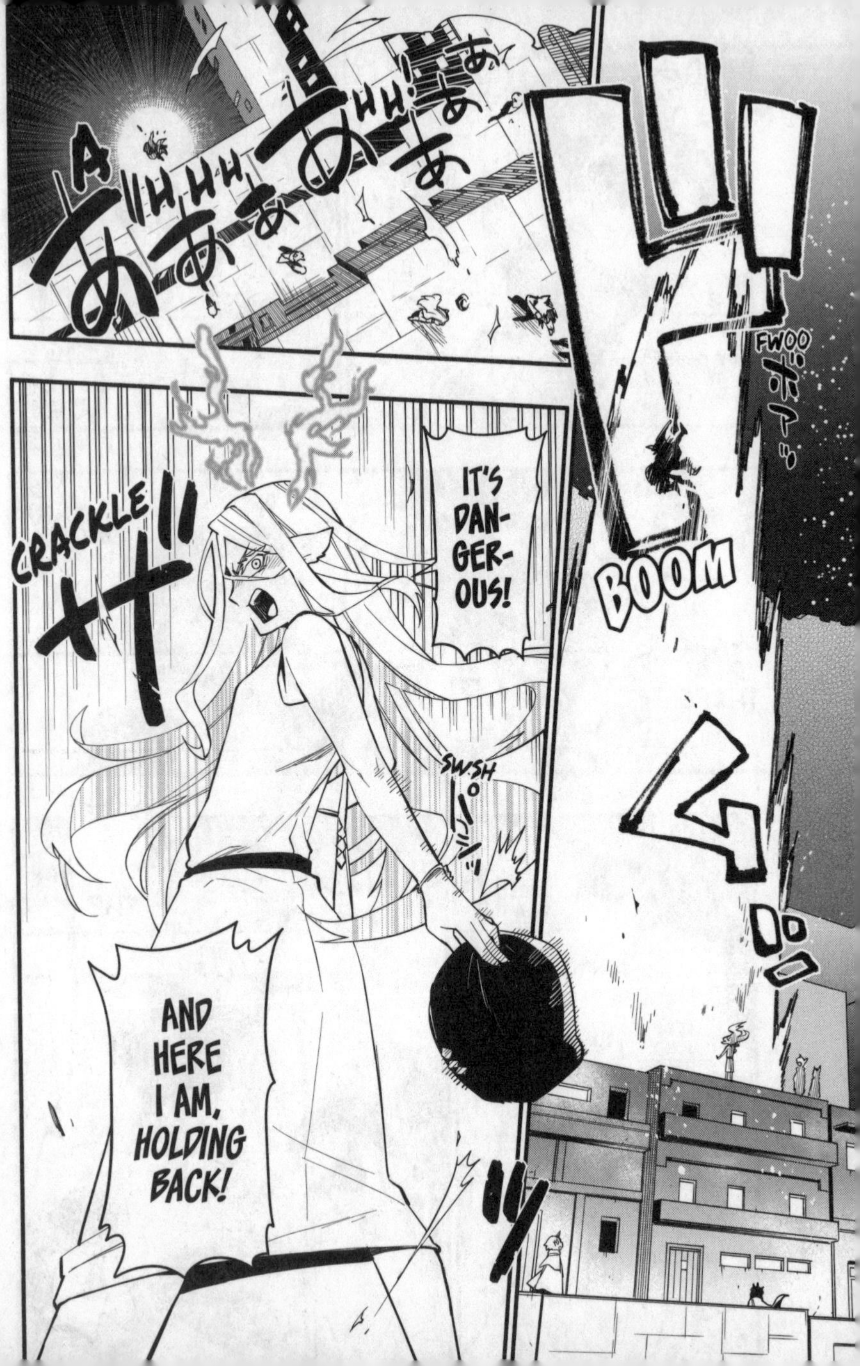

DOOOM
BOOM
FWOO ボアッ
A あああああ HHHH! AHH! ああ
CRACKLE ザザ
IT'S DAN-GER-OUS!
AND HERE I AM, HOLDING BACK!
SWISH パシッ

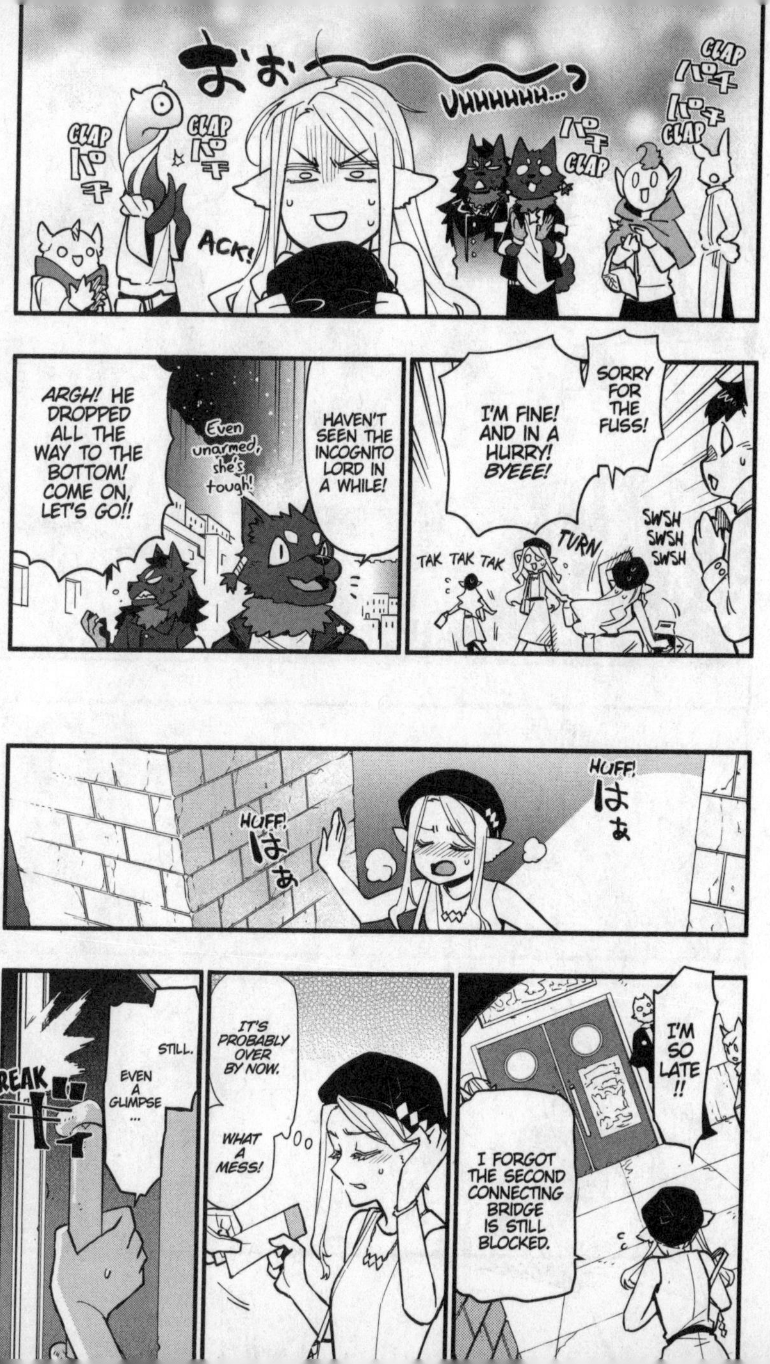
おお〜〜〜〜っ
UHHHHHH...?
CLAP パチ
CLAP パチ
ACK!
パチ CLAP
CLAP パチ
パチ CLAP
SORRY FOR THE FUSS!
I'M FINE! AND IN A HURRY! BYEEE!
SWSH SWSH SWSH
TURN
TAK TAK TAK
HAVEN'T SEEN THE INCOGNITO LORD IN A WHILE!
Even unarmed, she's tough!
ARGH! HE DROPPED ALL THE WAY TO THE BOTTOM! COME ON, LET'S GO!!
HUFF! はぁ
HUFF! はぁ
I'M SO LATE!!
I FORGOT THE SECOND CONNECTING BRIDGE IS STILL BLOCKED.
IT'S PROBABLY OVER BY NOW.
WHAT A MESS!
STILL.
EVEN A GLIMPSE...
CREAK

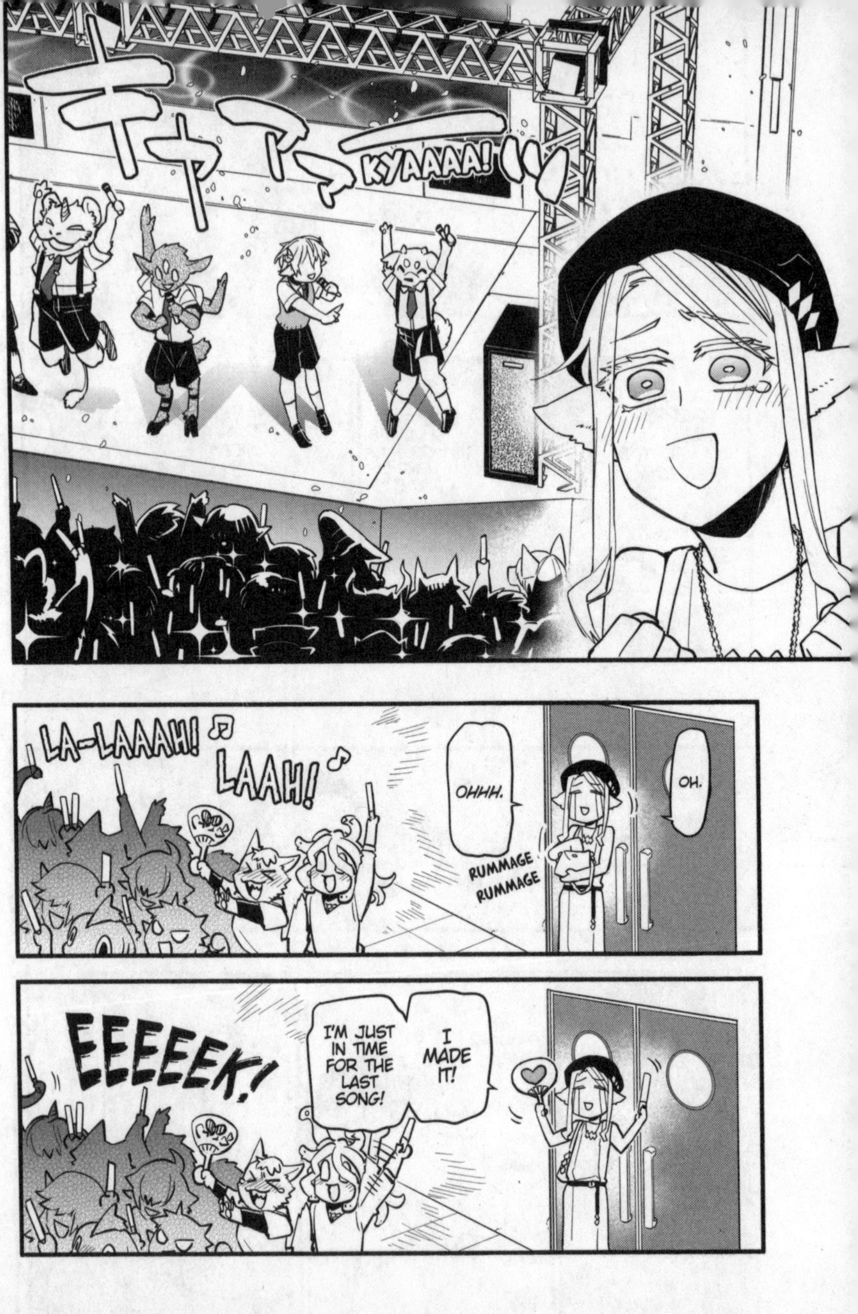
キャアーッ
KYAAAA!
LA-LAAAH!
LAAH!
OH.
OHHH.
RUMMAGE RUMMAGE
I MADE IT!
I'M JUST IN TIME FOR THE LAST SONG!
EEEEEK!

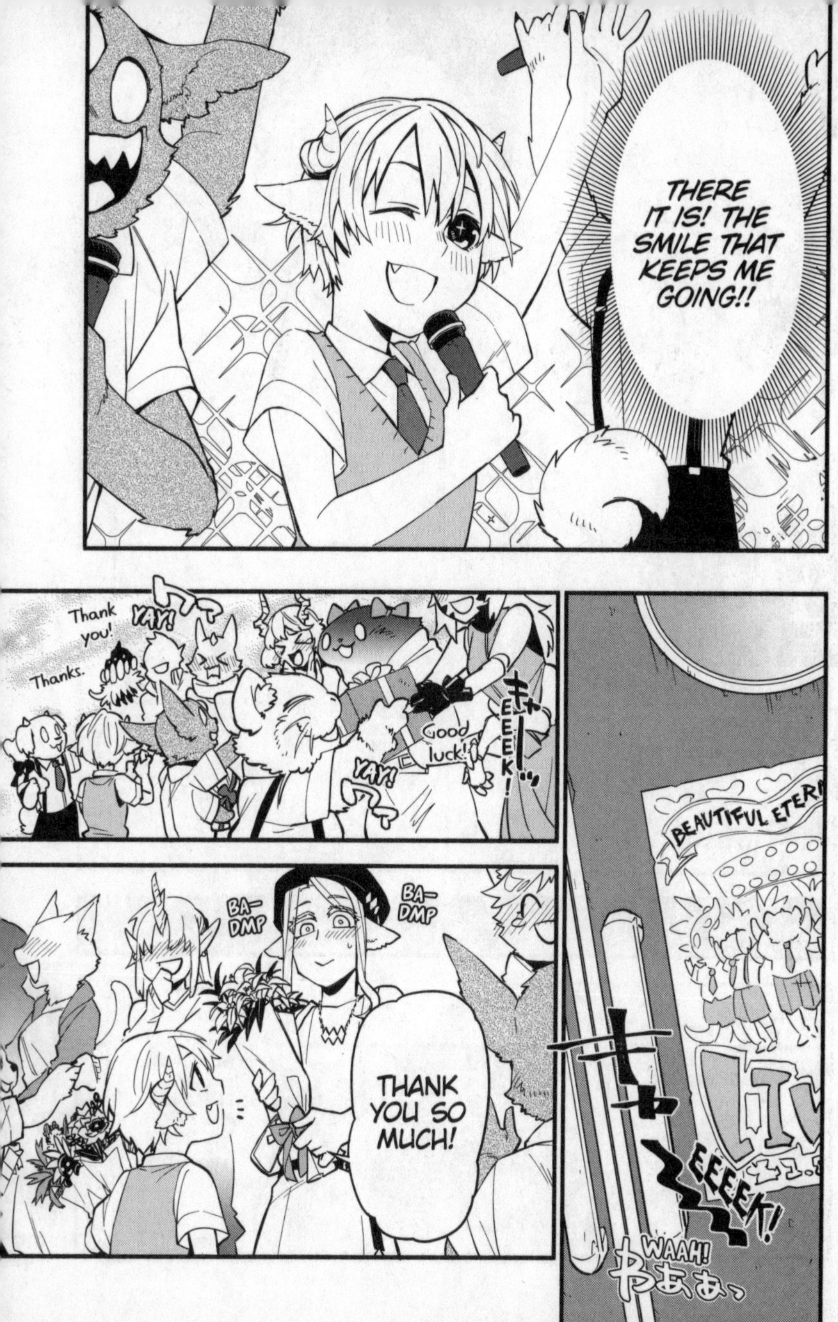
THERE IT IS! THE SMILE THAT KEEPS ME GOING!!
Thank you!
YAY!
Thanks.
EEEEK!
Good luck!
YAY!
BEAUTIFUL ETER
EEEEK!
WAAH!
BA-DMP
BA-DMP
THANK YOU SO MUCH!

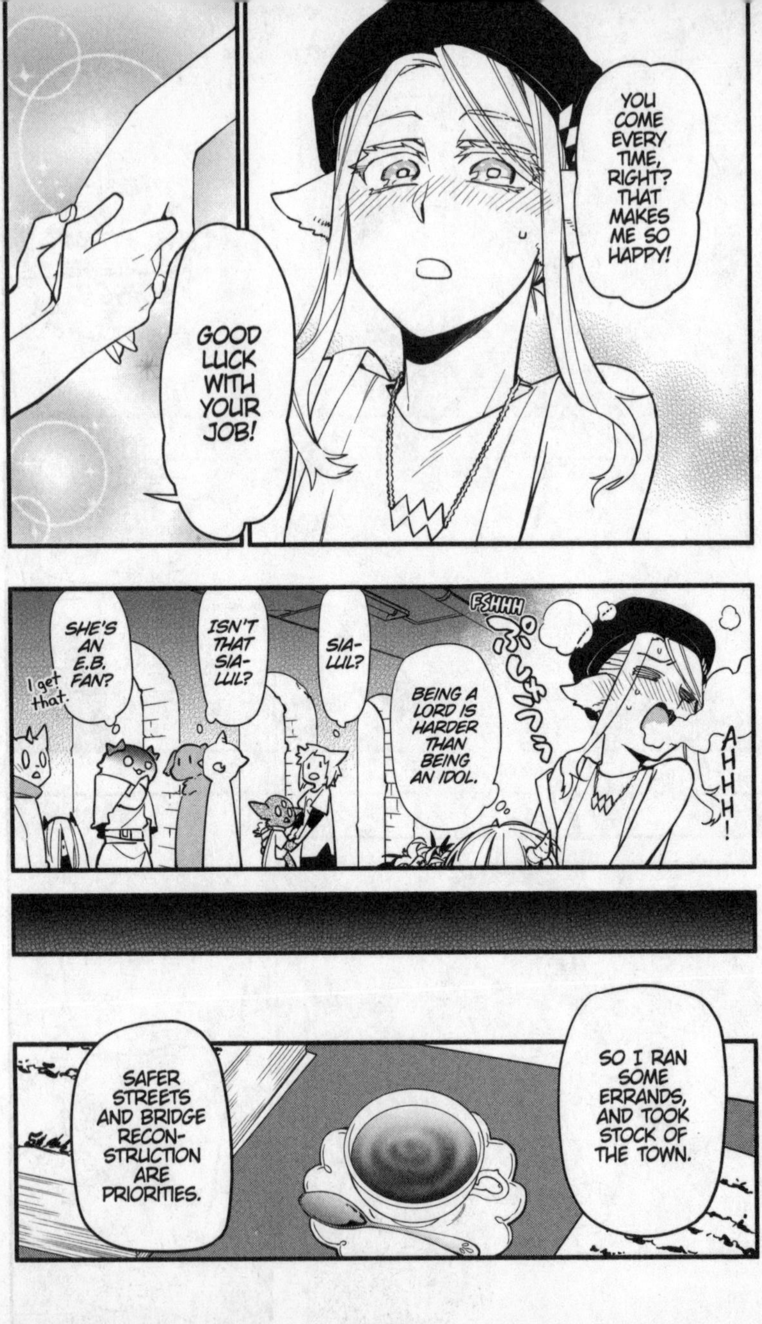
YOU COME EVERY TIME, RIGHT? THAT MAKES ME SO HAPPY!
GOOD LUCK WITH YOUR JOB!
FSHHH
AHHHH!
BEING A LORD IS HARDER THAN BEING AN IDOL.
SIA-LUL?
ISN'T THAT SIA-LUL?
SHE'S AN E.B. FAN?
I get that.
SO I RAN SOME ERRANDS, AND TOOK STOCK OF THE TOWN.
SAFER STREETS AND BRIDGE RECON-STRUCTION ARE PRIORITIES.

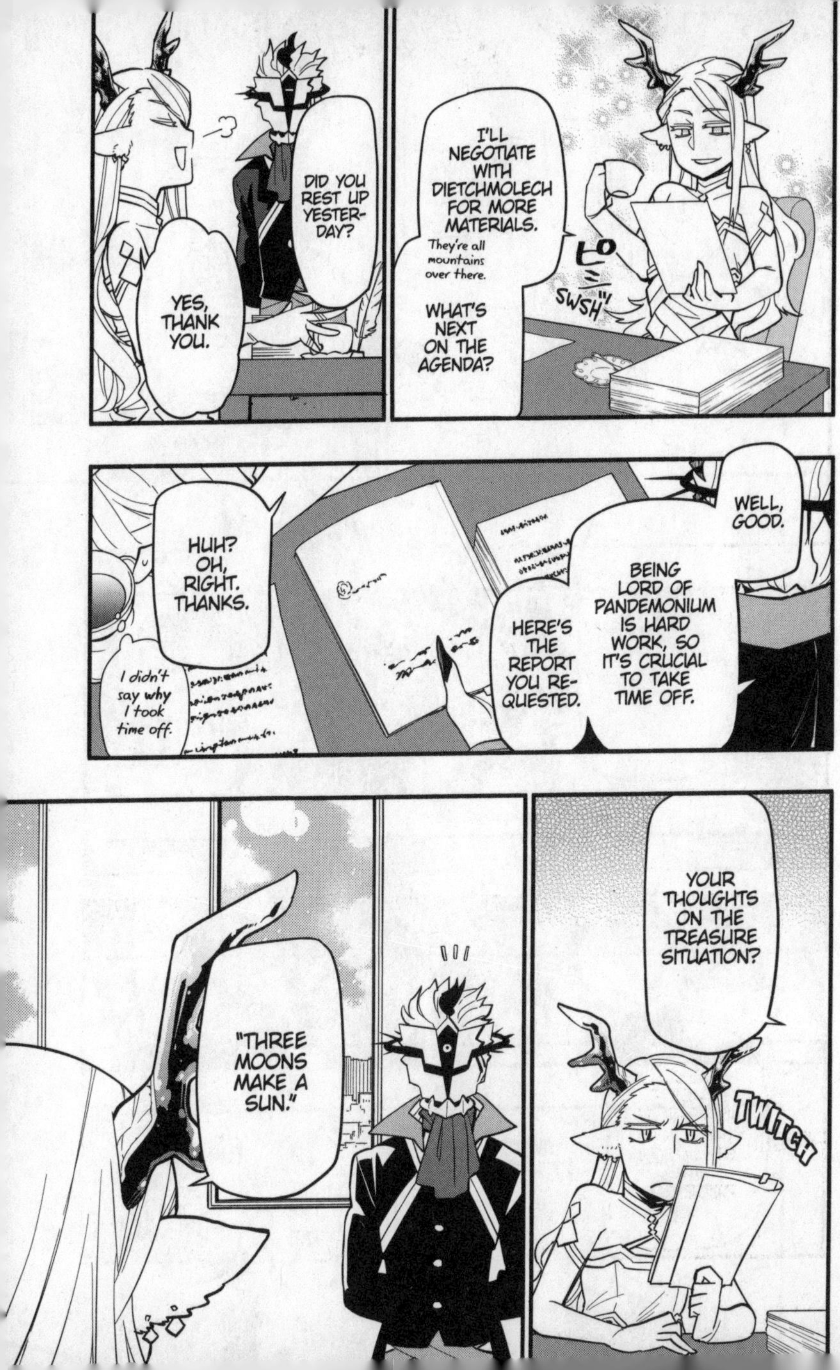
I'LL NEGOTIATE WITH DIETCHMOLECH FOR MORE MATERIALS.
They're all mountains over there.
WHAT'S NEXT ON THE AGENDA?
SWSH
DID YOU REST UP YESTER-DAY?
YES, THANK YOU.
WELL, GOOD.
BEING LORD OF PANDEMONIUM IS HARD WORK, SO IT'S CRUCIAL TO TAKE TIME OFF.
HERE'S THE REPORT YOU RE-QUESTED.
HUH? OH, RIGHT. THANKS.
I didn't say why I took time off.
YOUR THOUGHTS ON THE TREASURE SITUATION?
TWITCH
"THREE MOONS MAKE A SUN."

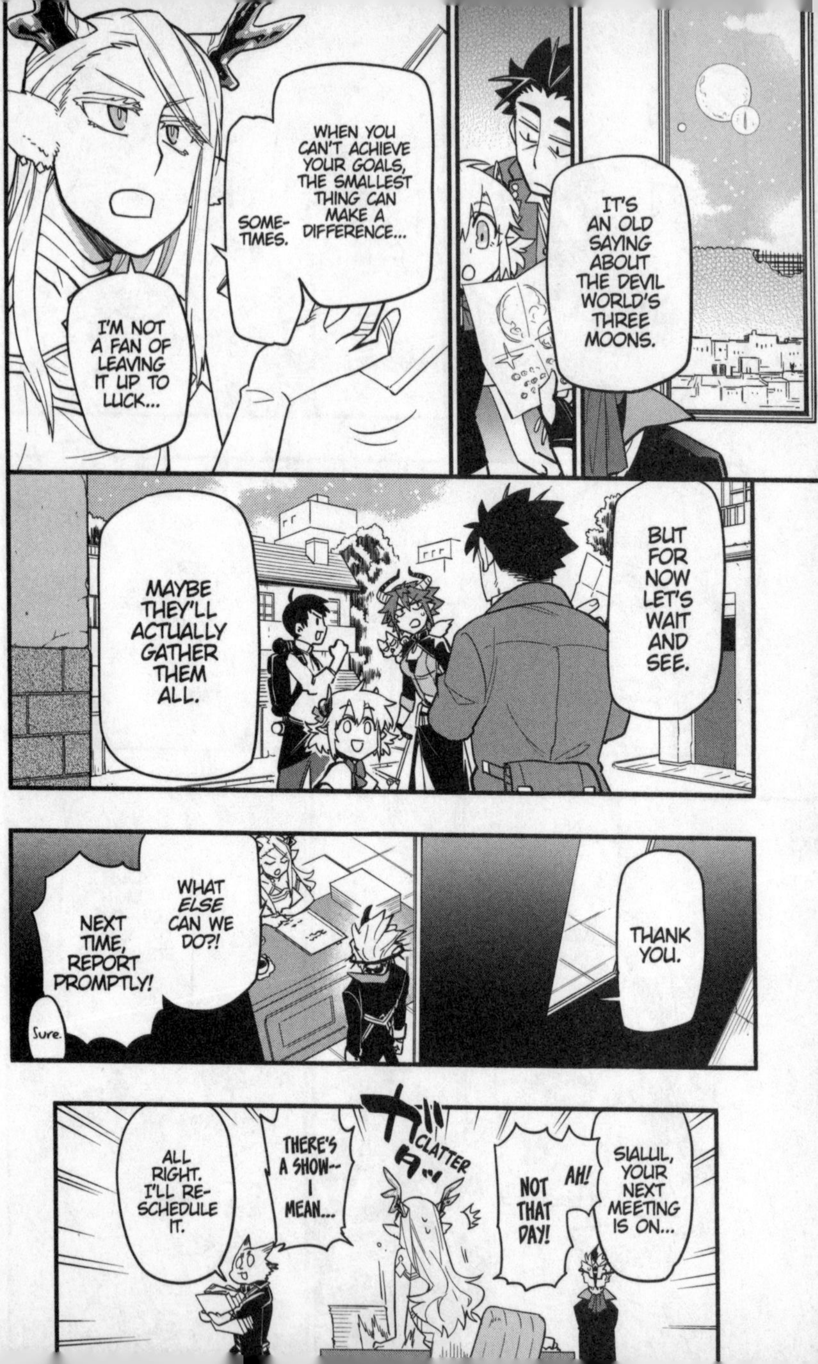
IT'S AN OLD SAYING ABOUT THE DEVIL WORLD'S THREE MOONS.
WHEN YOU CAN'T ACHIEVE YOUR GOALS, THE SMALLEST THING CAN MAKE A DIFFERENCE...
SOME-TIMES.
I'M NOT A FAN OF LEAVING IT UP TO LUCK...
BUT FOR NOW LET'S WAIT AND SEE.
MAYBE THEY'LL ACTUALLY GATHER THEM ALL.
THANK YOU.
WHAT ELSE CAN WE DO?!
NEXT TIME, REPORT PROMPTLY!
Sure.
SIALUL, YOUR NEXT MEETING IS ON...
AH!
NOT THAT DAY!
CLATTER
THERE'S A SHOW-- I MEAN...
ALL RIGHT. I'LL RE-SCHEDULE IT.

Sorry For My Familiar

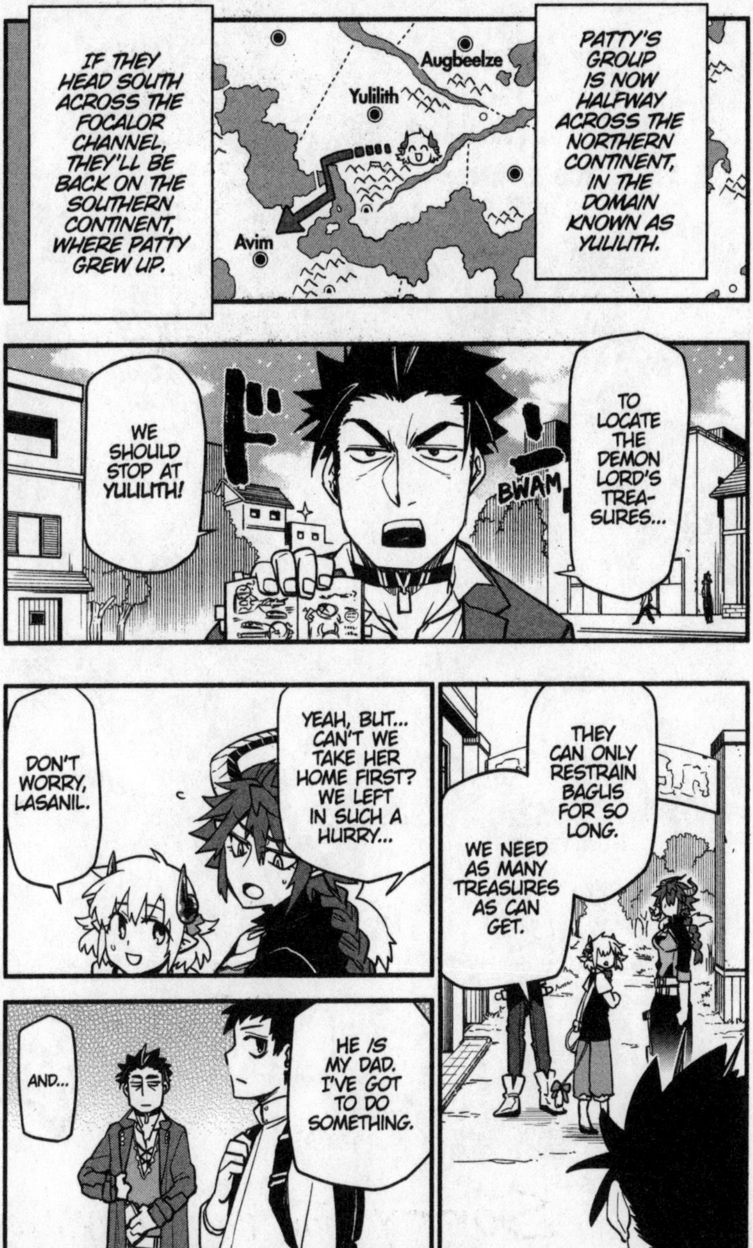
PATTY'S GROUP IS NOW HALFWAY ACROSS THE NORTHERN CONTINENT, IN THE DOMAIN KNOWN AS YULILITH.
Augbeelze
Yulilith
Avim
IF THEY HEAD SOUTH ACROSS THE FOCALOR CHANNEL, THEY'LL BE BACK ON THE SOUTHERN CONTINENT, WHERE PATTY GREW UP.
TO LOCATE THE DEMON LORD'S TREA-SURES...
BWAM
WE SHOULD STOP AT YULILITH!
THEY CAN ONLY RESTRAIN BAGLIS FOR SO LONG.
WE NEED AS MANY TREASURES AS CAN GET.
YEAH, BUT... CAN'T WE TAKE HER HOME FIRST? WE LEFT IN SUCH A HURRY...
DON'T WORRY, LASANIL.
HE IS MY DAD. I'VE GOT TO DO SOMETHING.
AND...

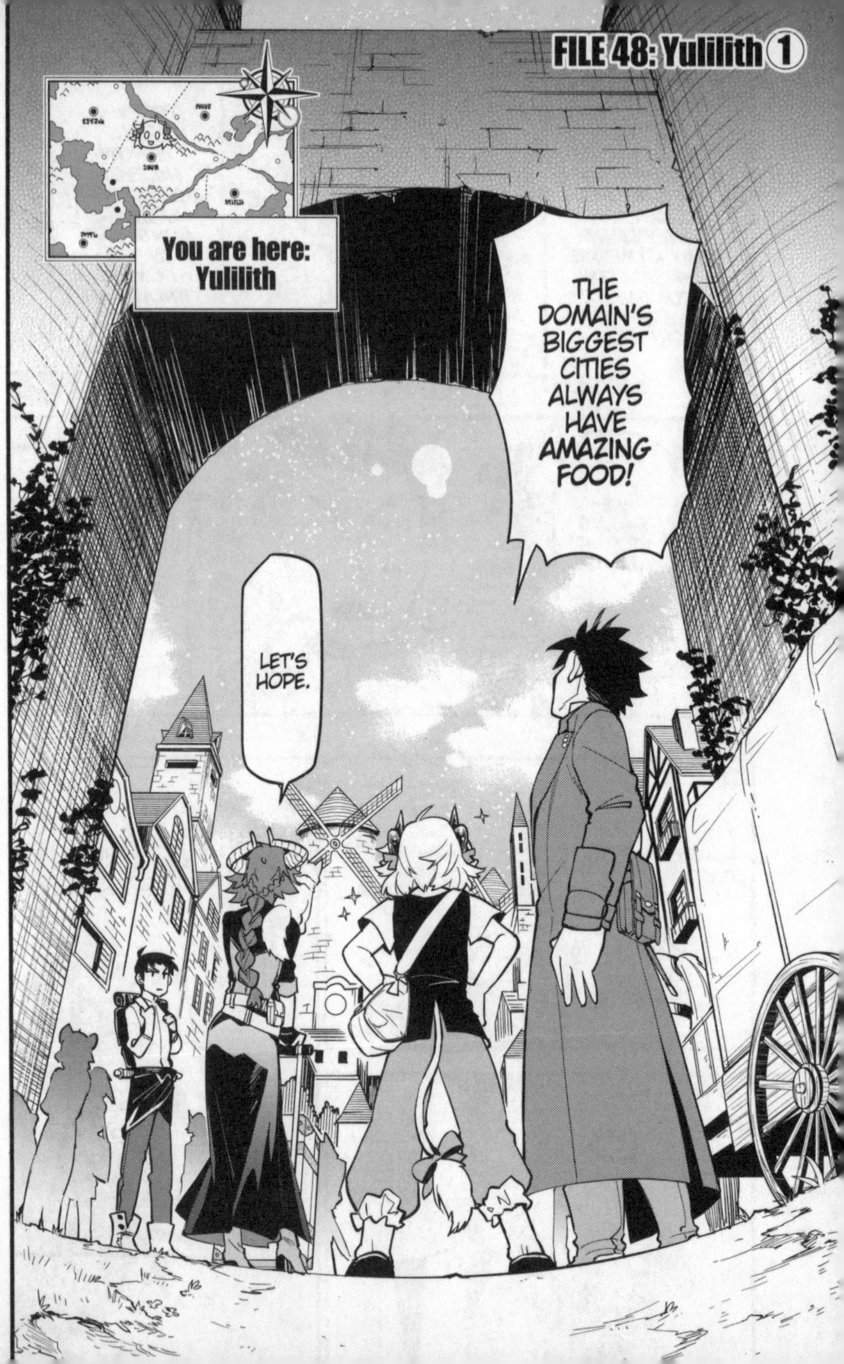
FILE 48: Yulilith 1
You are here: Yulilith
THE DOMAIN'S BIGGEST CITIES ALWAYS HAVE AMAZING FOOD!
LET'S HOPE.

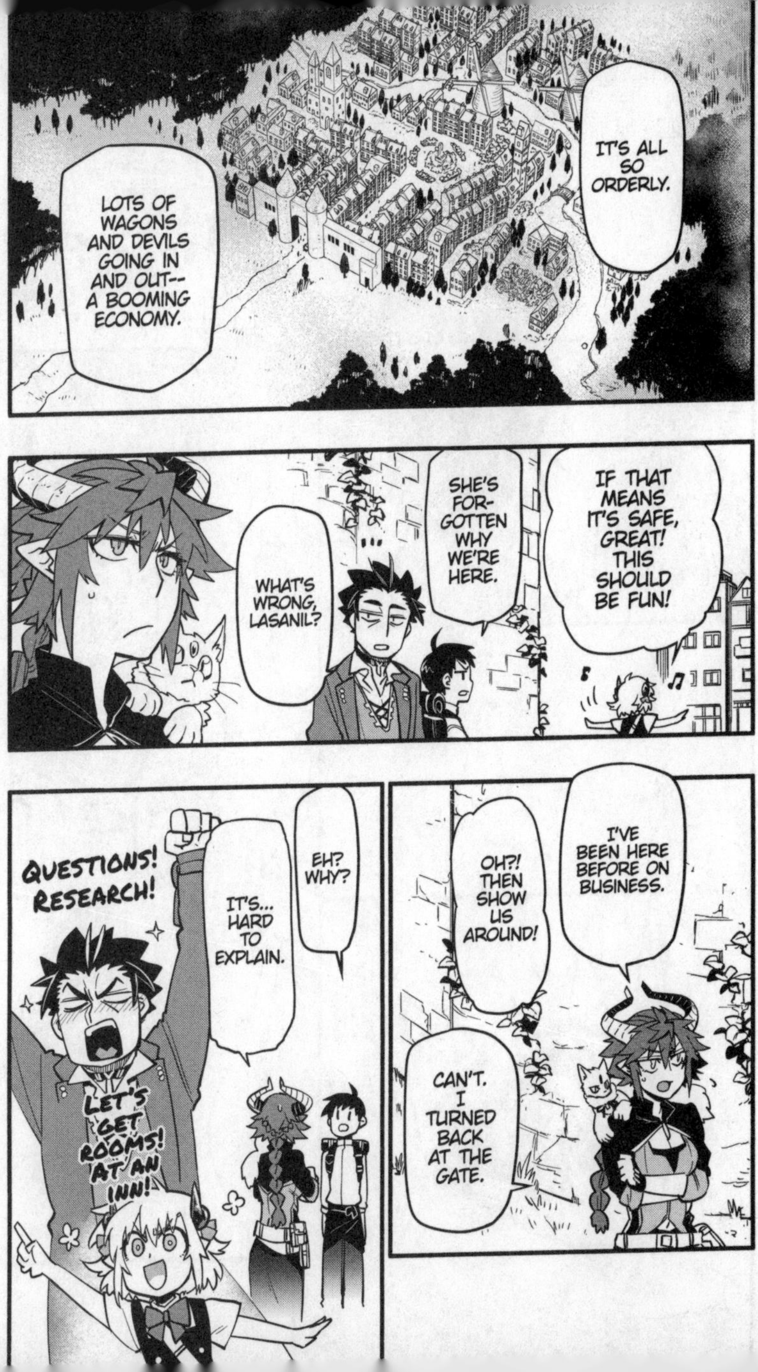
IT'S ALL SO ORDERLY.
LOTS OF WAGONS AND DEVILS GOING IN AND OUT-- A BOOMING ECONOMY.
IF THAT MEANS IT'S SAFE, GREAT! THIS SHOULD BE FUN!
SHE'S FOR-GOTTEN WHY WE'RE HERE.
...
WHAT'S WRONG, LASANIL?
I'VE BEEN HERE BEFORE ON BUSINESS.
OH?! THEN SHOW US AROUND!
CAN'T. I TURNED BACK AT THE GATE.
EH? WHY?
IT'S... HARD TO EXPLAIN.
QUESTIONS! RESEARCH!
LET'S GET ROOMS! AT AN INN!

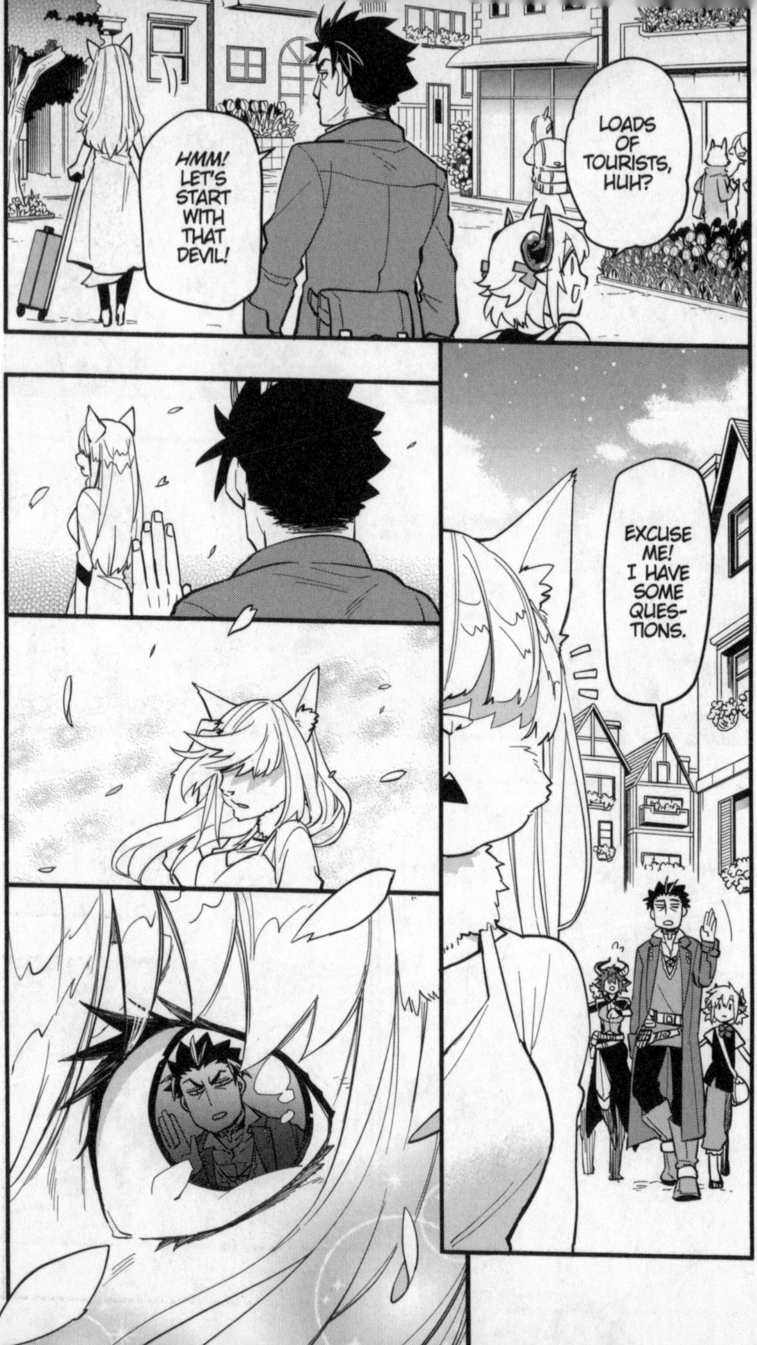
LOADS OF TOURISTS, HUH?
HMM! LET'S START WITH THAT DEVIL!
EXCUSE ME! I HAVE SOME QUES-TIONS.

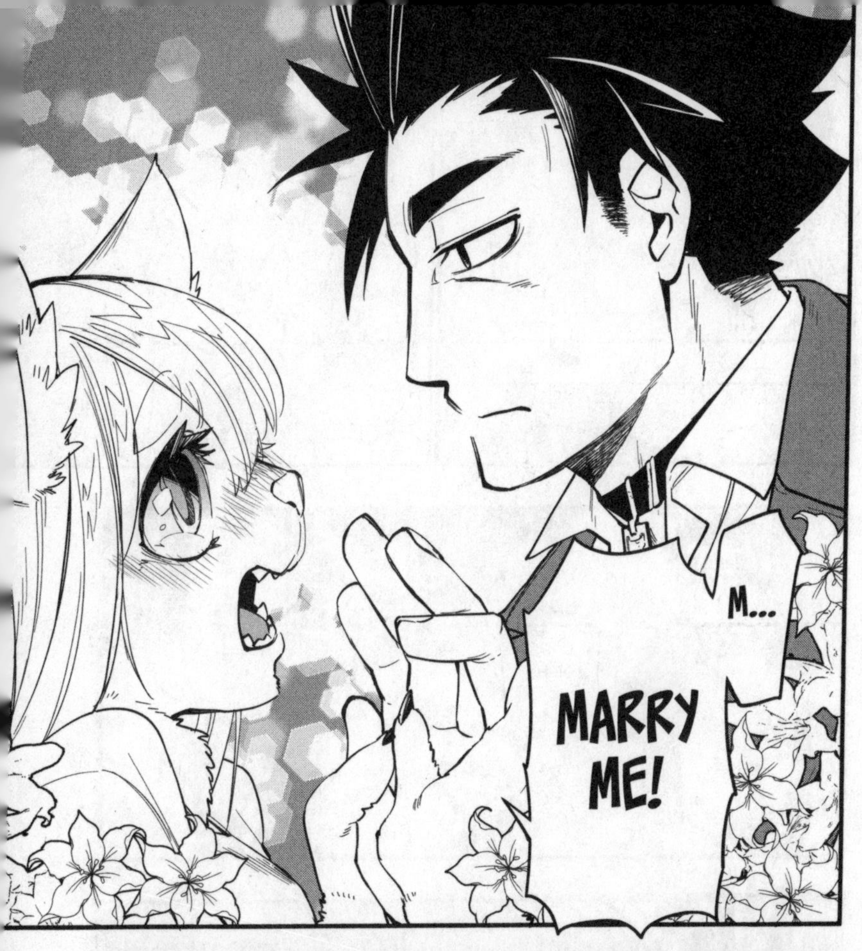
M...
MARRY ME!

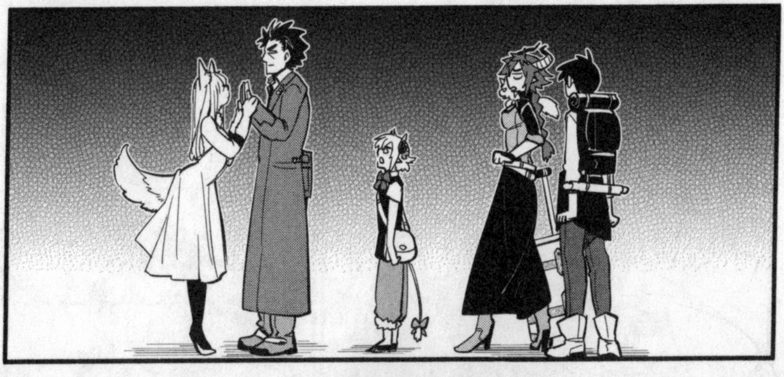

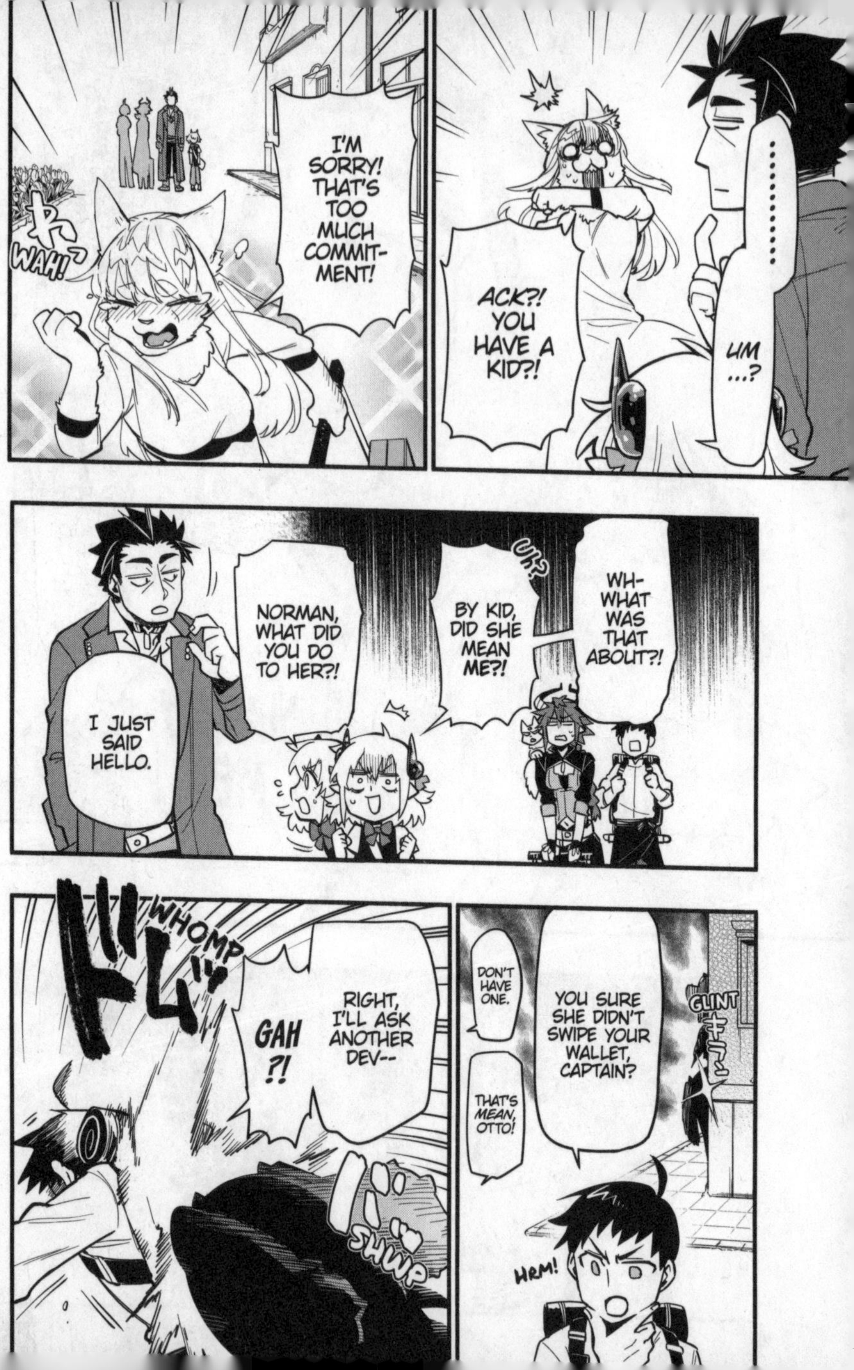
......
UM ...?
ACK?! YOU HAVE A KID?!
WAH!
I'M SORRY! THAT'S TOO MUCH COMMIT-MENT!
WH-WHAT WAS THAT ABOUT?!
UH?
BY KID, DID SHE MEAN ME?!
NORMAN, WHAT DID YOU DO TO HER?!
I JUST SAID HELLO.
YOU SURE SHE DIDN'T SWIPE YOUR WALLET, CAPTAIN?
DON'T HAVE ONE.
THAT'S *MEAN*, OTTO!
GLINT
HRM!
RIGHT, I'LL ASK ANOTHER DEV--
GAH ?!
WHOMP
SHWP

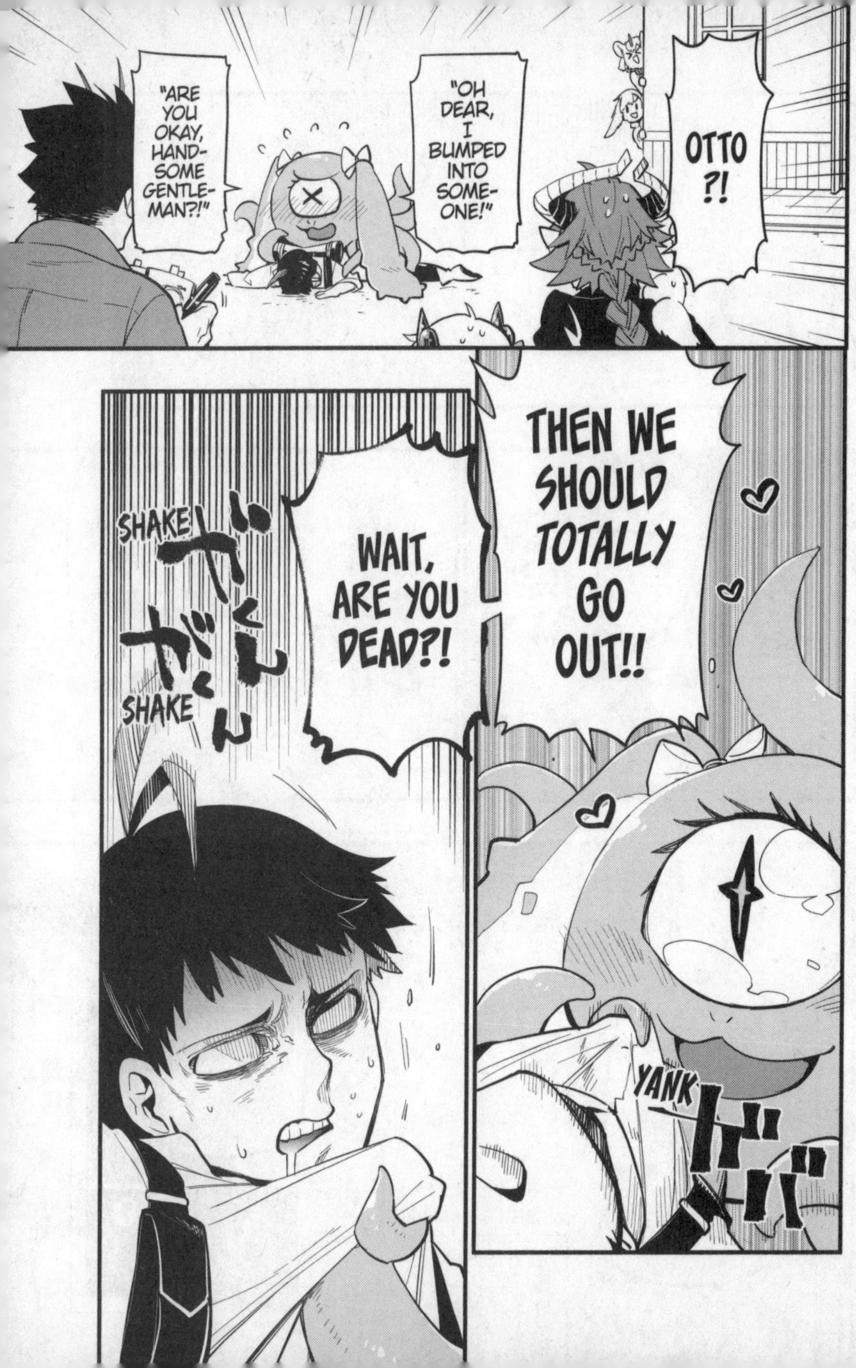
OTTO ?!
"OH DEAR, I BUMPED INTO SOME-ONE!"
"ARE YOU OKAY, HAND-SOME GENTLE-MAN?!"
THEN WE SHOULD TOTALLY GO OUT!!
YANK
WAIT, ARE YOU DEAD?!
SHAKE
SHAKE

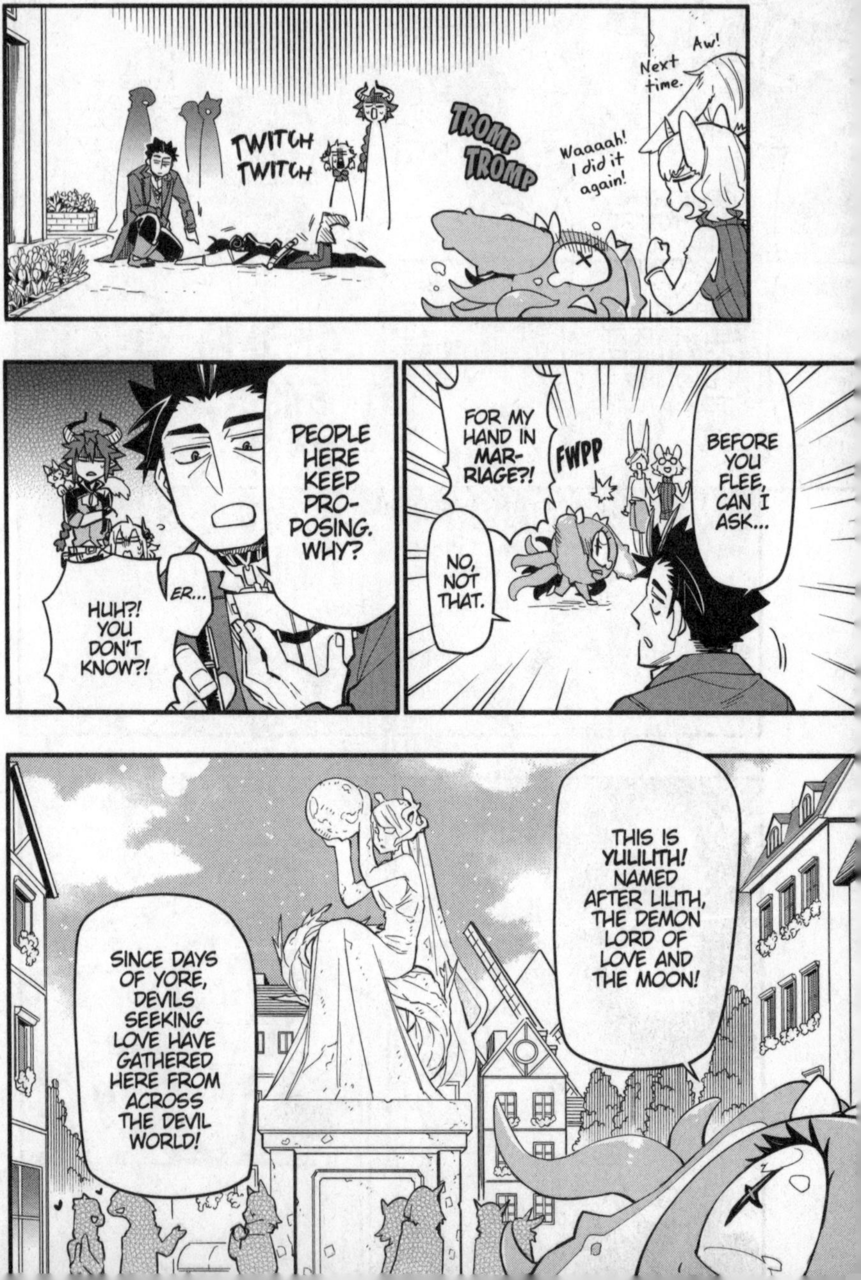
Aw!
Next time.
Waaaah! I did it again!
TROMP TROMP
TWITCH TWITCH
BEFORE YOU FLEE, CAN I ASK...
FOR MY HAND IN MAR-RIAGE?!
FWPP
NO, NOT THAT.
PEOPLE HERE KEEP PRO-POSING. WHY?
ER...
HUH?! YOU DON'T KNOW?!
THIS IS YULILITH! NAMED AFTER LILITH, THE DEMON LORD OF LOVE AND THE MOON!
SINCE DAYS OF YORE, DEVILS SEEKING LOVE HAVE GATHERED HERE FROM ACROSS THE DEVIL WORLD!

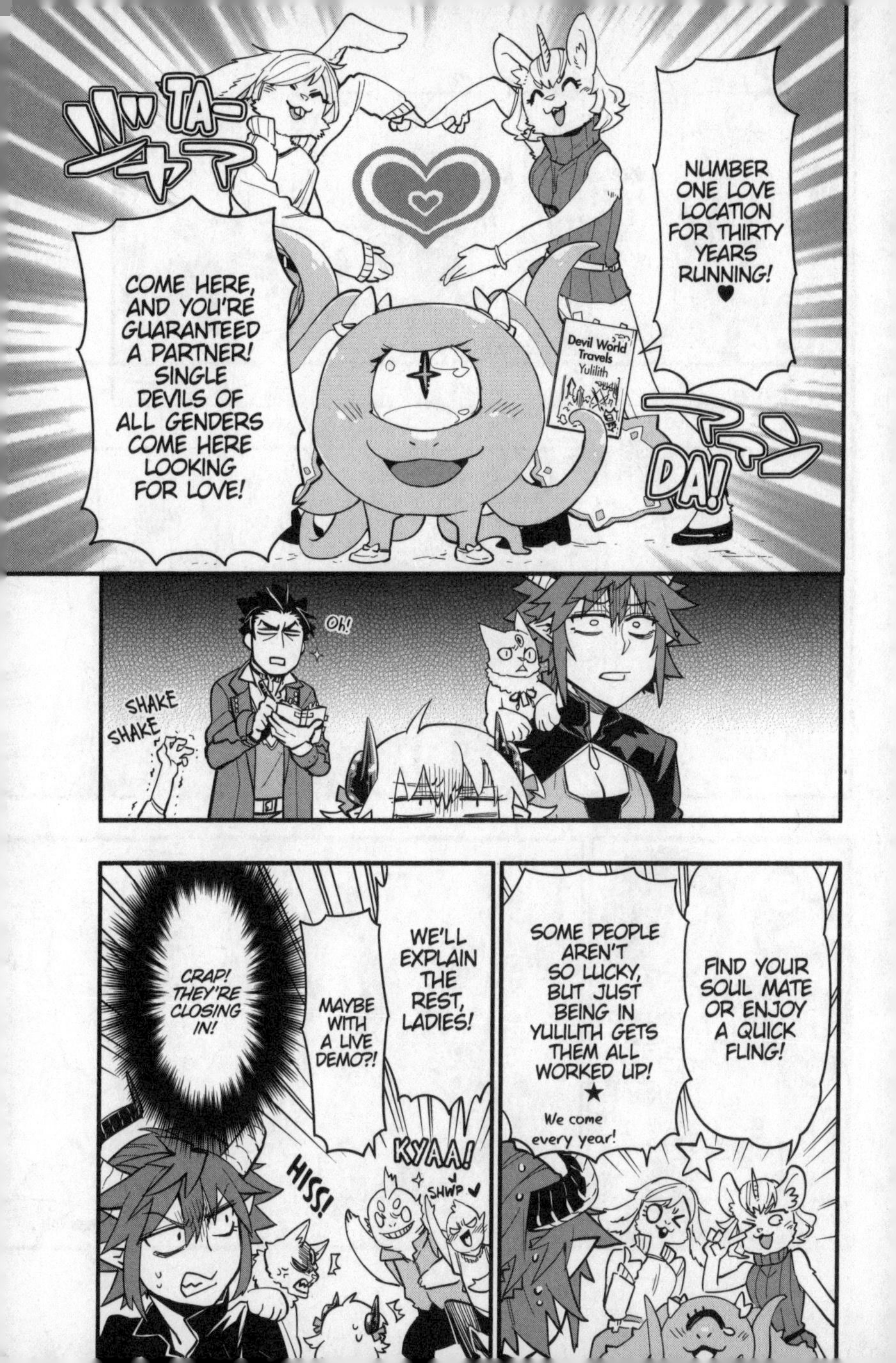

TA-
NUMBER ONE LOVE LOCATION FOR THIRTY YEARS RUNNING! ♥
COME HERE, AND YOU'RE GUARANTEED A PARTNER! SINGLE DEVILS OF ALL GENDERS COME HERE LOOKING FOR LOVE!
Devil World Travels
Yulilith
DA!
Oh!
SHAKE
SHAKE
FIND YOUR SOUL MATE OR ENJOY A QUICK FLING!
SOME PEOPLE AREN'T SO LUCKY, BUT JUST BEING IN YULILITH GETS THEM ALL WORKED UP! ★
We come every year!
WE'LL EXPLAIN THE REST, LADIES!
MAYBE WITH A LIVE DEMO?!
KYAA!
SHWP ♥
HISS!
CRAP! THEY'RE CLOSING IN!

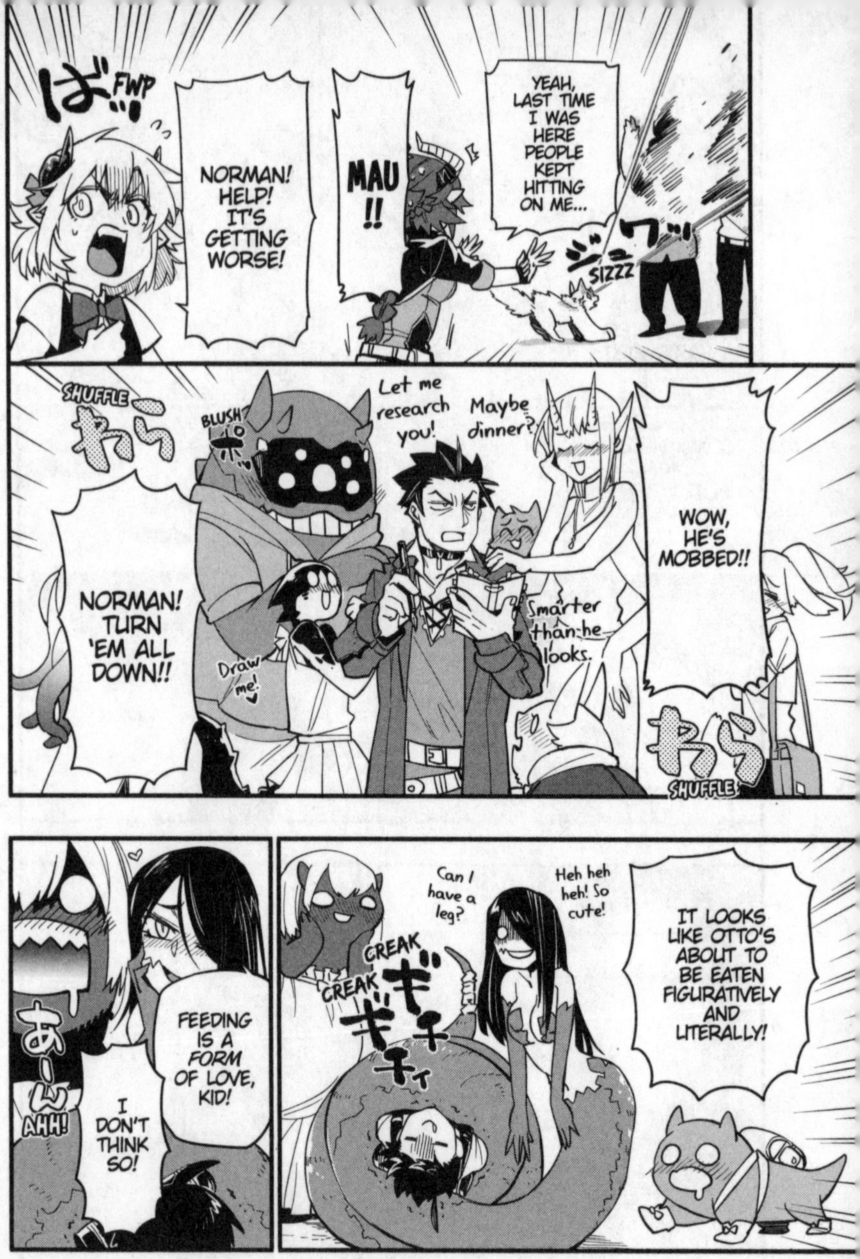
YEAH, LAST TIME I WAS HERE PEOPLE KEPT HITTING ON ME...
SIZZZ
MAU !!
NORMAN! HELP! IT'S GETTING WORSE!
FWP
WOW, HE'S MOBBED!!
SHUFFLE
Maybe dinner?
Smarter than he looks.
Let me research you!
BLUSH
Draw me!
NORMAN! TURN 'EM ALL DOWN!!
SHUFFLE
IT LOOKS LIKE OTTO'S ABOUT TO BE EATEN FIGURATIVELY AND LITERALLY!
Heh heh heh! So cute!
Can I have a leg?
CREAK
CREAK
FEEDING IS A FORM OF LOVE, KID!
I DON'T THINK SO!
AHH!

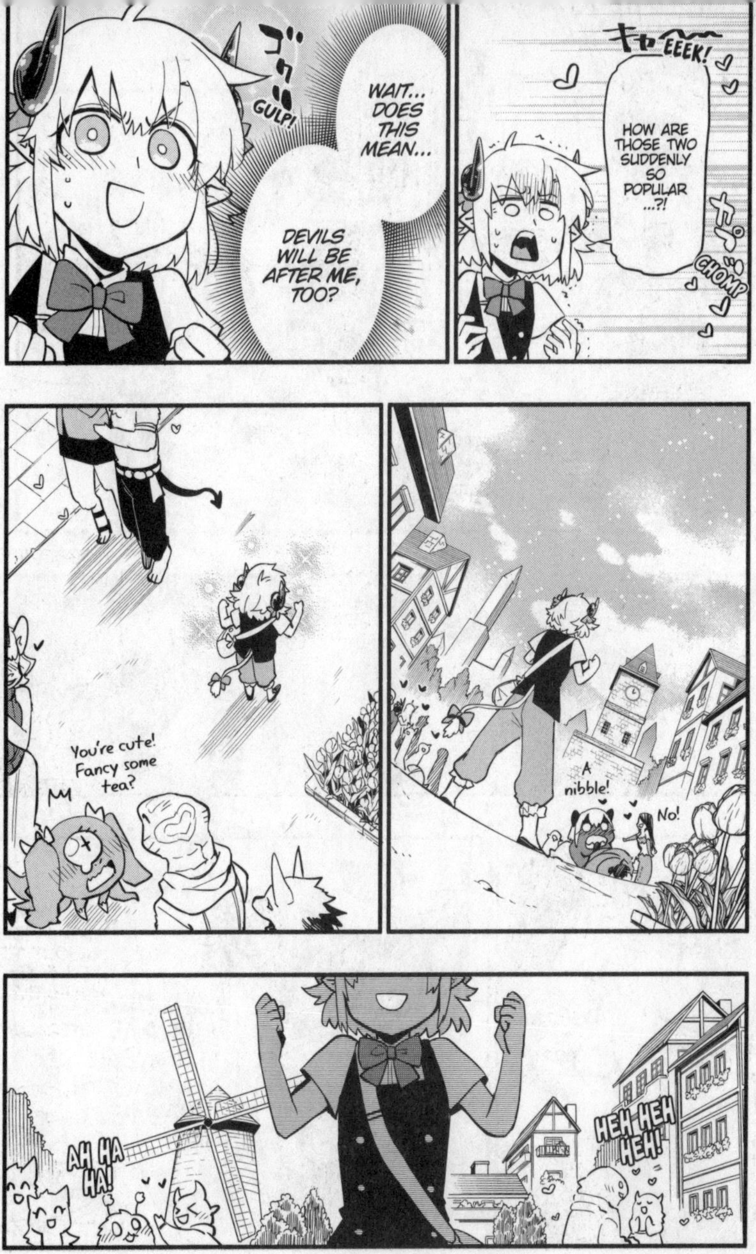

キャ EEEK!
HOW ARE THOSE TWO SUDDENLY SO POPULAR ...?!
CHOMP
GULP!
WAIT... DOES THIS MEAN...
DEVILS WILL BE AFTER ME, TOO?
A nibble!
No!
You're cute! Fancy some tea?
HEH HEH HEH!
AH HA HA!

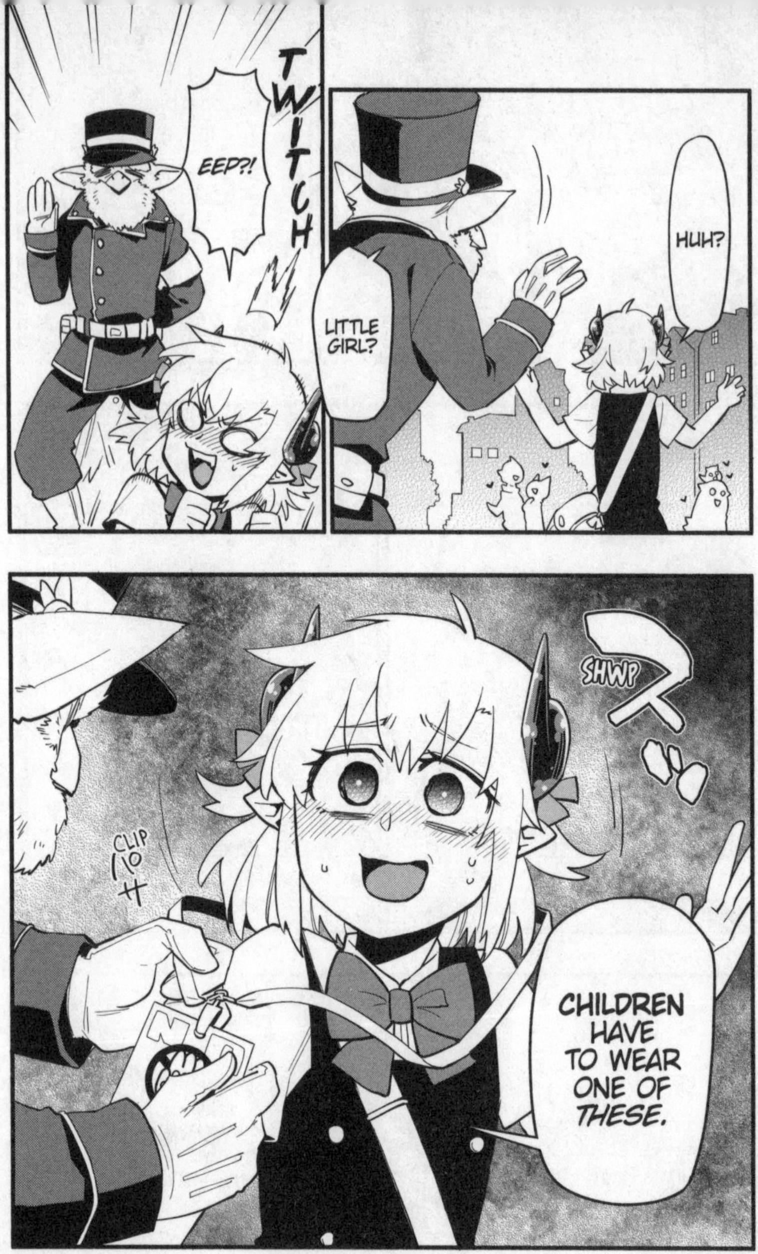
HUH?
LITTLE GIRL?
TWITCH
EEP?!
SHWP
CLIP
CHILDREN HAVE TO WEAR ONE OF *THESE.*

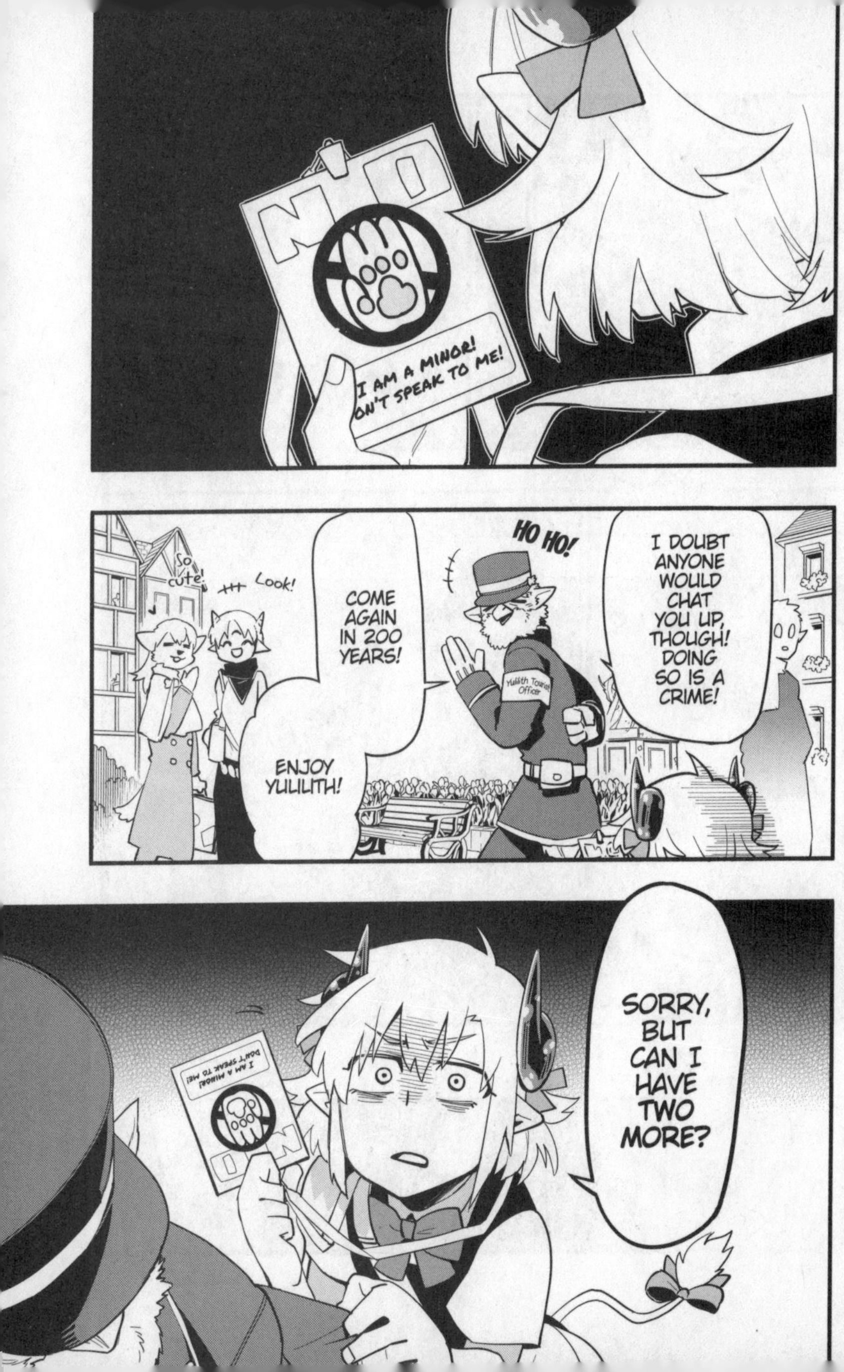
NO
I AM A MINOR!
ON'T SPEAK TO ME!
HO HO!
I DOUBT ANYONE WOULD CHAT YOU UP, THOUGH! DOING SO IS A CRIME!
COME AGAIN IN 200 YEARS!
ENJOY YULILITH!
Look!
So cute!
SORRY, BUT CAN I HAVE TWO MORE?

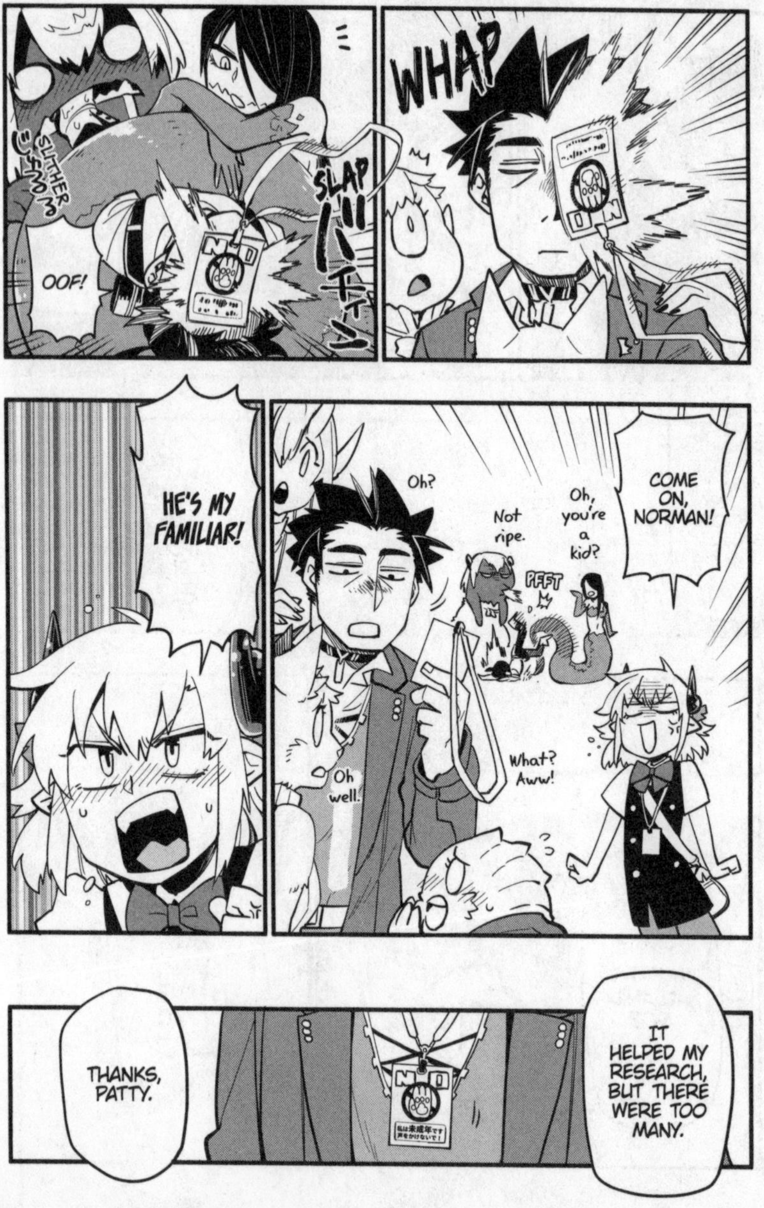
WHAP
My
SLAP
バチィン
SLITHER
じゅるる
OOF!
COME ON, NORMAN!
Oh, you're a kid?
Not ripe.
PFFT
Oh?
What? Aww!
Oh well.
HE'S MY FAMILIAR!
IT HELPED MY RESEARCH, BUT THERE WERE TOO MANY.
THANKS, PATTY.

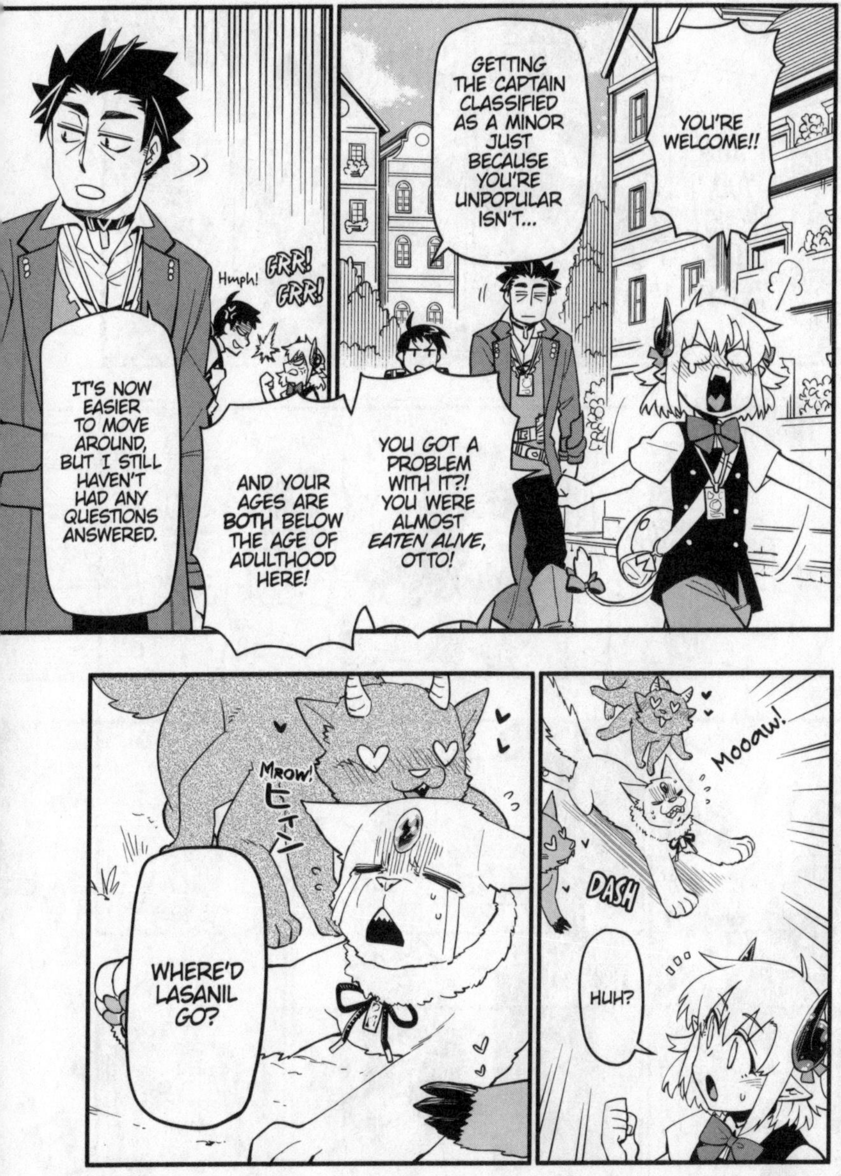
GETTING THE CAPTAIN CLASSIFIED AS A MINOR JUST BECAUSE YOU'RE UNPOPULAR ISN'T...
YOU'RE WELCOME!!
YOU GOT A PROBLEM WITH IT?! YOU WERE ALMOST EATEN ALIVE, OTTO!
AND YOUR AGES ARE BOTH BELOW THE AGE OF ADULTHOOD HERE!
GRR! GRR!
Humph!
IT'S NOW EASIER TO MOVE AROUND, BUT I STILL HAVEN'T HAD ANY QUESTIONS ANSWERED.
Mooaw!
DASH
HUH?
MROW!
WHERE'D LASANIL GO?

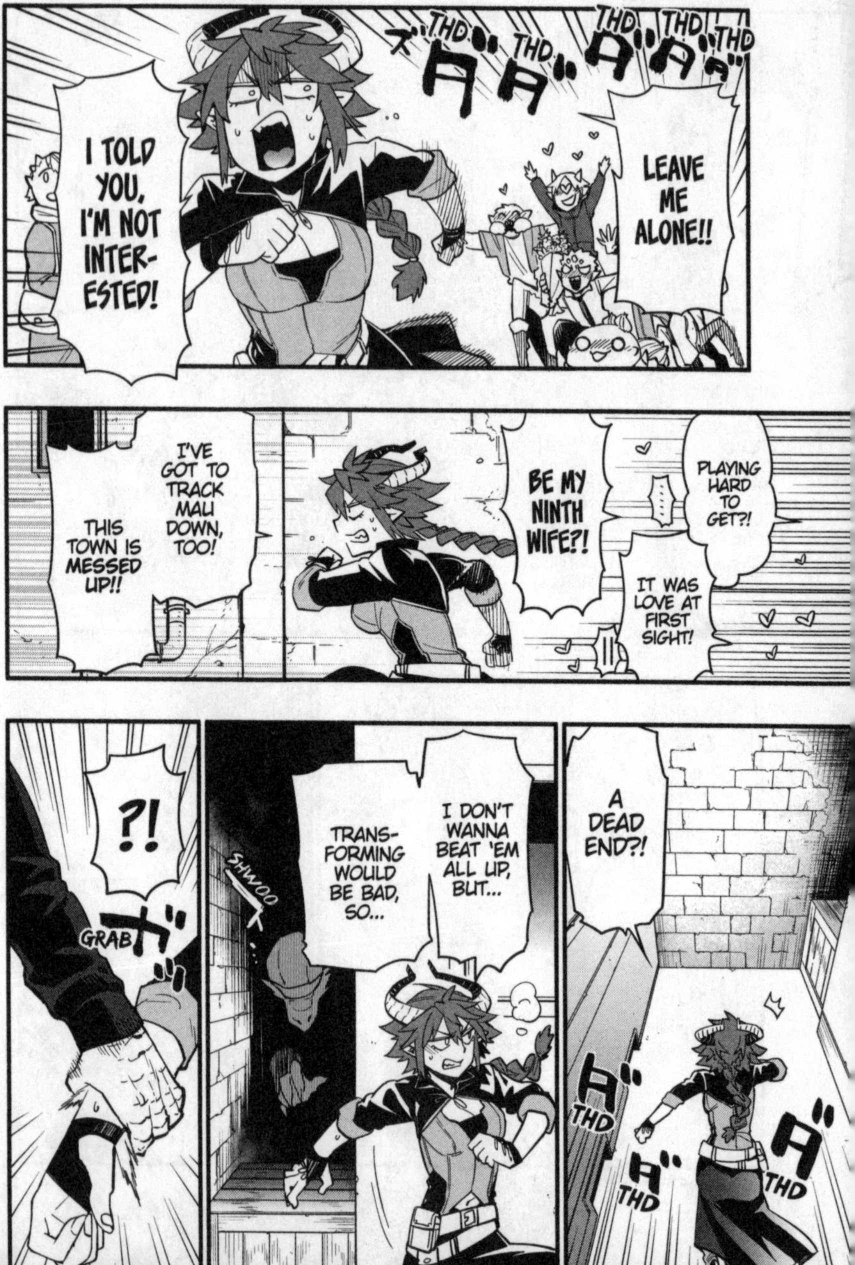
THD THD THD THD THD
LEAVE ME ALONE!!
I TOLD YOU, I'M NOT INTER-ESTED!
PLAYING HARD TO GET?!
IT WAS LOVE AT FIRST SIGHT!
BE MY NINTH WIFE?!
I'VE GOT TO TRACK MAU DOWN, TOO!
THIS TOWN IS MESSED UP!!
A DEAD END?!
THD THD THD
I DON'T WANNA BEAT 'EM ALL UP, BUT...
TRANS-FORMING WOULD BE BAD, SO...
SHWOO
?!
GRAB

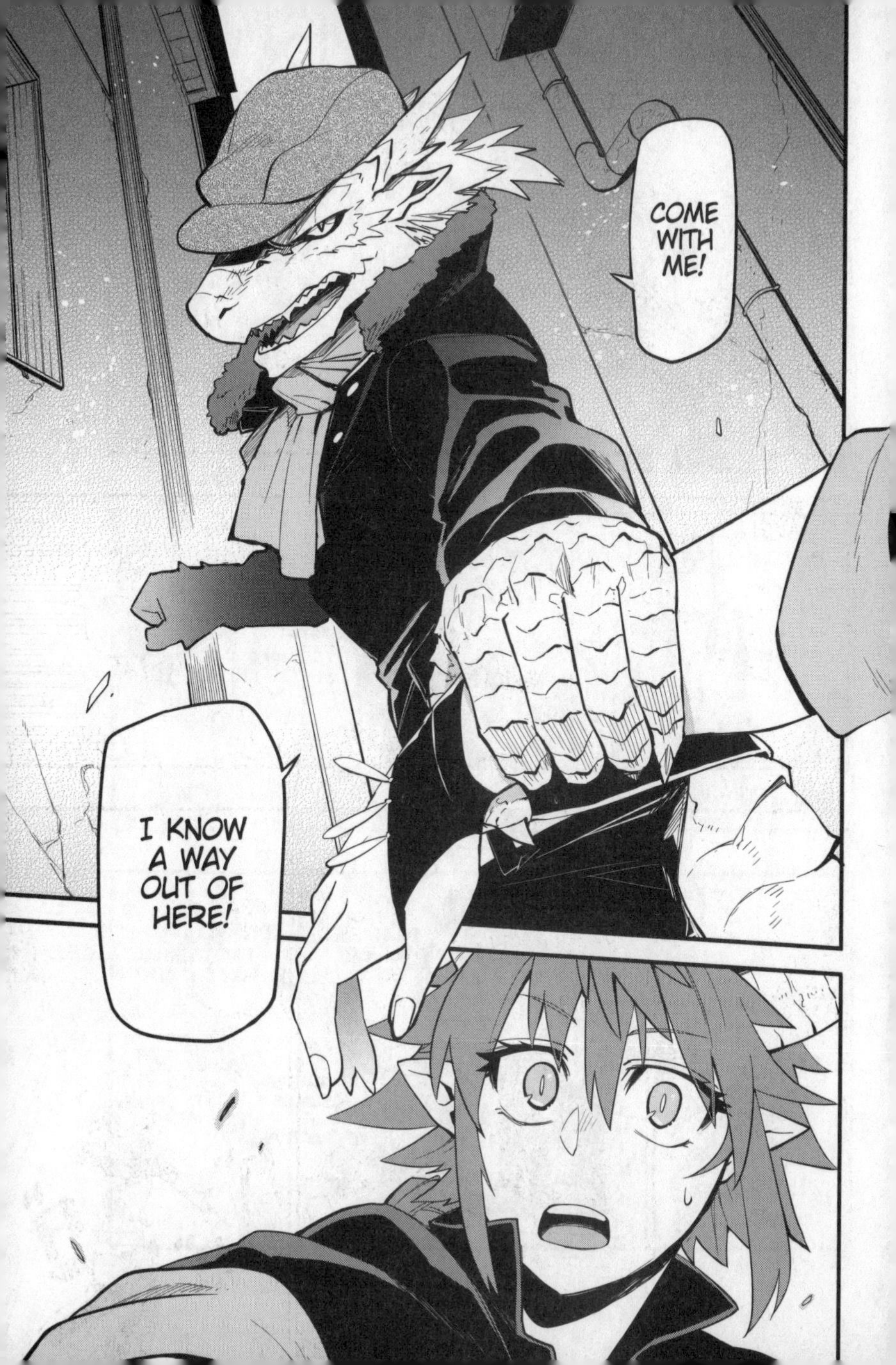
COME WITH ME!
I KNOW A WAY OUT OF HERE!

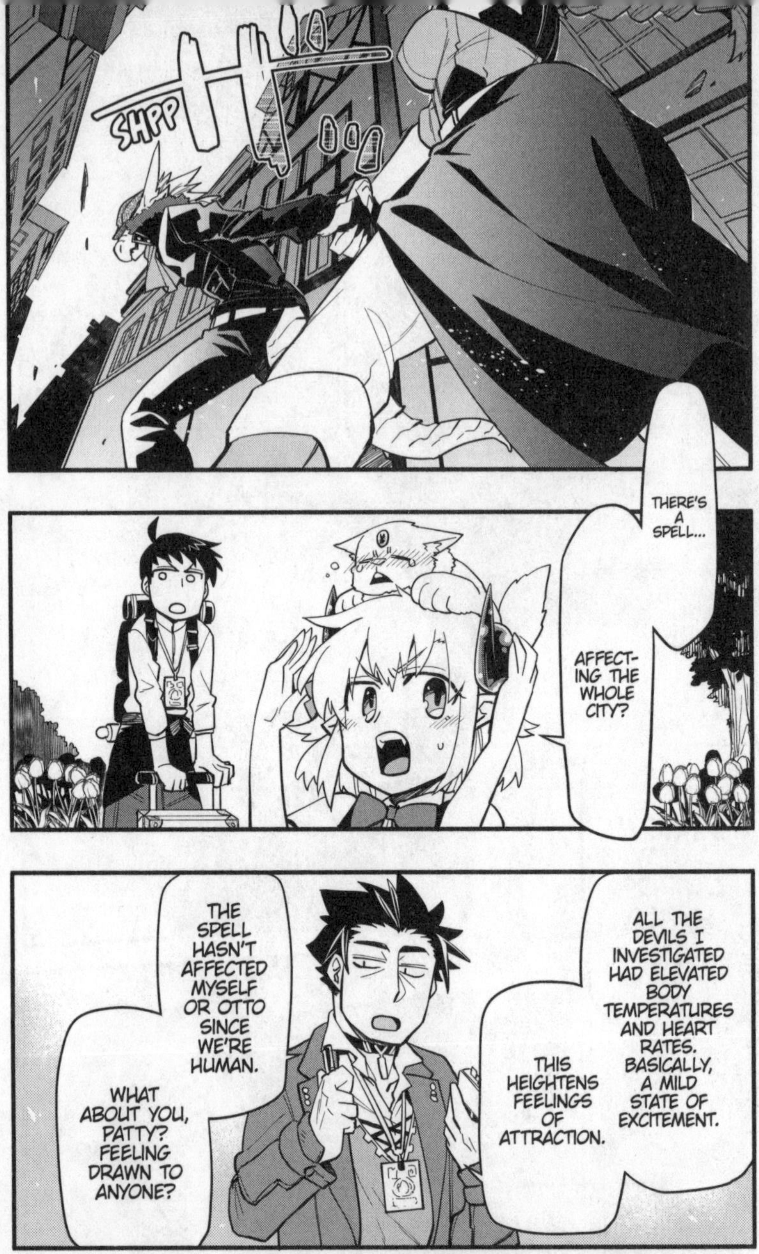
SHPP
THERE'S A SPELL...
AFFECTING THE WHOLE CITY?
ALL THE DEVILS I INVESTIGATED HAD ELEVATED BODY TEMPERATURES AND HEART RATES. BASICALLY, A MILD STATE OF EXCITEMENT.
THIS HEIGHTENS FEELINGS OF ATTRACTION.
THE SPELL HASN'T AFFECTED MYSELF OR OTTO SINCE WE'RE HUMAN.
WHAT ABOUT YOU, PATTY? FEELING DRAWN TO ANYONE?

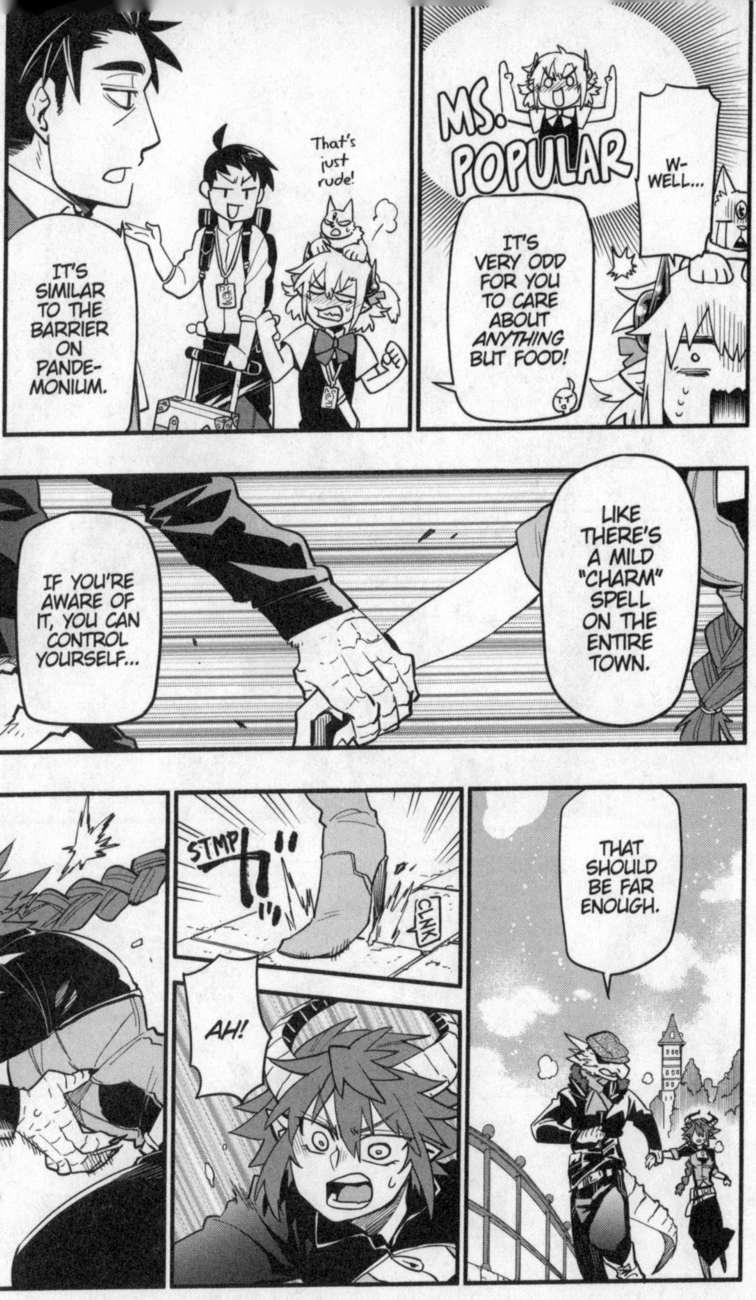
MS. POPULAR
IT'S VERY ODD FOR YOU TO CARE ABOUT *ANYTHING* BUT FOOD!
W-WELL...
IT'S SIMILAR TO THE BARRIER ON PANDEMONIUM.
That's just rude!
LIKE THERE'S A MILD "CHARM" SPELL ON THE ENTIRE TOWN.
IF YOU'RE AWARE OF IT, YOU CAN CONTROL YOURSELF...
THAT SHOULD BE FAR ENOUGH.
STMP
CLNK
AH!

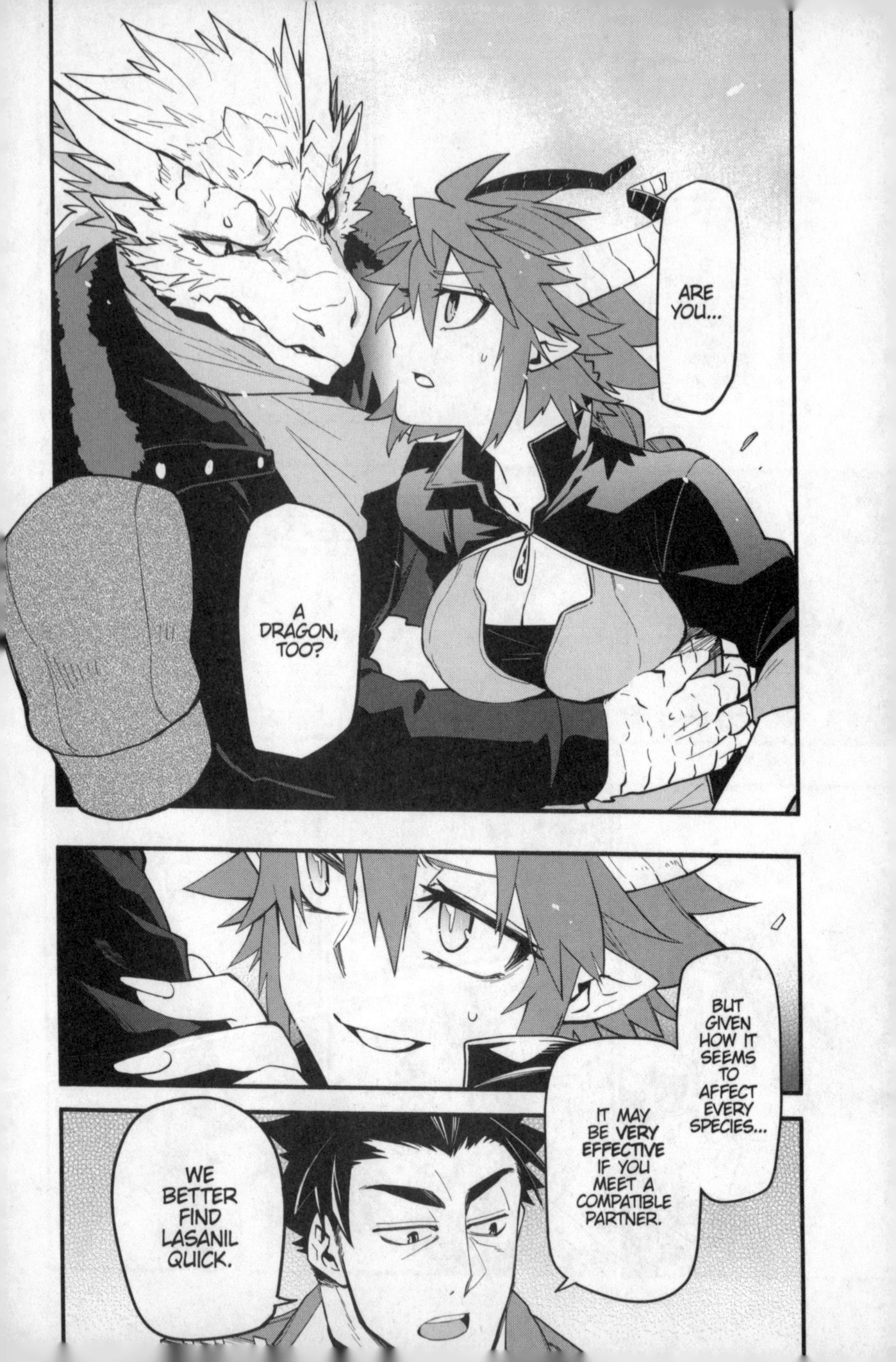
ARE YOU...
A DRAGON, TOO?
BUT GIVEN HOW IT SEEMS TO AFFECT EVERY SPECIES...
IT MAY BE VERY EFFECTIVE IF YOU MEET A COMPATIBLE PARTNER.
WE BETTER FIND LASANIL QUICK.

Sorry For My Familiar

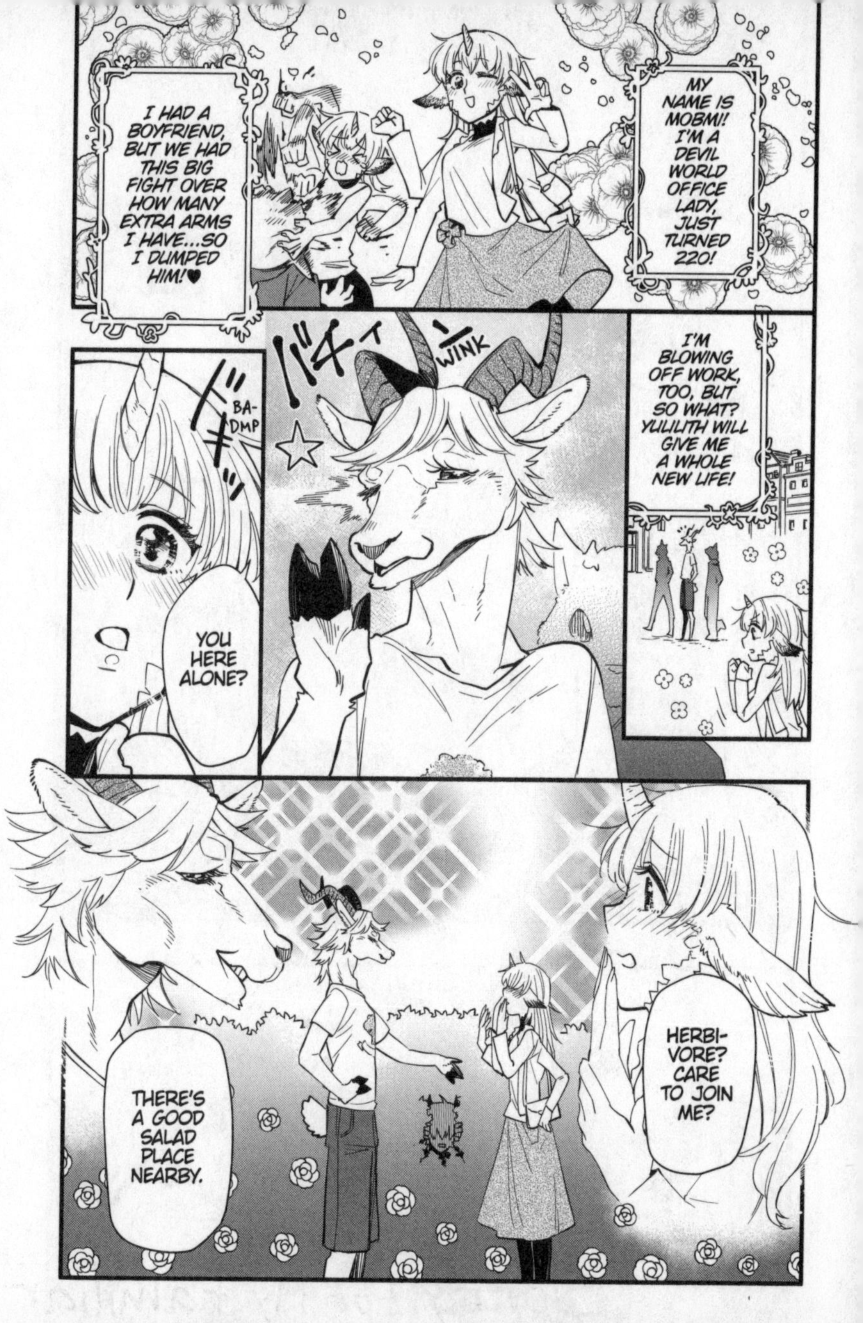
MY NAME IS MOBMI! I'M A DEVIL WORLD OFFICE LADY, JUST TURNED 220!
I HAD A BOYFRIEND, BUT WE HAD THIS BIG FIGHT OVER HOW MANY EXTRA ARMS I HAVE...SO I DUMPED HIM!♥
I'M BLOWING OFF WORK, TOO, BUT SO WHAT? YULILITH WILL GIVE ME A WHOLE NEW LIFE!
WINK
BA-DMP
YOU HERE ALONE?
HERBI-VORE? CARE TO JOIN ME?
THERE'S A GOOD SALAD PLACE NEARBY.

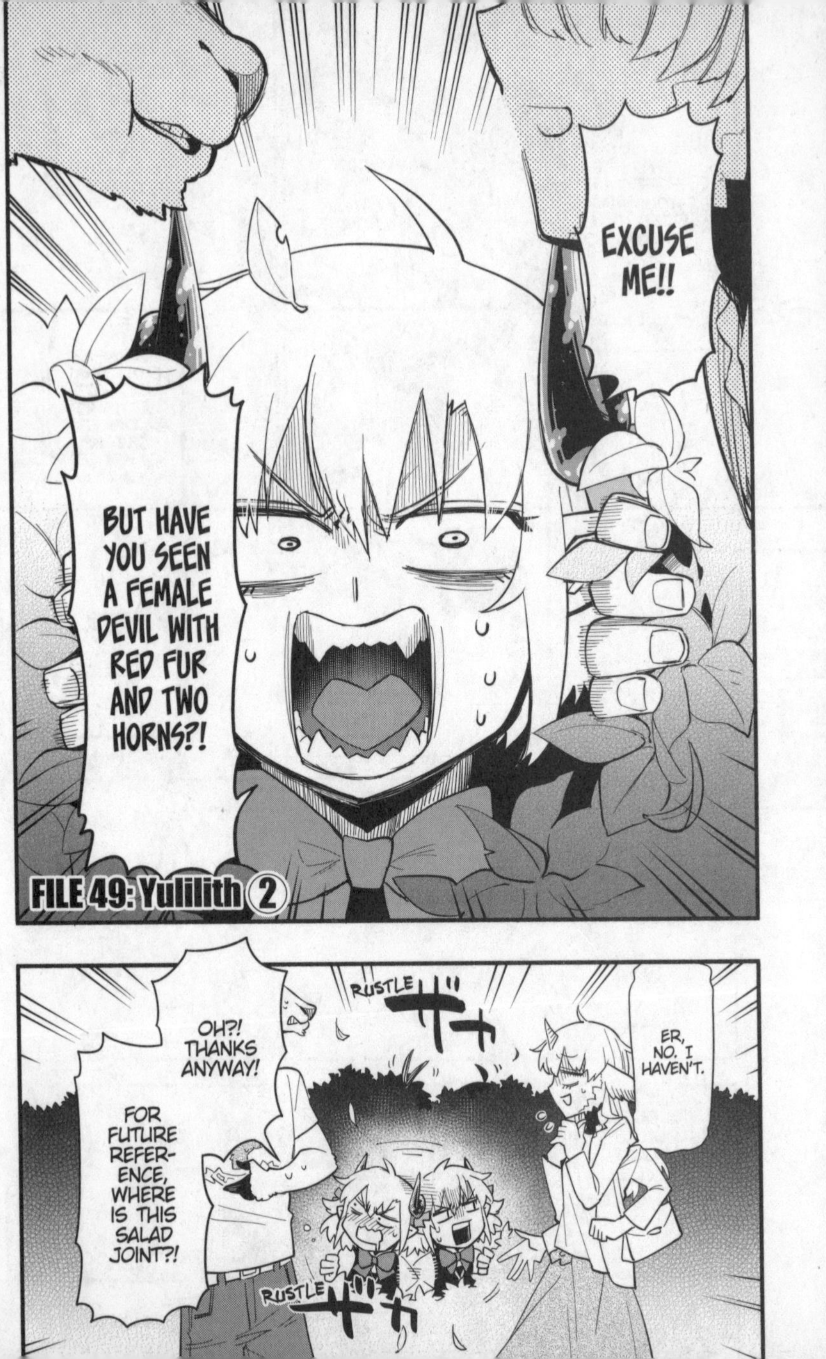
EXCUSE ME!!
BUT HAVE YOU SEEN A FEMALE DEVIL WITH RED FUR AND TWO HORNS?!
FILE 49: Yulilith ②
ER, NO. I HAVEN'T.
RUSTLE
OH?! THANKS ANYWAY!
FOR FUTURE REFERENCE, WHERE IS THIS SALAD JOINT?!
RUSTLE

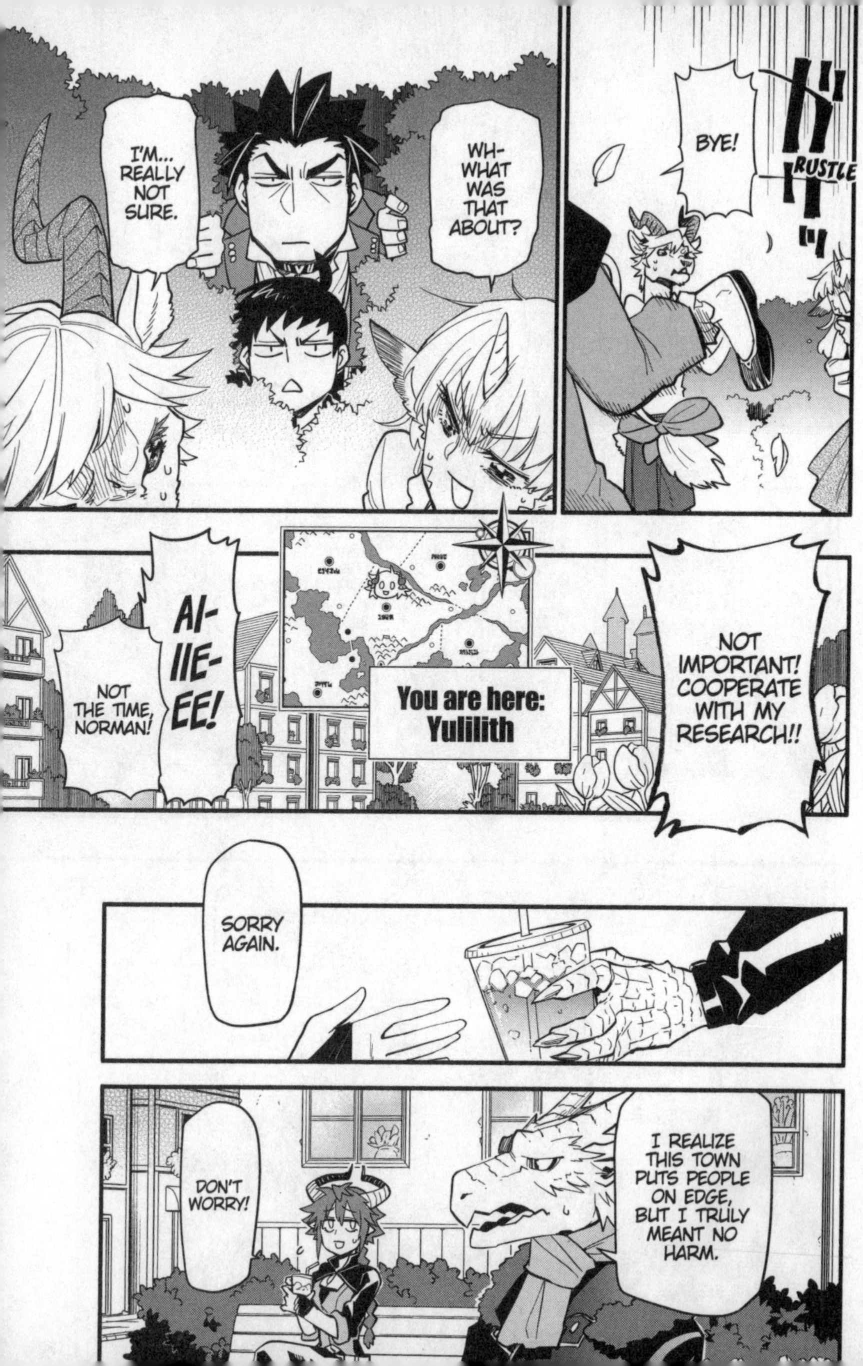
BYE!
RUSTLE
WH- WHAT WAS THAT ABOUT?
I'M... REALLY NOT SURE.
NOT IMPORTANT! COOPERATE WITH MY RESEARCH!!
You are here: Yulilith
AI- IIE- EE!
NOT THE TIME, NORMAN!
SORRY AGAIN.
I REALIZE THIS TOWN PUTS PEOPLE ON EDGE, BUT I TRULY MEANT NO HARM.
DON'T WORRY!

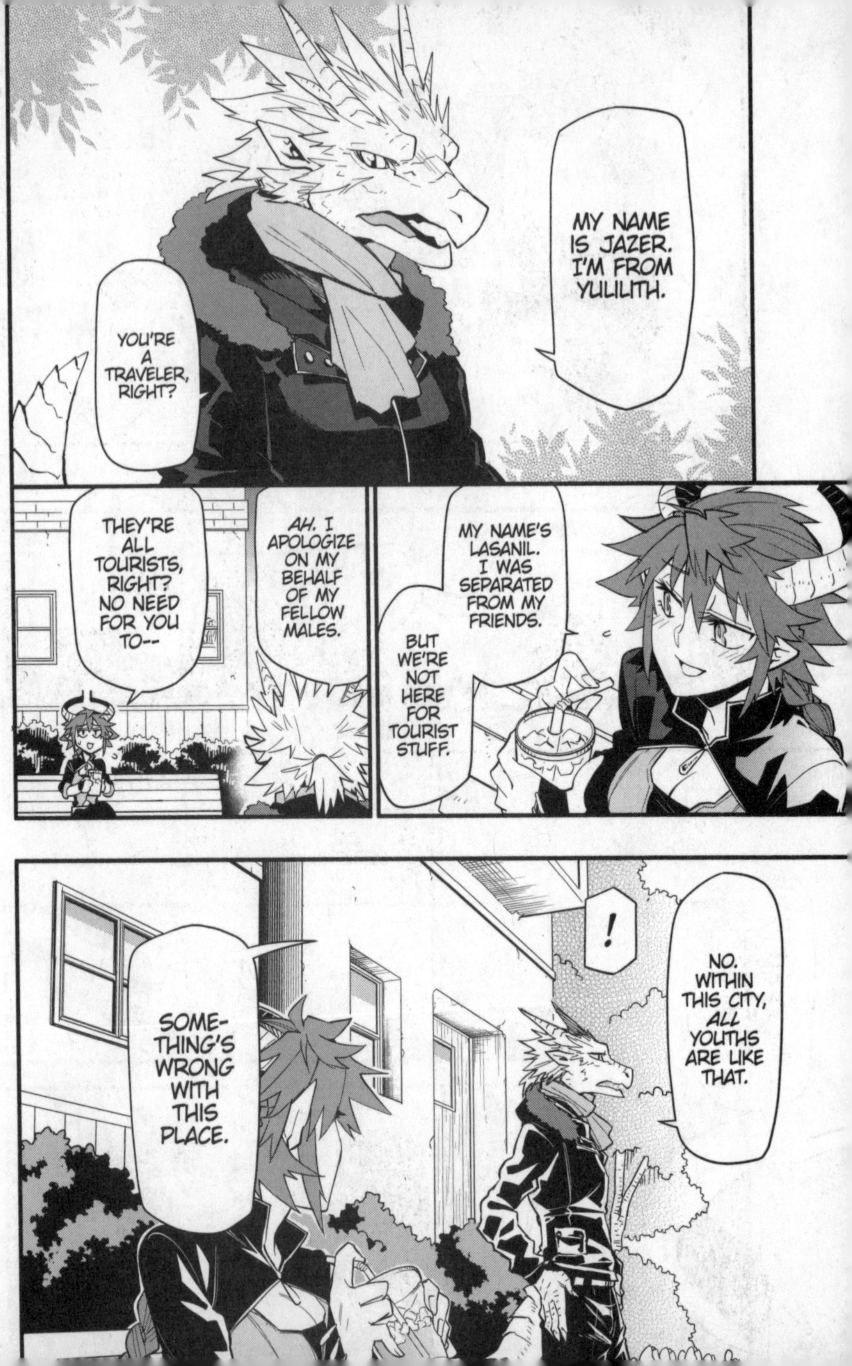
MY NAME IS JAZER. I'M FROM YULILITH.
YOU'RE A TRAVELER, RIGHT?
MY NAME'S LASANIL. I WAS SEPARATED FROM MY FRIENDS.
BUT WE'RE NOT HERE FOR TOURIST STUFF.
AH. I APOLOGIZE ON MY BEHALF OF MY FELLOW MALES.
THEY'RE ALL TOURISTS, RIGHT? NO NEED FOR YOU TO--
!
NO. WITHIN THIS CITY, ALL YOUTHS ARE LIKE THAT.
SOME-THING'S WRONG WITH THIS PLACE.

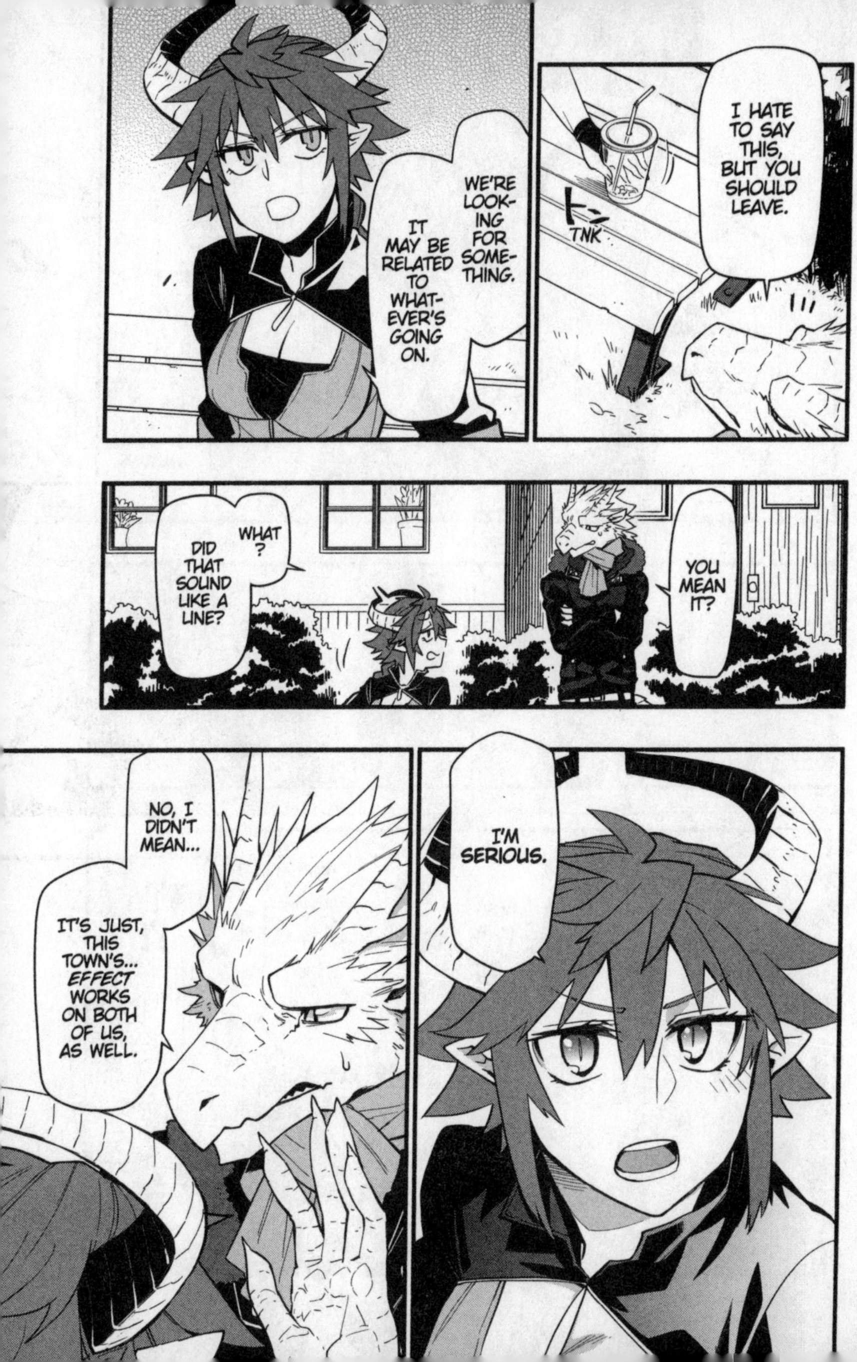
I HATE TO SAY THIS, BUT YOU SHOULD LEAVE.
トン
TNK
WE'RE LOOKING FOR SOMETHING.
IT MAY BE RELATED TO WHATEVER'S GOING ON.
YOU MEAN IT?
WHAT? DID THAT SOUND LIKE A LINE?
I'M SERIOUS.
NO, I DIDN'T MEAN...
IT'S JUST, THIS TOWN'S... *EFFECT* WORKS ON BOTH OF US, AS WELL.

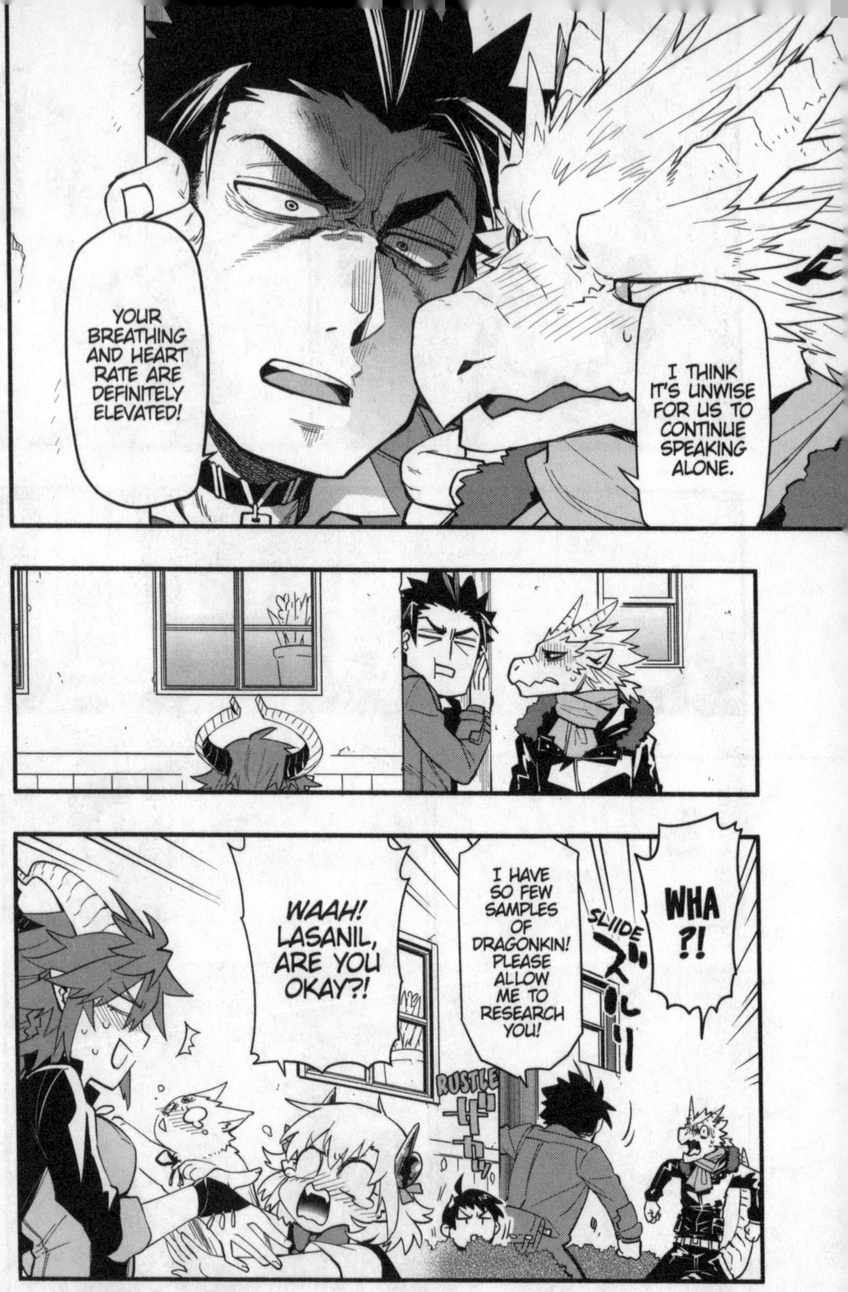
I THINK IT'S UNWISE FOR US TO CONTINUE SPEAKING ALONE.
YOUR BREATHING AND HEART RATE ARE DEFINITELY ELEVATED!
WHA ?!
SLIIDE
I HAVE SO FEW SAMPLES OF DRAGONKIN! PLEASE ALLOW ME TO RESEARCH YOU!
WAAH! LASANIL, ARE YOU OKAY?!
RUSTLE

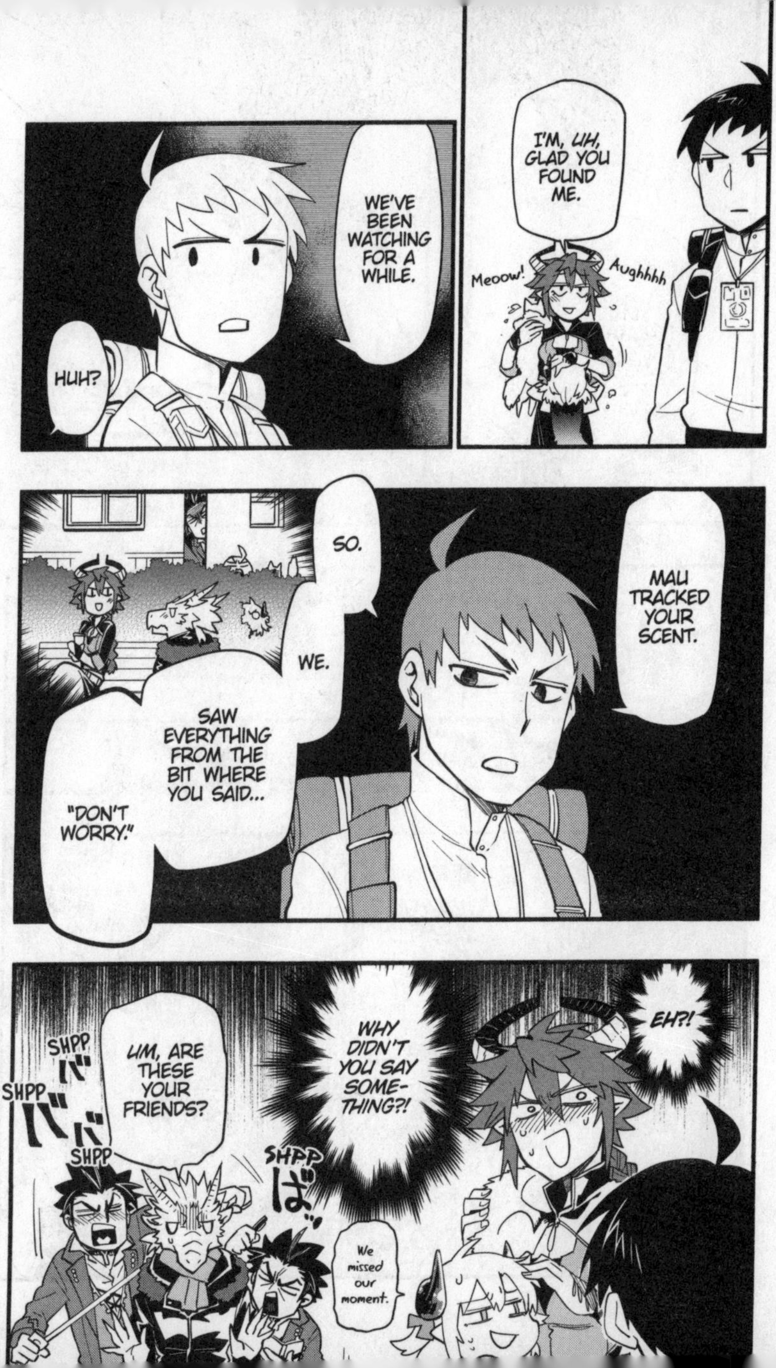
I'M, UH, GLAD YOU FOUND ME.
Meoow!
Aughhhh
WE'VE BEEN WATCHING FOR A WHILE.
HUH?
MAU TRACKED YOUR SCENT.
SO.
WE.
SAW EVERYTHING FROM THE BIT WHERE YOU SAID...
"DON'T WORRY."
EH?!
WHY DIDN'T YOU SAY SOME-THING?!
We missed our moment.
SHPP
ば
UM, ARE THESE YOUR FRIENDS?
SHPP
バ
SHPP
バ
SHPP
バ

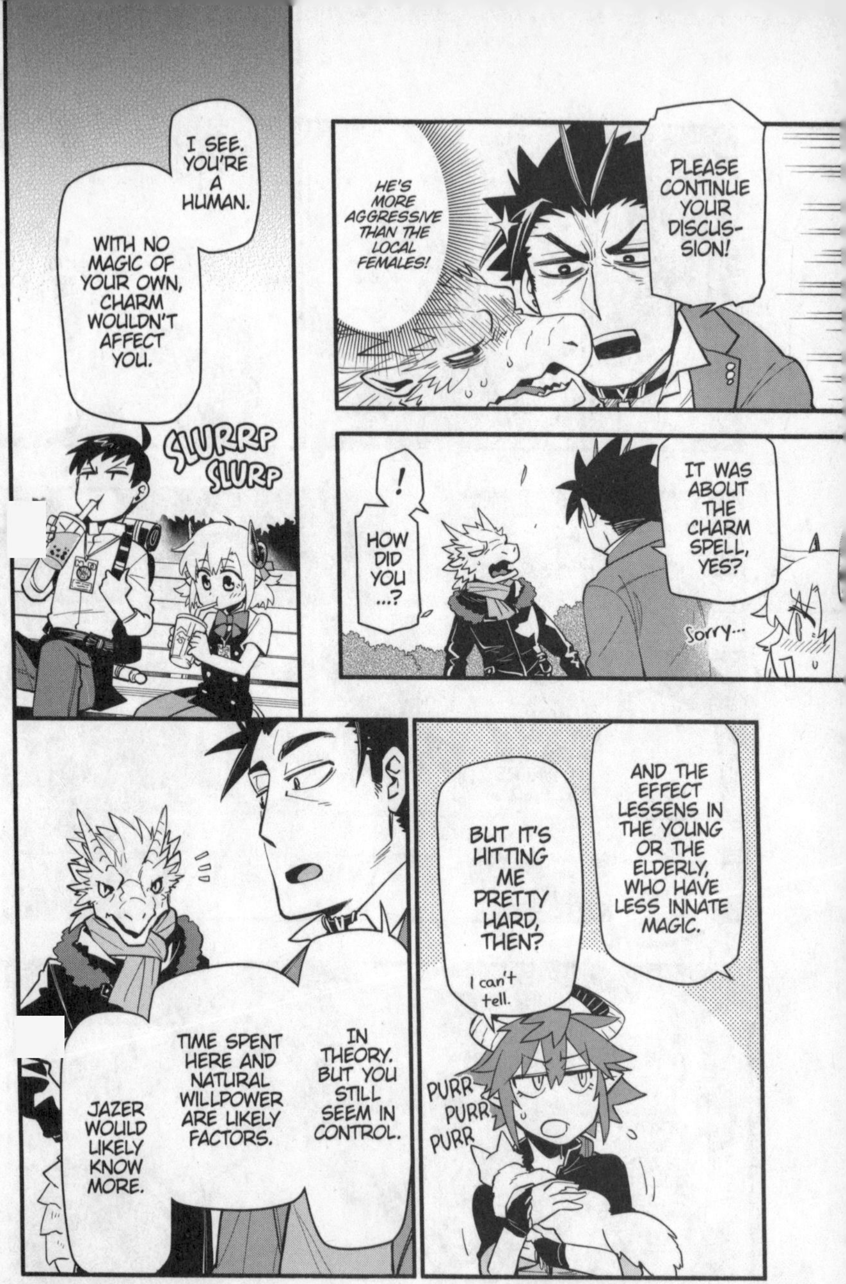
PLEASE CONTINUE YOUR DISCUS-SION!
HE'S MORE AGGRESSIVE THAN THE LOCAL FEMALES!
IT WAS ABOUT THE CHARM SPELL, YES?
!
HOW DID YOU ...?
Sorry...
I SEE. YOU'RE A HUMAN.
WITH NO MAGIC OF YOUR OWN, CHARM WOULDN'T AFFECT YOU.
SLURRP SLURP
AND THE EFFECT LESSENS IN THE YOUNG OR THE ELDERLY, WHO HAVE LESS INNATE MAGIC.
BUT IT'S HITTING ME PRETTY HARD, THEN?
I can't tell.
PURR PURR PURR
IN THEORY. BUT YOU STILL SEEM IN CONTROL.
TIME SPENT HERE AND NATURAL WILLPOWER ARE LIKELY FACTORS.
JAZER WOULD LIKELY KNOW MORE.

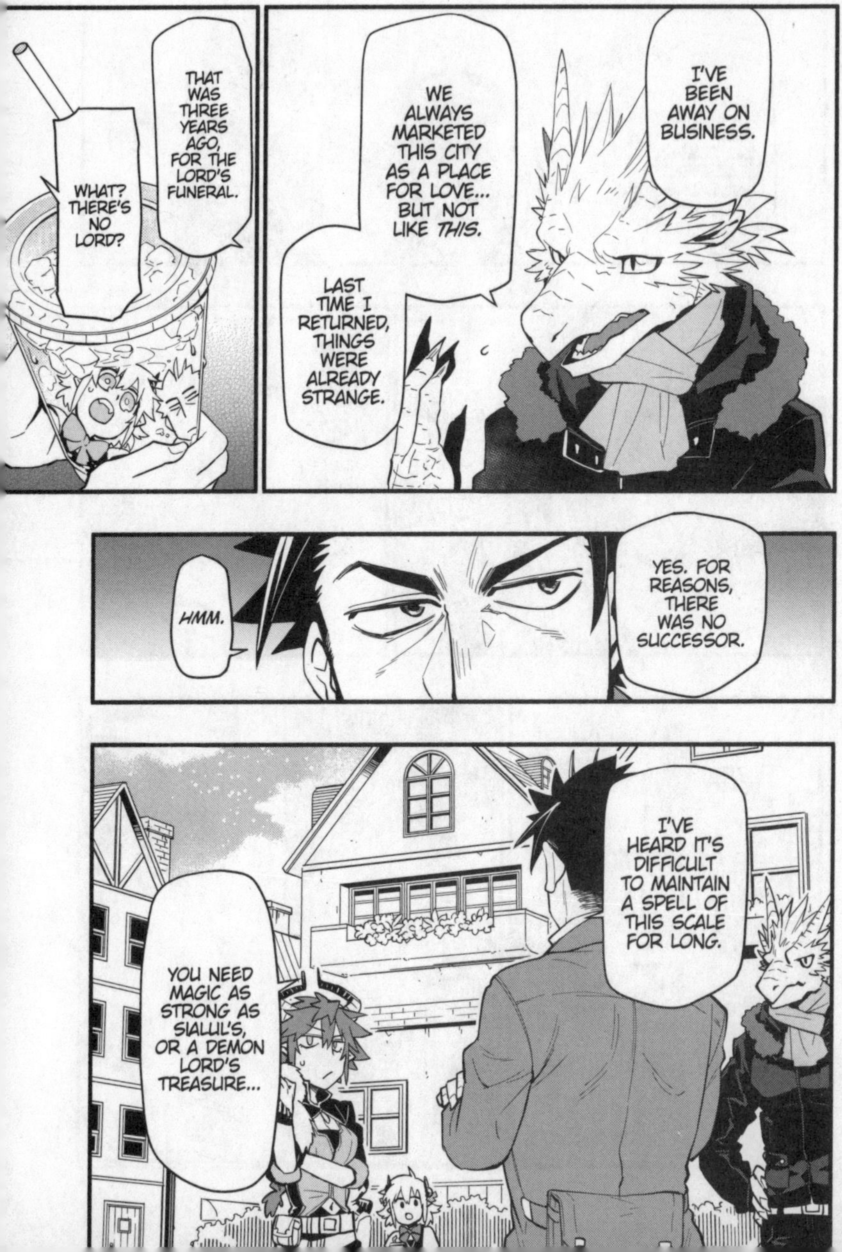
I'VE BEEN AWAY ON BUSINESS.
WE ALWAYS MARKETED THIS CITY AS A PLACE FOR LOVE... BUT NOT LIKE *THIS*.
LAST TIME I RETURNED, THINGS WERE ALREADY STRANGE.
THAT WAS THREE YEARS AGO, FOR THE LORD'S FUNERAL.
WHAT? THERE'S NO LORD?
YES. FOR REASONS, THERE WAS NO SUCCESSOR.
HMM.
I'VE HEARD IT'S DIFFICULT TO MAINTAIN A SPELL OF THIS SCALE FOR LONG.
YOU NEED MAGIC AS STRONG AS SIALUL'S, OR A DEMON LORD'S TREASURE...

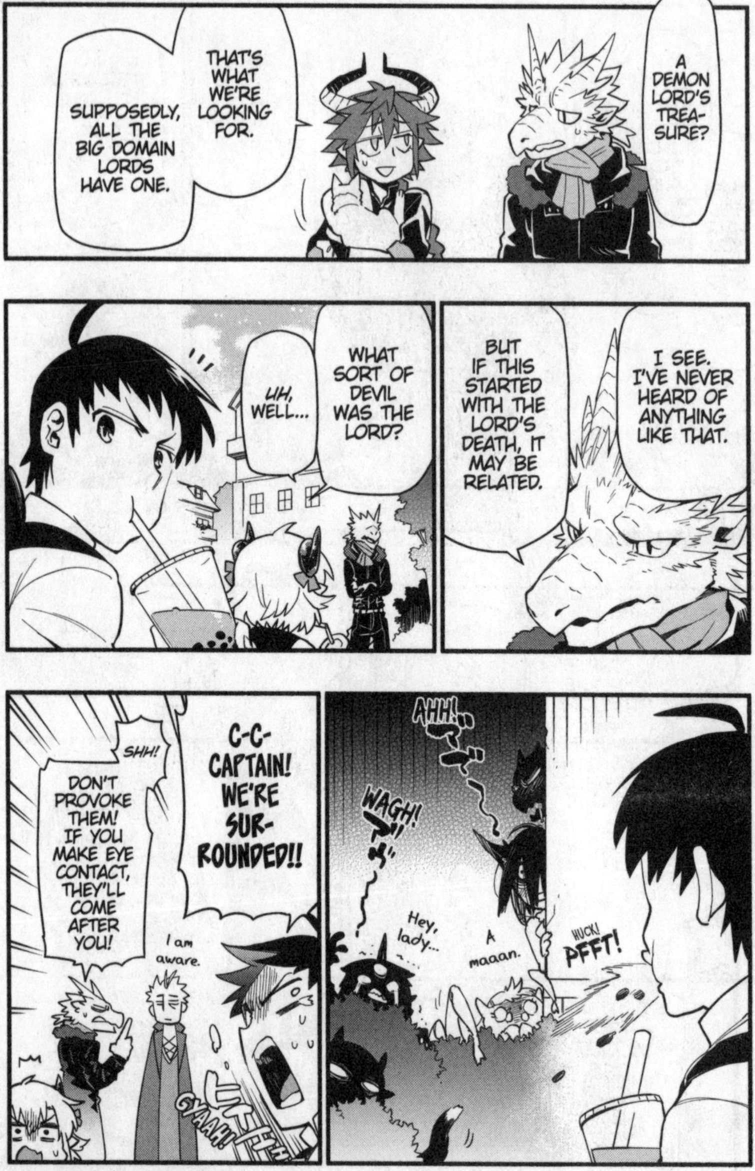
A DEMON LORD'S TREA-SURE?
THAT'S WHAT WE'RE LOOKING FOR.
SUPPOSEDLY, ALL THE BIG DOMAIN LORDS HAVE ONE.
I SEE. I'VE NEVER HEARD OF ANYTHING LIKE THAT.
BUT IF THIS STARTED WITH THE LORD'S DEATH, IT MAY BE RELATED.
WHAT SORT OF DEVIL WAS THE LORD?
UH, WELL...
AHH!
WAGH!
Hey, lady...
A maaan.
HUCK!
PFFT!
C-C-CAPTAIN! WE'RE SUR-ROUNDED!!
SHH!
DON'T PROVOKE THEM! IF YOU MAKE EYE CONTACT, THEY'LL COME AFTER YOU!
I am aware.
GYAAH!

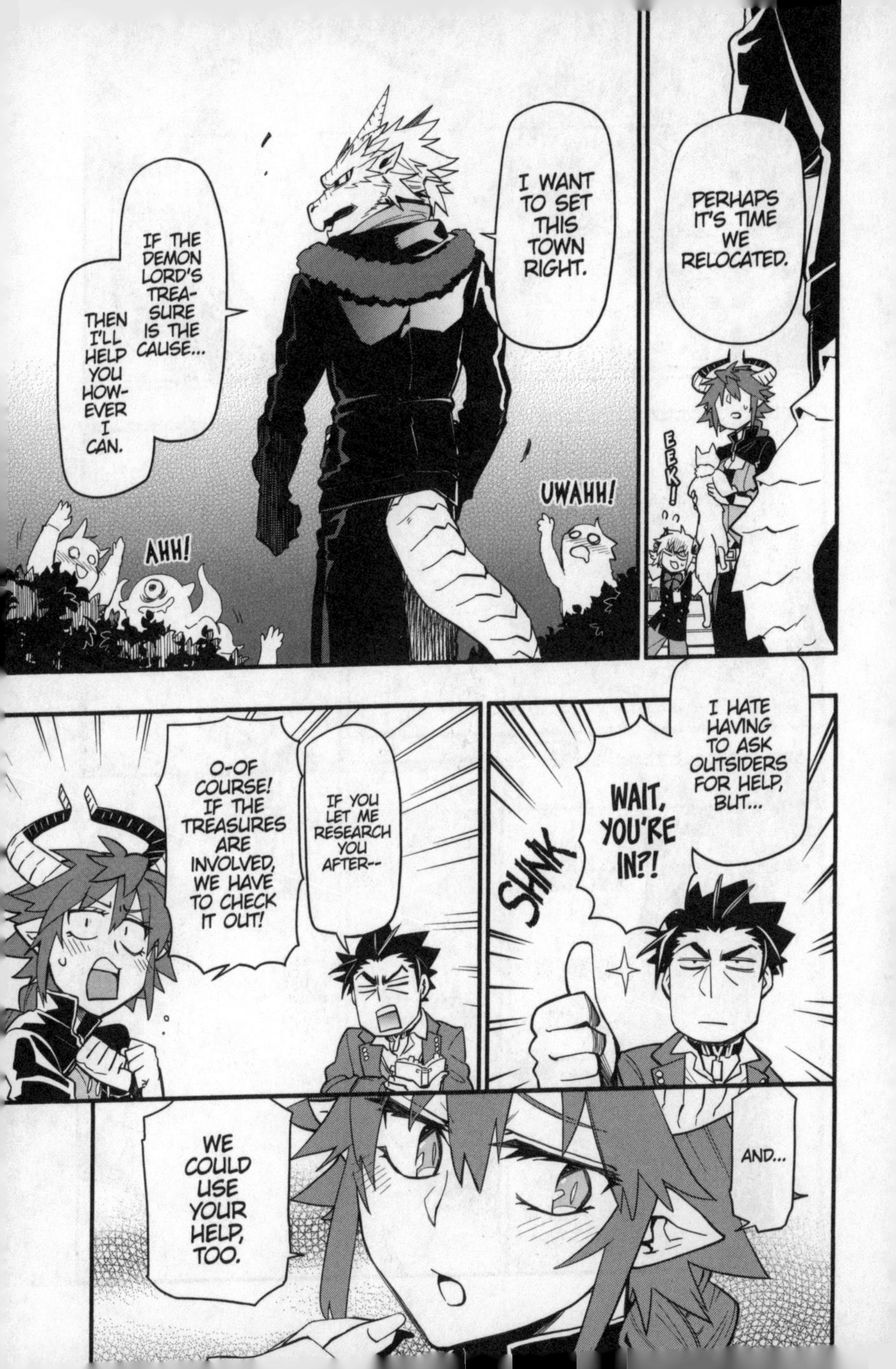
PERHAPS IT'S TIME WE RELOCATED.
EEK!
I WANT TO SET THIS TOWN RIGHT.
UWAHH!
IF THE DEMON LORD'S TREA-SURE IS THE CAUSE...
THEN I'LL HELP YOU HOW-EVER I CAN.
AHH!
I HATE HAVING TO ASK OUTSIDERS FOR HELP, BUT...
WAIT, YOU'RE IN?!
SHNK
IF YOU LET ME RESEARCH YOU AFTER--
O-OF COURSE! IF THE TREASURES ARE INVOLVED, WE HAVE TO CHECK IT OUT!
AND...
WE COULD USE YOUR HELP, TOO.

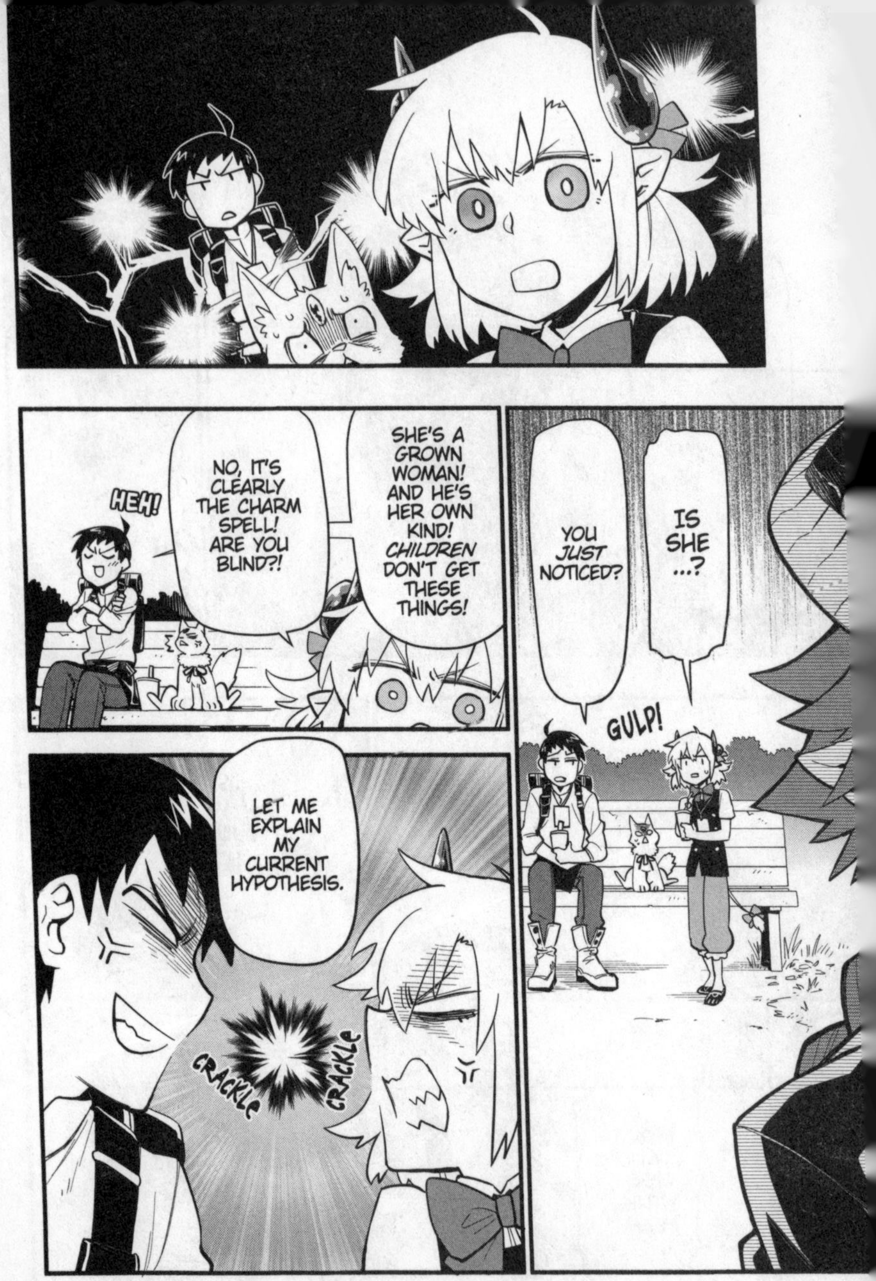
IS SHE ...?
YOU JUST NOTICED?
GULP!
SHE'S A GROWN WOMAN! AND HE'S HER OWN KIND! CHILDREN DON'T GET THESE THINGS!
NO, IT'S CLEARLY THE CHARM SPELL! ARE YOU BLIND?!
HEH!
LET ME EXPLAIN MY CURRENT HYPOTHESIS.
CRACKLE
CRACKLE

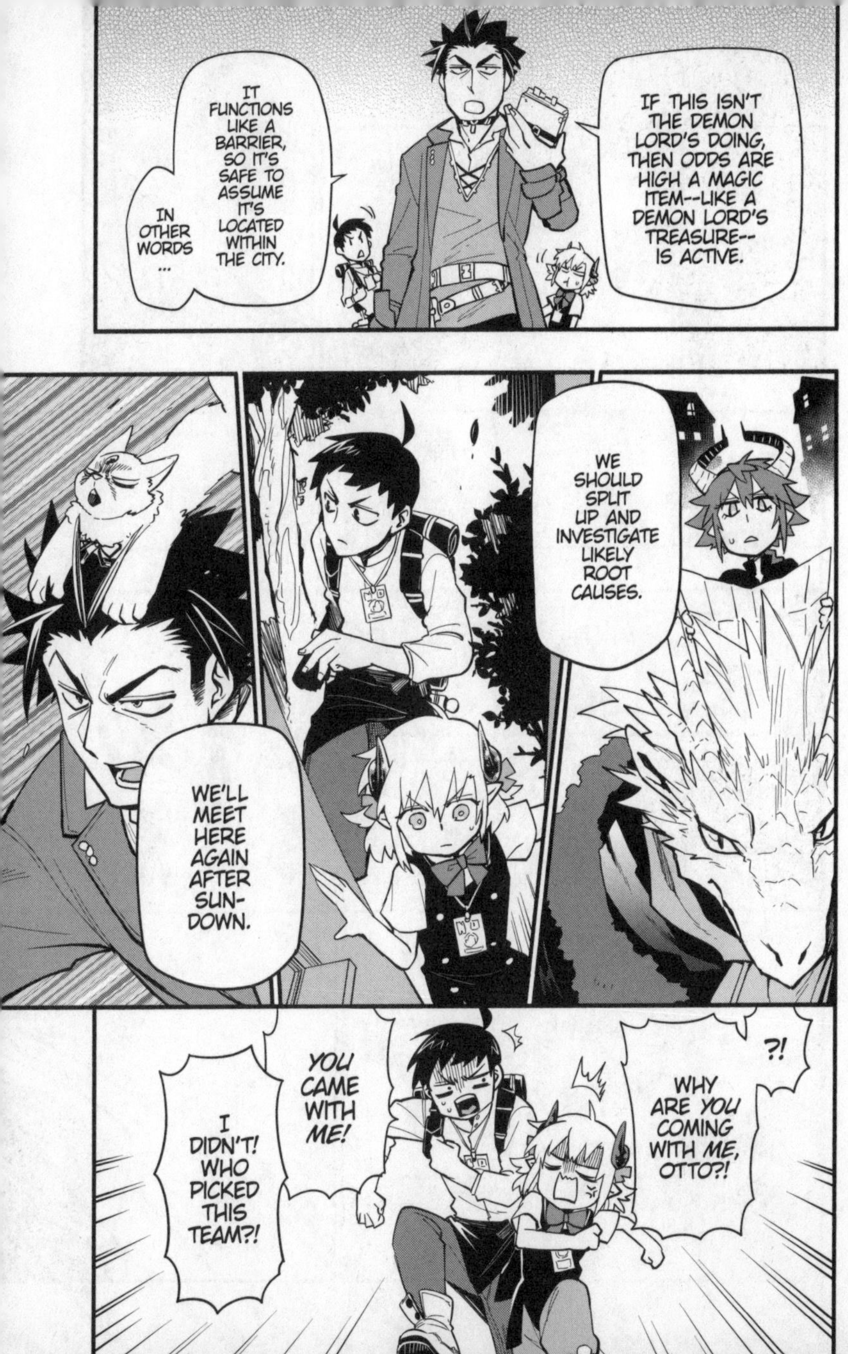
IF THIS ISN'T THE DEMON LORD'S DOING, THEN ODDS ARE HIGH A MAGIC ITEM--LIKE A DEMON LORD'S TREASURE--IS ACTIVE.
IT FUNCTIONS LIKE A BARRIER, SO IT'S SAFE TO ASSUME IT'S LOCATED WITHIN THE CITY.
IN OTHER WORDS...
WE SHOULD SPLIT UP AND INVESTIGATE LIKELY ROOT CAUSES.
WE'LL MEET HERE AGAIN AFTER SUN-DOWN.
?!
WHY ARE *YOU* COMING WITH *ME*, OTTO?!
YOU CAME WITH *ME*!
I DIDN'T! WHO PICKED THIS TEAM?!

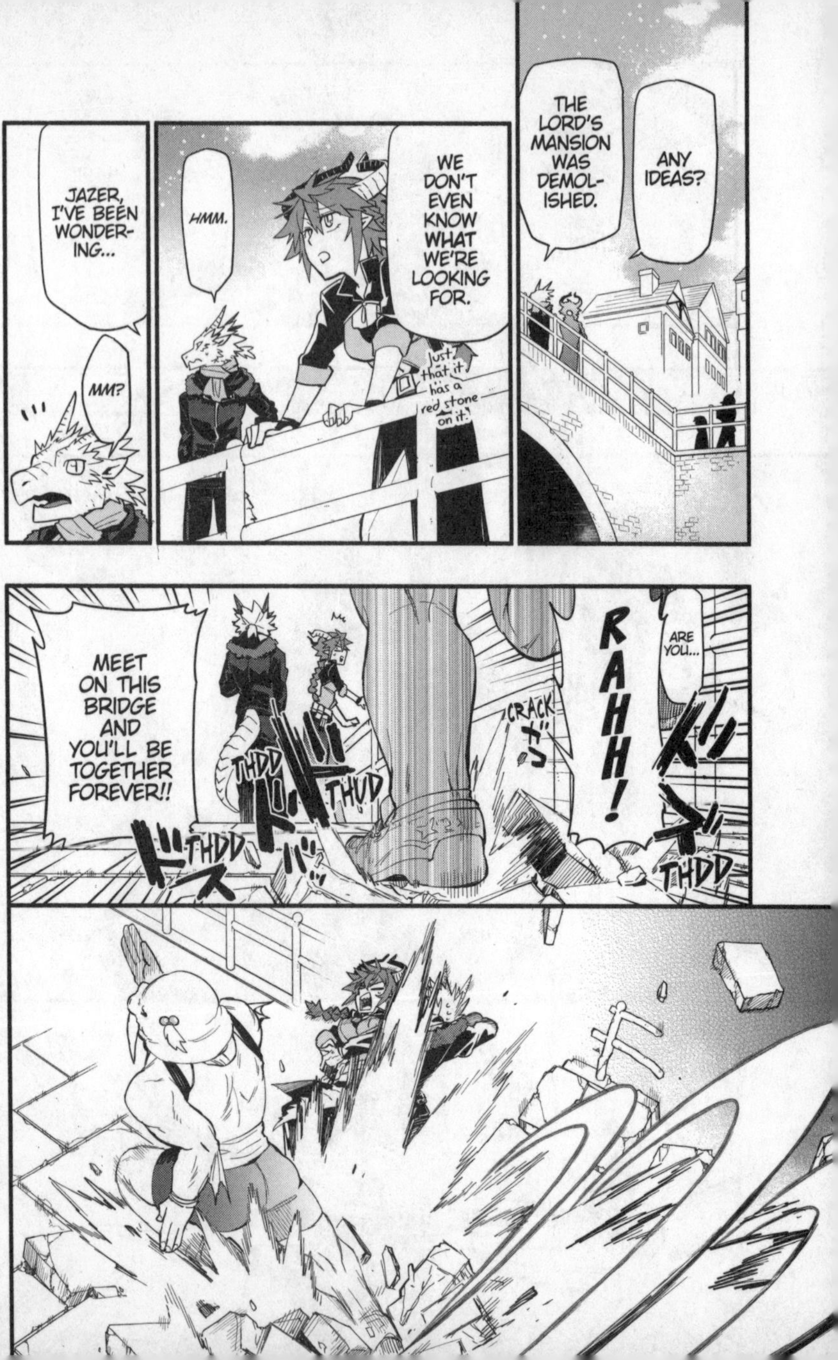
ANY IDEAS?
THE LORD'S MANSION WAS DEMOLISHED.
WE DON'T EVEN KNOW WHAT WE'RE LOOKING FOR.
Just that it has a red stone on it.
HMM.
JAZER, I'VE BEEN WONDERING...
MM?
ARE YOU...
RAHH!
THDD
CRACK
THUD
THDD
THDD
MEET ON THIS BRIDGE AND YOU'LL BE TOGETHER FOREVER!!

ザパァァァン
SPLAAAASH

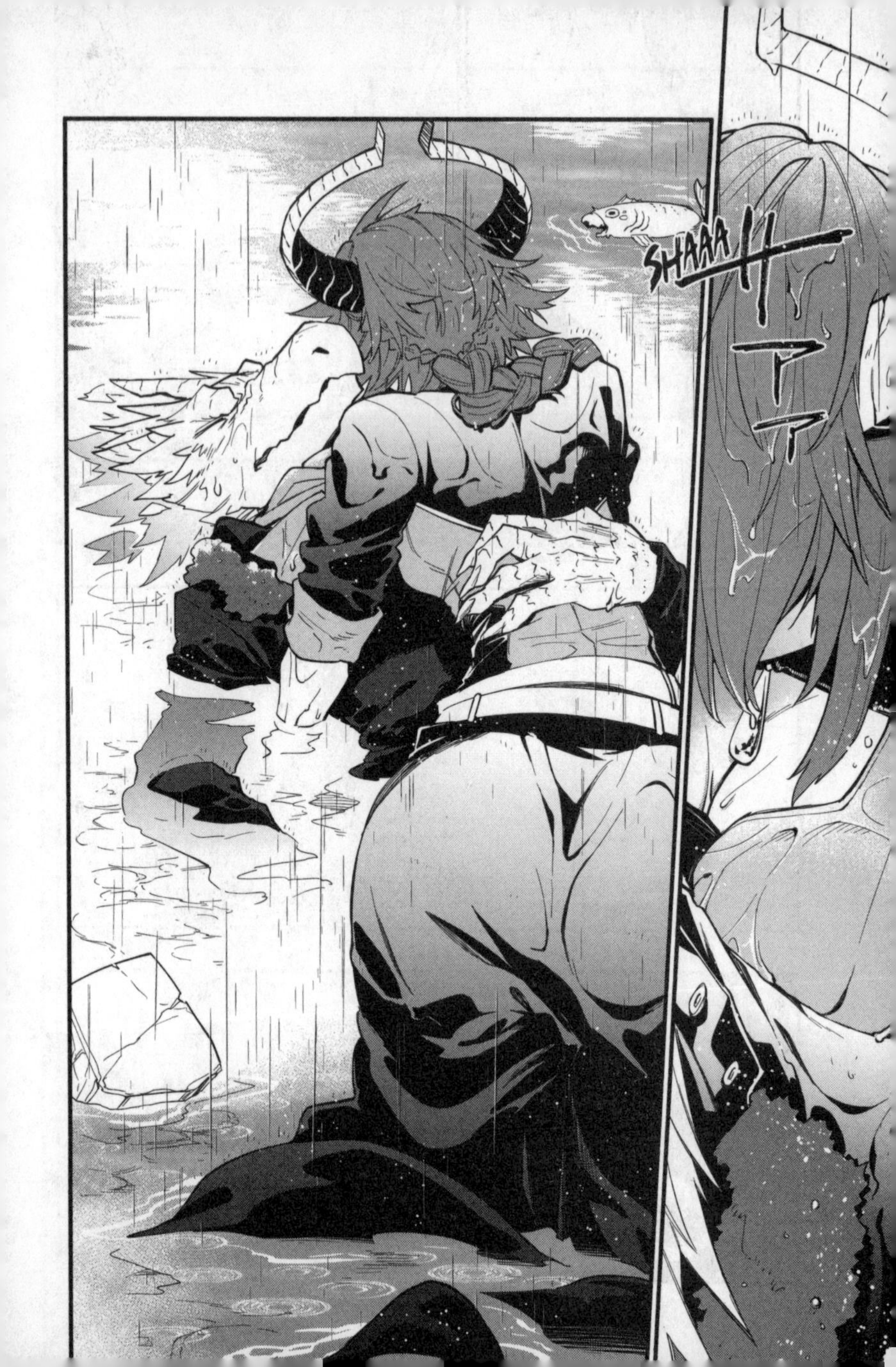
SHAAA
ザァァ

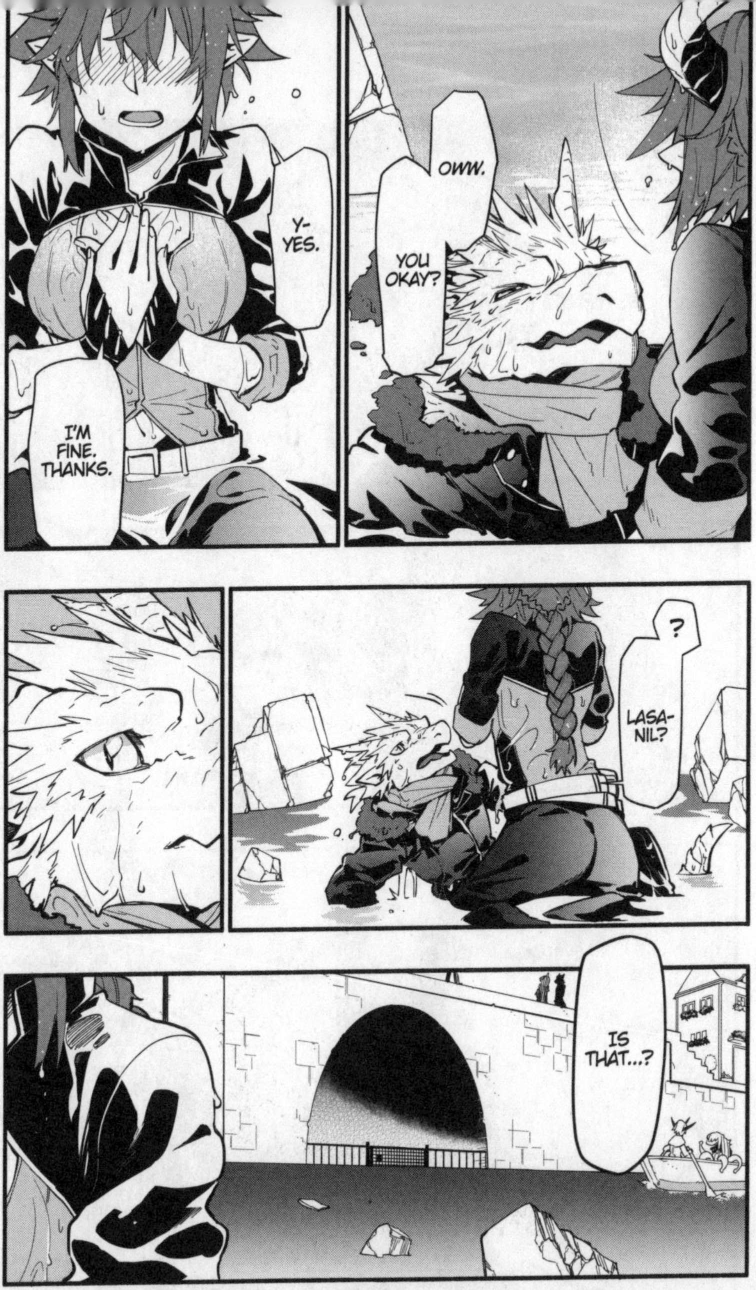
OWW.
YOU OKAY?
Y-YES.
I'M FINE. THANKS.
?
LASA-NIL?
IS THAT...?

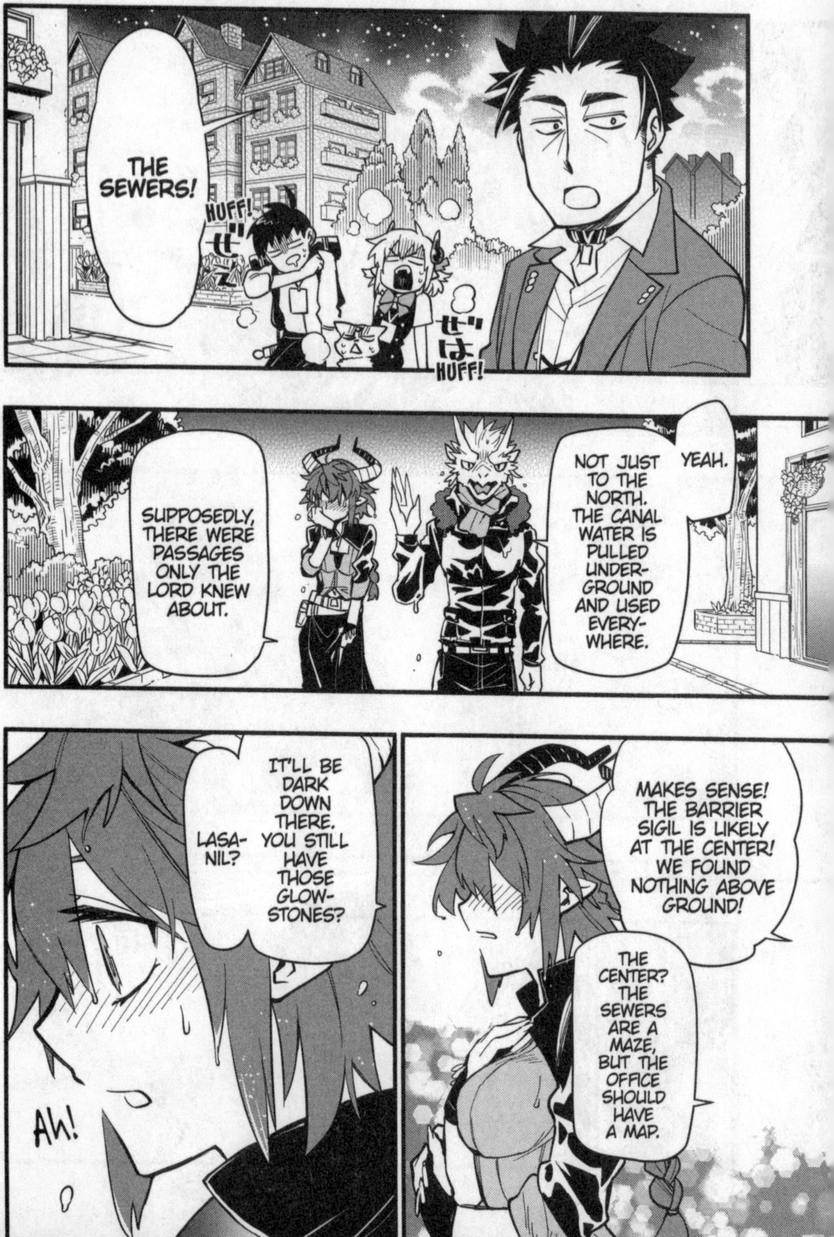
THE SEWERS!
HUFF!
ぜ
ぜは
HUFF!
YEAH.
NOT JUST TO THE NORTH. THE CANAL WATER IS PULLED UNDER-GROUND AND USED EVERY-WHERE.
SUPPOSEDLY, THERE WERE PASSAGES ONLY THE LORD KNEW ABOUT.
MAKES SENSE! THE BARRIER SIGIL IS LIKELY AT THE CENTER! WE FOUND NOTHING ABOVE GROUND!
THE CENTER? THE SEWERS ARE A MAZE, BUT THE OFFICE SHOULD HAVE A MAP.
IT'LL BE DARK DOWN THERE. YOU STILL HAVE THOSE GLOW-STONES?
LASA-NIL?
AH!

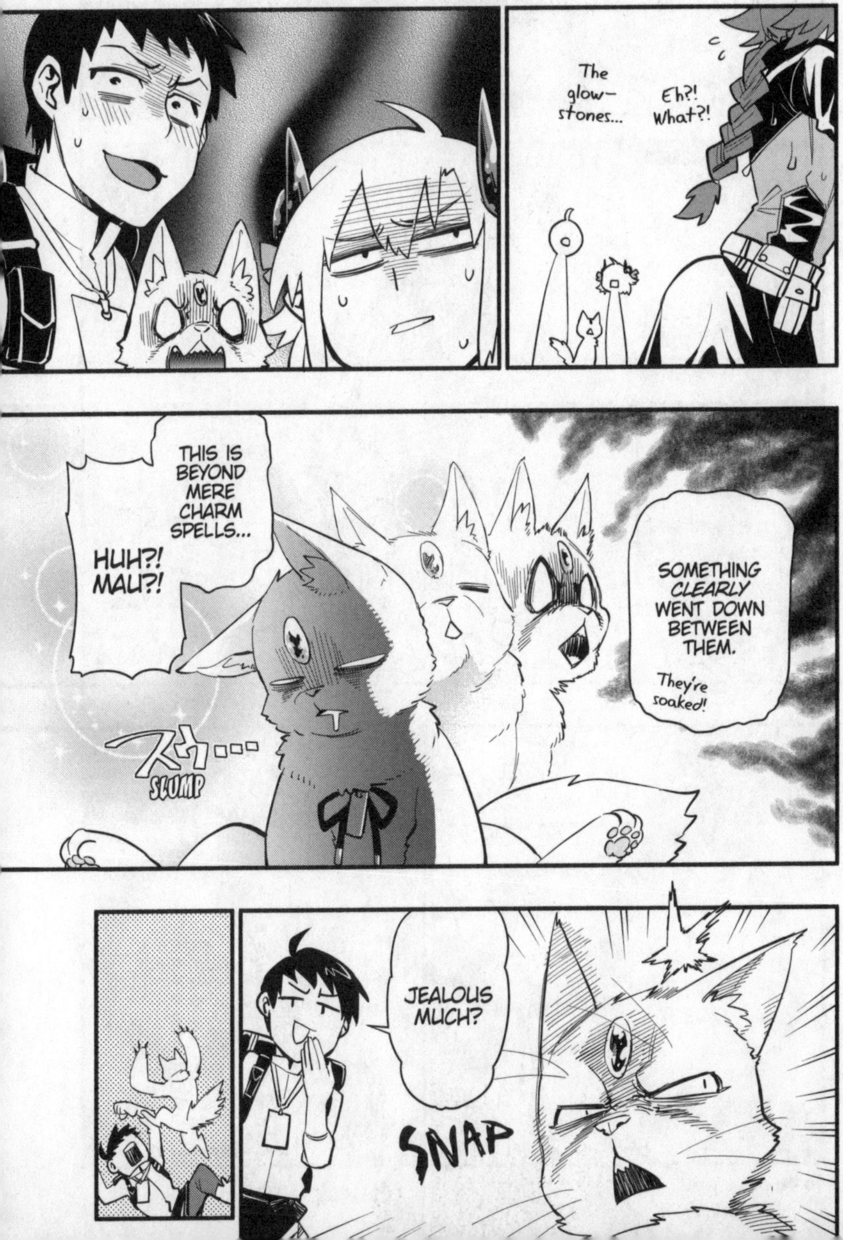
Eh?! What?!
The glow-stones...
SOMETHING CLEARLY WENT DOWN BETWEEN THEM.
They're soaked!
THIS IS BEYOND MERE CHARM SPELLS...
HUH?! MAU?!
スゥ…
SLUMP
JEALOUS MUCH?
SNAP

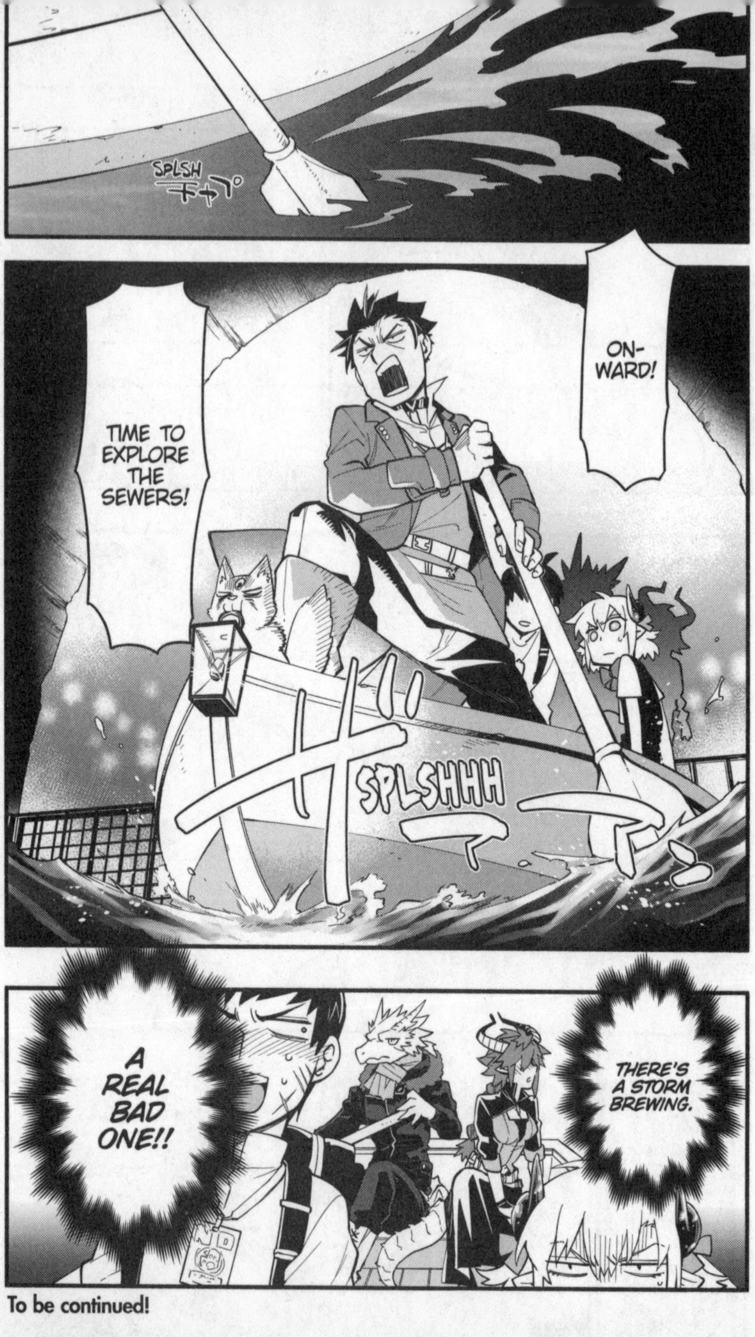
SPLSH
キャプ
ON-WARD!
TIME TO EXPLORE THE SEWERS!
SPLSHHH
THERE'S A STORM BREWING.
A REAL BAD ONE!!

To be continued!

AT THE AMUSEMENT PARK

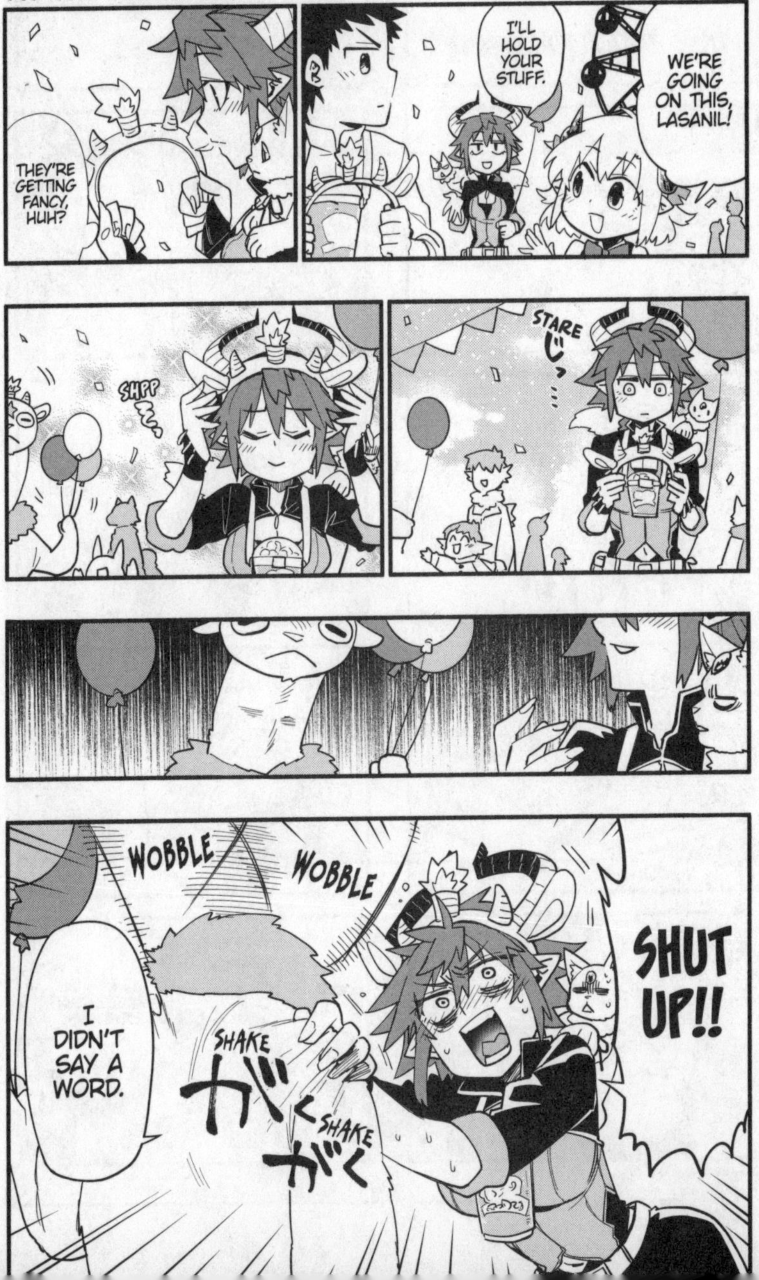
WE'RE GOING ON THIS, LASANIL!
I'LL HOLD YOUR STUFF.
THEY'RE GETTING FANCY, HUH?
STARE
じっ
SHPP
SHUT UP!!
WOBBLE
WOBBLE
SHAKE
がく
SHAKE
がく
I DIDN'T SAY A WORD.

NICKNAMES

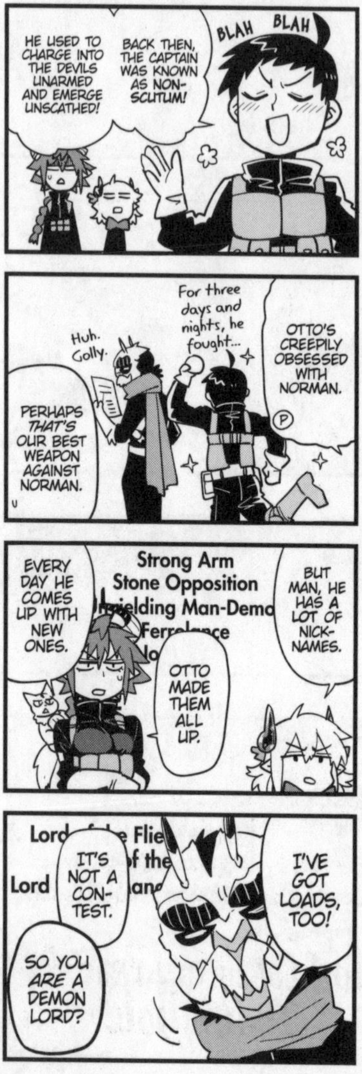
BLAH BLAH
BACK THEN, THE CAPTAIN WAS KNOWN AS NON-SCUTUM!
HE USED TO CHARGE INTO THE DEVILS UNARMED AND EMERGE UNSCATHED!
OTTO'S CREEPILY OBSESSED WITH NORMAN.
For three days and nights, he fought...
Huh. Golly.
PERHAPS THAT'S OUR BEST WEAPON AGAINST NORMAN.
BUT MAN, HE HAS A LOT OF NICK-NAMES.
Strong Arm
Stone Opposition
OTTO MADE THEM ALL UP.
EVERY DAY HE COMES UP WITH NEW ONES.
I'VE GOT LOADS, TOO!
IT'S NOT A CON-TEST.
SO YOU ARE A DEMON LORD?

FOUR AND A HALF SPINS

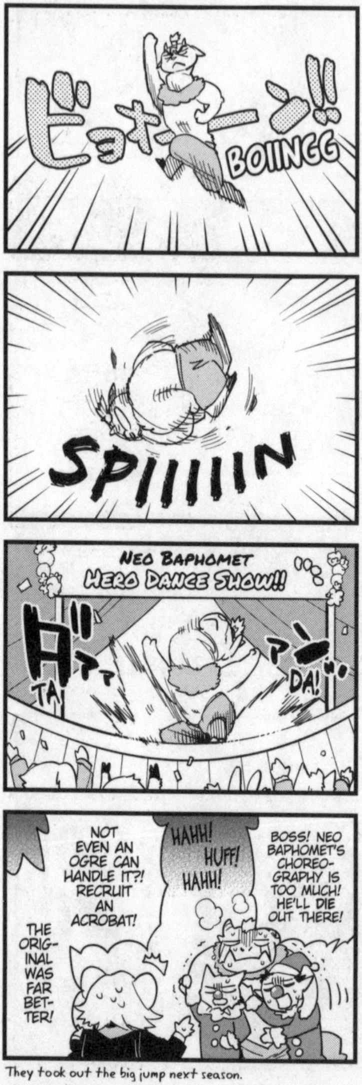
ビョオーーン!!
BOIINGG
SPIIIIIN
NEO BAPHOMET HERO DANCE SHOW!!
TA
DA!
BOSS! NEO BAPHOMET'S CHOREO-GRAPHY IS TOO MUCH! HE'LL DIE OUT THERE!
HAHH! HUFF! HAHH!
NOT EVEN AN OGRE CAN HANDLE IT?! RECRUIT AN ACROBAT!
THE ORIGI-NAL WAS FAR BET-TER!

They took out the big jump next season.

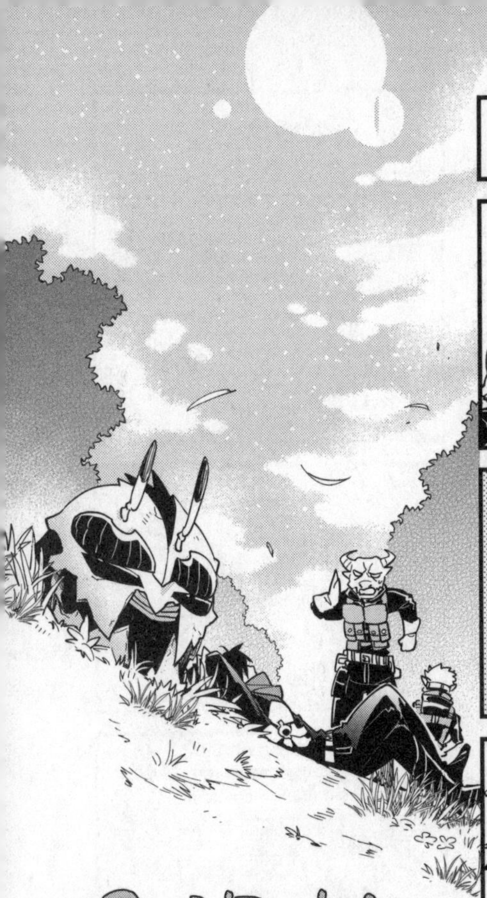

LEGAL IDOL

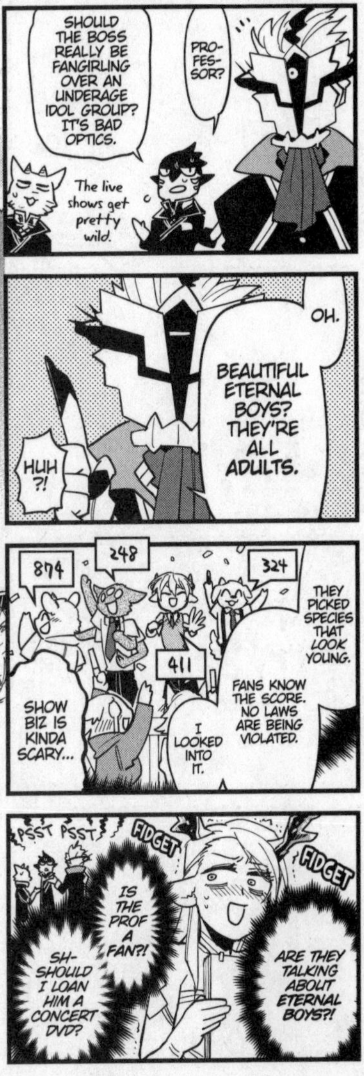
PROFESSOR?
SHOULD THE BOSS REALLY BE FANGIRLING OVER AN UNDERAGE IDOL GROUP? IT'S BAD OPTICS.
The live shows get pretty wild.
OH.
BEAUTIFUL ETERNAL BOYS? THEY'RE ALL ADULTS.
HUH?!
324
248
874
411
THEY PICKED SPECIES THAT LOOK YOUNG.
FANS KNOW THE SCORE. NO LAWS ARE BEING VIOLATED.
I LOOKED INTO IT.
SHOW BIZ IS KINDA SCARY...
FIDGET
FIDGET
ARE THEY TALKING ABOUT ETERNAL BOYS?!
PSST PSST
IS THE PROF A FAN?!
SH-SHOULD I LOAN HIM A CONCERT DVD?

Special Thanks!

Assistant: Nanami-san
Kuroichi-san
Editor: F-hata-san, M-ta-san
Cover/Logo Design: Sugita-san

And-to-all-my-readers
Thank you!

Yagura

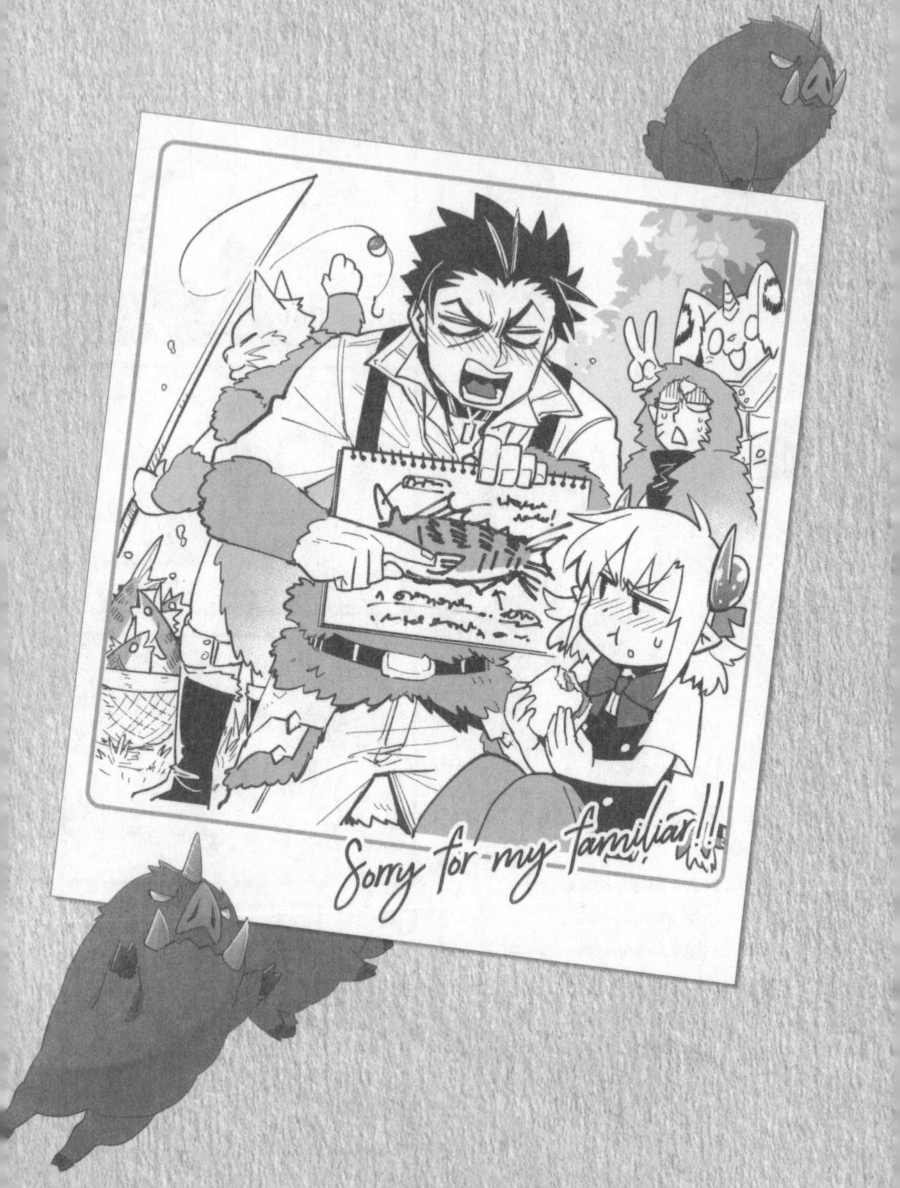
Sorry for my familiar!!

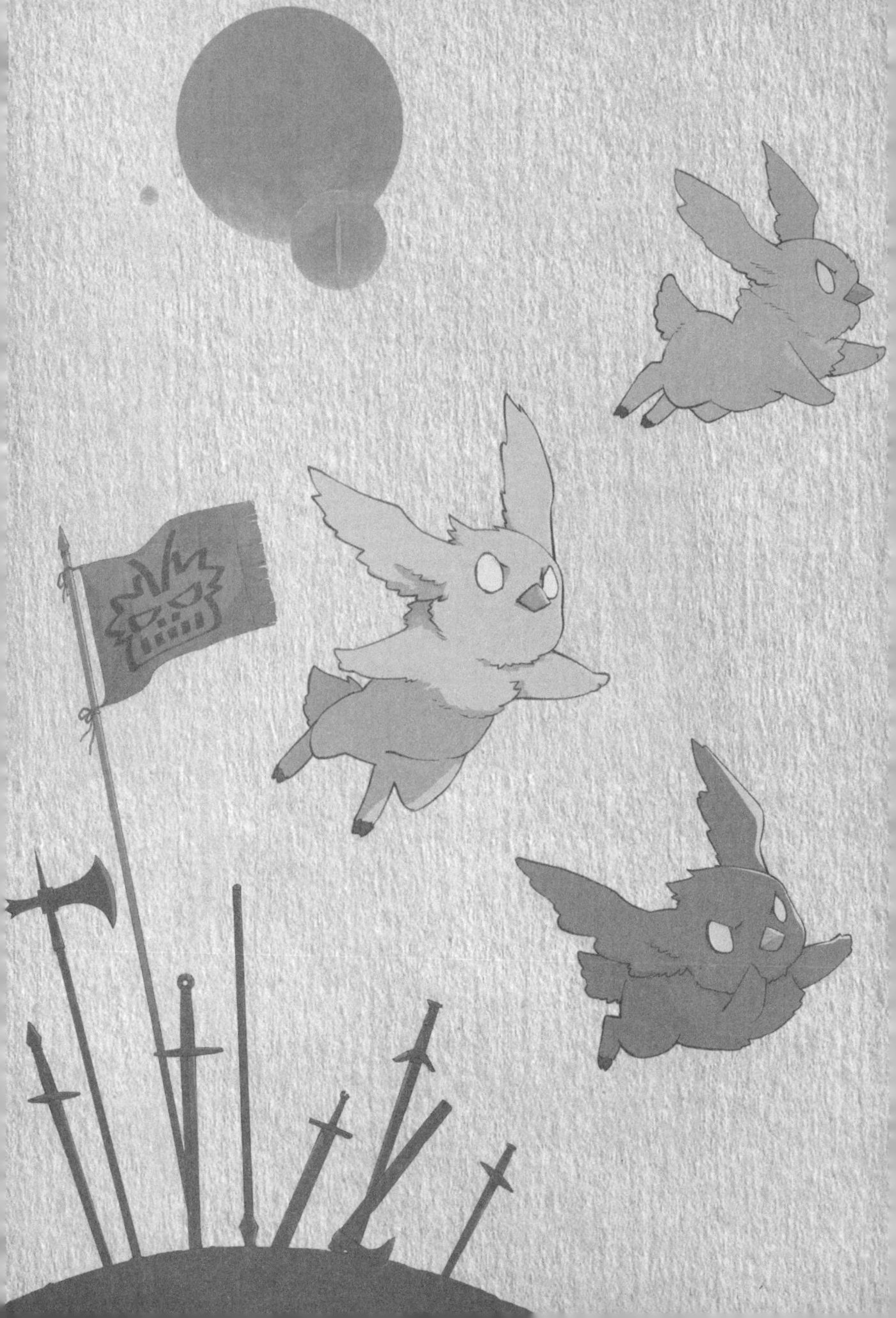

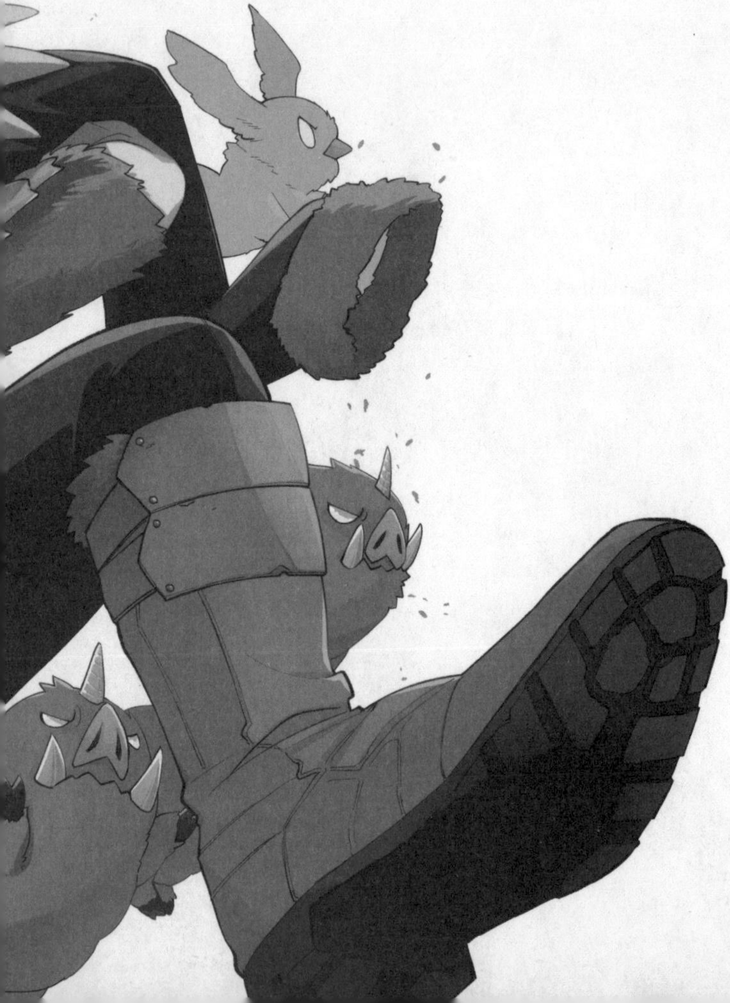

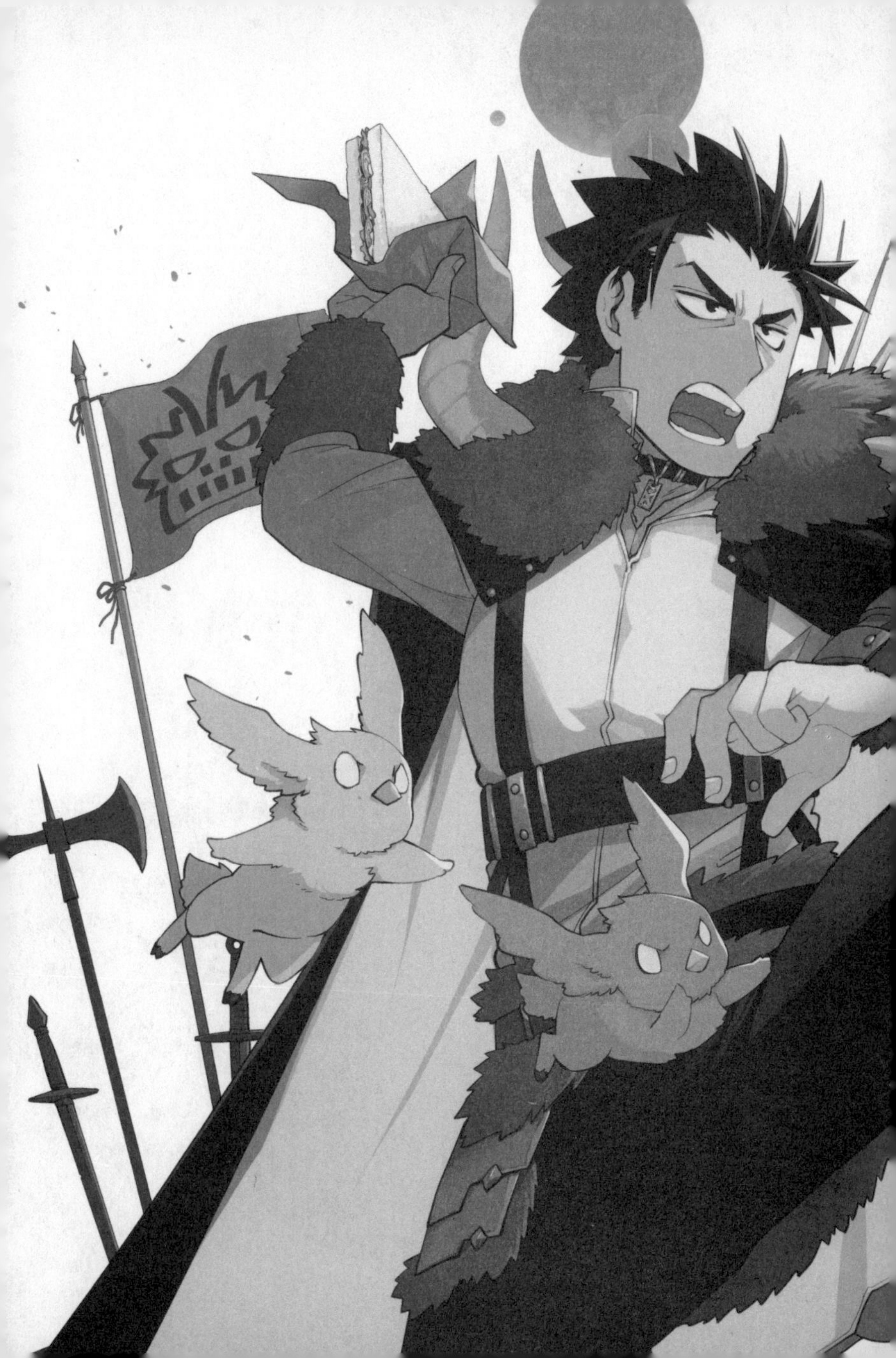

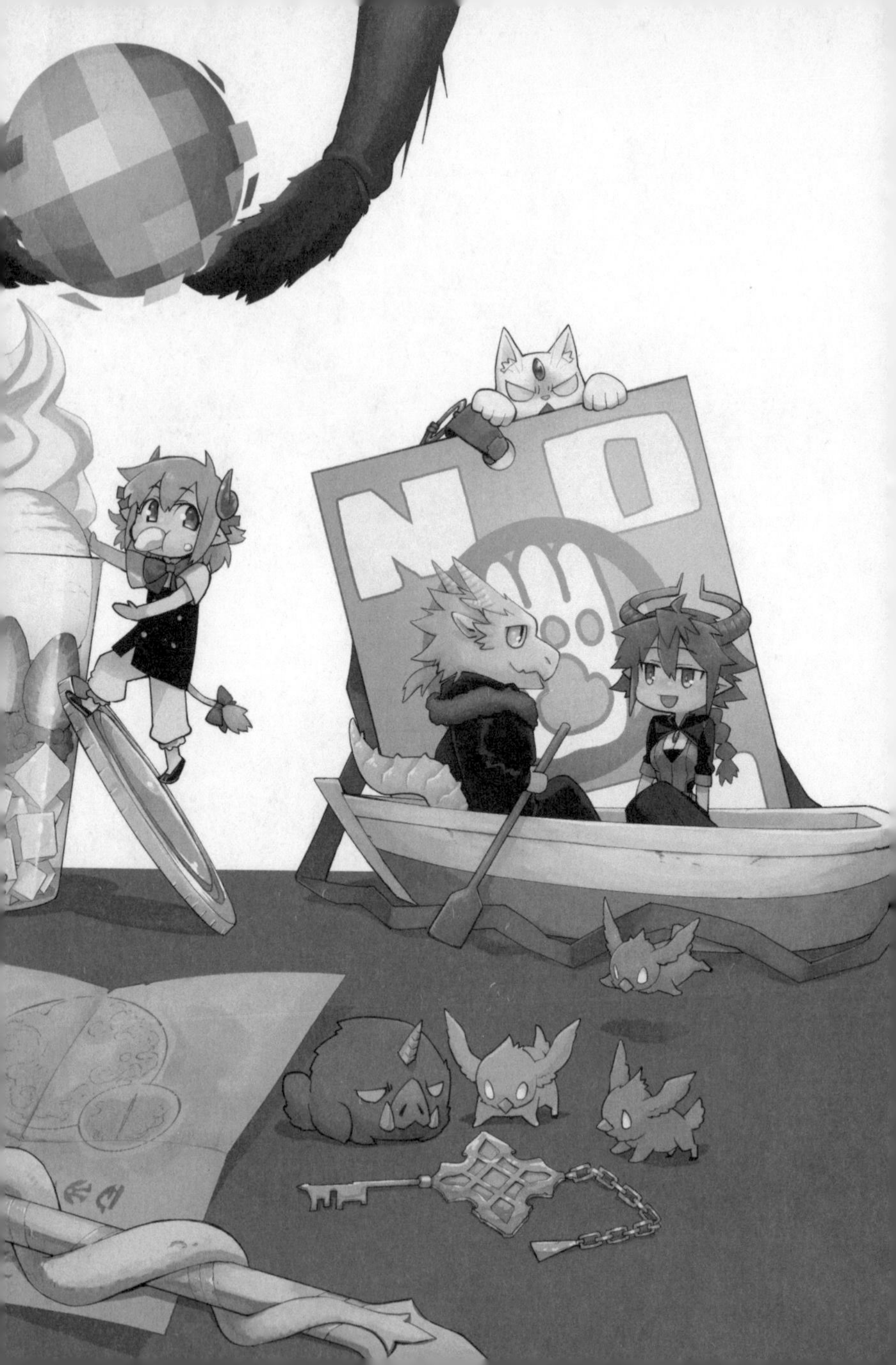
NO

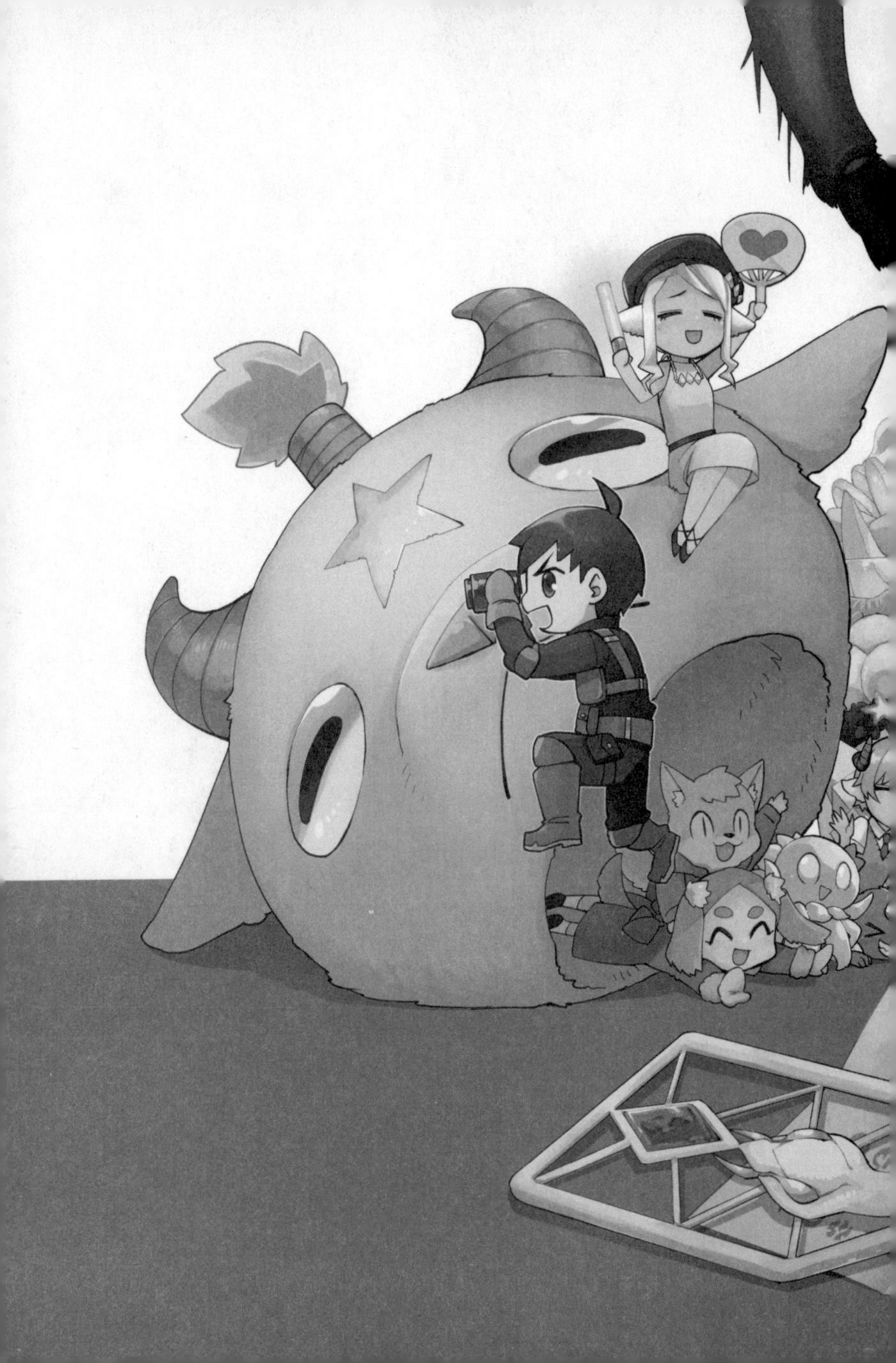

Sorry For My Familiar